Home Plans

Publisher
Jim Schiekofer
The Family Handyman

Editor
Eric Englund
*Homestore™
Plans and Publications*

Marketing Manager
Andrea Vecchio
The Family Handyman

Production Manager
Judy Rodriguez
The Family Handyman

Production Associate
Lynn Colbjornsen
*Homestore™
Plans and Publications*

Graphic Designer
Jeff Harrison
*Homestore™
Plans and Publications*

The homes pictured here and on the cover may have been modified by the homeowners. Please refer to the floor plan and/or the drawn elevation for actual blueprint details.

Contents

Featured Homes

Breland & Farmer Designers, Inc.

Plan E-1626   page 90

Plan DD-1696   page 183

Sections

Home-Plan Chapters

Ordering Your Plans

Next-Day Delivery Available on All Plans
TO ORDER, CALL ANYTIME, TOLL-FREE:
1-800-820-1296

The Family Handyman magazine and Homestore™ Plans and Publications are pleased to join together to bring you this outstanding collection of home designs. Through our combined efforts, we have compiled the finest work from 40 of North America's leading home-design firms.

This edition features our top-rated designs, arranged to make it easier to find the home that meets your needs.

With an inventory of more than 11,000 plans, Homestore™ Plans and Publications has supplied blueprints for more than 250,000 new homes. We look forward to helping you find your dream home.

On the Cover

Plan L-1994-FA   page 269

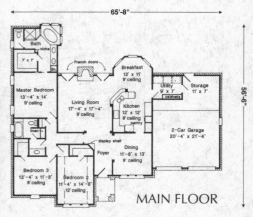

MAIN FLOOR

Except where noted, all photos on this page and on the cover are by Mark Englund/Homestore™ Plans and Publications.

Scenic Hideaway

- The perfect complement to any scenic hideaway spot, this A-frame is as affordable as it is adorable.
- A large deck embraces the front of the chalet, providing ample space for outdoor dining and recreation. Inside, vaulted ceilings and high windows lend a feeling of spaciousness.
- The living room is dramatically expanded by a high, vaulted ceiling and soaring windows facing the deck. This room also boasts a woodstove with a masonry hearth.
- The open, galley-style kitchen is well organized and includes a stacked washer/dryer unit and easy outdoor access. Nearby is a skylighted full bath.
- Upstairs, the romantic bedroom/loft overlooks the living room below, and features a vaulted ceiling. Windows at both ends of the bedroom provide stunning views.
- On both floors, areas with limited headroom are utilized effectively as extra storage space.

Plan H-968-1A	
Bedrooms: 1	**Baths:** 1
Living Area:	
Upper floor	144 sq. ft.
Main floor	391 sq. ft.
Total Living Area:	**535 sq. ft.**
Exterior Wall Framing:	2x6
Foundation Options:	

Crawlspace
(All plans can be built with your choice of foundation and framing. A generic conversion diagram is available. See order form.)

BLUEPRINT PRICE CODE:	**AA**

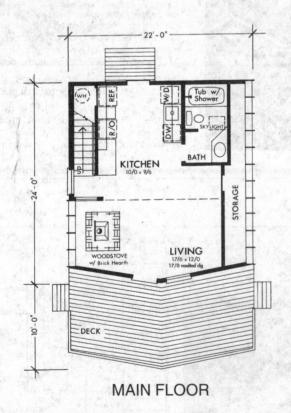

MAIN FLOOR

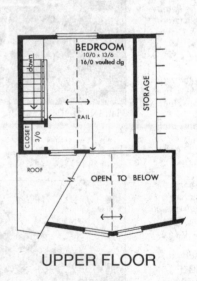

UPPER FLOOR

ORDER BLUEPRINTS ANYTIME!
CALL TOLL-FREE 1-800-820-1296

Plan H-968-1A

Plan copyright held by home designer/architect

PRICES AND DETAILS
ON PAGES 12-15

16 DEW LANE ▶

234 juice spills

28 sleepover parties

22 games of basketball in the kitchen

4 litters of puppies

24,854 door slams

18 happy childhoods

©2002 Wood Promotion Network. Be Constructive

WOOD HAS LIFE

There's nothing like wood to add warmth, beauty, enduring value and character to a home. Choose the affordable, energy-efficient, renewable building material that North America's homes have been made from for hundreds of years. Wood loves life. And lives love wood.

Build It Yourself

- Everything you need for a leisure or retirement retreat is neatly packaged in this affordable, easy-to-build design.
- The basic rectangular shape features a unique wraparound deck, entirely covered by a projecting roofline.
- A central fireplace and a vaulted ceiling visually enhance the cozy living and dining rooms.
- The efficient kitchen offers convenient service to the adjoining dining room. In the crawlspace version, the kitchen also includes a snack bar.
- Two main-floor bedrooms share a large full bath.
- The daylight-basement option is suitable for building on a sloping lot and consists of an extra bedroom, a general-purpose area and a garage.

Plans H-833-7 & -7A

Bedrooms: 2+	Baths: 1
Living Area:	
Main floor	952 sq. ft.
Daylight basement	676 sq. ft.
Total Living Area:	**952/1,628 sq. ft.**
Tuck-under garage	276 sq. ft.
Exterior Wall Framing:	2x6
Foundation Options:	**Plan #**
Daylight basement	H-833-7
Crawlspace	H-833-7A

(All plans can be built with your choice of foundation and framing. A generic conversion diagram is available. See order form.)

BLUEPRINT PRICE CODE:	**AA/B**

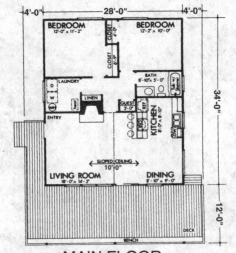

MAIN FLOOR
Crawlspace Version

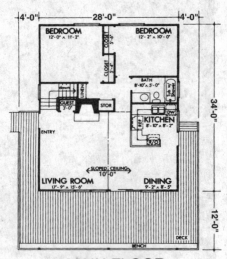

MAIN FLOOR
Basement Version

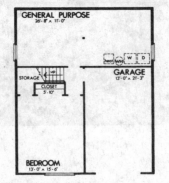

DAYLIGHT BASEMENT

REAR VIEW

Plans H-833-7 & -7A
Plan copyright held by home designer/architect

PRICES AND DETAILS
ON PAGES 12-15

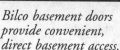

Adorable and Affordable

- This charming one-story home has much to offer, despite its modest size and economical bent.
- The lovely full-width porch boasts old-fashioned detailing, such as the round columns, decorative railings and ornamental molding.
- An open floor plan maximizes the home's square footage. The front door opens to the living room, where a railing creates a hallway effect while using very little space.
- Straight ahead, the dining room adjoins the island kitchen, while offering a compact laundry closet and sliding glass doors to a large rear patio.
- Focusing on quality, the home also offers features such as a 10-ft. tray ceiling in the living room and a 9-ft. stepped ceiling in the dining room.
- The three bedrooms are well proportioned. The master bedroom includes a private bathroom, while the two smaller bedrooms share a full bath.

Plan AX-91316

Bedrooms: 3	Baths: 2
Living Area:	
Main floor	1,097 sq. ft.
Total Living Area:	**1,097 sq. ft.**
Basement	1,097 sq. ft.
Garage	461 sq. ft.
Exterior Wall Framing:	2x4

Foundation Options:
Daylight basement
Standard basement
Crawlspace
Slab
(All plans can be built with your choice of foundation and framing. A generic conversion diagram is available. See order form.)

BLUEPRINT PRICE CODE: A

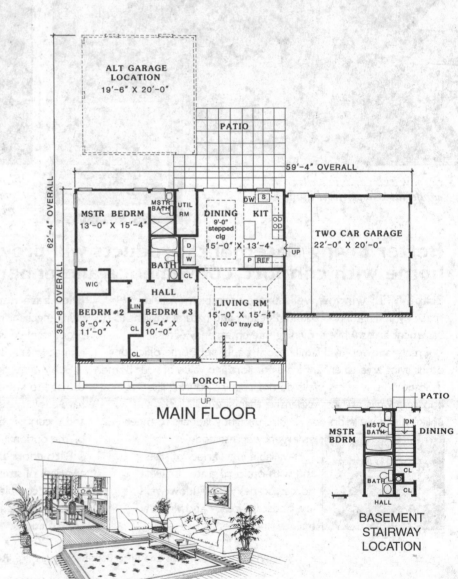

MAIN FLOOR

VIEW INTO LIVING AND DINING ROOMS

BASEMENT STAIRWAY LOCATION

Plan AX-91316
Plan copyright held by home designer/architect

PRICES AND DETAILS
ON PAGES 12-15

300 Reasons to Own One

40 House Washes   200 Car Washes   60 Deck Cleanings

ZERO BREAKDOWNS*

The Most Important Reason of All

For the ultimate in durability, all Campbell Hausfeld pressure washers are Built to Last. And the fact that they provide the ultimate in versatility doesn't hurt either. Use them to clean decks, siding, cars, patios, and more. The pressure washer pictured above features a 5.5 HP Honda overhead cam engine and a durable axial pump with a long life brass manifold, all in a compact design. (Accessories sold separately.) Every one is Built to Last, so you can count on them 300 times. And beyond!

*Campbell Hausfeld stands by its reputation for quality and durability subject to conditions of our one, two, or three-year limited product warranties. Usage claims are estimates based upon product review and analysis.

CAMPBELL HAUSFELD
BUILT TO LAST
© 2002 Campbell Hausfeld
CODE A45

Visit **www.chtools.com/washers** to get a free catalog and join the Powered Equipment Club for special offers.
Call toll-free: **1-866-CHTOOLS (1-866-248-6657)**

Active Living Made Easy

- This home is perfect for active living. Its rectangular design allows the use of truss roof framing, which makes construction easy and economical.
- The galley-style kitchen and the sunny dining area are kept open to the living room, forming one huge activity space. Two sets of sliding glass doors expand the living area to the large deck.
- The secluded master bedroom offers a private bath, while the remaining bedrooms share a hall bath.
- The two baths, the laundry facilities and the kitchen are clustered to allow common plumbing walls.
- Plan H-921-1A has a standard crawlspace foundation and an optional solar-heating system. Plan H-921-2A has a Plen-Wood system, which utilizes the sealed crawlspace as a chamber for distributing heated or cooled air. Both versions of the design call for energy-efficient 2x6 exterior walls.

Plans H-921-1A & -2A	
Bedrooms: 3	Baths: 2
Living Area:	
Main floor	1,164 sq. ft.
Total Living Area:	1,164 sq. ft.
Exterior Wall Framing:	2x6
Foundation Options:	Plan #
Crawlspace	H-921-1A
Plen-Wood crawlspace	H-921-2A
(All plans can be built with your choice of foundation and framing. A generic conversion diagram is available. See order form.)	
BLUEPRINT PRICE CODE:	A

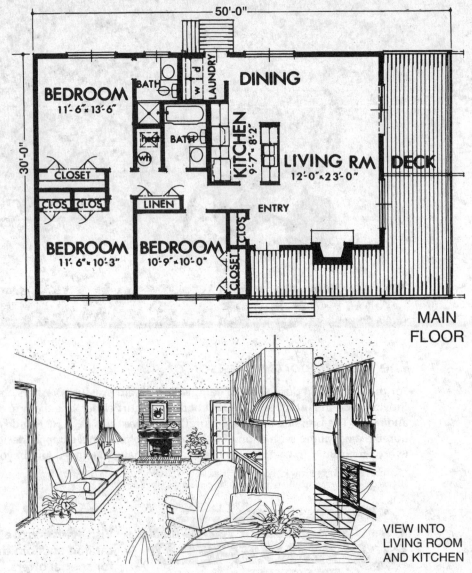

MAIN FLOOR

VIEW INTO LIVING ROOM AND KITCHEN

Plans H-921-1A & -2A

Plan copyright held by home designer/architect

PRICES AND DETAILS ON PAGES 12-15

Fight Allergens, Mold Spores and Dust, and Create a HEPA Healthy Home™

GuardianPlus™

AIR SYSTEMS

Now, one affordable unit improves the environment throughout your home.

Introducing GuardianPlus™ Air Systems with HEPA Filtration, Fresh Air Ventilation and Heat Recovery, a revolutionary way to increase air quality in your home. Quiet and lightweight, this unit can operate independently or attach to your HVAC system, where it stays out of sight. With GuardianPlus Air Systems, you can fight back against the microscopic dust, pollen, mold spores and pet dander that can worsen allergies and asthma. In short,

GuardianPlus Air Systems create dramatically cleaner air throughout your home, benefiting every member of your family. Better still, GuardianPlus Air Systems cost less than the multiple single-room units that you would need for filtration alone. To learn more about how you can keep your entire home cleaner and healthier, call 1-800-637-1453 (Broan) or 1-888-336-6151 (NuTone), or visit www.guardianplusairsystems.com.

Broan-NuTone™ GuardianPlus™ and HEPA Healthy Home™ are trademarks of Broan-NuTone LLC. HEPA (High Efficiency Particulate Air) filters capture 99.97% of all particles that are 0.3 microns or larger.

BROAN·NUTONE
A NORTEK COMPANY

Taking CONTROL of Indoor Air Quality

Scientific research has shown that indoor air can be up to 100 times more polluted than the air outside.

When your home has poor indoor air quality, airborne particles, gases and other pollutants are circulated throughout every room. This can lead to an unhealthy and uncomfortable environment and can put your family's health at risk. Resulting problems range from recurring colds and aggravated allergies to persistent coughs, headaches and poor concentration.

Now, there's a way to avoid these risks and provide a cleaner, healthier environment for you and your family through the innovative GuardianPlus™ Air Systems with Whole-House HEPA filtration, Fresh Air Ventilation and Heat Recovery.

HEPA filters capture 99.97% of all particles, even those as small as 0.3 microns (a human hair is 150 microns). Both HEPA filtration and fresh air ventilation are very important to improve indoor air quality, and the GuardianPlus™ Air Systems are the most effective and affordable ways to ensure fresh, clean indoor air throughout your home.

Options for *Every* Home

Unlike portable room air cleaners which can only cover isolated areas, GuardianPlus™ Air Systems address your entire indoor environment. The GuardianPlus™ family of products offers three types of customized systems to fit your needs:

*   **HEPA filtration throughout the house;**

*   **HEPA filtration with Fresh Air Ventilation;**

*   **HEPA filtration with Fresh Air Ventilation and Heat Recovery.**

Breath Easier

GuardianPlus™ Air Systems are lightweight, and each unit will provide whole-house ventilation for up to 2,500 square feet. They can be installed in all types of homes, anywhere in the country, in approximately three hours. They are also efficient, using as much energy as two 100-watt lightbulbs. Best of all, they're affordable, with complete installation starting at under $600.

Your sales consultant will help you choose the system solution for your indoor air quality problem. Call 1-800-637-1453 (Broan) or 1-888-336-6151 (NuTone) or visit **www.guardianplusairsystems.com** for more information.

The Package

what our plans include

Our construction blueprints are detailed, clear and concise. All blueprints are designed by licensed architects or members of the American Institute of Building Design (AIBD) or the Council of Publishing Home Designers (CPHD), and all plans are designed to meet one of the recognized North American building codes (the Uniform Building Code, the Standard Building Code, the Basic Building Code or the National Building Code of Canada) in effect at the time and place they are drawn.

The blueprints for most home designs include the elements listed below, but the presentation of these elements may vary depending on the size and complexity of the home and the style of the individual designer.

Exterior Elevations

Exterior elevations show the front, rear and sides of the house, including exterior materials, details and measurements.

Foundation Plans

Foundation plans include drawings for a full, daylight or partial basement, crawlspace, slab, or pole foundation. All necessary notations and dimensions are included. (Foundation options will vary for each plan. If the home you want does not have the type of foundation you desire, a foundation conversion diagram is available.)

Detailed Floor Plans

Detailed floor plans show the placement of interior walls and the dimensions for rooms, doors, windows, stairways, etc., of each level of the house.

Cross Sections

Cross sections show details of the house as though it were cut in slices from the roof to the foundation. The cross sections specify the home's construction, insulation, flooring and roofing details.

Interior Elevations

Interior elevations show the specific details of cabinets (kitchen, bathroom and utility room), fireplaces, built-in units, and other special interior features, depending on the nature and complexity of the item.

Note: To save money and to accommodate your own style and taste, we suggest contacting local cabinet and fireplace distributors for sizes and styles.

Roof Details

Roof details show slope, pitch and location of dormers, gables and other roof elements, including clerestory windows and skylights.

Other Helpful Building Aids

Every set of plans that you order will contain the details your builder needs. However, additional guides and information are also available:

Planning Sets

Planning sets are a great way to research the home that interests you. A planning set includes all four exterior elevations and the floor plans, shown to scale. Planning sets are stamped "Not for Construction," and may not be used to build a home. Receive full credit for the price of the planning set when you purchase a 4-, 8-, 12- or reproducible-set package of blueprints for that home within 60 days of your planning set purchase. See the chart on page 14 to see if a planning set is available for your design.

Reproducible Blueprint Set

Reproducible sets are useful if you will be making changes to the stock home plan you've chosen. This set consists of line drawings produced on erasable, reproducible paper for the purpose of modification. When alterations are complete, working copies can be made. *Bonus: Includes free working set

Mirror-Reversed Plans

Mirror-reversed plans are used when building the home in reverse of the illustrated floor plan. Reversed plans are available for an additional one-time surcharge. Since the lettering and dimensions read backward, we recommend ordering only one or two reversed sets in addition to the regular-reading sets.

Note: Full-reverse blueprints are available for a limited number of plans. Because lettering and dimensions read normally, all sets in your order will be reversed if your plan is available in full reverse. There is a $50 one-time surcharge for all reversed plans.

Itemized List of Materials

An itemized list of materials details the quantity, type and size of materials needed to build your home. This list is helpful in acquiring

These details may be shown on the elevation sheet or on a separate diagram.

Note: If trusses are used, we suggest using a local truss manufacturer to design your trusses to comply with local codes and regulations.

Electrical Layouts

Schematic electrical layouts show the suggested locations for switches, fixtures and outlets. These details may be shown on the floor plan or on a separate diagram.

General Specifications

General specifications provide general instructions and information regarding structure, excavating and grading, masonry and concrete work, carpentry and wood, thermal and moisture protection, and specifications about drywall, tile, flooring, glazing, caulking and sealants.

Note: Due to regional variations, local availability of materials, local codes, methods of installation, and individual preferences, it is impossible to include much detail on heating, plumbing and electrical work on your plans. The duct work, venting and other details will vary depending on the type of heating and cooling system (forced air, hot water, electric, solar) and the type of energy (gas, oil, electricity, solar) that you use. These details and specifications are easily obtained from your builder, contractor and/or local suppliers.

an accurate construction estimate. An expanded material workbook is available for some plans. Call for details.

Description of Materials

A description of materials may be required by your bank in order to secure a loan through the Federal Housing Administration or the Department of Veterans Affairs. The list specifies the minimum grade of building materials required to meet FHA or VA standards.

Generic "How-To" Diagrams

Plumbing, wiring, solar heating, and framing and foundation conversion diagrams are available. These diagrams detail the basic tools and techniques needed to plumb; wire; install a solar-heating system; convert plans with 2x4 exterior walls to 2x6 (or vice versa); or adapt a plan for a basement, crawlspace or slab foundation.

Note: These diagrams are general and not specific to any one plan.

Ordering Information

read before you buy

Blueprint Prices

Our pricing schedule is based on total heated living space. Garages, porches, decks and unfinished basements are not included in the total square footage.

Architectural and Engineering Seals

The increased concern over energy costs and safety has prompted many cities and states to require an architect or engineer to review and "seal" a blueprint prior to construction. There may be a fee for this service. Contact your local lumberyard, municipal building department, builders association, or local chapter of the AIBD or the American Institute of Architects (AIA).

Note: Plans for homes to be built in Nevada, Delaware, New Jersey or New York may have to be re-drawn and sealed by a design professional licensed in the state in which they are to be built.

Foundation Options and Exterior Construction

Depending on your location and climate, your home will normally be built with a slab, crawlspace or basement foundation; the exterior walls will usually be of 2x4 or 2x6 framing. Most professional contractors and builders can easily adapt a home to meet the foundation and exterior wall requirements that you desire.

If the home you select does not offer your preferred type of foundation or exterior walls, you may wish to purchase a generic foundation and framing conversion diagram.

Note: These diagrams are not specific to any one plan.

Exchange Information

We want you to be happy with your home plans. If, for some reason, the blueprints that you ordered cannot be used, we will be pleased to exchange them within 30 days of the purchase date. A handling fee will be assessed for all exchanges. For more information, call toll-free.

Note: Reproducible sets may not be exchanged for any reason.

Estimating Building Costs

Building costs vary widely with the style and size of the home, the finishing materials you select and the local rates for labor and materials. A local average cost per square foot can give you a rough estimate. Contact a local contractor, your state or local builders association, the National Association of Home Builders (NAHB), or the AIBD. A more accurate estimate will require a professional review of the working blueprints and the materials you will be using.

How Many Blueprints Do You Need?

A single planning set is sufficient to study and review a home in greater detail (see page 12). However, to get cost estimates or to build, you will need at least four sets (see the checklist on page 15). If you plan to modify your home plan, we recommend ordering a reproducible set.

Customization and Modifications

The designers at Homestore™ Plans & Publications Design Services can make your dream home uniquely yours. They'll customize virtually any plan to better suit your budget, lifestyle and design preferences.

Call toll-free 1-888-266-3439 or e-mail customize@homeplans.com describing the changes you'd like. Tell us the state in which you are building and the foundation type and exterior wall framing you desire. Be sure to include a daytime phone number so our consultants can reach you with any questions they may have. A Design Services associate will prepare an estimate for the cost and turnaround time of customizing your plan—FREE! Then, with your approval, Design Services will go to work and make that plan uniquely yours.

Compliance with Codes

Every state, county and municipality has its own codes, zoning requirements, ordinances and building regulations. Modifications may be needed to comply with your specific requirements—snow loads, energy codes, seismic zones, etc. All of our plans are designed to meet the specifications of seismic zones I or II. We authorize the use of our blueprints expressly conditioned upon your obligation and agreement to strictly comply with all local building codes, ordinances, regulations and requirements, including permits and inspections at the time of construction.

License Agreement and Copyright

When you purchase a blueprint or reproducible set, we grant you a license to use it to construct a single unit. Our plans are protected under the Federal Copyright Act, Title XVII of the United States Code and Chapter 37 of the Code of Federal Regulations. Each designer retains title and ownership of the original documents. The blueprints licensed to you may not be resold to or used by any other person, copied or reproduced by any means. When you purchase a reproducible set, you reserve the right to modify and reproduce the plan. Reproducible sets may not be resold or used by any other person. For more details, see page 16.

Order Form

three ways to order

1.
Call toll-free anytime:
1-800-820-1296.

2.
Fax order form to
(651) 602-5002.

3.
Mail your order to the address at the bottom of the form.

plan prefix	planning set	reproducible set	itemized list of materials	description of materials	next-day delivery
A	●	●	C		●
AGH	●	●			●
AHP	●	●	●	●	●
APS	●	●	C		●
AX		●	C		●
B	●	●	C		●
BRF	●	●			●
C	●	●	●		●
CC	●	●	C		●
CH		●			●
CHD		●			●
COA	●	●			●
DBI	●	●	●		●
DD	●	●	C		●
DHI	●	●			●
DP	●	●			●
DW	●	●	●		●
E	C	●	C		●
EOF	●	●	C		●
GL	●	●			●
GS	●	●			●
H	●	●	●	●	●
HDS	●	●	C		●
HFL	●	●			●
HWG	●	●			●
I	●	●	C		●
ICON	●	●			●
J	●	●	C		●
JWB	●				●
K	●	●	●	●	●
KD	●	●			●
KP	●	●			●
L	●	●	C		●
LM	C	●			●
LRK	●	●			●
LS	●	●			●
NW	●	●	C		●
OH	●	●			●
P	●		●	●	●
PI	●	●			●
PIC		US	●		●
PJG	●	●			●
PSC	●	●			●
RD	●	●			●
RLA	●	●			●
S	●	●	C		●
SDC	●	●			●
SDG	●	●			●
SUN	●	●	●		●
UD	●	●	C		●
WAA	●	●			●

Legend

● Available
C Call for availability.
US U.S. customers only

PRICING

Blueprints & Accessories

Price Code	Planning Set	4 Sets	8 Sets	12 Sets	Reproducible Set*
AAA	$99	$309	$349	$419	$484
AA	$99	$349	$389	$469	$524
A	$99	$419	$454	$529	$589
B	$99	$454	$494	$569	$629
C	$99	$494	$534	$609	$669
D	$99	$564	$609	$664	$704
E	$99	$619	$659	$739	$809
F	$99	$659	$699	$789	$854
G	$99	$704	$744	$829	$904
H	$99	$744	$789	$874	$949
I	$99	$789	$829	$914	$984

Prices subject to change

*A Reproducible Set is produced on erasable paper for the purpose of modification. See page 14 for availability.

Itemized List of Materials

Price Code	1 Set*	Price Code	1 Set*	Price Code	1 Set*
AAA	$60	C	$65	G	$75
AA	$60	D	$65	H	$75
A	$60	E	$70	I	$80
B	$60	F	$70		

See page 14 for availability.   *Additional sets are available for $15 each.

Generic How-To Diagrams

Quantity Price	Any 1 $20	Any 2 $30	Any 3 $40	All 4 $45

Shipping & Handling

	1-3 sets	4-7 sets	8 sets or more	Reproducible Set
U.S. Regular (5-6 WORKING DAYS)	$15.00	$17.50	$20.00	$20.00
U.S. Express (2-3 WORKING DAYS)	$30.00	$32.50	$35.00	$35.00
U.S. Next Day* (1 WORKING DAY*)	$45.00	$47.50	$50.00	$50.00
Canada Regular (5-7 WORKING DAYS)	$35.00	$40.00	$45.00	$45.00
Canada Express (2-4 WORKING DAYS)	$50.00	$55.00	$60.00	$60.00
International (7-10 WORKING DAYS)	$60.00	$70.00	$80.00	$80.00

*Order before noon Central Time for next-day delivery to most locations.

BLUEPRINT CHECKLIST

_____ **OWNER'S SET(S)**

_____ **BUILDER** (usually requires at least three sets; one for legal document, one for inspections and a minimum of one set for subcontractors)

_____ **BUILDING PERMIT DEPT.** (at least one set; check with your local governing body for number of sets required)

_____ **LENDING INSTITUTION** (usually one set for conventional mortgage; three sets for FHA or VA loans)

_____ **TOTAL NUMBER OF SETS**

BLUEPRINT ORDER FORM

Your Order

Plan Number: FHTR166- _____   **Price Code:** _____

Foundation: _____
(Carefully review the foundation option(s) available for your plan—basement, crawlspace, pole, pier or slab. If several options are offered, choose only one.)

Blueprints

❑ **Planning Set** See page 14 for availability. $ _____
RECOMMENDED FOR REVIEW/STUDY   (see left)
STAMPED "NOT FOR CONSTRUCTION"

❑ **Four Sets**
RECOMMENDED FOR BIDDING

❑ **Eight Sets**
RECOMMENDED FOR CONSTRUCTION

❑ **Twelve Sets**
RECOMMENDED FOR MULTIPLE CONTRACTOR BIDS

❑ **Reproducible Set** See page 14 for availability.
RECOMMENDED FOR CONSTRUCTION/MODIFICATION
INCLUDES ONE FREE BLUEPRINT

Additional Sets   QTY: _____ x $50 = $ _____
Additional sets of the plan ordered are $50 each.   ($50 per set)
Available on all plans. With minimum 4-set order only.

Reversed Sets   QTY: _____ $ _____
If you wish your home to be the mirror image of the illustrated   ($50 surcharge)
floor plan, please specify how many of your sets should be reversed. (Because the lettering on reversed plans reads backward, we recommend reversing only one or two of your sets.) There is a $50 one-time charge for any number of reversed sets.

Itemized List of Materials   QTY: _____ $ _____
See pricing at left. See page 14 for availability.   (see left)

Description of Materials $ _____
Sold only in sets of two for $60. See page 14 for availability.   ($60 for set of two)

Generic How-To Diagrams $ _____
General guides on plumbing, wiring and solar heating, plus   (see left)
information on how to convert from one foundation or exterior framing to another. See pricing at left.
Note: These diagrams are not specific to any one plan.

❑ PLUMBING   ❑ WIRING   ❑ SOLAR HEATING   ❑ FRAMING & FOUNDATION CONVERSION

Order Total

Subtotal $ _____

Sales Tax $ _____
All U.S. residents add appropriate sales tax.
Attention Canadian customers: All sales are final, FOB St. Paul, Minnesota.

Shipping/Handling $ _____
See chart at left.

Total $ _____

Payment Information

❑ CHECK OR MONEY ORDER ENCLOSED (IN U.S. FUNDS)
❑ VISA   ❑ MASTERCARD   ❑ AMEX   ❑ DISCOVER

CARD NUMBER _____ EXP. DATE _____

NAME _____

ADDRESS _____

CITY _____ STATE _____ COUNTRY _____

ZIP CODE _____ DAYTIME PHONE (_____) _____

❑ CHECK HERE IF YOU ARE A BUILDER   HOME PHONE (_____) _____

MAIL TO Homestore, Dept. FHTR166
P.O. Box 75488
St. Paul, MN 55175-0488

OR FAX TO (651) 602-5002

SOURCE CODE: FHTR166

Cozy, Rustic Country Home

- This cozy, rustic home offers a modern, open interior that efficiently maximizes the modest square footage.
- A simple front porch offers just enough room to set up a couple of rocking chairs and shoot the breeze.
- The large living room features a sloped ceiling accented by rustic beams. An eye-catching corner fireplace warms this inviting space.
- The living room flows into the adjoining dining room and the efficient U-shaped kitchen for a spacious, open feel.
- The master suite is separated from the two secondary bedrooms by the home's common living areas. The master suite includes a private bath and a separate dressing area with a dual-sink vanity.
- Extra storage boosts the garage's utility.

Plan E-1109

Bedrooms: 3	Baths: 2
Living Area:	
Main floor	1,191 sq. ft.
Total Living Area:	**1,191 sq. ft.**
Garage, storage and utility	572 sq. ft.
Exterior Wall Framing:	2x6

Foundation Options:

Crawlspace

Slab

(All plans can be built with your choice of foundation and framing. A generic conversion diagram is available. See order form.)

BLUEPRINT PRICE CODE: A

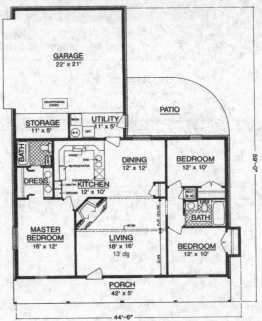

VIEW INTO LIVING ROOM, DINING ROOM AND KITCHEN

MAIN FLOOR

ORDER BLUEPRINTS ANYTIME! CALL TOLL-FREE 1-800-820-1296

Plan E-1109

Plan copyright held by home designer/architect

PRICES AND DETAILS ON PAGES 12-15

Appealing One-Story

- This appealing one-story design boasts a shady and inviting front porch accented by decorative railings. It's the perfect spot to chat with the neighbors or enjoy an inspiring sunset.
- Inside, a cathedral ceiling expands the living and dining rooms. This large area is brightened by multiple bay windows and is warmed by a unique two-way fireplace. Sliding glass doors lead to a sunny backyard patio.
- The U-shaped kitchen includes a pantry closet and plenty of cabinet space. The kitchen is fronted by a serving bar that makes itself available to the adjacent dining room.
- The master bedroom boasts a mirrored dressing area, a private bath and abundant closet space.
- Two additional bedrooms share another full bath. The third bedroom includes a cozy window seat.

Plan NW-521

Bedrooms: 3	Baths: 2
Living Area:	
Main floor	1,187 sq. ft.
Total Living Area:	**1,187 sq. ft.**
Garage	448 sq. ft.
Exterior Wall Framing:	2x6

Foundation Options:

Crawlspace
(All plans can be built with your choice of foundation and framing. A generic conversion diagram is available. See order form.)

BLUEPRINT PRICE CODE: A

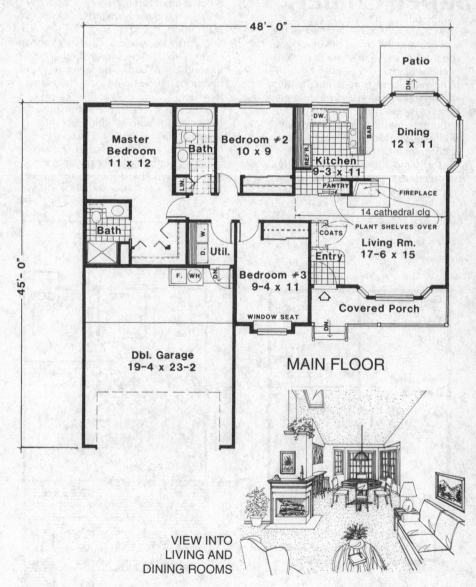

48'-0"

45'-0"

Patio

Master Bedroom 11 x 12

Bath

Bedroom #2 10 x 9

DW.

Dining 12 x 11

REFR.

Kitchen 9-3 x 11

BAR

LIN.

PANTRY

FIREPLACE

14 cathedral clg

PLANT SHELVES OVER

Bath

D. W.

Util.

COATS

Living Rm. 17-6 x 15

F.

WH

DN.

Bedroom #3 9-4 x 11

Entry

WINDOW SEAT

DN.

Covered Porch

Dbl. Garage 19-4 x 23-2

MAIN FLOOR

VIEW INTO LIVING AND DINING ROOMS

ORDER BLUEPRINTS ANYTIME!
CALL TOLL-FREE 1-800-820-1296

Plan NW-521

Plan copyright held by home designer/architect

PRICES AND DETAILS
ON PAGES 12-15

17

Super Chalet

- The charming Alpine detailing of the exterior and the open, flexible layout of the interior make this one of our most popular plans.
- In from the large front deck, the living room wraps around a central fireplace or woodstove, providing a warm and expansive multipurpose living space. Sliding glass doors open to the deck for outdoor entertaining.
- The adjoining dining room is easily serviced from the galley-style kitchen.

A convenient full bath serves a nearby bedroom and the remainder of the main floor.
- Two upper-floor bedrooms have vaulted ceilings, extra closet space and access to another full bath. The larger bedroom offers sliding glass doors to a lofty deck.
- The blueprints recommend finishing the interior walls with solid lumber paneling for a rich, rustic look.
- In addition to a large general-use area and a shop, the optional daylight basement has space for a car or a boat.

Plans H-26-1 & -1A	
Bedrooms: 3	**Baths:** 2
Living Area:	
Upper floor	476 sq. ft.
Main floor	728 sq. ft.
Daylight basement	410 sq. ft.
Total Living Area:	**1,204/1,614 sq. ft.**
Tuck-under garage	318 sq. ft.
Exterior Wall Framing:	2x4
Foundation Options:	**Plan #**
Daylight basement	H-26-1
Crawlspace	H-26-1A

(All plans can be built with your choice of foundation and framing. A generic conversion diagram is available. See order form.)

BLUEPRINT PRICE CODE:	**A/B**

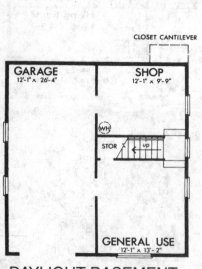

DAYLIGHT BASEMENT

STAIRWAY AREA IN CRAWLSPACE VERSION

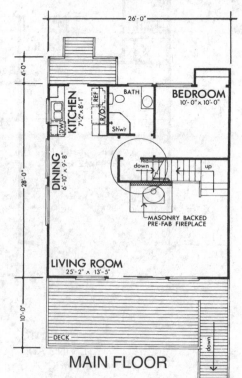

MAIN FLOOR

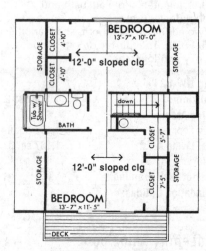

UPPER FLOOR

ORDER BLUEPRINTS ANYTIME!
CALL TOLL-FREE 1-800-820-1296

Plans H-26-1 & -1A

Plan copyright held by home designer/architect

PRICES AND DETAILS
ON PAGES 12-15

Comfortable L-Shaped Ranch

- From the covered entry to the beautiful and spacious family gathering areas, this comfortable ranch-style home puts many extras into a compact space.
- Straight off the central foyer, an inviting fireplace and a bright bay window highlight the living and dining area, while sliding glass doors open to a wide backyard terrace.
- The combination kitchen/family room features a large eating bar. The nearby mudroom offers a service entrance, laundry facilities, access to the garage and room for a half-bath.
- In the isolated sleeping wing, the master bedroom boasts a private bath and plenty of closet space. Two additional bedrooms share another full bath.

Plan K-276-R

Bedrooms: 3	Baths: 2–2½
Living Area:	
Main floor	1,245 sq. ft.
Total Living Area:	**1,245 sq. ft.**
Standard basement	1,245 sq. ft.
Garage	499 sq. ft.
Exterior Wall Framing:	2x4 or 2x6

Foundation Options:

Standard basement
Crawlspace
Slab

(All plans can be built with your choice of foundation and framing. A generic conversion diagram is available. See order form.)

BLUEPRINT PRICE CODE: **A**

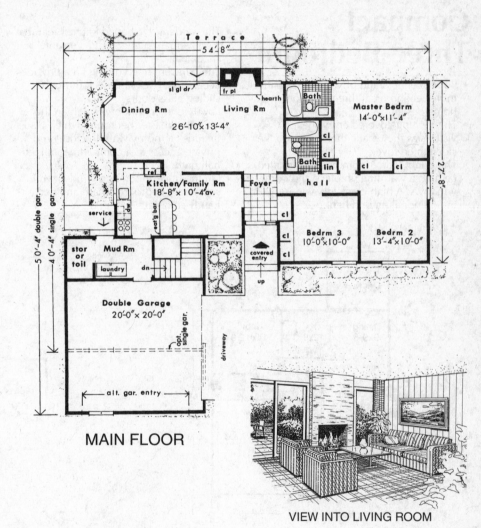

MAIN FLOOR

VIEW INTO LIVING ROOM

ORDER BLUEPRINTS ANYTIME!
CALL TOLL-FREE 1-800-820-1296

Plan K-276-R
Plan copyright held by home designer/architect

PRICES AND DETAILS
ON PAGES 12-15   19

Compact Three-Bedroom

- Both openness and privacy are possible in this economical three-bedroom home design.
- The inviting covered entry shelters visitors as they make their way into the sidelighted foyer.
- The bright living room boasts a vaulted ceiling, a warming fireplace and corner windows. A high clerestory window lets in additional natural light.

- The modern, U-shaped kitchen features a convenient pantry and a versatile snack bar.
- The adjacent open dining area provides access to a backyard deck through sliding glass doors.
- Lovely corner windows brighten the secluded master bedroom, which also includes a roomy walk-in closet and private access to a compartmentalized hall bath.
- On the upper floor, two good-sized secondary bedrooms share another handy split bath.

Plan B-101-8501

Bedrooms: 3	**Baths: 2**
Living Area:	
Upper floor	400 sq. ft.
Main floor	846 sq. ft.
Total Living Area:	**1,246 sq. ft.**
Garage	400 sq. ft.
Standard basement	846 sq. ft.
Exterior Wall Framing:	2x4
Foundation Options:	

Standard basement
(All plans can be built with your choice of foundation and framing. A generic conversion diagram is available. See order form.)

BLUEPRINT PRICE CODE:	**A**

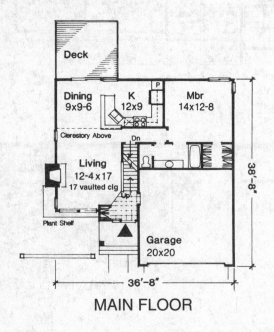

MAIN FLOOR

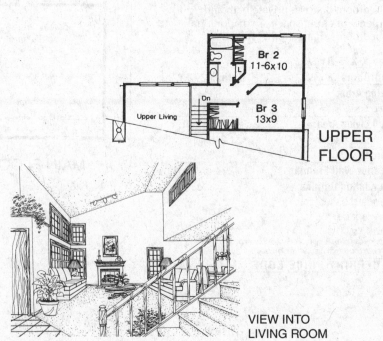

UPPER FLOOR

VIEW INTO LIVING ROOM

Plan B-101-8501
Plan copyright held by home designer/architect

PRICES AND DETAILS
ON PAGES 12-15

Unexpected Amenities

- Surprising interior amenities are found within the casual exterior of this good-looking design.
- A dramatic fireplace warms the comfortable formal areas. The living and dining rooms share a 20-ft. cathedral ceiling and high windows that flank the fireplace. Sliding glass doors access an expansive side patio.

- The efficient walk-through kitchen provides plenty of counter space, in addition to a windowed sink and a pass-through to the living areas.
- A large bedroom, a full bath and an oversized utility room complete the main floor. The utility room offers space for a washer and dryer, plus a sink and an extra freezer.
- Upstairs, the spacious and secluded master suite boasts a walk-in closet, a private bath and lots of storage space. A railed loft area overlooks the living and dining rooms.

Plan I-1249-A	
Bedrooms: 2	**Baths:** 2
Living Area:	
Upper floor	297 sq. ft.
Main floor	952 sq. ft.
Total Living Area:	**1,249 sq. ft.**
Standard basement	952 sq. ft.
Exterior Wall Framing:	2x6

Foundation Options:

Standard basement
Crawlspace
(All plans can be built with your choice of foundation and framing. A generic conversion diagram is available. See order form.)

BLUEPRINT PRICE CODE: A

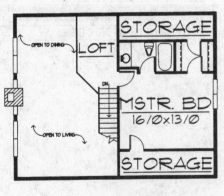

UPPER FLOOR

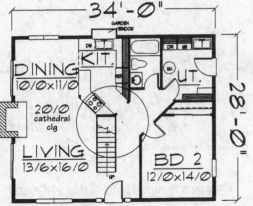

MAIN FLOOR

BASEMENT STAIRWAY LOCATION

VIEW INTO DINING ROOM AND KITCHEN

ORDER BLUEPRINTS ANYTIME!
CALL TOLL-FREE 1-800-820-1296

Plan I-1249-A
Plan copyright held by home designer/architect

PRICES AND DETAILS
ON PAGES 12-15

21

Soft Allure

- Arched windows, combined with distinctive keystones and soldier coursing, give a soft allure to the front of this lovely two-story home.
- The pretty front porch features a pair of columns that nicely frame the living room's beautiful picture window.
- Inside, the oversized living room is the main attraction; it features a soaring vaulted ceiling to create an astounding

sense of openness. A corner fireplace adds a touch of cozy comfort.
- Gourmet meals get grand treatment in the unique bay-windowed dining room, which accesses the back patio.
- An enormous walk-in closet gives the occupants of the spacious master suite freedom to expand their wardrobe. The room's charm is enhanced by a linen closet and a private tub.
- Two additional bedrooms upstairs share a full-sized bath.

Plan DD-1218-1	
Bedrooms: 3	**Baths: 2**
Living Area:	
Upper floor	373 sq. ft.
Main floor	889 sq. ft.
Total Living Area:	**1,262 sq. ft.**
Standard basement	889 sq. ft.
Garage	403 sq. ft.
Exterior Wall Framing:	2x4
Foundation Options:	
Standard basement	
Crawlspace	
Slab	

(All plans can be built with your choice of foundation and framing. A generic conversion diagram is available. See order form.)

BLUEPRINT PRICE CODE:	A

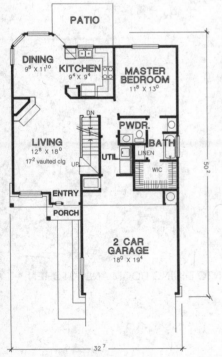

MAIN FLOOR

UPPER FLOOR

VIEW INTO LIVING AND DINING ROOMS

ORDER BLUEPRINTS ANYTIME!
CALL TOLL-FREE 1-800-820-1296

Plan DD-1218-1

Plan copyright held by home designer/architect

PRICES AND DETAILS
ON PAGES 12-15

Covered Porch Invites Visitors

- This nice home welcomes visitors with its covered front porch and its wide-open living areas. Watch happily as your new neighbors drop by for a chat, and your relatives stream in at the holidays, their arms full of gifts.
- Detailed columns, railings and shutters decorate the front porch, which guides guests to the central entry.

- Just off the entry, the bright living room merges with the dining room. What a fantastic place to gather! The side wall is lined with glass, including a glass door that opens to the yard.
- The angled kitchen features a serving counter facing the dining room. A handy laundry closet and access to a storage area and the garage are nearby.
- An angled hall leads to the bedroom wing. The master suite offers a private bath, a walk-in closet and a dressing area with a vanity. Two more bedrooms and another full bath are off the hall.

Plan E-1217

Bedrooms: 3	**Baths:** 2

Living Area:	
Main floor	1,266 sq. ft.
Total Living Area:	**1,266 sq. ft.**
Garage and storage	550 sq. ft.
Exterior Wall Framing:	2x6

Foundation Options:
Crawlspace
Slab
(All plans can be built with your choice of foundation and framing. A generic conversion diagram is available. See order form.)

BLUEPRINT PRICE CODE:	**A**

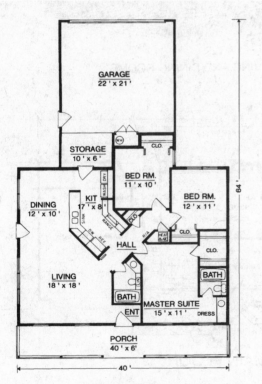

MAIN FLOOR

VIEW INTO KITCHEN AND LIVING ROOM FROM DINING ROOM

ORDER BLUEPRINTS ANYTIME!
CALL TOLL-FREE 1-800-820-1296

Plan E-1217
Plan copyright held by home designer/architect

PRICES AND DETAILS
ON PAGES 12-15   23

Comfortable Ranch Design

- This affordable ranch design offers numerous amenities and is ideally structured for comfortable living, both indoors and out.
- A tiled reception hall leads into the spacious living and dining rooms, which feature a handsome brick fireplace, a sloped ceiling and two sets of sliding glass doors to a lovely backyard terrace.
- The adjacent family room, designed for privacy, showcases a large boxed-out window with a built-in seat. The kitchen features an efficient U-shaped counter, an eating bar and a pantry.
- The master suite enjoys its own terrace, plus a private bath with a whirlpool tub.
- Two additional bedrooms share a second full bath.
- The garage has two separate storage areas, one accessible from the interior and the other from the backyard.

Plan K-518-A

Bedrooms: 3	Baths: 2
Living Area:	
Main floor	1,276 sq. ft.
Total Living Area:	**1,276 sq. ft.**
Standard basement	1,247 sq. ft.
Garage and storage	567 sq. ft.
Enclosed storage	12 sq. ft.
Exterior Wall Framing:	2x4 or 2x6

Foundation Options:

Standard basement
Slab
(All plans can be built with your choice of foundation and framing. A generic conversion diagram is available. See order form.)

BLUEPRINT PRICE CODE: A

VIEW INTO LIVING AND DINING ROOMS

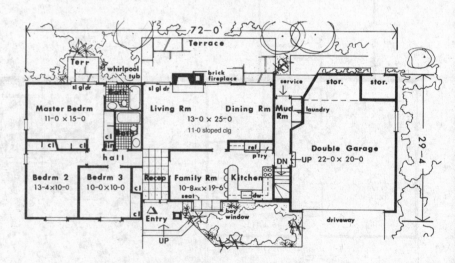

MAIN FLOOR

Plan K-518-A

Plan copyright held by home designer/architect

PRICES AND DETAILS ON PAGES 12-15

Family-Style Leisure Living

- This handsome ranch-style home features a floor plan that is great for family living and entertaining.
- In from the front porch, the formal areas flow together for a dramatic impact. The living room is enhanced by a fireplace and a 15-ft. sloped ceiling. A patio door in the dining room extends activities to the outdoors.
- The efficient U-shaped kitchen opens to the dining room and offers a pantry, a

window above the sink and abundant counter space.
- A good-sized utility room with convenient laundry facilities opens to the carport. This area also includes a large storage room and disappearing stairs to even more storage space.
- Three bedrooms and two baths occupy the sleeping wing. The master suite features a large walk-in closet and a private bath.
- The two remaining bedrooms are well proportioned and share a hall bath. Storage space is well accounted for here as well, with two linen closets and a coat closet in the bedroom hall.

Plan E-1308

Bedrooms: 3	Baths: 2
Living Area:	
Main floor	1,375 sq. ft.
Total Living Area:	**1,375 sq. ft.**
Carport	430 sq. ft.
Storage	95 sq. ft.
Exterior Wall Framing:	2x4

Foundation Options:

Crawlspace
Slab
(All plans can be built with your choice of foundation and framing. A generic conversion diagram is available. See order form.)

BLUEPRINT PRICE CODE: **A**

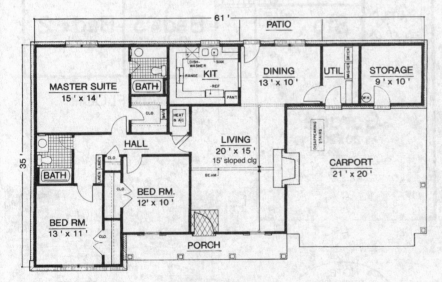

MAIN FLOOR

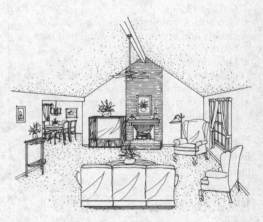

VIEW INTO LIVING ROOM

ORDER BLUEPRINTS ANYTIME!
CALL TOLL-FREE 1-800-820-1296

Plan E-1308
Plan copyright held by home designer/architect

PRICES AND DETAILS
ON PAGES 12-15

25

Janet Steyer

Bold, New Economic Plan

- The inviting entry of this economical three-bedroom ranch flows directly into the spacious living areas for an immediate welcome to the home. Bold angles inside and out add interest and functionality to the design.
- Warmed by a fireplace, the living room is easily served from the kitchen's angled snack counter. The adjoining dining area enjoys access to a covered backyard patio that's perfect for grilling out or enjoying a fine meal outdoors.
- The charming master bedroom offers a private bath, a dressing area with a vanity and kneespace, and a roomy walk-in closet.
- Two additional bedrooms boast walk-in closets and are served by a full hall bath nearby.
- The convenient laundry/utility room accesses the two-car garage, which includes extra storage space.
- At only 46 ft. wide, this design would be suitable for a narrow lot.

Plan SDG-81115

Bedrooms: 3	Baths: 2
Living Area:	
Main floor	1,296 sq. ft.
Total Living Area:	**1,296 sq. ft.**
Garage	400 sq. ft.
Exterior Wall Framing:	2x4
Foundation Options:	

Slab
(All plans can be built with your choice of foundation and framing. A generic conversion diagram is available. See order form.)

BLUEPRINT PRICE CODE:	A

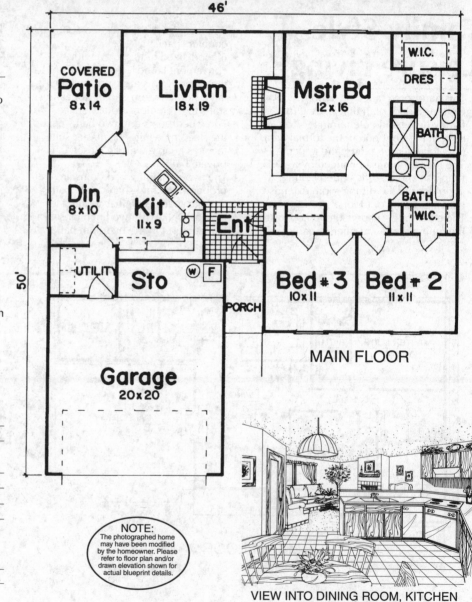

MAIN FLOOR

46'

50'

COVERED Patio 8 x 14

LivRm 18 x 19

MstrBd 12 x 16

W.I.C.

DRES

BATH

Din 8 x 10

Kit 11 x 9

Ent

BATH

W.I.C.

UTILITY

Sto

W F

PORCH

Bed # 3 10 x 11

Bed # 2 11 x 11

Garage 20 x 20

NOTE:
The photographed home may have been modified by the homeowner. Please refer to floor plan and/or drawn elevation shown for actual blueprint details.

VIEW INTO DINING ROOM, KITCHEN AND LIVING ROOM

ORDER BLUEPRINTS ANYTIME! CALL TOLL-FREE 1-800-820-1296

Plan SDG-81115

Plan copyright held by home designer/architect

PRICES AND DETAILS ON PAGES 12-15

A Chalet for Today

- With its wraparound deck and soaring windows, this chalet-style home is ideal for recreational living and scenic sites.
- The living and dining rooms combine to take advantage of the cathedral ceiling, the rugged stone fireplace and the view through the spectacular windows.
- The open kitchen features a bright corner sink and a nifty breakfast bar that adjoins the living area.
- The handy main-floor laundry area is near two bedrooms and a full bath.
- A vaulted ceiling crowns the quiet, versatile study.
- The master suite and a storage area share the upper floor. A high ceiling, a whirlpool bath and sweeping views give this space an elegant feel.
- The basement option has a tuck-under garage and additional storage space.

Plan AHP-9340

Bedrooms: 3+	Baths: 2
Living Area:	
Upper floor	332 sq. ft.
Main floor	974 sq. ft.
Total Living Area:	**1,306 sq. ft.**
Daylight basement	624 sq. ft.
Garage	350 sq. ft.
Exterior Wall Framing:	2x4 or 2x6

Foundation Options:
Daylight basement
Crawlspace
Slab
(All plans can be built with your choice of foundation and framing. A generic conversion diagram is available. See order form.)

BLUEPRINT PRICE CODE:	**A**

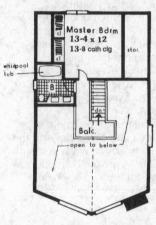

UPPER FLOOR

VIEW INTO LIVING AND DINING ROOMS

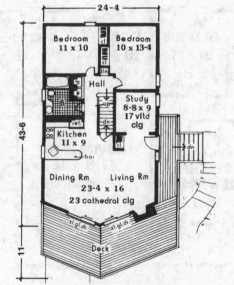

MAIN FLOOR

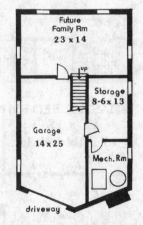

DAYLIGHT BASEMENT

ORDER BLUEPRINTS ANYTIME!
CALL TOLL-FREE 1-800-820-1296

Plan AHP-9340
Plan copyright held by home designer/architect

PRICES AND DETAILS
ON PAGES 12-15

27

It's All in the Details

- It's the mouthwatering details that give this home its distinctively country character. Its facade is a marvel; the graceful columns, railings, dormer windows and high transoms accentuate the inviting porch.
- Brightened by radiant windows, the large living room hosts a warming fireplace. Two high dormers admit additional natural light.

- Straight back, a bay window punctuated by French doors livens the dining area. A snack bar links it to the kitchen, which you'll find adaptable to both casual and formal meals.
- A sizable terrace overlooking the backyard is the perfect arena for lazy summer picnics and frolicsome Sunday afternoons.
- The sprawling master bedroom is blessed with a pair of windows in the sleeping chamber that wake you with morning light. A private bath offers a zesty whirlpool tub and a separate shower for busy weekday mornings.

Plan AHP-9615	
Bedrooms: 3	**Baths: 2**
Living Area:	
Main floor	1,331 sq. ft.
Total Living Area:	**1,331 sq. ft.**
Standard basement	1,377 sq. ft.
Garage	459 sq. ft.
Exterior Wall Framing:	2x4 or 2x6

Foundation Options:
Standard basement
Crawlspace
Slab
(All plans can be built with your choice of foundation and framing. A generic conversion diagram is available. See order form.)

BLUEPRINT PRICE CODE:	A

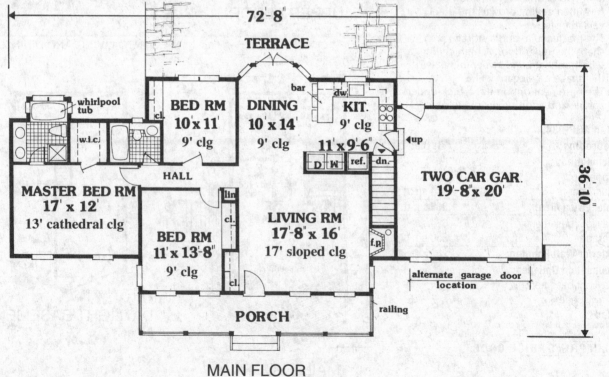

MAIN FLOOR

Plan AHP-9615

Plan copyright held by home designer/architect

PRICES AND DETAILS
ON PAGES 12-15

High-Profile Contemporary

- This design does away with wasted space, putting the emphasis on quality rather than on size.
- The angled floor plan minimizes hall space and creates smooth traffic flow. The roof framing is square, allowing for economical construction.
- The living and dining rooms share a cathedral ceiling, a fireplace and a spectacular view of a rear terrace.
- The dining room includes a glass-filled alcove and sliding patio doors topped by transom windows. Tall windows frame the living room fireplace and trace the slope of the ceiling.
- A pass-through joins the dining room to the combination kitchen and family room, which features a snack bar and a clerestory window.
- The sleeping wing hosts a super master suite, which boasts a skylighted dressing area and a private bath. The vaulted second bedroom shares a hall bath with the den or third bedroom.

Plan K-688-D

Bedrooms: 2+	Baths: 2½
Living Area:	
Main floor	1,340 sq. ft.
Total Living Area:	**1,340 sq. ft.**
Standard basement	1,235 sq. ft.
Garage and storage	500 sq. ft.
Exterior Wall Framing:	2x4 or 2x6

Foundation Options:

Standard basement

Slab

(All plans can be built with your choice of foundation and framing. A generic conversion diagram is available. See order form.)

BLUEPRINT PRICE CODE: **A**

VIEW INTO DINING AND LIVING ROOMS

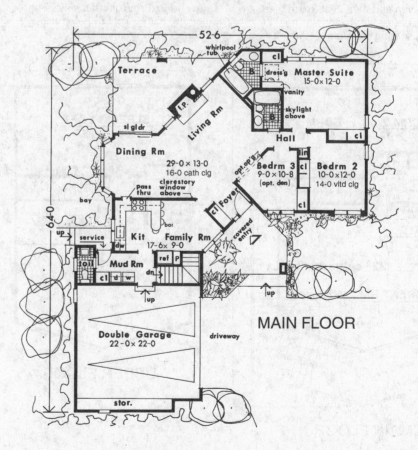

MAIN FLOOR

ORDER BLUEPRINTS ANYTIME!
CALL TOLL-FREE 1-800-820-1296

Plan K-688-D
Plan copyright held by home designer/architect

PRICES AND DETAILS
ON PAGES 12-15

29

A Prowed Plan to Be Proud of

- This attractive, open design, with its wonderful prowed Great Room, can function as a cabin, a mountain retreat or a permanent residence.
- A split-landing stairway ascends to a wraparound deck that leads to the home's entry. The deck cleverly conceals the home's tuck-under garage.
- The kitchen and the Great Room merge to form a huge family activity area under a soaring cathedral ceiling. Its

angled windows offer enviable views, while its woodstove lends warmth to any occasion.
- Two quiet main-floor bedrooms share a full bath and are great for kids or for guests.
- Upstairs, an open balcony loft offers elevated views through the front windows. This area may serve nicely as a reading or study alcove, or as a hobby/craft area.
- The large sleeping loft could be divided into two smaller bedrooms or used as a large and luxurious master suite. The adjoining bath is split to help make mornings more manageable.

Plan I-1354-B

Bedrooms: 3	Baths: 2
Living Area:	
Upper floor	366 sq. ft.
Main floor	988 sq. ft.
Total Living Area:	**1,354 sq. ft.**
Daylight basement	658 sq. ft.
Tuck-under garage	260 sq. ft.
Exterior Wall Framing:	2x6

Foundation Options:

Daylight basement
(All plans can be built with your choice of foundation and framing. A generic conversion diagram is available. See order form.)

BLUEPRINT PRICE CODE:	**A**

MAIN FLOOR

- 26'-0"
- BDRM 2 12⁴ x 9³
- BDRM 1 12⁴ x 10²
- DN UP
- KIT. 8² x 10²
- 22² cathedral clg
- GREAT RM 25² x 16²
- WOOD STOVE
- UP
- DN DN
- DECK
- 48'-0"

UPPER FLOOR

- 26'-0"
- SLEEP'G LOFT 24² x 13²
- UP
- LOFT 16² x 6²
- OPEN TO BELOW
- 40'-0"

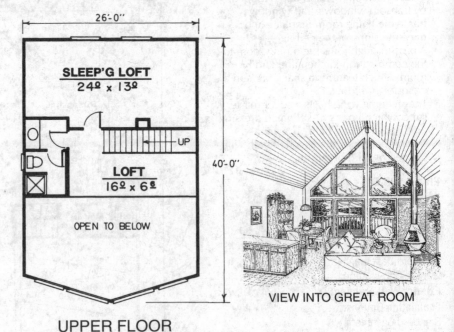

VIEW INTO GREAT ROOM

Plan I-1354-B

Plan copyright held by home designer/architect

PRICES AND DETAILS
ON PAGES 12-15

Inviting Windows

- This comfortable home presents an impressive facade, with its large and inviting front window arrangement.
- A step down from the front entry, the Great Room boasts a sloped ceiling with a barrel-vaulted area that outlines the half-round front window. The striking angled fireplace can be enjoyed from the adjoining dining area.
- The galley-style kitchen hosts a half-round cutout above the sink and a breakfast area that accesses a backyard deck and patio. The kitchen, breakfast area and dining area also are enhanced by vaulted ceilings.
- The master bedroom features a boxed-out window, a walk-in closet and a dramatic sloped ceiling. The private bath includes a garden tub, a separate shower and a private toilet compartment.
- Another full bath serves the two remaining bedrooms, one of which has sliding glass doors to the deck and would make an ideal den.

VIEW INTO GREAT ROOM

REAR VIEW

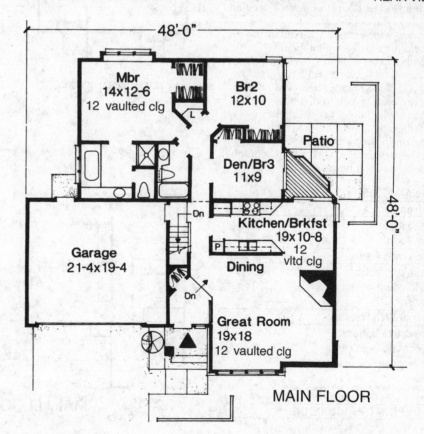

MAIN FLOOR

Plan B-902

Bedrooms: 2+	Baths: 2
Living Area:	
Main floor	1,368 sq. ft.
Total Living Area:	**1,368 sq. ft.**
Standard basement	1,368 sq. ft.
Garage	412 sq. ft.
Exterior Wall Framing:	2x4

Foundation Options:
Standard basement
(All plans can be built with your choice of foundation and framing. A generic conversion diagram is available. See order form.)

BLUEPRINT PRICE CODE: A

Plan B-902
Plan copyright held by home designer/architect

PRICES AND DETAILS ON PAGES 12-15

Formal Facade

- Formally balanced with twin dormers, gables and bay windows, a charming Southern-style exterior complements this home's informal interior. Its design boasts a compact, efficient plan with highly functional spaces.
- Featuring a fireplace, a built-in media center and a volume ceiling, the pavilion-style Great Room is flooded with light from the home's front and rear porches.
- Sliding glass doors to the back deck and a bay window highlight the dining room, which is easily served by the adjoining U-shaped kitchen.
- With a large walk-in closet, a private bath, a tray ceiling and a bay window, the secluded master bedroom offers wonderful respite from a busy day.
- Across the home, two secondary bedrooms share a full hall bath.
- An unfinished attic provides future expansion space, ideal for an additional bedroom or a home office.

Plan AX-97359

Bedrooms: 3+	Baths: 2
Living Area:	
Main floor	1,380 sq. ft.
Total Living Area:	**1,380 sq. ft.**
Future upper floor	385 sq. ft.
Standard basement	1,380 sq. ft.
Garage	427 sq. ft.
Exterior Wall Framing:	2x4

Foundation Options:
Standard basement
Crawlspace
Slab
(All plans can be built with your choice of foundation and framing. A generic conversion diagram is available. See order form.)

BLUEPRINT PRICE CODE:	A

FUTURE EXPANSION
20'-0"x 15'-4"

DN

DN

UPPER FLOOR

VIEW INTO GREAT ROOM

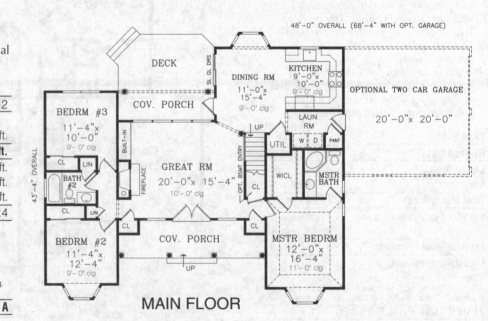

48'-0" OVERALL (68'-4" WITH OPT. GARAGE)

DECK

COV. PORCH

DINING RM
11'-0"x
15'-4"
9'-0" clg

KITCHEN
9'-0"x
10'-0"
9'-0" clg

OPTIONAL TWO CAR GARAGE
20'-0"x 20'-0"

BEDRM #3
11'-4"x
10'-0"
9'-0" clg

BUILT-IN

FIREPLACE

GREAT RM
20'-0"x 15'-4"
10'-0" clg

LAUN RM

UTIL

W D PANT

WICL

MSTR BATH

BATH #2

43'-4" OVERALL

CL LIN

CL LIN

CL

CL

CL

OPT. BSMT ENTRY

UP

BEDRM #2
11'-4"x
12'-4"
9'-0" clg

COV. PORCH

UP

MSTR BEDRM
12'-0"x
16'-4"
11'-0" clg

MAIN FLOOR

Plan AX-97359

Plan copyright held by home designer/architect

PRICES AND DETAILS
ON PAGES 12-15

A Place of Your Own

- This charming cottage serves as a cozy getaway home or as comfortable guest quarters adjoining a main residence. Quaint dormers, hexagonal porthole windows and spindle columns at the entry make it anything but ordinary.
- Don't let the minimal square footage fool you. The living room (with a sloped ceiling and a built-in media center), the kitchenette and the bayed dining area (with a pantry) are open and inviting. Multiple windows and the lofty ceiling increase the area's spacious feel.
- The master bedroom and its private bath are tucked just off the foyer. Close the door and no one need know that your bed is unmade and your workout clothes are strewn about!
- In the middle of all this convenience is an unexpected luxury. A spiral staircase leads to a loft that could become the perfect studio, exercise room, library or hobby room. The loft can also be expanded if your demand for space increases.

Plan L-564-CT	
Bedrooms: 1+	**Baths:** 1
Living Area:	
Upper floor	126 sq. ft.
Main floor	440 sq. ft.
Total Living Area:	**566 sq. ft.**
Exterior Wall Framing:	2x4
Foundation Options:	
Slab	

(All plans can be built with your choice of foundation and framing. A generic conversion diagram is available. See order form.)

BLUEPRINT PRICE CODE:	**AA**

MAIN FLOOR

Dining

pantry

Kitchenette

Bath

TV

Living Room
11' x 15'
17' vaulted clg

up

linen

display niche

Bedroom
10' x 10'-8"

19'-0"

27'-0"

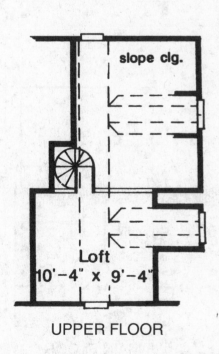

slope clg.

Loft
10'-4" x 9'-4"

UPPER FLOOR

Plan L-564-CT

Plan copyright held by home designer/architect

PRICES AND DETAILS
ON PAGES 12-15

This Porch Is Just Right

- This home's front porch offers just enough room for you to set out a couple of Adirondack chairs, cover yourself with a wool blanket or two, and wait for the stars to appear in the night sky.
- Inside, warm up in front of the family room's rustic stone fireplace. This spacious room also boasts a cathedral ceiling and is open to the upper floor.
- The island kitchen includes plenty of counter space for preparing gourmet meals. Serve them in the dining room, which is brightened by a Palladian window overlooking the front yard.
- The home's one large bedroom features a triple window arrangement looking out to a side porch. A walk-in closet stores your clothes. The nearby full bath sports a large soaking tub and room for a stackable washer and dryer.
- The side porch offers a covered walkway to the discreet carport.
- Upstairs, a handy loft can serve as sleeping quarters for the kids or for overnight guests. They'll appreciate the walk-in closet and views to the living areas below.

Plan J-9503	
Bedrooms: 1+	**Baths: 1**
Living Area:	
Upper floor	148 sq. ft.
Main floor	707 sq. ft.
Total Living Area:	**855 sq. ft.**
Standard basement	707 sq. ft.
Carport	256 sq. ft.
Exterior Wall Framing:	2x4

Foundation Options:
Standard basement
Crawlspace
Slab
(All plans can be built with your choice of foundation and framing. A generic conversion diagram is available. See order form.)

BLUEPRINT PRICE CODE:	**AA**

MAIN FLOOR

VIEW INTO FAMILY ROOM

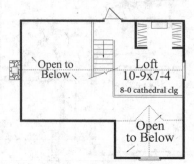

UPPER FLOOR

Plan J-9503
Plan copyright held by home designer/architect

PRICES AND DETAILS
ON PAGES 12-15

Cozy, Cost-Saving Retreat

- This cozy cabin is the perfect vacation retreat for that special mountain, lake or river location.
- The design is large enough to provide comfortable living quarters and small enough to fit a modest building budget.
- A vaulted ceiling and expanses of glass add volume to the living and dining area. Double doors provide access to an inviting deck or patio.
- The U-shaped kitchen offers a bright sink and a convenient pass-through to the dining area.
- A quiet bedroom and a hall bath complete the main floor.
- The upper floor consists of a vaulted loft that provides sweeping views of the living areas below and the scenery outside. The railed loft could serve as an extra sleeping area or a quiet haven for reading, relaxing and other activities.

Plan I-880-A

Bedrooms: 1+	Baths: 1
Living Area:	
Upper floor	308 sq. ft.
Main floor	572 sq. ft.
Total Living Area:	**880 sq. ft.**
Exterior Wall Framing:	2x6

Foundation Options:

Crawlspace

(All plans can be built with your choice of foundation and framing. A generic conversion diagram is available. See order form.)

BLUEPRINT PRICE CODE:	**AA**

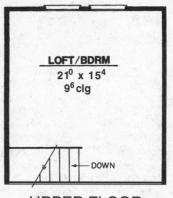

UPPER FLOOR

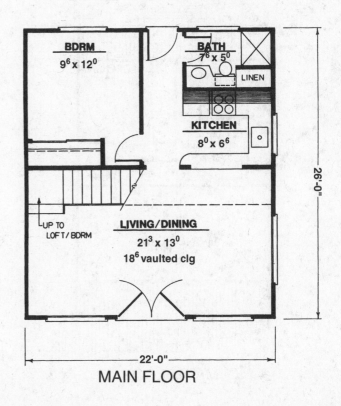

MAIN FLOOR

ORDER BLUEPRINTS ANYTIME!
CALL TOLL-FREE 1-800-820-1296

Plan I-880-A
Plan copyright held by home designer/architect

PRICES AND DETAILS
ON PAGES 12-15

35

Carefree Getaway

- Everything you need for a relaxing retreat can be found in this carefree getaway A-frame.
- A dramatic wall of glass allows sunshine to drench the expansive living room, which features a cozy woodstove and a soaring sloped ceiling.
- The U-shaped kitchen offers plenty of space for those essential appliances.

- The main-floor bedroom boasts a large rear-facing window and an ample closet with a handy storage area. Access to an expansive rear deck is nearby.
- Conveniently located right across the hall, the full bath includes a shower and easy access to a generous storage space.
- Upstairs, glorious views to both the front and rear can be enjoyed from the airy balcony room or extra bedroom. A dramatic ceiling slopes above.
- Sliding glass doors open to a romantic private deck—the perfect spot for an evening rendezvous.

Plan H-15-1

Bedrooms: 1+	Baths: 1

Living Area:

Upper floor	254 sq. ft.
Main floor	654 sq. ft.

Total Living Area:	**908 sq. ft.**

Exterior Wall Framing:	2x4

Foundation Options:

Crawlspace
(All plans can be built with your choice of foundation and framing. A generic conversion diagram is available. See order form.)

BLUEPRINT PRICE CODE: **AA**

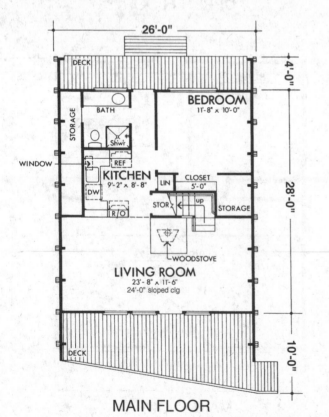

MAIN FLOOR

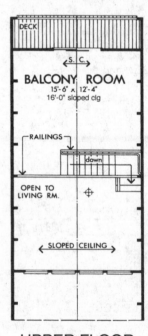

UPPER FLOOR

Plan H-15-1

Plan copyright held by home designer/architect

PRICES AND DETAILS
ON PAGES 12-15

Relax in the Country

- This country home provides plenty of room to relax, with its expansive porches and wide-open living spaces.
- Just off the front porch, the living room boasts a soothing fireplace with a raised brick hearth. The cathedral ceiling is shared with the adjoining dining room, which offers French-door access to the backyard porch.
- The walk-through kitchen features a handy pantry, plus a laundry closet that houses a stackable washer and dryer.
- A convenient pocket door leads to the secluded full bath.
- The master bedroom boasts two closets and private access to the bath.
- An open stairway with an oak handrail leads up to another bedroom, with a cozy seat under an arched window arrangement. Other features include a high ceiling, a pair of closets and access to extra storage space.

Plan J-90016

Bedrooms: 2	Baths: 1
Living Area:	
Upper floor	203 sq. ft.
Main floor	720 sq. ft.
Total Living Area:	**923 sq. ft.**
Standard basement	720 sq. ft.
Exterior Wall Framing:	2x6

Foundation Options:

Standard basement
Crawlspace
Slab
(All plans can be built with your choice of foundation and framing. A generic conversion diagram is available. See order form.)

BLUEPRINT PRICE CODE: AA

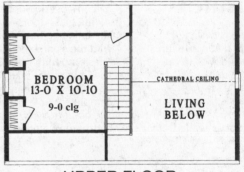

UPPER FLOOR

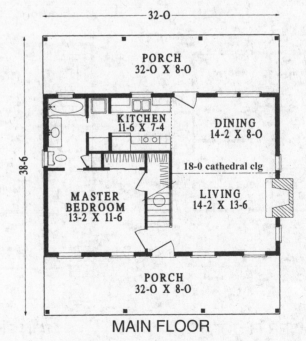

MAIN FLOOR

Plan J-90016

Plan copyright held by home designer/architect

PRICES AND DETAILS
ON PAGES 12-15

Sunny Chalet

- This captivating home is designed to maximize indoor and outdoor living. It features expansive windows, an open main floor and a large deck.
- The lower-level entry leads up a staircase to the spacious living room, which features a cathedral ceiling, an energy-efficient fireplace, a railed balcony overlooking the foyer and sliding glass doors to the deck.
- The adjacent bayed dining room merges with the skylighted kitchen, which also boasts a handy serving bar.
- The lower floor features two spacious bedrooms that share a full bath, complete with a whirlpool tub.
- The quiet den could serve as a third bedroom or a guest room.

Plan K-532-L

Bedrooms: 2+	Baths: 1½
Living Area:	
Main floor	492 sq. ft.
Lower floor	488 sq. ft.
Total Living Area:	**980 sq. ft.**
Exterior Wall Framing:	2x4 or 2x6

Foundation Options:

Crawlspace
(All plans can be built with your choice of foundation and framing. A generic conversion diagram is available. See order form.)

BLUEPRINT PRICE CODE: **AA**

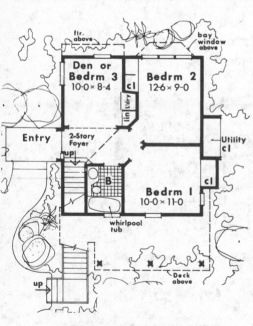

LOWER FLOOR

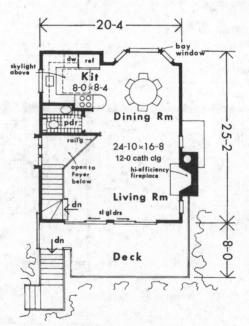

MAIN FLOOR

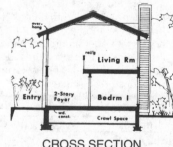

CROSS SECTION

VIEW INTO LIVING
AND DINING ROOMS

Plan K-532-L

Plan copyright held by home designer/architect

PRICES AND DETAILS
ON PAGES 12-15

Classic Cottage with Style

- Nicely finished in striking stucco, this cozy cottage features classic, space-efficient style.
- Beyond the columned front porch, the angled entry opens to the elegant living room, with its handsome fireplace and dramatic vaulted ceiling.
- The adjoining dining room is brightened by a trio of French doors, one of which opens to the backyard.
- The uniquely shaped kitchen hosts a sprawling serving bar that facilitates holiday entertaining. You'll love the convenience of the adjacent laundry area, which doubles as a mudroom.
- A rear porch accesses a handy outdoor storage room, which is perfect for all of your gardening necessities.
- Just off the kitchen, the sizable and secluded master suite boasts an angled entrance, while the luxurious private bath offers a garden spa tub and a roomy walk-in closet.
- The secondary bedroom enjoys a bright boxed-out window and private access to another full bath.

Plan E-901

Bedrooms: 2	Baths: 2
Living Area:	
Main floor	984 sq. ft.
Total Living Area:	**984 sq. ft.**
Storage	113 sq. ft.
Exterior Wall Framing:	2x4

Foundation Options:

Crawlspace
Slab
(All plans can be built with your choice of foundation and framing. A generic conversion diagram is available. See order form.)

BLUEPRINT PRICE CODE: **AA**

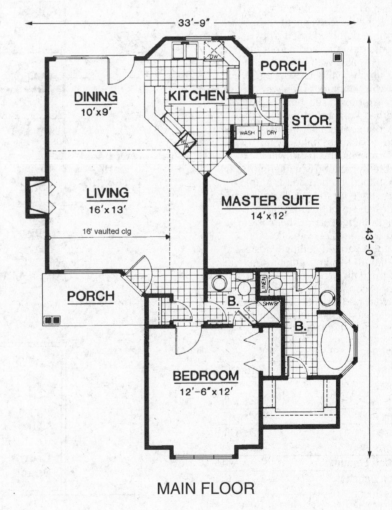

MAIN FLOOR

ORDER BLUEPRINTS ANYTIME!
CALL TOLL-FREE 1-800-820-1296

Plan E-901
Plan copyright held by home designer/architect

PRICES AND DETAILS
ON PAGES 12-15

39

Home at Last

- This split-level home will serve as the backdrop to memorable and everyday family activities for years to come.
- A charming porch adorned by two handsome columns and a front-facing gable serves as a warm welcome home.
- Inside, a high ceiling crowns the living room, which includes plenty of windows for extra sunshine.
- An overhead plant shelf leads to the dining room, where sliding glass doors open to a backyard patio. When summer arrives, this patio will undoubtedly be a busy gathering spot.
- The U-shaped kitchen boasts ample counter space for the family cook. The open design simplifies mealtime.
- Up a half-flight of stairs, the master bedroom features private access to a hall bath. A vaulted ceiling lends a stylish flair to this important room.
- Across the hall, two good-sized bedrooms complete the floor plan.
- When your budget and needs dictate, add the optional garage and finish the versatile basement level.

Plan B-92009

Bedrooms: 3	Baths: 1
Living Area:	
Main floor	992 sq. ft.
Total Living Area:	**992 sq. ft.**
Partial basement	532 sq. ft.
Garage (optional)	225 sq. ft.
Exterior Wall Framing:	2x4

Foundation Options:

Partial basement

(All plans can be built with your choice of foundation and framing. A generic conversion diagram is available. See order form.)

BLUEPRINT PRICE CODE:	**AA**

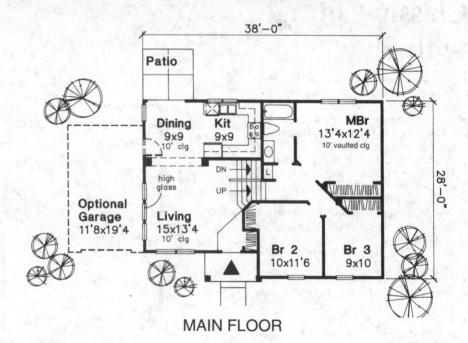

MAIN FLOOR

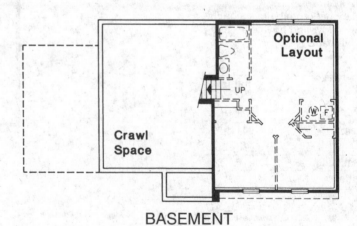

BASEMENT

**ORDER BLUEPRINTS ANYTIME!
CALL TOLL-FREE 1-800-820-1296**

Plan B-92009
Plan copyright held by home designer/architect

**PRICES AND DETAILS
ON PAGES 12-15**

A Room with a View

- The window wall in this chalet-style home's Great Room ensures that no matter where you're sitting, you have a fantastic view of the outdoors. A vaulted two-story ceiling with two skylights provides a window to the heavens also.
- Convenience is key in the kitchen. Everything's within reach, and the washer and dryer are a just few steps away. Prepare some afternoon snacks and take them to the nature-watchers in the Great Room.
- On those beautiful evenings that are meant for barbecues, move outside to the extravagant deck and soak up the sights from there.
- The entire upstairs is dedicated to the master bedroom. An overlook to the Great Room, a walk-in closet, two skylights in the vaulted ceiling, and a full attached bath all provide rustic luxury.
- Guests have comfortable quarters in the downstairs bedroom, seconds away from the other full bath.

Plan SUN-2940

Bedrooms: 2	Baths: 2

Living Area:	
Upper floor	336 sq. ft.
Main floor	672 sq. ft.
Total Living Area:	**1,008 sq. ft.**
Exterior Wall Framing:	2x6

Foundation Options:

Crawlspace
(All plans can be built with your choice of foundation and framing. A generic conversion diagram is available. See order form.)

BLUEPRINT PRICE CODE: A

VIEW INTO GREAT ROOM

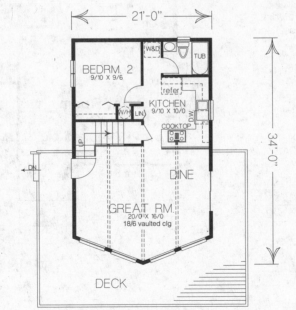

MAIN FLOOR

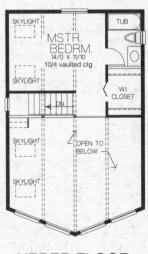

UPPER FLOOR

ORDER BLUEPRINTS ANYTIME!
CALL TOLL-FREE 1-800-820-1296

Plan SUN-2940
Plan copyright held by home designer/architect

PRICES AND DETAILS
ON PAGES 12-15

41

Designed for Today's Family

- Compact and affordable, this home is designed for today's young families.
- The Great Room features corner windows, an impressive fireplace and a vaulted ceiling. A built-in bookcase holds novels, family photos and special mementos.
- The open kitchen/dining room combination offers plenty of space for two people to share food preparation and clean-up chores. A convenient pantry is a nice extra.
- Sliding glass doors open to a sunny deck and a handy storage area for gardening tools or sports equipment.
- The master suite is impressive for a home of this size, and includes a cozy window seat, a large walk-in closet and a private bath.
- Another full bath serves the roomy second bedroom, as well as the rest of the main floor. The optional third bedroom could be used as a den or as an expanded dining area.

Plan B-8317

Bedrooms: 2+	Baths: 2
Living Area:	
Main floor	1,016 sq. ft.
Total Living Area:	**1,016 sq. ft.**
Exterior Wall Framing:	2x4

Foundation Options:

Slab

(All plans can be built with your choice of foundation and framing. A generic conversion diagram is available. See order form.)

BLUEPRINT PRICE CODE: A

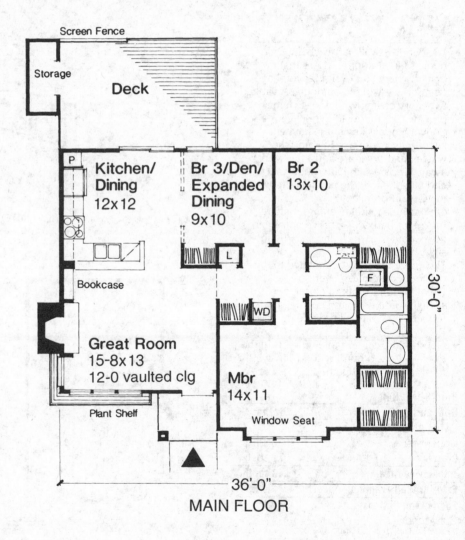

Screen Fence

Storage

Deck

P

Kitchen/ Dining
12x12

Br 3/Den/ Expanded Dining
9x10

Br 2
13x10

L

F

Bookcase

WD

Great Room
15-8x13
12-0 vaulted clg

Mbr
14x11

Plant Shelf

Window Seat

30'-0"

36'-0"

MAIN FLOOR

Plan B-8317

Plan copyright held by home designer/architect

PRICES AND DETAILS ON PAGES 12-15

Stylish Cottage

- This delightful, cottage-style home conceals a spacious, up-to-date interior behind its timeless facade.
- A recessed, arched entry adds interest to the stucco facade.
- Inside, the living room flaunts a lofty cathedral ceiling. Exposed wood trusses add a rustic air. You'll love gathering in this majestic space with family and friends.
- The intimate dining area, flooded with light from its surrounding windows, adjoins an efficient, L-shaped kitchen. A door to the rear garden makes it easy for the family chef to snip fresh herbs.
- The loft, an exciting retreat accessed from the living room by an incline ladder, can become whatever type of sanctuary you envision: a home office, an artist's studio or perhaps a writer's quiet getaway.
- Ample closet space and attractive sloped ceilings enhance the two bedrooms.
- The roomy two-car garage features extra storage space.

Plan L-902-SA

Bedrooms: 2	Baths: 1

Living Area:

Upper floor	127 sq. ft.
Main floor	902 sq. ft.
Total Living Area:	**1,029 sq. ft.**
Detached garage and storage	510 sq. ft.
Exterior Wall Framing:	**2x4**

Foundation Options:

Slab
(All plans can be built with your choice of foundation and framing. A generic conversion diagram is available. See order form.)

BLUEPRINT PRICE CODE:	**A**

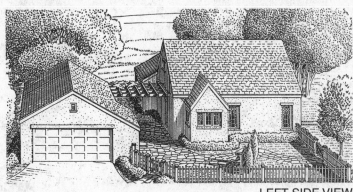

LEFT SIDE VIEW

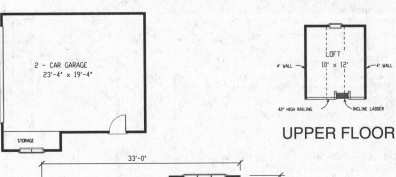

2 - CAR GARAGE
23'-4" x 19'-4"

STORAGE

LOFT
10' x 12'

4' WALL   4' WALL

42" HIGH RAILING   INCLINE LADDER

UPPER FLOOR

33'-0"

SLOPE CEILING

DINING TABLE

KITCHEN
11' x 11'

BEDROOM 1
11'-4" x 12'-8"
9'-0" clg

LINEN

OPTIONAL INCLINE
LADDER TO LOFT

LIVING ROOM
16'-4" x 16'-8"
18'-6" cathedral clg

BEDROOM 2
11'-4" x 11'-4"
9'-0" clg

CATHEDRAL CEILING WITH
EXPOSED WOOD TRUSSES

SLOPE CLG.

33'-4"

MAIN FLOOR

Plan L-902-SA

Plan copyright held by home designer/architect

PRICES AND DETAILS
ON PAGES 12-15

Country-Style Coziness

- Designed as a starter or retirement home, this delightful plan has a charming exterior and an open, airy interior.
- The spacious front porch gives guests a warm welcome and provides added space for relaxing or entertaining. The modified hip roof, half-round louver vent and decorative porch railings are other distinguishing features of the facade.
- Inside, the open dining and living rooms are heightened by dramatic vaulted ceilings. The streamlined kitchen has a snack counter joining it to the dining room. All three rooms reap the benefits of the fireplace.
- A laundry closet is in the hall leading to the three bedrooms. The main bath is close by.
- The master bedroom suite offers its own bath, plus a private patio sequestered behind the garage.

Plan APS-1002

Bedrooms: 3	Baths: 2
Living Area:	
Main floor	1,050 sq. ft.
Total Living Area:	**1,050 sq. ft.**
Standard basement	1,050 sq. ft.
Garage	288 sq. ft.
Exterior Wall Framing:	2x4

Foundation Options:

Standard basement
Slab

(All plans can be built with your choice of foundation and framing. A generic conversion diagram is available. See order form.)

BLUEPRINT PRICE CODE:	A

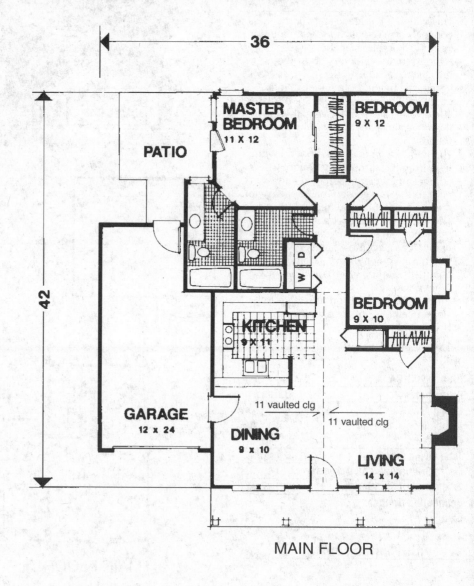

MAIN FLOOR

Plan APS-1002

Plan copyright held by home designer/architect

PRICES AND DETAILS
ON PAGES 12-15

Family Living

- When you walk into this home's 17-ft.-high side entry, you will meet all the sights and smells of family life: a crackling fire in the living room's fireplace, something delicious cooking in the kitchen and the dining room table set with your finest china.

- The kitchen features an optional island countertop and a serving bar that looks into the sunny living room. Sliding glass doors in the dining room open to the starry night sky.

- Tucked into the corner of the house, the sun-soaked study features a large window seat for quiet reading. Sliding glass doors lead onto the rear patio, a perfect spot for sipping iced tea in the warm months.

- The main-floor master bedroom enjoys a substantial measure of privacy from the rest of the home. Ample closet space, a boxed-out window and private access to a full bath lengthen its list of luxuries.

- Two more bedrooms and a full bath upstairs give the kids plenty of room for themselves.

Plan BRF-1070

Bedrooms: 3	Baths: 2
Living Area:	
Upper floor	327 sq. ft.
Main floor	743 sq. ft.
Total Living Area:	**1,070 sq. ft.**
Garage	252 sq. ft.
Exterior Wall Framing:	2x4

Foundation Options:

Slab

(All plans can be built with your choice of foundation and framing. A generic conversion diagram is available. See order form.)

BLUEPRINT PRICE CODE: A

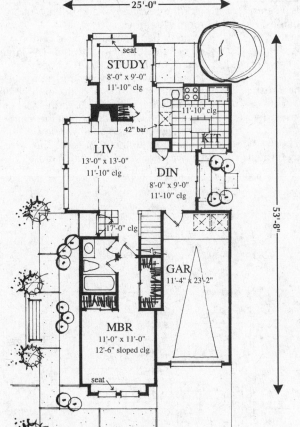

MAIN FLOOR

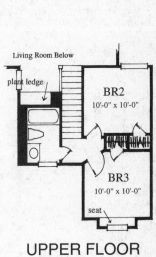

UPPER FLOOR

ORDER BLUEPRINTS ANYTIME!
CALL TOLL-FREE 1-800-820-1296

Plan BRF-1070

Plan copyright held by home designer/architect

PRICES AND DETAILS
ON PAGES 12-15

45

Great Highlight

- The highlight of this design is a central Great Room that's ideal for parties! A serving bar from the kitchen offers a spot for an appetizer spread, while a backyard patio provides overflow space when the weather is right.
- Because of its openness to the Great Room, the bright dining room can accommodate a small table as easily as a large one.
- The efficient, galley-style kitchen benefits from the light coming through the dining room's large windows, and

its proximity to the garage means a short breakfast-to-car run in the morning! A handy—and bright—utility room is nearby.

- A trio of bedrooms is located on the other side of the Great Room. The large bedroom at the back of the home features a walk-in closet and a private half-bath. Plans for an optional full bath are included with the blueprints.
- Each of the two bedrooms at the front of the home sports a tall window looking out to the front yard. The hallway houses a wide linen closet, along with a full bath.

Plan KD-1022	
Bedrooms: 3	**Baths:** 1½–2
Living Area:	
Main floor	1,022 sq. ft.
Total Living Area:	**1,022 sq. ft.**
Garage and storage	460 sq. ft.
Exterior Wall Framing:	2x4
Foundation Options:	
Slab	

(All plans can be built with your choice of foundation and framing. A generic conversion diagram is available. See order form.)

BLUEPRINT PRICE CODE:	A

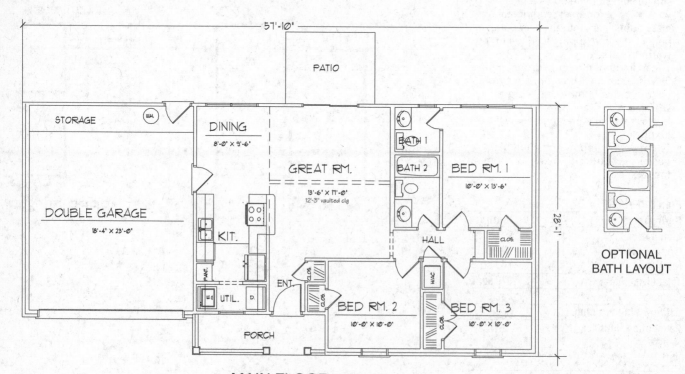

MAIN FLOOR

OPTIONAL BATH LAYOUT

Plan KD-1022

Plan copyright held by home designer/architect

PRICES AND DETAILS ON PAGES 12-15

A Family Affair

- The thoughtful design of the sleeping wing in this one-story home makes it ideal for families with young children.
- The front porch serves as an inviting entry point to the spacious floor plan.
- Inside, the central living area is topped by a cathedral ceiling and features a fireplace. This natural hub of family life is sized to accommodate both casual and formal living and dining.
- A French door next to the fireplace leads to a sun deck that extends the living space into the backyard. The deck's proximity to the kitchen makes it a handy spot for outdoor grilling.
- A sunny breakfast nook lies just past the galley kitchen. Enjoy your Saturday coffee here, and keep an eye on backyard activities through an optional bay window.
- A washer and dryer are close at hand, yet tucked away from view.
- The master suite includes a private bath and a walk-in closet, and is reassuringly close to the secondary bedrooms, which share a full bath.

Plan APS-1004	
Bedrooms: 3	**Baths:** 2
Living Area:	
Main floor	1,069 sq. ft.
Total Living Area:	**1,069 sq. ft.**
Garage	460 sq. ft.
Exterior Wall Framing:	2x4

Foundation Options:

Crawlspace
(All plans can be built with your choice of foundation and framing. A generic conversion diagram is available. See order form.)

BLUEPRINT PRICE CODE:	**A**

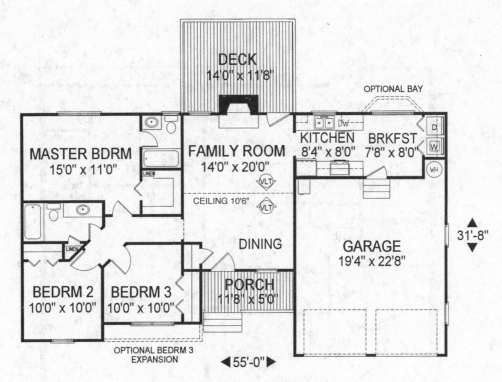

MAIN FLOOR

ORDER BLUEPRINTS ANYTIME!
CALL TOLL-FREE 1-800-820-1296

Plan APS-1004
Plan copyright held by home designer/architect

PRICES AND DETAILS
ON PAGES 12-15

47

Central Design

- This home's central design places the common rooms together and in close proximity to the bedrooms—perfect for a growing family.
- A railed front porch contributes to the attractive facade and is just the right size for a comfortable swing or a rocker. Just inside the entry, a handy closet houses coats and shoes.
- The stunning vaulted Great Room offers a corner fireplace with a wide hearth and access to a rear patio. It's easy to envision yourself entertaining guests or

enjoying family meals in the sun-filled dining room nearby.
- The efficient, galley-style kitchen features a garden window above the sink and a breakfast bar for quick meals or an appetizer spread.
- Enjoy the vaulted ceiling, the walk-in closet and the private bath of the master suite, which is allotted generous space considering the home's total square footage.
- Two additional bedrooms share a convenient hall bath. One of them boasts a vaulted ceiling and a fantastic window with an arched transom.

Plan KD-1086

Bedrooms: 3	Baths: 2
Living Area:	
Main floor	1,086 sq. ft.
Total Living Area:	**1,086 sq. ft.**
Garage and storage	439 sq. ft.
Exterior Wall Framing:	2x4

Foundation Options:
Crawlspace
Slab
(All plans can be built with your choice of foundation and framing. A generic conversion diagram is available. See order form.)

BLUEPRINT PRICE CODE:	A

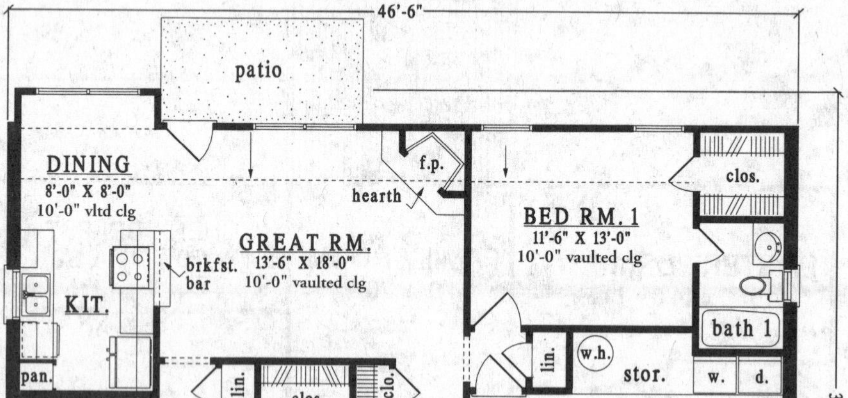

MAIN FLOOR

Plan floor diagram labels:
46'-6"
patio
DINING 8'-0" X 8'-0" 10'-0" vltd clg
f.p.
hearth
clos.
GREAT RM. 13'-6" X 18'-0" 10'-0" vaulted clg
brkfst. bar
BED RM. 1 11'-6" X 13'-0" 10'-0" vaulted clg
KIT.
bath 1
pan.
lin.
w.h.
stor.
w. d.
clos.
clos.
hall
bath 2
entry
BED RM. 3 10'-0" X 10'-0"
BED RM. 2 10'-0" X 11'-8" 12'-0" vaulted clg
clos.
porch
DOUBLE GARAGE 18'-6" X 20'-0"
38'-7"

Plan KD-1086
Plan copyright held by home designer/architect

PRICES AND DETAILS ON PAGES 12-15

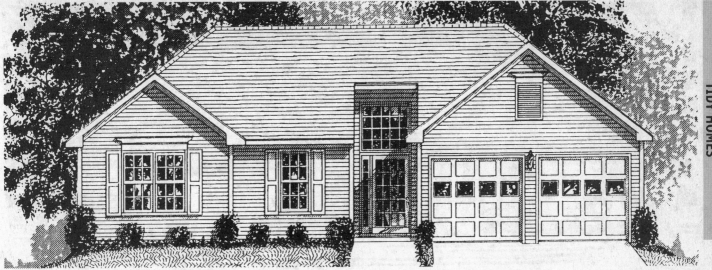

Striking Windows

- A dramatic covered entry with a tall, striking window arrangement draws attention to this modest-sized home.
- A bright French door opens directly into the spacious family room, which features a soaring vaulted ceiling and a cozy fireplace for winter nights. A hardwood floor adds a beautiful touch at the front of the room.
- To the right of the family room, the inviting dining area offers two options

—a sunny bay window or sliding glass doors that open to the backyard.
- The efficient galley-style kitchen boasts enclosed laundry facilities and convenient access to the dining area. The kitchen's handy garage access will make unloading groceries a snap.
- The spacious master bedroom boasts a huge walk-in closet and a private bath with an airy vaulted ceiling. The bath includes an inviting garden tub, a separate shower and a dual-sink vanity.
- A hall bath, which is centrally located for added convenience, serves two secondary bedrooms nearby. Both rooms include good-sized closets.

Plan APS-1003	
Bedrooms: 3	**Baths:** 2
Living Area:	
Main floor (slab version)	1,093 sq. ft.
Main floor (basement version)	1,188 sq. ft.
Total Living Area:	**1,093/1,188 sq. ft.**
Standard basement	1,188 sq. ft.
Garage	364 sq. ft.
Exterior Wall Framing:	2x4
Foundation Options:	
Standard basement	
Slab	

(All plans can be built with your choice of foundation and framing. A generic conversion diagram is available. See order form.)

BLUEPRINT PRICE CODE:	**A**

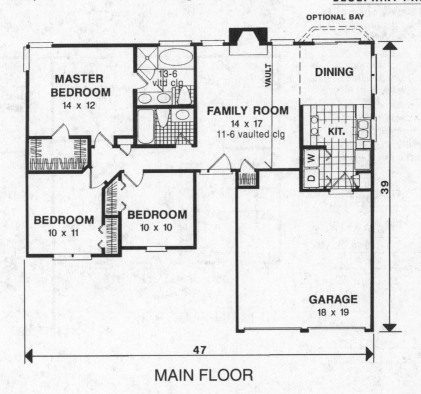

MAIN FLOOR

ORDER BLUEPRINTS ANYTIME!
CALL TOLL-FREE 1-800-820-1296

Plan APS-1003

Plan copyright held by home designer/architect

PRICES AND DETAILS
ON PAGES 12-15

49

Small Wonder

- This very affordable one-story home boasts an extremely efficient floor plan that maximizes the compact square footage. High ceilings in the shared living areas and in the master suite give the illusion of even more space.
- An elegant columned porch with gorgeous arched windows greets visitors and welcomes you home every day. Plenty of room is available here to sit and watch the day go by.
- The front entry opens directly into the good-sized living room, where you will enjoy years of memories in the making. A vaulted ceiling soars above, while a warm fireplace flanked by decorative plant shelves serves as the room's comforting focal point.
- The tiled dining room and U-shaped kitchen nearby share a vaulted ceiling. Easy access to the dining room will make family meals quick and easy. A patio provides a pleasing setting to enjoy a glass of fresh lemonade.
- The secluded master bedroom features a 10-ft. vaulted ceiling and a private bath.

Plan DD-1100-B

Bedrooms: 3	Baths: 2
Living Area:	
Main floor	1,100 sq. ft.
Total Living Area:	**1,100 sq. ft.**
Garage and utility	416 sq. ft.
Exterior Wall Framing:	2x4

Foundation Options:

Crawlspace
Slab
(All plans can be built with your choice of foundation and framing. A generic conversion diagram is available. See order form.)

BLUEPRINT PRICE CODE:	**A**

VIEW INTO LIVING
AND DINING ROOMS

MAIN FLOOR

ORDER BLUEPRINTS ANYTIME!
CALL TOLL-FREE 1-800-820-1296

Plan DD-1100-B
Plan copyright held by home designer/architect

PRICES AND DETAILS
ON PAGES 12-15

Beautiful Bay Window!

- A beautiful bay window beneath a charming gable highlights the front of this single-level home.
- Just beyond the entry, the living room invites family members to gather around the warming fireplace. The windows draw in plenty of sunlight while a high ceiling soars above.
- An exit to the garage between the living room and the kitchen offers access to laundry facilities and makes it especially easy to unload groceries.
- The kitchen includes a vast expanse of counter space, as well as a raised bar that's perfect for buffet-style meals. A pantry maximizes storage space.
- On more formal occasions, guests will linger over after-dinner coffee in the bayed dining room.
- Across the home, the spacious master suite features a high sloped ceiling, two walk-in closets, a dressing area and a private bath.
- Two additional bedrooms share a compartmentalized bath.

Plan RD-1091	
Bedrooms: 3	**Baths:** 2
Living Area:	
Main floor	1,091 sq. ft.
Total Living Area:	**1,091 sq. ft.**
Garage	528 sq. ft.
Exterior Wall Framing:	2x4

Foundation Options:

Crawlspace
Slab
(All plans can be built with your choice of foundation and framing. A generic conversion diagram is available. See order form.)

BLUEPRINT PRICE CODE: **A**

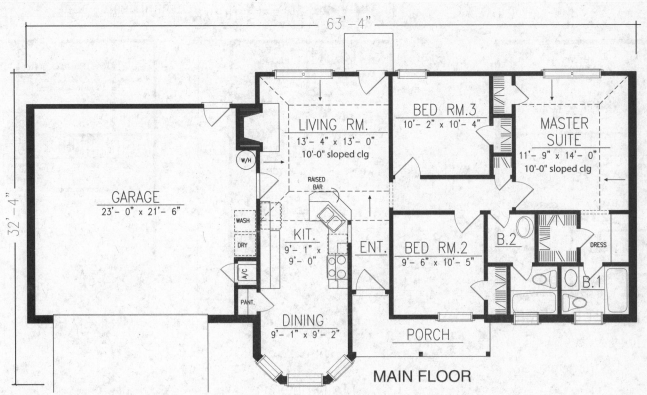

MAIN FLOOR

ORDER BLUEPRINTS ANYTIME!
CALL TOLL-FREE 1-800-820-1296

Plan RD-1091
Plan copyright held by home designer/architect

PRICES AND DETAILS
ON PAGES 12-15

51

Chalet Charm

- A cathedral ceiling and a warm fireplace grace the Great Room of this rustic chalet. Two sets of sliding glass doors lead to a wide wraparound deck. Large windows above the doors provide a breathtaking panoramic view.
- The Great Room unfolds to the open kitchen, which features a six-person snack bar that is perfect for casual dining. Stacked laundry facilities are just steps away, as is a full bath that is shared by the two main-floor bedrooms.
- An open stairway leads to a balcony that overlooks the Great Room and the scenery beyond.
- The master bedroom is enhanced by a beautiful cathedral ceiling, a private bath and roomy closets. Attic storage space is also available.
- The optional basement plan offers a tuck-under garage, additional storage space and a large area for a future family room.

Plan AHP-9501

Bedrooms: 3	Baths: 2
Living Area:	
Upper floor	260 sq. ft.
Main floor	854 sq. ft.
Total Living Area:	**1,114 sq. ft.**
Daylight basement	344 sq. ft.
Tuck-under garage/storage	510 sq. ft.
Exterior Wall Framing:	2x4 or 2x6

Foundation Options:
Daylight basement
Crawlspace
Slab
(All plans can be built with your choice of foundation and framing. A generic conversion diagram is available. See order form.)

BLUEPRINT PRICE CODE:	**A**

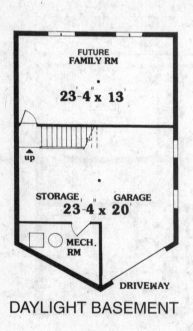

DAYLIGHT BASEMENT

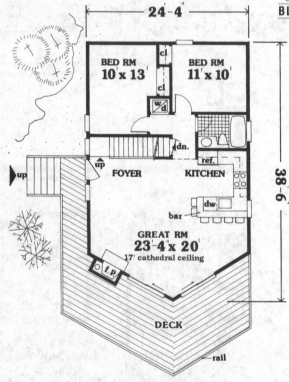

MAIN FLOOR

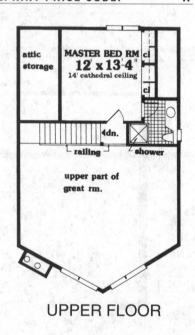

UPPER FLOOR

ORDER BLUEPRINTS ANYTIME! CALL TOLL-FREE 1-800-820-1296

Plan AHP-9501

Plan copyright held by home designer/architect

PRICES AND DETAILS ON PAGES 12-15

Elegant from Every Angle

- A stately Palladian window gives this delightful home great curb appeal. Tucked to the side, the main entry provides both privacy and a look at this home's attractive second face.

- The tiled foyer flows gracefully into the spacious living room. Sure to become the favorite site for communal gatherings and family fun, this space features a handsome fireplace flanked by windows, and a cheery plant shelf.

- The dining room includes sliding glass doors that open to the backyard, and adjoins the efficient, U-shaped kitchen. Here, ample counter space and a bright window sink make food preparation a unique pleasure.

- Built-in bookshelves and a skylighted bath add elegance to the master suite. You'll also enjoy a roomy walk-in closet and the added spaciousness of a volume ceiling.

- Two secondary bedrooms share another full bath. The foremost bedroom showcases the Palladian window that gives the facade its graceful air.

Plan L-86-A

Bedrooms: 3	Baths: 2
Living Area:	
Main floor	1,119 sq. ft.
Total Living Area:	**1,119 sq. ft.**
Garage and utility	377 sq. ft.
Exterior Wall Framing:	2x4

Foundation Options:

Slab

(All plans can be built with your choice of foundation and framing. A generic conversion diagram is available. See order form.)

BLUEPRINT PRICE CODE: A

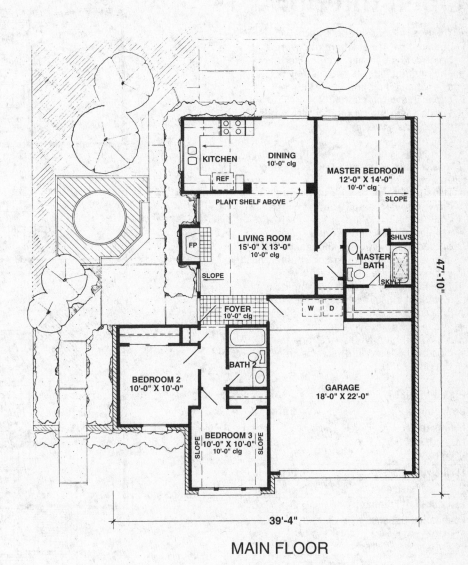

MAIN FLOOR

KITCHEN
REF
DINING 10'-0" clg
MASTER BEDROOM 12'-0" X 14'-0" 10'-0" clg
SLOPE
PLANT SHELF ABOVE
SHLVS
FP
LIVING ROOM 15'-0" X 13'-0" 10'-0" clg
MASTER BATH
SKYLT
SLOPE
FOYER 10'-0" clg
W D
BATH 2
BEDROOM 2 10'-0" X 10'-0"
GARAGE 18'-0" X 22'-0"
SLOPE
BEDROOM 3 10'-0" X 10'-0" 10'-0" clg
SLOPE
47'-10"
39'-4"

ORDER BLUEPRINTS ANYTIME!
CALL TOLL-FREE 1-800-820-1296

Plan L-86-A
Plan copyright held by home designer/architect

PRICES AND DETAILS
ON PAGES 12-15

53

Cottage with Open Interior

- The exterior of this contemporary cottage features a delightful covered porch and a pair of matching dormers.
- The inviting entry is crowned by a dramatic ceiling and flows into the expansive vaulted Great Room. Tall windows brighten both corners, while a fireplace serves as a handsome centerpiece.
- Sliding glass doors between the Great Room and the breakfast nook open to an angled deck.
- The sunny nook provides a bright and cozy setting for family dining with a view of the backyard.
- Ample cabinets and counter space are offered in the efficient kitchen, which also features a handy snack counter that extends into the nook.
- The main-floor master bedroom boasts a walk-in closet and easy access to the full bath beyond.
- The upper floor offers another bedroom, plus a full bath with space for a laundry closet. The loft could serve as an extra sleeping space.

Plan JWB-9307

Bedrooms: 2+	Baths: 2
Living Area:	
Upper floor	349 sq. ft.
Main floor	795 sq. ft.
Total Living Area:	**1,144 sq. ft.**
Standard basement	712 sq. ft.
Exterior Wall Framing:	2x4 or 2x6

Foundation Options:

Standard basement

(All plans can be built with your choice of foundation and framing. A generic conversion diagram is available. See order form.)

BLUEPRINT PRICE CODE: A

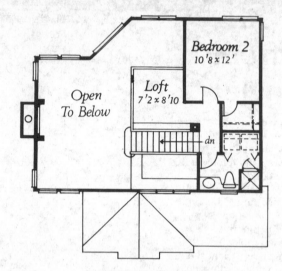

UPPER FLOOR

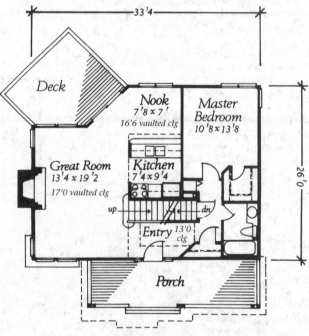

MAIN FLOOR

ORDER BLUEPRINTS ANYTIME!
CALL TOLL-FREE 1-800-820-1296

Plan JWB-9307

Plan copyright held by home designer/architect

PRICES AND DETAILS
ON PAGES 12-15

Nostalgic Getaway

- Porches in the front and back of this country-style home make tempting mid-afternoon getaways in the summertime. Camp out with friends on the front porch and visit over a pitcher of lemonade and a plate of gingersnaps.
- As it cools off later in the evening, come in and sit by the living-room fireplace. Windows on either side of the hearth provide a view to the outdoors—though you'll hardly regret not being there.
- The setup of the dining room and kitchen allows for the easy flow of conversation.
- A nearby utility room and a snack bar servicing the living room highlight the kitchen. A door near the dining room invites you to enjoy your meals outside.
- Take advantage of the secluded master bedroom, which boasts a walk-in closet, a dressing area and private access to a full bath.

Plan DD-1141

Bedrooms: 3	Baths: 2
Living Area:	
Upper floor	338 sq. ft.
Main floor	819 sq. ft.
Total Living Area:	**1,157 sq. ft.**
Standard basement	819 sq. ft.
Exterior Wall Framing:	2x4

Foundation Options:

Standard basement
Crawlspace
Slab

(All plans can be built with your choice of foundation and framing. A generic conversion diagram is available. See order form.)

BLUEPRINT PRICE CODE:	A

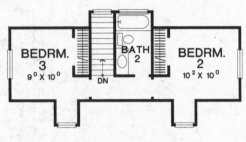

UPPER FLOOR

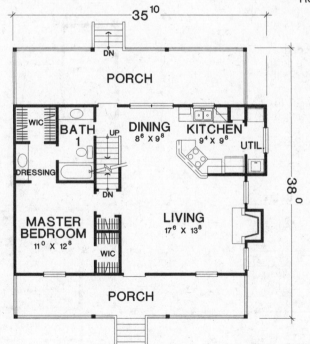

VIEW INTO LIVING ROOM, DINING ROOM AND KITCHEN

MAIN FLOOR

Beautifully Timeless

- Beautifully timeless and effortlessly practical, this two-story's wonderful charm will endure through the ages.
- The huge front porch adds attractiveness and functionality. Railings, columns and graceful arches give the exterior an undeniable appeal, while the plentiful space the porch provides lets you enjoy a variety of activities in the open air.
- Though economically sized, the floor plan is surprisingly spacious and open.
- A pair of big windows keeps the family room filled with warm sunshine. Roomy and pleasant, it's the perfect spot for all your holiday gatherings.
- Just a few steps away is the gourmet kitchen. Enjoy breakfast while poring over your morning newspaper in the adjoining nook.
- With a private bath and a large closet, the master suite offers a sweet taste of well-deserved luxury.
- Two additional bedrooms and a full bath are found on the upper floor.

Plan HDS-99-333	
Bedrooms: 3	**Baths:** 2
Living Area:	
Upper floor	350 sq. ft.
Main floor	820 sq. ft.
Total Living Area:	**1,170 sq. ft.**
One-car garage	240 sq. ft.
Optional two-car garage	400 sq. ft.
Exterior Wall Framing: 8-in. concrete block	
Foundation Options:	

Crawlspace
(All plans can be built with your choice of foundation and framing. A generic conversion diagram is available. See order form.)

| **BLUEPRINT PRICE CODE:** | **A** |

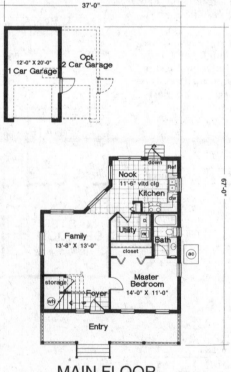

UPPER FLOOR

MAIN FLOOR

ORDER BLUEPRINTS ANYTIME! CALL TOLL-FREE 1-800-820-1296

Plan HDS-99-333
Plan copyright held by home designer/architect

PRICES AND DETAILS ON PAGES 12-15

Love at First Sight!

- Upon seeing its covered front porch and bright brick and siding exterior, it's easy to fall in love with this adorable home.
- Past the ornate and inviting entry, the spacious family room and its decorative plant shelf and dramatic fireplace offer an impressive introduction to the interior. Tall windows and a vaulted ceiling add to the ambience.
- The adjoining dining room is great for casual or formal occasions. The sliding glass doors that access the backyard may be built into a sunny window bay for a more dramatic effect.
- The efficient galley-style kitchen offers a pantry, an attached laundry room and a door to the garage.
- The master bedroom includes a roomy walk-in closet. The private master bath features a vaulted ceiling, a garden tub, a separate shower and a dual-sink vanity. A second full bath services two secondary bedrooms.

Plan APS-1103

Bedrooms: 3	Baths: 2
Living Area:	
Main floor	1,197 sq. ft.
Total Living Area:	**1,197 sq. ft.**
Garage	380 sq. ft.
Exterior Wall Framing:	2x4

Foundation Options:

Crawlspace

Slab

(All plans can be built with your choice of foundation and framing. A generic conversion diagram is available. See order form.)

BLUEPRINT PRICE CODE:	**A**

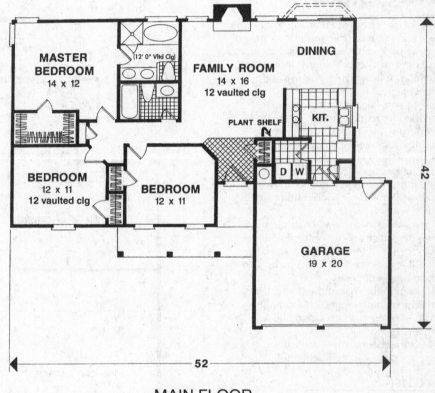

MAIN FLOOR

ORDER BLUEPRINTS ANYTIME!
CALL TOLL-FREE 1-800-820-1296

Plan APS-1103
Plan copyright held by home designer/architect

PRICES AND DETAILS
ON PAGES 12-15

57

Economy with Class

- This classy one-story home puts a new twist on the word "economy." Its paned bay window and attractive garage appointments exude sunny appeal, and its interior keeps your comfort and convenience firmly in mind.
- Living and sleeping areas are neatly divided for extra privacy.
- Step from the entry to the generous living room, where a cozy fireplace warms family gatherings, and a sloped ceiling creates a feeling of space.
- Separated from the living room by a half-wall, the dining room hosts any meal with airy style.
- The U-shaped kitchen boasts plenty of counter space and a corner sink under windows. On grocery-shopping days, you'll appreciate its close proximity to the garage entrance!
- A haven in the rear of the home, the master suite privileges its occupants with a roomy walk-in closet and a private bath.
- Two other bedrooms—one with a lovely bay window—share another full bath.

Plan L-1198

Bedrooms: 3	Baths: 2
Living Area:	
Main floor	1,198 sq. ft.
Total Living Area:	**1,198 sq. ft.**
Garage and storage	431 sq. ft.
Exterior Wall Framing:	2x4

Foundation Options:

Slab

(All plans can be built with your choice of foundation and framing. A generic conversion diagram is available. See order form.)

BLUEPRINT PRICE CODE: A

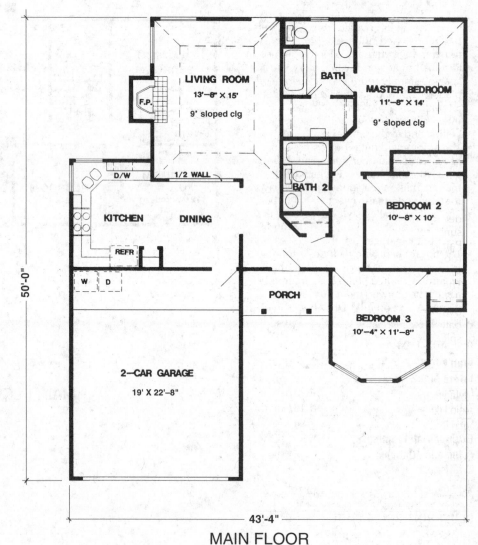

MAIN FLOOR

ORDER BLUEPRINTS ANYTIME!
CALL TOLL-FREE 1-800-820-1296

Plan L-1198
Plan copyright held by home designer/architect

PRICES AND DETAILS
ON PAGES 12-15

Great Expectations

- If a growing family is in your future, give thought to this charming home, which offers a bonus space in its daylight basement that can be finished off as a rollicking family room.
- From the split entry, stairs lead up to the formal gathering areas. In the living room, a fireplace teams up with a trio of windows to create stylish ambience. A vaulted ceiling shows these features off nicely and adds to the home's airy feel.
- Decorative columns gracefully frame the dining room's entrance. Beyond, sliding glass doors introduce a backyard deck that practically begs you to enjoy summer with zest and spontaneity!
- Pair up with your favorite cook in the roomy kitchen and serve up a feast fit for royalty.
- The master suite resides at the end of the hall, and features a vaulted ceiling over the sleeping chamber. A private bath livens you each morning with a splashy shower.

Plan B-90067

Bedrooms: 3+	Baths: 2–2½
Living Area:	
Main floor	1,203 sq. ft.
Total Living Area:	**1,203 sq. ft.**
Daylight basement	510 sq. ft.
Garage	560 sq. ft.
Exterior Wall Framing:	2x4

Foundation Options:

Daylight basement

(All plans can be built with your choice of foundation and framing. A generic conversion diagram is available. See order form.)

BLUEPRINT PRICE CODE: A

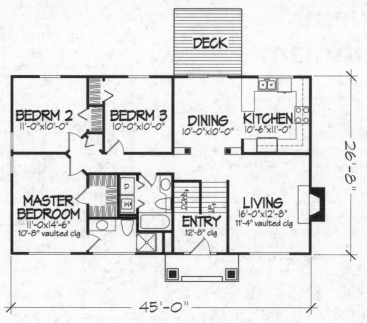

MAIN FLOOR

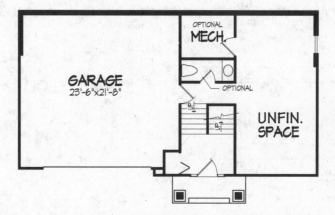

DAYLIGHT BASEMENT

ORDER BLUEPRINTS ANYTIME!
CALL TOLL-FREE 1-800-820-1296

Plan B-90067
Plan copyright held by home designer/architect

PRICES AND DETAILS
ON PAGES 12-15

59

Modern Craftsman

- Don't get turned around by the fact that this home has traditional Craftsman-style railings, classic shingles, decorative beams below the eaves—and a modern floor plan.
- What you will notice is that the floor plan itself appears to be upside down—all the primary living areas are located upstairs, atop a cute carport.
- The lower level hosts ample storage, including a mechanical room with laundry facilities, and a large secondary bedroom. A clever, angled closet and a corner sink make use of space in the bedroom, which has a private bath.
- Upstairs, the sunny, open living room blends seamlessly with the island kitchen and a cozy dining nook, as well as a sizable deck, lending a sense of spaciousness. A big pantry rounds out the space.
- The secluded master suite is a delightful retreat. It offers a large walk-in closet and private access to a full bath that features a generous tub.

Plan COA-1-0

Bedrooms: 2	Baths: 2
Living Area:	
Main floor	774 sq. ft.
Lower floor	358 sq. ft.
Mechanical	80 sq. ft.
Total Living Area:	**1,212 sq. ft.**
Carport	230 sq. ft.
Exterior Wall Framing:	2x4

Foundation Options:

Slab

(All plans can be built with your choice of foundation and framing. A generic conversion diagram is available. See order form.)

BLUEPRINT PRICE CODE: A

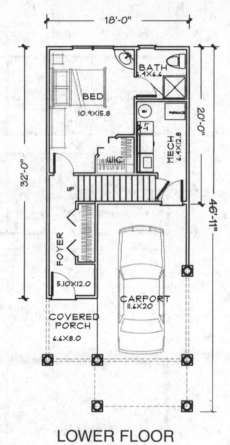

LOWER FLOOR

MAIN FLOOR

ORDER BLUEPRINTS ANYTIME!
CALL TOLL-FREE 1-800-820-1296

Plan COA-1-0

Plan copyright held by home designer/architect

PRICES AND DETAILS
ON PAGES 12-15

Versatile A-Frame

- This traditional A-frame is designed for optimum comfort and minimum cost. The versatile interior can vary from plush to rustic, allowing the home to serve equally well as a weekend cabin, a summer retreat or a ski chalet.
- The highlight of the floor plan is the spacious living room, with its high vaulted ceiling and dramatic stone fireplace. The fireplace extends to the outdoors, where it doubles as a barbecue. A stunning window wall parallels the angles of the A-frame and includes sliding glass doors that access a huge deck. The adjoining U-shaped kitchen is open to the dining room.
- To the rear are two bedrooms and a full bath. Between the bedrooms is a hallway to a backyard deck.
- Upstairs is a third bedroom with a private deck and a half-bath. The balcony area that overlooks the living room can sleep overnight guests.

Plan H-6	
Bedrooms: 3+	**Baths:** 1½
Living Area:	
Upper floor	375 sq. ft.
Main floor	845 sq. ft.
Total Living Area:	**1,220 sq. ft.**
Exterior Wall Framing:	2x4
Foundation Options:	

Crawlspace
(All plans can be built with your choice of foundation and framing. A generic conversion diagram is available. See order form.)

BLUEPRINT PRICE CODE:	**A**

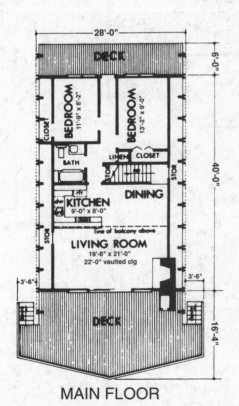

MAIN FLOOR

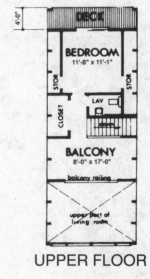

UPPER FLOOR

Plan H-6

Plan copyright held by home designer/architect

PRICES AND DETAILS
ON PAGES 12-15

Affordable Charm

- An inviting columned porch introduces this affordable home.
- Inside, soaring ceilings and attention to detail highlight the efficient floor plan.
- The foyer leads to an eat-in kitchen, which includes a handy built-in pantry. A great high ceiling enhances this sunny space.
- A convenient serving counter connects the kitchen to the open dining room. A beautiful bay window is topped by a half-round transom.
- The adjacent living room features an energy-efficient fireplace and French-door access to an inviting rear deck.
- A dramatic vaulted ceiling soars above the living and dining rooms.
- The spacious master bedroom boasts a striking vaulted ceiling, a large walk-in closet and private access to the hall bath.
- Two additional bedrooms and a linen closet round out the floor plan.

Plan B-93015

Bedrooms: 3	Baths: 1
Living Area:	
Main floor	1,227 sq. ft.
Total Living Area:	**1,227 sq. ft.**
Standard basement	1,217 sq. ft.
Garage	385 sq. ft.
Exterior Wall Framing:	2x6

Foundation Options:

Standard basement

(All plans can be built with your choice of foundation and framing. A generic conversion diagram is available. See order form.)

BLUEPRINT PRICE CODE: A

MAIN FLOOR

Plan B-93015

Plan copyright held by home designer/architect

PRICES AND DETAILS
ON PAGES 12-15

Classic Country

- This charming country-style home features a classic exterior and a luxurious interior design in an economical floor plan.
- A covered front porch leads through a sidelighted entry directly to the living room. A coat closet is close by.
- Stylish windows brighten the spacious living room, where a handsome recessed fireplace crackles. A marvelous vaulted ceiling soars overhead and extends to the dining room and kitchen.

- Stately columns set off the entry to the dining room, which offers French-door access to a backyard terrace that is perfect for summertime entertainment.
- The dining room and the efficient kitchen share a stylish serving bar.
- The secluded master suite is graced by a cathedral ceiling. A French door opens to a private terrace.
- The master bath flaunts a refreshing whirlpool tub and a separate shower.
- Lovely windows bring natural light into two more bedrooms. A hall bath easily services both rooms.

Plan AHP-9507	
Bedrooms: 3	**Baths: 2**
Living Area:	
Main floor	1,232 sq. ft.
Total Living Area:	**1,232 sq. ft.**
Standard basement	1,183 sq. ft.
Garage and storage	324 sq. ft.
Exterior Wall Framing:	2x4 or 2x6

Foundation Options:

Standard basement
Crawlspace
Slab
(All plans can be built with your choice of foundation and framing. A generic conversion diagram is available. See order form.)

BLUEPRINT PRICE CODE:	**A**

MAIN FLOOR

ORDER BLUEPRINTS ANYTIME!
CALL TOLL-FREE 1-800-820-1296

Plan AHP-9507
Plan copyright held by home designer/architect

PRICES AND DETAILS
ON PAGES 12-15   63

Modest and Inviting

- A neat front porch and a cheery shuttered window highlight this design's inviting facade. Despite a modest square footage, the floor plan provides ample room for a family.
- A coat closet keeps the entry tidy. The expansive family room beyond boasts a cozy fireplace and convenient proximity to the kitchen, making this a great space for entertaining or casual family times.
- Sliding glass doors open to the backyard and allow light into the dining room. A half-wall separates the dining room and the kitchen, which features a wide pantry and a window over the sink.
- Isolated from the other bedrooms, the master suite is a comforting sanctuary. The private bath with a walk-in closet easily services two.
- Two secondary bedrooms—one with a walk-in closet—reside on the other side of the home and share a full bath.
- For your convenience, the laundry room is located on the main floor.

Plan LS-98850-GW

Bedrooms: 3	Baths: 2
Living Area:	
Main floor	1,269 sq. ft.
Total Living Area:	**1,269 sq. ft.**
Standard basement	1,242 sq. ft.
Garage	400 sq. ft.
Exterior Wall Framing:	2x4
Foundation Options:	

Standard basement
(All plans can be built with your choice of foundation and framing. A generic conversion diagram is available. See order form.)

BLUEPRINT PRICE CODE:	**A**

MAIN FLOOR

Plan LS-98850-GW
Plan copyright held by home designer/architect

PRICES AND DETAILS
ON PAGES 12-15

That Familiar Country Feeling

- A railed porch and twin dormers give this city home the look of a country dwelling. Its wide-open kitchen will give you the same familiar feeling.
- Bright corner windows illuminate the generous-sized living room, where a fireplace adds style and warmth.
- The kitchen is also a great place to gather, with its open island/snack bar, plus its sunny breakfast nook. A door around the corner is a convenient passage for transporting groceries from the attached two-car garage.
- A covered deck to the rear is a lovely continuation of the outdoor living space provided by the front porch. Here, you may host a picnic, barbecue with the neighbors or read your favorite book.
- The master bedroom offers a sizable sleeping area, a walk-in closet and private access to the hall bath, which is shared with the two secondary bedrooms. The smaller bedroom would also make a nice home office.

Plan LS-99004-B

Bedrooms: 3	Baths: 1
Living Area:	
Main floor	1,231 sq. ft.
Total Living Area:	**1,231 sq. ft.**
Standard basement	1,231 sq. ft.
Garage	495 sq. ft.
Exterior Wall Framing:	2x4

Foundation Options:
Standard basement
(All plans can be built with your choice of foundation and framing. A generic conversion diagram is available. See order form.)

BLUEPRINT PRICE CODE: **A**

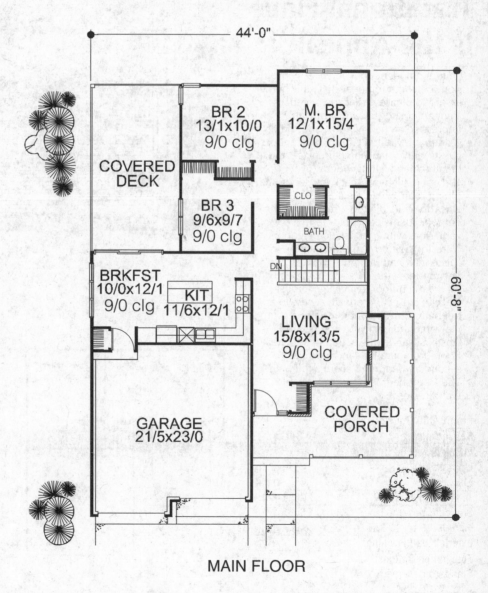

MAIN FLOOR

Plan LS-99004-B

Plan copyright held by home designer/architect

PRICES AND DETAILS
ON PAGES 12-15

Traditional Flair Is the Appeal

- Offering modern conveniences without skimping on traditional style, this home is sure to please. Its facade of cedar shingles creates texture, while an impressive arched window adds flair.
- A dramatic vaulted Great Room entices guests with a handsome fireplace and a breathtaking wall of windows.
- The open kitchen's snack bar serves the dining room, which features sliding glass doors leading to a rear deck. This outdoor spot is perfect for festive gatherings with friends and neighbors. A clerestory window fills the interior space with natural light.
- The master suite, conveniently located on the main floor, offers a generous walk-in closet and private access to a full bath. Corner windows offer a sunny view into the backyard and beyond.
- Upstairs, survey the action in the Great Room from a railed landing. Two secondary bedrooms share a full bath. The larger bedroom boasts a sizable walk-in closet.

REAR VIEW

Plan B-88017

Bedrooms: 3	**Baths: 2**
Living Area:	
Upper floor	431 sq. ft.
Main floor	858 sq. ft.
Total Living Area:	**1,289 sq. ft.**
Standard basement	858 sq. ft.
Garage	400 sq. ft.
Exterior Wall Framing:	2x4

Foundation Options:

Standard basement

(All plans can be built with your choice of foundation and framing. A generic conversion diagram is available. See order form.)

BLUEPRINT PRICE CODE: A

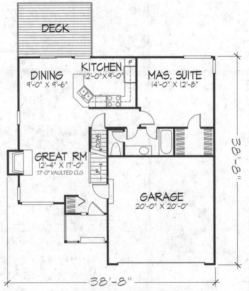

MAIN FLOOR

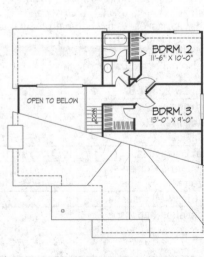

UPPER FLOOR

ORDER BLUEPRINTS ANYTIME! CALL TOLL-FREE 1-800-820-1296

Plan B-88017

Plan copyright held by home designer/architect

PRICES AND DETAILS ON PAGES 12-15

Charming Accents

- Traditional accents add warmth and charm to the facade of this affordable one-story home.
- Decorative, beveled oval glass adorns the elegant entry, which is flanked by sidelights.
- The tiled foyer introduces the spacious family room, which is enhanced by a vaulted ceiling and a nice fireplace. A French door provides easy access to the backyard.
- The galley-style kitchen flows into the sunny dining area, which can be extended with an optional bay window.
- The secluded master bedroom features plenty of closet space. The private master bath boasts a corner garden tub, a separate shower and two sinks. The bath may be expanded with a vaulted ceiling.
- Two additional bedrooms share a hall bath in the opposite wing. A nice-sized laundry room is centrally located.

Plan APS-1205

Bedrooms: 3	Baths: 2
Living Area:	
Main floor	1,296 sq. ft.
Total Living Area:	**1,296 sq. ft.**
Standard basement	1,296 sq. ft.
Garage	413 sq. ft.
Exterior Wall Framing:	2x4

Foundation Options:

Standard basement
Crawlspace
Slab
(All plans can be built with your choice of foundation and framing. A generic conversion diagram is available. See order form.)

BLUEPRINT PRICE CODE: **A**

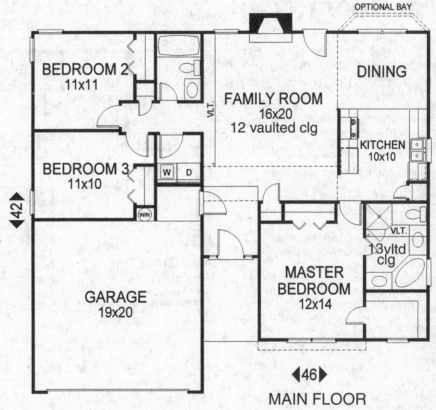

OPTIONAL BAY

BEDROOM 2
11x11

DINING

FAMILY ROOM
16x20
12 vaulted clg

KITCHEN
10x10

BEDROOM 3
11x10

W D

WH

GARAGE
19x20

MASTER BEDROOM
12x14

VLT.

13vltd clg

◄42►

◄46►

MAIN FLOOR

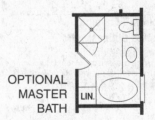

OPTIONAL MASTER BATH

LIN.

ORDER BLUEPRINTS ANYTIME!
CALL TOLL-FREE 1-800-820-1296

Plan APS-1205
Plan copyright held by home designer/architect

PRICES AND DETAILS
ON PAGES 12-15   67

Intriguing Great Room

- The focal point of this open, economical home is its comfortable Great Room and dining area. An inviting fireplace, a dramatic arched window and a vaulted ceiling spark conversation.
- The roomy kitchen incorporates a sunny breakfast room with a vaulted ceiling. Sliding glass doors open to the backyard deck. The kitchen also has a pantry and a handy pass-through to the dining room.
- The bedroom wing includes a lovely master suite and two secondary bedrooms. The master suite boasts a private bath with a separate tub and shower, while the secondary bedrooms share another full bath.
- The washer and dryer are conveniently located near the bedroom wing and the entrance from the garage.

Plan B-90008

Bedrooms: 3	Baths: 2
Living Area:	
Main floor	1,325 sq. ft.
Total Living Area:	**1,325 sq. ft.**
Standard basement	1,325 sq. ft.
Garage	390 sq. ft.
Exterior Wall Framing:	2x6

Foundation Options:

Standard basement

(All plans can be built with your choice of foundation and framing. A generic conversion diagram is available. See order form.)

BLUEPRINT PRICE CODE: A

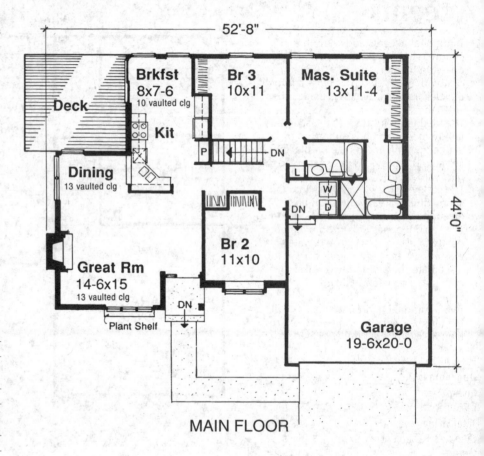

MAIN FLOOR

Plan B-90008

Plan copyright held by home designer/architect

PRICES AND DETAILS
ON PAGES 12-15

World at Your Feet

- With a vaulted ceiling, a handsome fireplace and sliding glass doors that open to a rear terrace and the wide world beyond, this one-story home's central Great Room dominates its family-friendly floor plan.

- The smart country kitchen features a bayed eating nook and a convenient snack bar. The bayed formal dining area is just steps away.

- A versatile room to the right of the foyer can serve as either a casual den or a third bedroom. The second bedroom and the hall bath are nearby.

- The luxurious master suite's extras include a tray ceiling and a full bath with a tub and a separate shower. The sleeping area boasts access to a private rear terrace.

- The side-entry, two-car garage offers ample storage space and opens to the home's mudroom. The mudroom houses laundry facilities and can also be accessed via a side service entrance.

VIEW INTO GREAT ROOM

Plan K-824-V

Bedrooms: 2+	Baths: 2
Living Area:	
Main floor	1,325 sq. ft.
Total Living Area:	**1,325 sq. ft.**
Standard basement	1,373 sq. ft.
Garage and storage	489 sq. ft.
Exterior Wall Framing:	2x4 or 2x6

Foundation Options:

Standard basement

Slab

(All plans can be built with your choice of foundation and framing. A generic conversion diagram is available. See order form.)

BLUEPRINT PRICE CODE: A

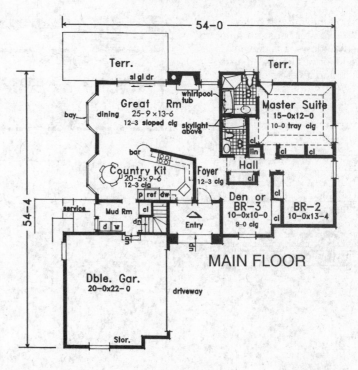

MAIN FLOOR

ORDER BLUEPRINTS ANYTIME!
CALL TOLL-FREE 1-800-820-1296

Plan K-824-V

Plan copyright held by home designer/architect

PRICES AND DETAILS
ON PAGES 12-15

69

Smart One-Story Home

- The smart exterior design of this home gives it great looks, whether it's finished with stucco, brick or wood siding (all options are provided in the blueprints).
- The living room makes an impressive first statement, with its vaulted ceiling and a fireplace framed by tall windows. More windows line the rear wall of the bayed dining area, with French doors opening to a patio.
- The galley-style kitchen is efficiently arranged next to the dining room, and a laundry/pantry area lies between the kitchen and the garage.
- A full bath is off the hall to the three bedrooms. The master bedroom suite offers corner windows, a large walk-in closet and a luxurious bath with a step-up garden tub and a separate shower.

Plan APS-1304

Bedrooms: 3	Baths: 2
Living Area:	
Main floor	1,338 sq. ft.
Total Living Area:	**1,338 sq. ft.**
Garage	440 sq. ft.
Exterior Wall Framing:	2x4
Foundation Options:	
Slab	

(All plans can be built with your choice of foundation and framing. A generic conversion diagram is available. See order form.)

BLUEPRINT PRICE CODE:	A

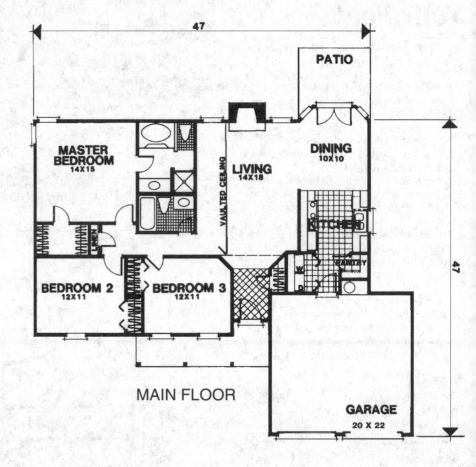

MAIN FLOOR

ORDER BLUEPRINTS ANYTIME!
CALL TOLL-FREE 1-800-820-1296

Plan APS-1304

Plan copyright held by home designer/architect

PRICES AND DETAILS ON PAGES 12-15

Maximum Livability

- Compact and easy to build, this appealing ranch-style home is big on charm and livability.
- The entry of the home opens to the dramatic vaulted living room with exposed beams, a handsome fireplace and access to a patio.
- Wood post dividers set off the large raised dining room, which is brightened by a stunning window wall.
- The adjoining kitchen offers a spacious snack bar and easy access to the utility room and the two-car garage. A nice storage area is also included.
- Three bedrooms and two baths occupy the sleeping wing. One of the baths is private to the master suite, which features a walk-in closet and a dressing area with a sit-down makeup table. The two remaining bedrooms also have walk-in closets.

Plan E-1305

Bedrooms: 3	Baths: 2
Living Area:	
Main floor	1,346 sq. ft.
Total Living Area:	**1,346 sq. ft.**
Garage	441 sq. ft.
Storage	44 sq. ft.
Exterior Wall Framing:	2x4

Foundation Options:
Crawlspace
Slab
(All plans can be built with your choice of foundation and framing. A generic conversion diagram is available. See order form.)

BLUEPRINT PRICE CODE: A

MAIN FLOOR

ORDER BLUEPRINTS ANYTIME!
CALL TOLL-FREE 1-800-820-1296

Plan E-1305
Plan copyright held by home designer/architect

PRICES AND DETAILS
ON PAGES 12-15

71

Striking Stone Chimney

- With tall windows and a rustic stone chimney, the striking facade of this home demands attention.
- The sheltered entry leads into a raised foyer, which steps down to the sunny living room and its dramatic vaulted ceiling.
- A handsome fireplace warms the living room and the adjoining dining room, which offers access to an inviting deck.
- A cozy breakfast nook is included in the efficient, open-design kitchen. A special feature is the convenient pass-through to the dining room.
- A skylighted staircase leads upstairs to the master suite, with its private bath and large walk-in closet.
- A second bedroom shares another full bath with a loft or third bedroom.
- A dramatic balcony overlooks the living room below.

Plan B-224-8512

Bedrooms: 2+	Baths: 2½
Living Area:	
Upper floor	691 sq. ft.
Main floor	668 sq. ft.
Total Living Area:	**1,359 sq. ft.**
Standard basement	668 sq. ft.
Garage	458 sq. ft.
Exterior Wall Framing:	2x4

Foundation Options:

Standard basement

(All plans can be built with your choice of foundation and framing. A generic conversion diagram is available. See order form.)

BLUEPRINT PRICE CODE:	**A**

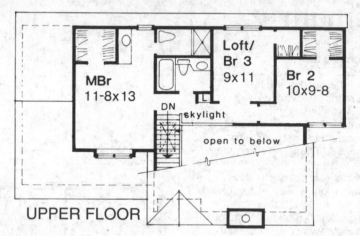

UPPER FLOOR

MBr 11-8x13

Loft/ Br 3 9x11

Br 2 10x9-8

DN skylight

open to below

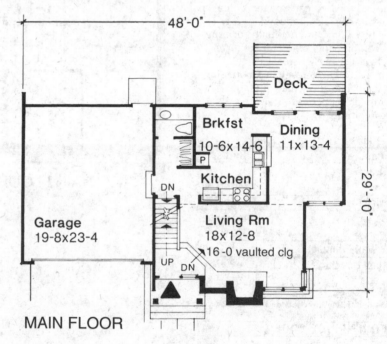

MAIN FLOOR

48'-0"

29'-10"

Deck

Brkfst 10-6x14-6

Dining 11x13-4

Kitchen

Garage 19-8x23-4

Living Rm 18x12-8

16-0 vaulted clg

UP DN

DN

ORDER BLUEPRINTS ANYTIME! *CALL TOLL-FREE 1-800-820-1296*

Plan B-224-8512

Plan copyright held by home designer/architect

PRICES AND DETAILS *ON PAGES 12-15*

Outdoor Spaces

- You'll love the way this home incorporates indoor and outdoor living. A front porch draws you in, while a rear deck beckons you back outside.
- Inside, the spacious, central living room boasts a handsome corner fireplace and a voluminous cathedral ceiling—it's a perfect place for gathering your family together.
- A charming plant ledge separates the living room from the dining room.

- The kitchen features a pantry, a nearby utility closet and a handy snack bar serving the dining room, which boasts French-door access to a comfortable backyard deck.
- The opulent master suite provides a cathedral ceiling in the bedroom. The private bath flaunts a large walk-in closet, a dual-sink vanity, a relaxing garden tub and a separate oversized shower.
- Across the home, two additional bedrooms, each with ample closet space, share a full hall bath, which enjoys an inviting tub and a roomy linen closet.

Plan HWG-1362-N

Bedrooms: 3	Baths: 2
Living Area:	
Main floor	1,362 sq. ft.
Total Living Area:	**1,362 sq. ft.**
Exterior Wall Framing:	2x4

Foundation Options:

Crawlspace
(All plans can be built with your choice of foundation and framing. A generic conversion diagram is available. See order form.)

BLUEPRINT PRICE CODE: A

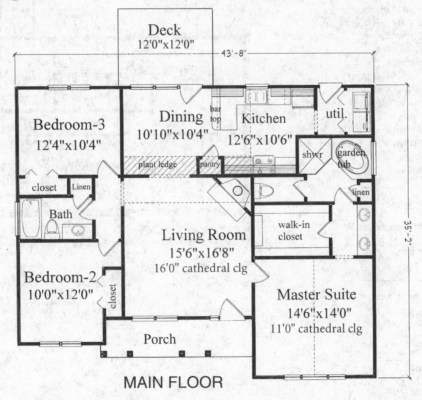

Deck 12'0"x12'0"

43'-8"

Bedroom-3 12'4"x10'4"

Dining 10'10"x10'4"

bar top

Kitchen 12'6"x10'6"

util.

closet Linen

plant ledge pantry

shwr garden tub

linen

Bath

Living Room 15'6"x16'8" 16'0" cathedral clg

walk-in closet

35'-2"

Bedroom-2 10'0"x12'0"

closet

Master Suite 14'6"x14'0" 11'0" cathedral clg

Porch

MAIN FLOOR

Plan HWG-1362-N

Plan copyright held by home designer/architect

PRICES AND DETAILS ON PAGES 12-15

Special Delivery

- This compact, country-style home delivers a beguiling front porch and a floor plan full of special touches.
- The front entry opens to the vast living room, which enjoys the warmth of a fireplace and the rustic ambience of a vaulted ceiling with false beams.
- Open to the living room and the kitchen, the dining room is a convenient spot for casual and elegant meals. Two windows overlook the backyard and draw in natural light.
- Its efficient layout endears the U-shaped kitchen to the family chef, who will make use of the pantry closet and abundant counter space. Close proximity to the carport eases the pain of carrying groceries on shopping days.
- Nicely secluded from the living areas, the master bedroom features a walk-in closet and a private bath with a separate dressing area. Two secondary bedrooms include walk-in closets.

Plan E-1301

Bedrooms: 3	Baths: 2
Living Area:	
Main floor	1,365 sq. ft.
Total Living Area:	**1,365 sq. ft.**
Carport	441 sq. ft.
Storage	87 sq. ft.
Exterior Wall Framing:	2x4

Foundation Options:
Crawlspace
Slab
(All plans can be built with your choice of foundation and framing. A generic conversion diagram is available. See order form.)

BLUEPRINT PRICE CODE:	**A**

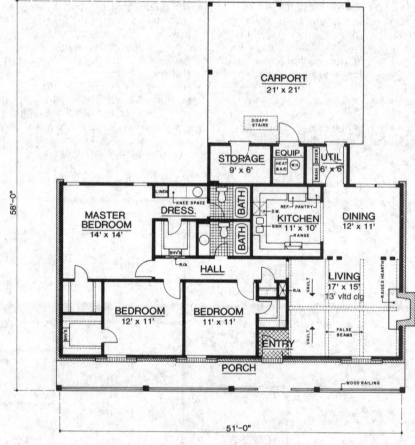

MAIN FLOOR

ORDER BLUEPRINTS ANYTIME!
CALL TOLL-FREE 1-800-820-1296

Plan E-1301
Plan copyright held by home designer/architect

PRICES AND DETAILS
ON PAGES 12-15

All in One!

- This plan puts today's most luxurious home-design features into one attractive, economical package.
- The covered front porch and the gabled roofline, accented by an arched window and a round louver vent, give the exterior a homey yet stylish appeal.
- Just inside the front door, the raised ceiling offers an impressive greeting. The living room is flooded with light through a central skylight and a pair of French doors that frame the fireplace.
- The living room flows into the nice-sized dining room, also with a raised ceiling. The adjoining kitchen offers a handy laundry closet, lots of counter space and a sunny dinette that opens to an expansive backyard terrace.
- The bedroom wing includes a wonderful master suite with a dressing area and two closets. Glass blocks above the dual-sink vanity in the master bath let in light yet maintain privacy. A whirlpool tub completes the suite.
- The larger of the two remaining bedrooms boasts a high ceiling and an arched window.

Plan HFL-1680-FL

Bedrooms: 3	Baths: 2
Living Area:	
Main floor	1,367 sq. ft.
Total Living Area:	**1,367 sq. ft.**
Standard basement	1,367 sq. ft.
Garage	431 sq. ft.
Exterior Wall Framing:	2x6

Foundation Options:
Standard basement
Slab
(All plans can be built with your choice of foundation and framing. A generic conversion diagram is available. See order form.)

BLUEPRINT PRICE CODE:	A

VIEW INTO LIVING ROOM

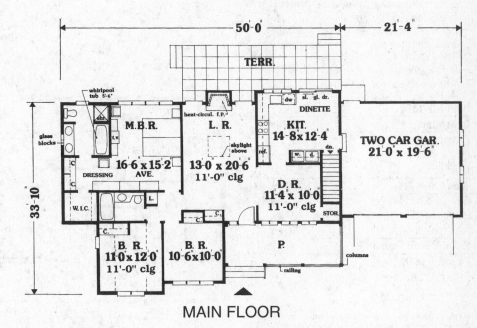

MAIN FLOOR

Plan HFL-1680-FL

Plan copyright held by home designer/architect

PRICES AND DETAILS
ON PAGES 12-15

Colonial Touch

- Matching dormers and shuttered windows add a Colonial touch to this inviting home. The front door opens directly into the living room, welcoming visitors right into family space.
- The living room sprawls to the broad hearth of the warming fireplace. Just a step away, the dining room overlooks the backyard through corner windows.
- Serving is simple beyond the snack bar, where the kitchen handles any meal with ease. Ample counters give the cook plenty of elbow room, and the step-in pantry is certain to please.
- Insulated from the busy family areas by a hall door, the main-floor master suite is a quiet retreat. Pamper yourself with a generous walk-in closet and private access to a full bath.
- Upstairs, two bedrooms overlook the front yard through dormer windows. They share a full hall bath.
- Below, the garage sets aside plenty of storage space for tools or bikes.

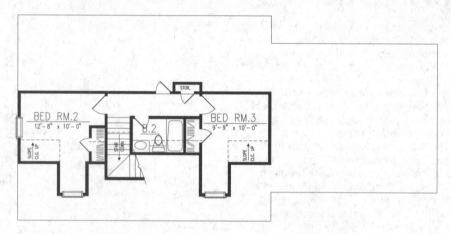

UPPER FLOOR

Plan RD-1360

Bedrooms: 3	Baths: 2

Living Area:

Upper floor	400 sq. ft.
Main floor	960 sq. ft.
Total Living Area:	**1,360 sq. ft.**
Standard basement	970 sq. ft.
Garage and storage	494 sq. ft.
Mechanical	10 sq. ft.
Exterior Wall Framing:	**2 x 4**

Foundation Options:

Standard basement
Crawlspace
Slab

(All plans can be built with your choice of foundation and framing. A generic conversion diagram is available. See order form.)

BLUEPRINT PRICE CODE:	**A**

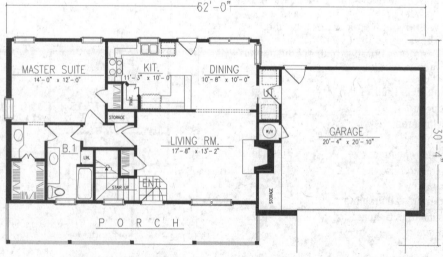

MAIN FLOOR

ORDER BLUEPRINTS ANYTIME!
CALL TOLL-FREE 1-800-820-1296

Plan RD-1360

Plan copyright held by home designer/architect

PRICES AND DETAILS
ON PAGES 12-15

Get Away— or Stay

- This rustic charmer is the right size for a vacation getaway or a starter home, and it's well equipped for day-to-day living.
- A deep porch at the front and and a covered patio out back are irresistible outdoor living spaces, not to mention delightful spots to watch a summer rain.
- The spacious living room with a focal-point fireplace can accommodate intimate gatherings or small parties with equal ease. The room flows freely into the dining area, which is served by the galley-style kitchen and topped by a rugged wood beam.
- Note the smart placement of the laundry facilities at the edge of the kitchen—do all your chores in one handy spot!
- The main-floor master bedroom includes private access to the back patio, plus a well-planned private bath.
- On the upper floor, two bedrooms share a full bath. A cute play area for the little ones rounds out the design.

Plan DD-1341

Bedrooms: 3	Baths: 2½

Living Area:	
Upper floor	504 sq. ft.
Main floor	866 sq. ft.
Total Living Area:	**1,370 sq. ft.**
Standard basement	866 sq. ft.
Exterior Wall Framing:	2x4

Foundation Options:

Standard basement

Crawlspace

Slab

(All plans can be built with your choice of foundation and framing. A generic conversion diagram is available. See order form.)

BLUEPRINT PRICE CODE:	A

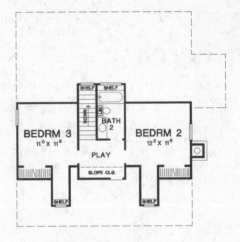

UPPER FLOOR

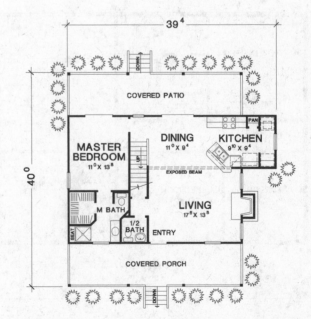

MAIN FLOOR

ORDER BLUEPRINTS ANYTIME!
CALL TOLL-FREE 1-800-820-1296

Plan DD-1341
Plan copyright held by home designer/architect

PRICES AND DETAILS
ON PAGES 12-15

77

Inviting Country Porch

- A columned porch with double doors invites you into the rustic living areas of this ranch-style home.
- Inside, the entry allows views back to the expansive, central living room and the backyard beyond.
- The living room boasts an exposed-beam ceiling and a massive fireplace

with a wide stone hearth, a wood box and built-in bookshelves. A sunny patio offers additional entertaining space.
- The dining room and the efficient kitchen combine for easy meal service, with a serving bar separating the two.
- The main hallway leads to the sleeping wing, which offers a large master bedroom with a walk-in closet and a private bath.
- Two additional bedrooms share another full bath, and a laundry closet is easily accessible to the entire bedroom wing.

Plan E-1304	
Bedrooms: 3	**Baths:** 2
Living Area:	
Main floor	1,395 sq. ft.
Total Living Area:	**1,395 sq. ft.**
Garage	451 sq. ft.
Storage	30 sq. ft.
Exterior Wall Framing:	2x4

Foundation Options:
Crawlspace
Slab
(All plans can be built with your choice of foundation and framing. A generic conversion diagram is available. See order form.)

BLUEPRINT PRICE CODE:	A

MAIN FLOOR

73'-0"

37'-0"

MASTER BEDROOM 14 x 13'

KNEE SPACE

DRESSING ROOM

CLOSET

WASH DRY

LIVING 18' x 17'

BEAM

BEAM

PATIO

WOOD BOX

STONE

CLOSET

LINEN

HALL

STORAGE 7'-6" x 4'

DISAPPEARING STAIRS

HEAT & A.C.

BEDROOM 12' x 11'

BEDROOM 12' x 11'

CLOSET

ENTRY

DINING 12' x 11'

REF.

RANGE

W.H.

KITCHEN 12' x 10'

BAR

D.W. SINK

GARAGE 21' x 21'

PORCH 42' x 7'

Plan E-1304

Plan copyright held by home designer/architect

ORDER BLUEPRINTS ANYTIME!
CALL TOLL-FREE 1-800-820-1296

PRICES AND DETAILS
ON PAGES 12-15

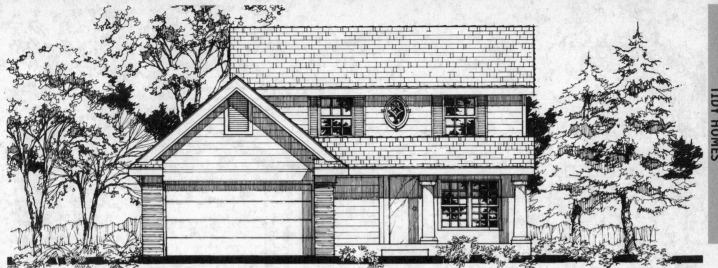

Affordable Livability

- An outstanding combination of affordability and livability are packaged under one roof in this transitional home.
- On the main floor, the smart L-shaped kitchen leaves room for a breakfast table, and accesses a backyard patio.
- Quiet formal occasions are at home in the dining room, which is visible from the foyer over a half-wall anchored by bold decorative posts.
- The living room, set off from the kitchen by a beautifully brightened central stairway, can be expanded behind the two-car garage for extra space.
- Three good-sized bedrooms and two full baths serve the family and cluster around a convenient laundry closet on the upper floor. The master bedroom shows off an airy vaulted ceiling and a big walk-in closet.

Plan B-90061

Bedrooms: 3	Baths: 2½
Living Area:	
Upper floor	727 sq. ft.
Main floor	669 sq. ft.
Total Living Area:	**1,396 sq. ft.**
Standard basement	669 sq. ft.
Garage	400 sq. ft.
Exterior Wall Framing:	2x4

Foundation Options:

Standard basement

(All plans can be built with your choice of foundation and framing. A generic conversion diagram is available. See order form.)

BLUEPRINT PRICE CODE: **A**

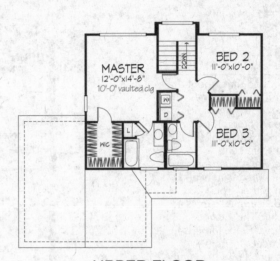

UPPER FLOOR

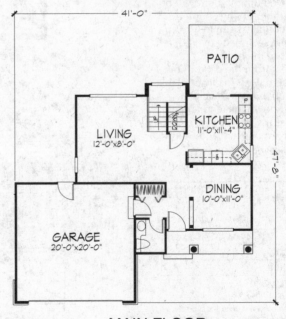

MAIN FLOOR

Plan B-90061

Plan copyright held by home designer/architect

PRICES AND DETAILS
ON PAGES 12-15

Compact Splendor

- Splendid details abound throughout this compact—and affordable!—home.
- Stunning arched windows greet and welcome impressed visitors. The durable brick exterior will stand the test of both time and the elements.
- Inside, the massive Great Room serves as the home's focal point. Family and friends will love to gather around the central fireplace to visit, play games or relax after a long day. The kitchen's breakfast bar is a great place for kids to enjoy after-school treats.
- The U-shaped kitchen allows the family cook plenty of room to maneuver. Meals in the bayed dining room will be a bit easier with the serving counter.
- You will enjoy countless summer afternoons on the secluded covered patio at the rear of the home.
- Adults can retreat from the patio to the master suite. Large walk-in closets flank the refreshing tub, while a dual-sink vanity with a sit-down makeup area eases morning stress.
- Walk-in closets are unusual additions to the two secondary bedrooms.

Plan KD-1398

Bedrooms: 3	Baths: 2
Living Area:	
Main floor	1,398 sq. ft.
Total Living Area:	**1,398 sq. ft.**
Garage and storage	465 sq. ft.
Exterior Wall Framing:	2x4

Foundation Options:

Slab

(All plans can be built with your choice of foundation and framing. A generic conversion diagram is available. See order form.)

BLUEPRINT PRICE CODE:	A

MAIN FLOOR

VIEW INTO GREAT ROOM

Plan KD-1398

Plan copyright held by home designer/architect

PRICES AND DETAILS
ON PAGES 12-15

Stylish Exterior, Open Floor Plan

- With its simple yet stylish exterior, this modest-sized design is suitable for country or urban settings.
- A covered front porch and a gabled roof extension accent the facade while providing plenty of sheltered space for outdoor relaxation.
- Inside, the open floor plan puts available space to efficient use.
- The living room, which offers a warm fireplace, is expanded by a cathedral ceiling. The addition of the kitchen and the bayed dining room creates an expansive gathering space.
- The master suite features a private bath and a large walk-in closet.
- Two more good-sized bedrooms share a second full bath.
- A utility area leads to the carport, which incorporates extra storage space.

Plan J-86155

Bedrooms: 3	Baths: 2
Living Area:	
Main floor	1,385 sq. ft.
Total Living Area:	**1,385 sq. ft.**
Standard basement	1,385 sq. ft.
Carport	380 sq. ft.
Storage	40 sq. ft.
Exterior Wall Framing:	2x4

Foundation Options:

Standard basement
Crawlspace
Slab

(All plans can be built with your choice of foundation and framing. A generic conversion diagram is available. See order form.)

BLUEPRINT PRICE CODE: A

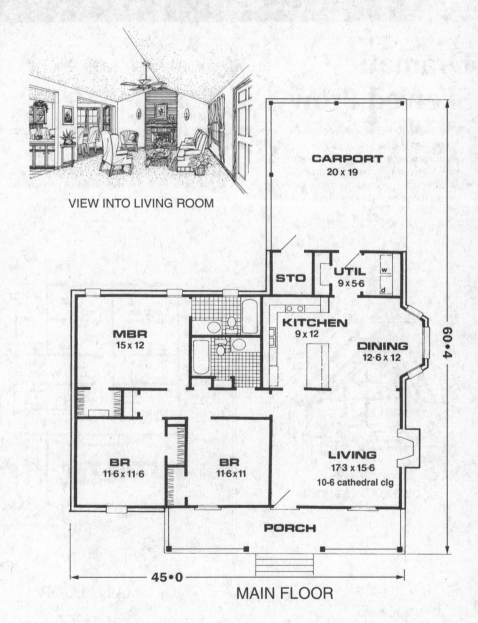

VIEW INTO LIVING ROOM

MAIN FLOOR

CARPORT 20 x 19

STO

UTIL 9 x 5·6

w
d

KITCHEN 9 x 12

DINING 12·6 x 12

MBR 15 x 12

BR 11·6 x 11·6

BR 11·6 x 11

LIVING 17·3 x 15·6 10·6 cathedral clg

PORCH

60·4

45·0

ORDER BLUEPRINTS ANYTIME!
CALL TOLL-FREE 1-800-820-1296

Plan J-86155

Plan copyright held by home designer/architect

PRICES AND DETAILS
ON PAGES 12-15

81

Dramatic Skewed Prow

- This cleverly modified A-frame design combines a dramatic exterior with an exciting interior that offers commanding views through its many windows.
- The central foyer opens to a spacious living room and dining room

combination with a soaring cathedral ceiling and a massive stone fireplace. Sliding glass doors open to an inviting wraparound deck.
- Directly ahead is the L-shaped kitchen, which also accesses the deck.
- Two bedrooms are located at the rear, near the laundry room and a full bath.
- A third bedroom, a second bath and a balcony loft that could sleep overnight guests are found on the upper level.

Plan HFL-1160-CW

Bedrooms: 3+	Baths: 2
Living Area:	
Upper floor	400 sq. ft.
Main floor	1,016 sq. ft.
Total Living Area:	**1,416 sq. ft.**
Exterior Wall Framing:	2x4

Foundation Options:

Crawlspace
(All plans can be built with your choice of foundation and framing. A generic conversion diagram is available. See order form.)

BLUEPRINT PRICE CODE: A

VIEW INTO DINING/LIVING ROOM

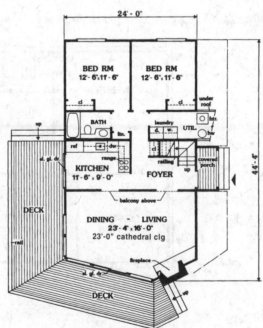

MAIN FLOOR

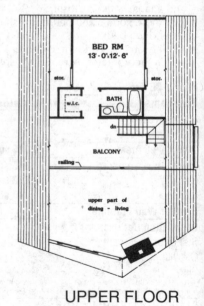

UPPER FLOOR

Plan HFL-1160-CW

Plan copyright held by home designer/architect

PRICES AND DETAILS
ON PAGES 12-15

Splendid Split-Foyer

- This popular split-foyer home offers soaring vaulted formal areas and a splendid master suite.
- The foyer leads up to the airy living room, which is brightened by broad windows and warmed by a fireplace
- The adjoining dining room merges with the breakfast area and accesses the back deck though sliding glass doors.

- Double windows warm the breakfast nook and provide views to the backyard. The kitchen also boasts an angled sink area with a plant shelf.
- The master suite features a large closet, a corner window and a deluxe master bath that boasts another closet, a step-up spa tub and a separate shower. Two additional bedrooms share a full bath.
- The lower level provides space for expansion with the inclusion of an unfinished family room. The tuck-under garage and the laundry room share this level.

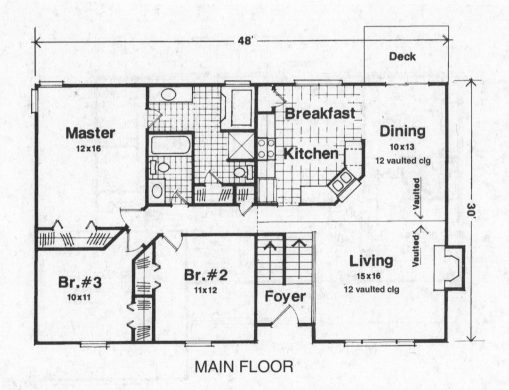

MAIN FLOOR

ORDER BLUEPRINTS ANYTIME!
CALL TOLL-FREE 1-800-820-1296

Plan APS-1410
Plan copyright held by home designer/architect

PRICES AND DETAILS
ON PAGES 12-15

83

Rustic Ranch-Style Design

- This ranch-style home offers a rustic facade that is warm and inviting. The railed front porch and stone accents are especially appealing.
- The interior is warm as well, with the focal point being the attractive living room. Features here include built-in shelves, an eye-catching fireplace, patio access and a dramatic sloped ceiling with exposed beams.

- The open dining room lies off the foyer and adjoins the efficient U-shaped kitchen, which includes a pantry and a broom closet. Nearby garage access makes unloading groceries convenient. The side-entry garage includes generous storage space.
- The master suite features a large walk-in closet and a roomy master bath, plus a nice view of the patio.
- At the other end of the home, two secondary bedrooms with abundant closet space share another full bath. One of the bedrooms offers a charming window seat.

Plan E-1410	
Bedrooms: 3	**Baths:** 2
Living Area:	
Main floor	1,418 sq. ft.
Total Living Area:	**1,418 sq. ft.**
Garage	484 sq. ft.
Storage	38 sq. ft.
Exterior Wall Framing:	2x4

Foundation Options:
Crawlspace
Slab
(All plans can be built with your choice of foundation and framing. A generic conversion diagram is available. See order form.)

BLUEPRINT PRICE CODE: A

MAIN FLOOR

Plan E-1410
Plan copyright held by home designer/architect

**PRICES AND DETAILS
ON PAGES 12-15**

Catch of the Day

- Inspired by the late 19th century summer cottages along the East Coast, this versatile shingle-style design is suitable as a primary residence or as a cozy weekend retreat.
- The floor plan is practically sized and is expanded by a deep veranda and a screened porch, which serve as additional entertaining areas. Hardwood floors and high ceilings lend beauty and volume to the living spaces.
- At the entry, a leaded glass door opens to a dramatic two-story foyer and turned staircase. A view into the living area reveals a warm woodstove and plenty of space for unwinding after work or a long day of fishing.
- A dining area is nestled between two sets of sliding French doors—one to the veranda and one to the porch.
- Its central location and convenient serving bar to the living area make the kitchen simple yet functional.
- Enticing double doors access the master bedroom on the main floor. Enjoy stepping out to the porch or into your private bath with a handy pocket door to the laundry room.
- Two more bedrooms, each with a raised ceiling and lots of space, share another bath on the upper floor.
- The blueprints include plans for a detached two-car garage.

Plan L-444-VACA	
Bedrooms: 3	**Baths:** 2
Living Area:	
Upper floor	464 sq. ft.
Main floor	978 sq. ft.
Total Living Area:	**1,442 sq. ft.**
Screened porch	100 sq. ft.
Detached garage	528 sq. ft.
Exterior Wall Framing:	2x4
Foundation Options:	
Slab	

(All plans can be built with your choice of foundation and framing. A generic conversion diagram is available. See order form.)

| **BLUEPRINT PRICE CODE:** | **A** |

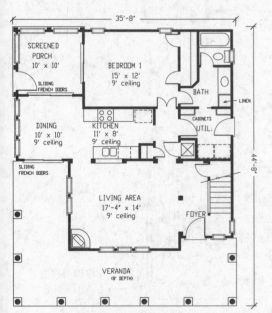

MAIN FLOOR

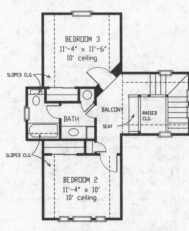

UPPER FLOOR

REAR VIEW

ORDER BLUEPRINTS ANYTIME!
CALL TOLL-FREE 1-800-820-1296

Plan L-444-VACA
Plan copyright held by home designer/architect

PRICES AND DETAILS
ON PAGES 12-15

85

Luxury in a Small Package

- The elegant exterior of this design sets the tone for the luxurious spaces within.
- The foyer opens to the centrally located living room, which features a cathedral ceiling, a handsome fireplace and access to a lovely rear terrace.
- The unusual kitchen design includes an angled snack bar that lies between the bayed breakfast den and the formal dining room. Sliding glass doors open to another terrace.
- The master suite is a dream come true, with its romantic fireplace, built-in desk and tray ceiling. The private bath includes a whirlpool tub and a dual-sink vanity.
- Another full bath serves the remaining two bedrooms, one of which boasts a cathedral ceiling and a beautiful arched window.

Plan AHP-9300

Bedrooms: 3	Baths: 2
Living Area:	
Main floor	1,513 sq. ft.
Total Living Area:	**1,513 sq. ft.**
Standard basement	1,360 sq. ft.
Garage	400 sq. ft.
Exterior Wall Framing:	2x4 or 2x6

Foundation Options:

Standard basement
Crawlspace
Slab

(All plans can be built with your choice of foundation and framing. A generic conversion diagram is available. See order form.)

BLUEPRINT PRICE CODE:	B

MAIN FLOOR

Terrace
51-8
sl.gl.dr.
Terrace
Dining Rm 12 x 10
Living Rm 14 x 21 15 cathedral clg
wic
whirlpool tub
Master Suite 14 x 14 9 tray clg
bay
bar
Den 10 x 9
Kitchen 12 x 11-6
ref. p
Mud Rm
d w
dn
Foyer
Hall
lin
up
Double Garage 20 x 20
Porch
Bedroom 2 12 x 11
Bedroom 3 11 x 11 11 cathedral clg
46-4

VIEW INTO
MASTER
SUITE

ORDER BLUEPRINTS ANYTIME!
CALL TOLL-FREE 1-800-820-1296

Plan AHP-9300
Plan copyright held by home designer/architect

PRICES AND DETAILS
ON PAGES 12-15

Elegant Touch

- A stunning exterior of brick, siding and copper flashing adds an elegant touch to this feature-filled one-story home.
- The recessed, sidelighted entry opens directly into the bright and airy family room, which boasts a high ceiling and a striking window-flanked fireplace.
- The adjacent formal dining room features a tray ceiling and includes a French door to a backyard patio.
- Designed with the gourmet in mind, the kitchen offers a pantry, an angled eating bar and a sunny breakfast area. A French door accesses a rear porch.
- Enhanced by a cathedral ceiling and decorative plant shelves, the master suite unfolds to a sitting area and a roomy walk-in closet. The vaulted master bath showcases a garden tub, a separate shower and a functional dual-sink vanity with knee space.
- On the opposite side of the home, two more bedrooms share another full bath.
- A laundry room is conveniently located between the entry and the garage.

Plan APS-1516

Bedrooms: 3	Baths: 2
Living Area:	
Main floor	1,593 sq. ft.
Total Living Area:	**1,593 sq. ft.**
Standard basement	1,593 sq. ft.
Garage/storage/mechanical	482 sq. ft.
Exterior Wall Framing:	2x4

Foundation Options:

Standard basement
Crawlspace
Slab
(All plans can be built with your choice of foundation and framing. A generic conversion diagram is available. See order form.)

BLUEPRINT PRICE CODE: **B**

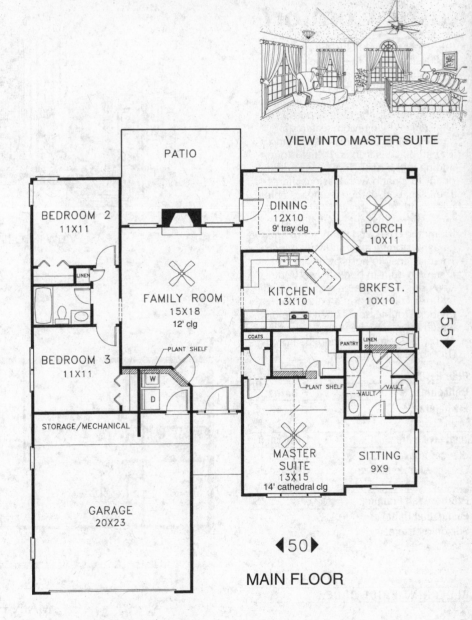

VIEW INTO MASTER SUITE

MAIN FLOOR

ORDER BLUEPRINTS ANYTIME!
CALL TOLL-FREE 1-800-820-1296

Plan APS-1516
Plan copyright held by home designer/architect

PRICES AND DETAILS
ON PAGES 12-15   87

Rustic Comfort

SENSIBLE HOMES

- Rustic charm highlights the exterior of this design, while the interior is filled with all the latest comforts.
- The front porch opens to the entry, where dividers with decorative railings offer views into the dining room.
- The sunken living room features a vaulted ceiling with exposed beams. The fireplace is fronted by fieldstone, adding to the rustic look. A rear door opens to a patio with luscious planters.
- The U-shaped kitchen features a china niche with glass shelves. Other bonuses include the adjacent sewing/hobby room, the oversized utility room and the garage's storage area and workbench.
- The master suite hosts a sunken sleeping area with built-in bookshelves. One step up is a sitting area that is defined by brick columns and a railed room divider. Double doors open to the bath, which offers a niche with glass shelves.
- Across the home, two more bedrooms share a second full bath.

Plan E-1607

Bedrooms: 3	Baths: 2
Living Area:	
Main floor	1,600 sq. ft.
Total Living Area:	**1,600 sq. ft.**
Standard basement	1,600 sq. ft.
Garage and workbench	484 sq. ft.
Storage	132 sq. ft.
Exterior Wall Framing:	2x6

Foundation Options:

Standard basement
Crawlspace
Slab

(All plans can be built with your choice of foundation and framing. A generic conversion diagram is available. See order form.)

BLUEPRINT PRICE CODE: **B**

VIEW INTO LIVING ROOM

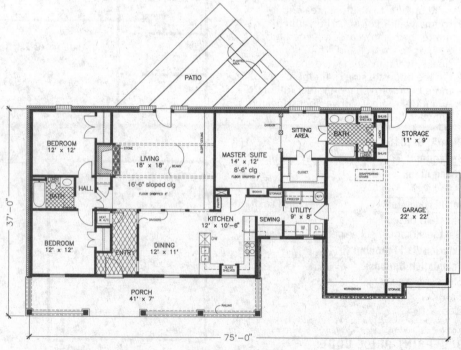

MAIN FLOOR

ORDER BLUEPRINTS ANYTIME!
CALL TOLL-FREE 1-800-820-1296

Plan E-1607
Plan copyright held by home designer/architect

PRICES AND DETAILS
ON PAGES 12-15

Good Looks, Great Views

- Wood shutters, glamorous half-round windows and durable brick give this home its good looks.
- Entry drama is created with the use of high ceilings in the foyer, dining room and Great Room. The dining room is set off by elegant columned openings; your formal meals can be kept warm and out of sight in the handy serving station around the corner.

- Over the kitchen's snack counter, the TV center and fireplace in the Great Room create an attractive wall that complements the sliding French door tandem to the rear.
- Half-round windows accentuate the radiant bays protruding from the breakfast room and the master suite, expanding the home's outdoor views.
- The master bedroom boasts a vaulted ceiling and a whirlpool bath.
- Wider doorways and an alternate garage plan with a ramp instead of a storage area make this home adaptable to wheelchair use.

Plan AX-95367	
Bedrooms: 3	**Baths:** 2
Living Area:	
Main floor	1,595 sq. ft.
Total Living Area:	**1,595 sq. ft.**
Standard basement	1,595 sq. ft.
Garage and storage	548 sq. ft.
Exterior Wall Framing:	2x4
Foundation Options:	
Standard basement	
Crawlspace	
Slab	

(All plans can be built with your choice of foundation and framing. A generic conversion diagram is available. See order form.)

BLUEPRINT PRICE CODE:	B

MAIN FLOOR

Plan dimensions and room labels:

- PORCH 10'-0" x 7'-0"
- 10'-9" HIGH VAULTED CLG
- BKFST RM 10'-0" x 8'-4"
- FR SL GL DRS
- BUILT-IN T.V.
- 10'-9" HIGH VAULTED CLG
- MSTR BEDRM 12'-4" x 15'-8"
- MSTR BATH
- STORAGE/ UTIL
- 10'-4" HIGH STEPPED CLG
- GREAT RM 14'-0" x 20'-0"
- WICL
- KITCHEN 10'-8" x 16'-0"
- 9'-0" HIGH CLG
- CL CL CL LIN
- TWO CAR GARAGE 20'-0" x 23'-4"
- SERVER
- STOR
- HALL
- BATH
- 37'-4" OVERALL
- OPT BSMT ENTRY
- 14' HIGH STEPPED CLG
- DINING RM 10'-6" x 14'-0"
- 14' HIGH FOYER
- 10'-6" HIGH VAULTED CLG
- BEDRM #3 10'-0" x 12'-0"
- BEDRM #2 11'-0" x 10'-0"
- 9'-0" HIGH CLG
- LAUN RM
- STORAGE
- 70'-0" OVERALL

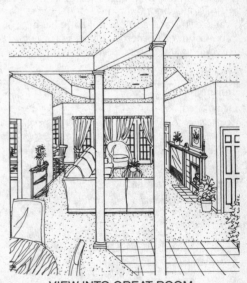

VIEW INTO GREAT ROOM FROM DINING ROOM

Breland & Farmer Designers, Inc.

Stylish and Compact

- This country-style home has a classic exterior and a space-saving and compact interior.
- A quaint columned porch extends along the front of the home. Through the front door, the entry leads to the spacious living room with a handsome fireplace, windows at either end and access to a big screened porch.
- The formal dining room flows from the living room and is easily served by the convenient U-shaped kitchen.
- A nice-sized laundry room and a full bath are nearby. The two-car garage offers a super storage area.
- The master suite features a huge walk-in closet. A separate dressing area leads to an adjoining, dual-access bath.
- The upper floor offers two more bedrooms and another full bath. Each bedroom has generous closet space and independent access to attic space.

Plan E-1626

Bedrooms: 3	Baths: 2
Living Area:	
Upper floor	464 sq. ft.
Main floor	1,136 sq. ft.
Total Living Area:	**1,600 sq. ft.**
Garage and storage	572 sq. ft.
Exterior Wall Framing:	2x6

Foundation Options:

Crawlspace
Slab
(All plans can be built with your choice of foundation and framing. A generic conversion diagram is available. See order form.)

BLUEPRINT PRICE CODE:	B

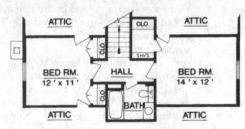

UPPER FLOOR

VIEW INTO LIVING ROOM

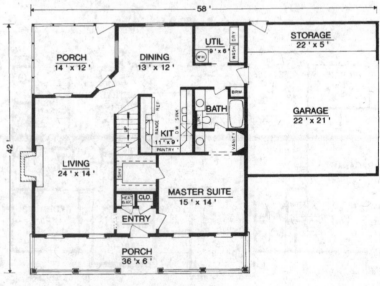

MAIN FLOOR

ORDER BLUEPRINTS ANYTIME!
CALL TOLL-FREE 1-800-820-1296

Plan E-1626

Plan copyright held by home designer/architect

PRICES AND DETAILS ON PAGES 12-15

Angled Solar Design

- This passive-solar design with a six-sided core is angled to capture as much sunlight as possible.
- Finished in natural vertical cedar planks and stone veneer, this contemporary three-bedroom requires a minimum of maintenance.
- Double doors at the entry open into the spacious living and dining areas.

- The formal area features a domed ceiling with skylights, a freestanding fireplace and three sets of sliding glass doors. The central sliding doors lead to a glass-enclosed sun room.
- The bright eat-in kitchen merges with the den, where sliding glass doors lead to one of three backyard terraces.
- The master bedroom, in the quiet sleeping wing, boasts ample closets, a private terrace and a luxurious bath, complete with a whirlpool tub.
- The two secondary bedrooms share a convenient hall bath.

Plan K-534-L

Bedrooms: 3	Baths: 2
Living Area:	
Main floor	1,647 sq. ft.
Sun room	109 sq. ft.
Total Living Area:	**1,756 sq. ft.**
Standard basement	1,505 sq. ft.
Garage and storage	417 sq. ft.
Exterior Wall Framing:	2x4 or 2x6

Foundation Options:

Standard basement
Slab
(All plans can be built with your choice of foundation and framing.
A generic conversion diagram is available. See order form.)

BLUEPRINT PRICE CODE: B

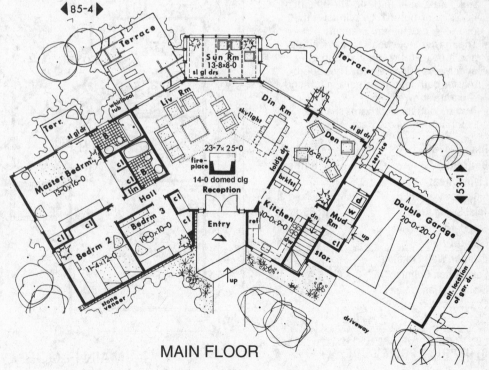

VIEW INTO LIVING AND DINING ROOMS

MAIN FLOOR

ORDER BLUEPRINTS ANYTIME!
CALL TOLL-FREE 1-800-820-1296

Plan K-534-L
Plan copyright held by home designer/architect

PRICES AND DETAILS
ON PAGES 12-15

91

Mark Englund/Homestore™ Plans and Publications

Planned to Perfection

- This attractive and stylish home offers an interior design that is planned to perfection.
- The covered entry and vaulted foyer create an impressive welcome.
- The Great Room features a corner fireplace, a wet bar and lots of windows. The adjoining dining room offers a bay window and access to a covered patio.
- The gourmet kitchen includes an island cooktop, a garden window above the sink and a built-in desk. The attached nook is surrounded by windows that overlook a delightful planter.
- The master suite boasts a tray ceiling and a peaceful reading area that accesses a private patio. The superb master bath features a garden tub and a separate shower.
- Two secondary bedrooms share a compartmentalized bath.

VIEW INTO
GREAT ROOM
AND DINING AREA

NOTE:
The photographed home may have been modified by the homeowner. Please refer to floor plan and/or drawn elevation shown for actual blueprint details.

Plan S-4789

Bedrooms: 3	Baths: 2
Living Area:	
Main floor	1,665 sq. ft.
Total Living Area:	**1,665 sq. ft.**
Standard basement	1,665 sq. ft.
Garage	400 sq. ft.
Exterior Wall Framing:	2x6

Foundation Options:

Standard basement
Crawlspace
Slab
(All plans can be built with your choice of foundation and framing. A generic conversion diagram is available. See order form.)

BLUEPRINT PRICE CODE: B

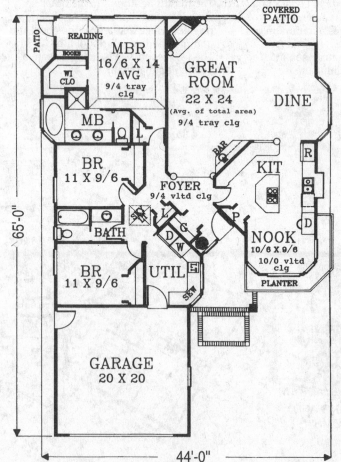

MAIN FLOOR

BASEMENT
STAIRWAY
LOCATION

ORDER BLUEPRINTS ANYTIME!
CALL TOLL-FREE 1-800-820-1296

Plan S-4789
Plan copyright held by home designer/architect

PRICES AND DETAILS
ON PAGES 12-15

LifeStyle HomeDesign

Relaxing Deck and Spa!

- Designed for relaxation as well as for active indoor/outdoor living, this popular home offers a gigantic deck and an irresistible spa room.
- A covered porch welcomes guests into the entry hall, which flows past the central, open-railed stairway to the spectacular Great Room.
- Sliding glass doors on each side of the Great Room open to the huge V-shaped deck. A dramatic vaulted ceiling and a woodstove add to the stunning effect.
- The vaulted master suite features a cozy window seat, a good-sized walk-in closet and private access to a full bath.
- The passive-solar spa room, enhanced by a vaulted ceiling and bright skylights, can be reached from both the master suite and the backyard deck.
- The upper floor hosts two additional vaulted bedrooms and a full bath; a balcony hall overlooks the Great Room.
- A fun recreation room, an extra bedroom and a versatile shop area are found in the optional basement.

REAR VIEW

SENSIBLE HOMES

Plans H-952-1A & -1B

Bedrooms: 3+	Baths: 2–3
Living Area:	
Upper floor	470 sq. ft.
Main floor	1,207 sq. ft.
Passive spa room	102 sq. ft.
Daylight basement	1,105 sq. ft.
Total Living Area:	**1,779/2,884 sq. ft.**
Garage	496 sq. ft.
Exterior Wall Framing:	2x6
Foundation Options:	**Plan #**
Daylight basement	H-952-1B
Crawlspace	H-952-1A

(All plans can be built with your choice of foundation and framing. A generic conversion diagram is available. See order form.)

BLUEPRINT PRICE CODE:	B/D

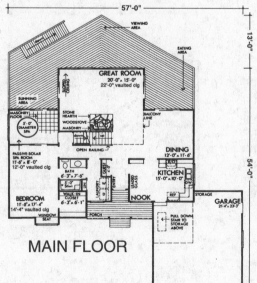

UPPER FLOOR

MAIN FLOOR

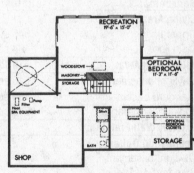

DAYLIGHT BASEMENT

ORDER BLUEPRINTS ANYTIME!
CALL TOLL-FREE 1-800-820-1296

Plans H-952-1A & -1B
Plan copyright held by home designer/architect

PRICES AND DETAILS
ON PAGES 12-15

93

Spacious Economy

- This economical country cottage features wide, angled spaces and 9-ft., 4-in. ceilings in both the Great Room and the master bedroom for roomy appeal and year-round comfort.
- The Great Room boasts a cozy fireplace with a raised hearth and a built-in niche for a TV, making this room perfect for winter gatherings. On warm nights, a homey covered porch at the rear can be accessed through sliding glass doors.
- Amenities in the luxurious master bedroom include a large walk-in closet, a private whirlpool bath and a dual-sink vanity.
- The nicely appointed kitchen offers nearby laundry facilities and porch access. A serving bar allows for casual dining and relaxed conversation.
- The optional daylight basement includes a tuck-under, two-car garage.

Plan AX-94322

Bedrooms: 3	Baths: 2½
Living Area:	
Upper floor	545 sq. ft.
Main floor	1,134 sq. ft.
Total Living Area:	**1,679 sq. ft.**
Daylight basement	618 sq. ft.
Standard basement	1,134 sq. ft.
Tuck-under garage	516 sq. ft.
Exterior Wall Framing:	2x4

Foundation Options:
Daylight basement
Standard basement
Crawlspace
Slab
(All plans can be built with your choice of foundation and framing. A generic conversion diagram is available. See order form.)

BLUEPRINT PRICE CODE:	**B**

VIEW INTO GREAT ROOM

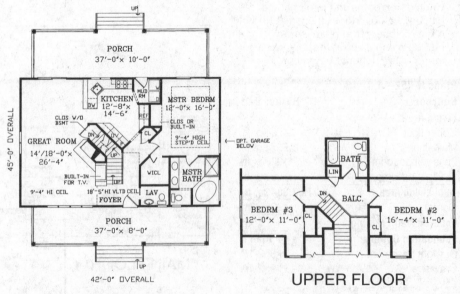

MAIN FLOOR

UPPER FLOOR

Plan AX-94322

Plan copyright held by home designer/architect

**PRICES AND DETAILS
ON PAGES 12-15**

To the Heart of the Matter

- Comfortable to the core, this home's highlight is its centrally located family room. As the years go by it remains the heart of activity, hosting cherished guests and offering a retreat from the daily grind.
- Plant shelves above the entry extend a lush welcome into the family room and the formal dining room. On chilly days, recline in front of the fireplace. On warm evenings, invite guests onto the backyard deck for a barbecue.
- A pass-through serving bar connects the family room with the kitchen, which features a handy pantry and a built-in desk. A breakfast bar in the light-filled nook offers extra counter space for buffet-style meals.
- The master suite flaunts a handsome tray ceiling, deck access and a roomy walk-in closet. The private master bath features a dual-sink vanity, a garden tub and a separate shower.
- Two secondary bedrooms share a full hall bath.

Plan APS-1614

Bedrooms: 3	Baths: 2
Living Area:	
Main floor	1,681 sq. ft.
Total Living Area:	**1,681 sq. ft.**
Garage	467 sq. ft.
Exterior Wall Framing:	2x4

Foundation Options:

Slab
(All plans can be built with your choice of foundation and framing. A generic conversion diagram is available. See order form.)

BLUEPRINT PRICE CODE: B

VIEW INTO KITCHEN

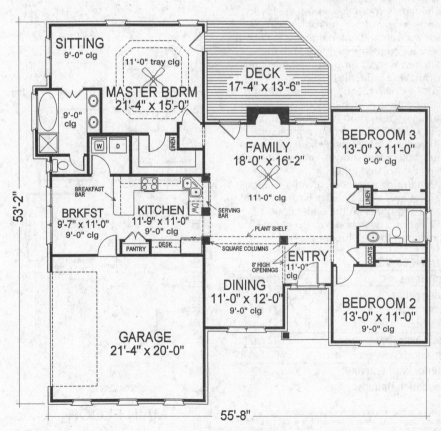

MAIN FLOOR

ORDER BLUEPRINTS ANYTIME!
CALL TOLL-FREE 1-800-820-1296

Plan APS-1614
Plan copyright held by home designer/architect

PRICES AND DETAILS
ON PAGES 12-15

95

Made for the Shade!

- Finely tuned interior features and vintage Victorian-style looks satisfy your appetite for relaxed, easy living. Time will seem to stand still when you enjoy it on the shady wraparound veranda.
- Inside, 9-ft. ceilings on both floors lend volume to every room.
- The family room flows from the foyer and serves as your indoor rendezvous for warmth and entertainment. A central serving counter extending from the kitchen is ideal for pouring drinks and displaying munchies.
- For sit-down meals, the dining room is quite fitting. A French door entices you to savor dessert on the cool veranda.
- Secluded to the rear, the master suite includes a large private bath with a spa tub, a separate shower, dual vanities and an isolated toilet.
- A charming sun room, a walk-in storage closet and a big bookshelf cater to the two bedrooms on the upper floor.
- Plans for a detached two-car garage are included in the blueprints.

VIEW INTO FAMILY ROOM

Plan L-680-VSA

Bedrooms: 3	Baths: 2½
Living Area:	
Upper floor	631 sq. ft.
Main floor	1,051 sq. ft.
Total Living Area:	**1,682 sq. ft.**
Detached garage	480 sq. ft.
Exterior Wall Framing:	2x4

Foundation Options:

Slab

(All plans can be built with your choice of foundation and framing. A generic conversion diagram is available. See order form.)

BLUEPRINT PRICE CODE:	B

MAIN FLOOR

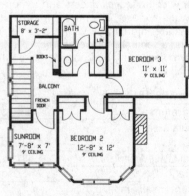

UPPER FLOOR

ORDER BLUEPRINTS ANYTIME! CALL TOLL-FREE 1-800-820-1296

Plan L-680-VSA

Plan copyright held by home designer/architect

PRICES AND DETAILS ON PAGES 12-15

Timeless Charm

- With exterior charm comparable to that of an English country cottage, this delightful home combines timeless beauty and modern amenities.
- The covered entry opens to a spacious living room. Illuminated by a bright bay window and a comforting fireplace, this space also features a media center.
- In the dining room, French doors open to a rear porch. Enjoy this elegant backdrop for formal or casual meals.

- A pantry, a serving counter and views to the rear garden highlight the kitchen, which accesses the sunny utility room.
- A walk-in closet and a set of French doors to the porch embellish the master suite. The bath includes dual sinks, a garden tub and a separate shower.
- The blueprints for this plan give you the option of adding French doors between the living room and the front-facing bedroom, to turn this space into a den.
- With its generous area, the garage is big enough to accommodate a workshop.

Plan L-373-CSA

Bedrooms: 3	**Baths:** 2

Living Area:	
Main floor	1,406 sq. ft.
Total Living Area:	**1,406 sq. ft.**
Garage	533 sq. ft.
Exterior Wall Framing:	2x4

Foundation Options:

Slab

(All plans can be built with your choice of foundation and framing. A generic conversion diagram is available. See order form.)

BLUEPRINT PRICE CODE: **A**

MAIN FLOOR

62'-0"

47'-8"

2-CAR GARAGE
19'-4" x 26'-0"

PORCH

KITCHEN
9' CLG.

DINING
10'-4" x 11'-8"
9' CLG.

FRENCH DOORS

MASTER BEDROOM
11'-4" x 16'-8"
9' CLG.

BATH
9' CLG.

BEDRM 3
10'-0" x 10'-4"
9' CLG.

BATH 2
9' CLG.

MEDIA CENTER

LIN

PAN

REF

UTIL
9' CLG.

W
D

FOYER

LIVING
14'-4" x 17'-8"
9' CLG.

42" HIGH WALL

BEDRM 2
12'-4" x 10'-8"
9' CLG.

ORDER BLUEPRINTS ANYTIME!
CALL TOLL-FREE 1-800-820-1296

Plan L-373-CSA
Plan copyright held by home designer/architect

PRICES AND DETAILS
ON PAGES 12-15

97

Media Savvy

- Video buffs will be in seventh heaven with the built-in media center in the spacious living room of this French country-style home. Enjoy your favorite video while a fire blazes in the fireplace.
- The convenient country kitchen features a pantry and a bayed nook that brings the outdoors in—the perfect place to start the day. The kitchen also features an angled counter that facilitates meal service in the adjacent window-lined dining room.
- Behind a pocket door in the master bedroom, a skylight fills the luxurious private bath with sunshine. A dual-sink vanity, a tub and a separate shower complete the amenities, while a roomy walk-in closet provides the finishing touch to this pampering suite.
- Across the home, a second bedroom is served by an additional full bath and enjoys the convenience of a nearby utility room.
- A storage space at the back of the two-car garage keeps the area tidy.

Plan L-101-HCC

Bedrooms: 2	Baths: 2
Living Area:	
Main floor	1,410 sq. ft.
Total Living Area:	**1,410 sq. ft.**
Garage	502 sq. ft.
Exterior Wall Framing:	2x4

Foundation Options:

Slab
(All plans can be built with your choice of foundation and framing. A generic conversion diagram is available. See order form.)

BLUEPRINT PRICE CODE: A

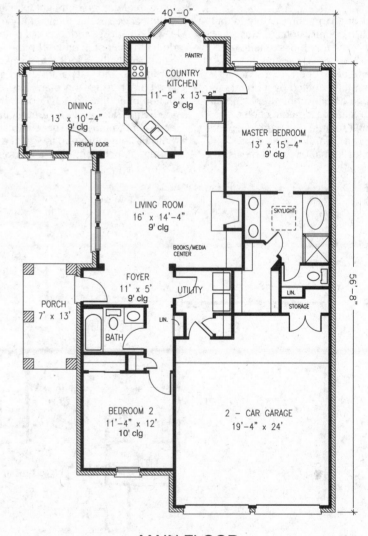

MAIN FLOOR

Plan L-101-HCC
Plan copyright held by home designer/architect

PRICES AND DETAILS
ON PAGES 12-15

Vacation Home with Views

- The octagonal shape and window-filled walls of this home create a powerful interior packed with panoramic views.
- Straight back from the angled entry, the Great Room is brightened by expansive windows and sliding glass doors leading to a huge wraparound deck. An impressive and unexpected spiral staircase at the center of the floor plan lends even more character.
- The walk-through kitchen offers a handy pantry. A sizable storage closet and a guest closet are located between the entry and the two-car garage, prime spots for grabbing or hanging up coats.
- A main-floor bedroom is conveniently located near a full bath.
- The upper-floor master suite is a raised sanctuary featuring lots of high glass, a walk-in closet, a private bath and access to concealed storage areas.
- Downstairs in the optional daylight basement is an extra bedroom, a full bath, a laundry closet and a large recreation room.

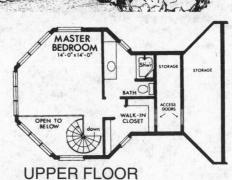

UPPER FLOOR

VIEW INTO GREAT ROOM

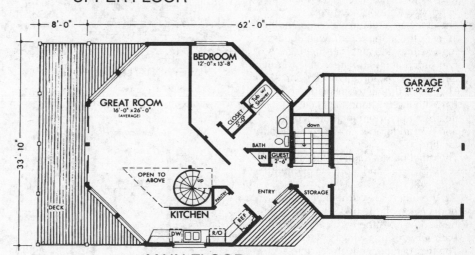

MAIN FLOOR

DAYLIGHT BASEMENT

Plans H-964-1A & -1B

Bedrooms: 2+	Baths: 2–3
Living Area:	
Upper floor	346 sq. ft.
Main floor	1,067 sq. ft.
Daylight basement	1,045 sq. ft.
Total Living Area:	**1,413/2,458 sq. ft.**
Garage	512 sq. ft.
Storage (upper floor)	134 sq. ft.
Exterior Wall Framing:	2x6
Foundation Options:	**Plan #**
Daylight basement	H-964-1B
Crawlspace	H-964-1A

(All plans can be built with your choice of foundation and framing. A generic conversion diagram is available. See order form.)

BLUEPRINT PRICE CODE:	A/C

Plans H-964-1A & -1B

Plan copyright held by home designer/architect

PRICES AND DETAILS
ON PAGES 12-15

Charming Traditional

- The attractive facade of this traditional home features decorative fretwork and louvers in the gables, plus eye-catching window and door treatments.
- The entry area features a commanding view of the living room, which boasts a high ceiling and a corner fireplace. A rear porch and patio are visible through large windows and a French door.
- The bayed dining room shares an eating bar with the U-shaped kitchen. The nearby utility room includes a pantry and two additional closets, plus laundry facilities.
- The quiet master suite includes a big walk-in closet and a private bath with a dual-sink vanity.
- On the other side of the home, double doors close off the two secondary bedrooms from the living areas. A full bath services this wing.
- The two-car garage features attic access and adjoins a nice-sized storage room.

Plan E-1428

Bedrooms: 3	Baths: 2
Living Area:	
Main floor	1,415 sq. ft.
Total Living Area:	**1,415 sq. ft.**
Garage	484 sq. ft.
Storage	60 sq. ft.
Exterior Wall Framing:	2x6

Foundation Options:

Crawlspace
Slab
(All plans can be built with your choice of foundation and framing. A generic conversion diagram is available. See order form.)

BLUEPRINT PRICE CODE: A

VIEW INTO LIVING ROOM

MAIN FLOOR

Plan E-1428

Plan copyright held by home designer/architect

PRICES AND DETAILS ON PAGES 12-15

The View from Saturday

- A tremendous deck and huge windows really bring the out-of-doors into this luxurious vacation retreat—ideal for the lakeshore or the ski hill.
- In between swims or fishing expeditions, spend time sunbathing and snacking on the wide deck.
- Matching sets of French doors flank the front windows and draw you into the family areas. The kitchen features a convenient island eating counter, while the skylighted Great Room offers a vaulted ceiling and a fireplace.
- Tucked into a corner at the rear of the home, the master bedroom provides a large closet and a view to the deck. A second bedroom on the first floor shares the full bath. Access to a rear porch is adjacent to the utility room.
- Upstairs, a vaulted loft reigns supreme. Perfect for guests, it enjoys an overlook to the Great Room, a full bath and a soaring ceiling.

Plan GS-1068	
Bedrooms: 2+	Baths: 2
Living Area:	
Upper floor	434 sq. ft.
Main floor	982 sq. ft.
Total Living Area:	**1,416 sq. ft.**
Exterior Wall Framing:	2x6
Foundation Options:	

Crawlspace
(All plans can be built with your choice of foundation and framing. A generic conversion diagram is available. See order form.)

BLUEPRINT PRICE CODE:	**A**

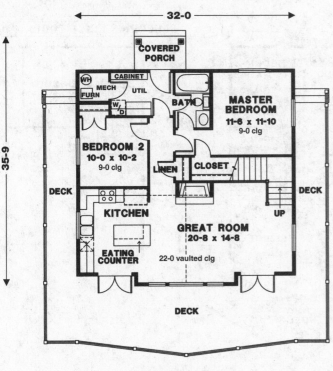

MAIN FLOOR

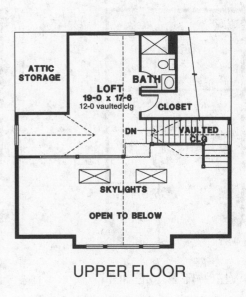

UPPER FLOOR

ORDER BLUEPRINTS ANYTIME!
CALL TOLL-FREE 1-800-820-1296

Plan GS-1068
Plan copyright held by home designer/architect

PRICES AND DETAILS
ON PAGES 12-15   101

Perfect Balance

- This home's handsome exterior strikes the perfect balance between the old and the new. A beautiful stone chimney and two impressive window walls clearly highlight this design.
- Walk through the foyer into the open living and dining area. Here, you can marvel at the elegant fireplace or enjoy the spectacular views through two sets of tall windows.
- The well-appointed kitchen boasts a handy serving bar as well as a convenient laundry closet nearby.

- Two bedrooms and a versatile den, along with an easily accessible hall bath, round out the the main floor.
- Cherish the seclusion offered by the spacious upper-floor master suite, which boasts a deluxe private bath, a roomy walk-in closet and plenty of nearby attic storage.
- Growing families will appreciate the expansion opportunities offered by the flexible basement.
- Take full advantage of the roomy wraparound deck, the perfect spot for barbecuing, suntanning or late-night gazing at the stars.

Plan AHP-9804

Bedrooms: 3+	Baths: 2
Living Area:	
Upper floor	396 sq. ft.
Main floor	1,072 sq. ft.
Total Living Area:	**1,468 sq. ft.**
Basement	760 sq. ft.
Tuck-under garage	312 sq. ft.
Exterior Wall Framing:	2x4 or 2x6

Foundation Options:

Daylight basement
Standard basement
Crawlspace
Slab
(All plans can be built with your choice of foundation and framing. A generic conversion diagram is available. See order form.)

BLUEPRINT PRICE CODE:	A

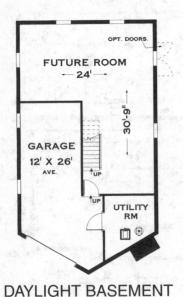

DAYLIGHT BASEMENT

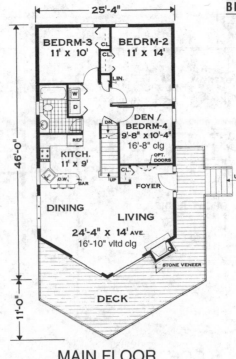

MAIN FLOOR

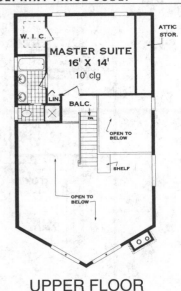

UPPER FLOOR

ORDER BLUEPRINTS ANYTIME! CALL TOLL-FREE 1-800-820-1296

Plan AHP-9804

Plan copyright held by home designer/architect

PRICES AND DETAILS ON PAGES 12-15

Tried and True

- Time-tested traditional touches abound in this appealing country-style home, which is fronted by a nostalgic railed porch and dormers.

- The spacious, central living room anchors the home. A tremendous fireplace flanked by built-in bookshelves serves as the focal-point of the room and adds warmth to family gatherings. Access to a cozy back porch is just steps away.

- An octagonal dining room borders the sunny kitchen, where you'll find a handy pantry and plenty of space to whip up any culinary masterpiece! The kitchen also adjoins a convenient utility room that leads to the attached garage.

- When you long for a good night's sleep, you'll appreciate the master suite, which offers a quiet sitting area that's perfect for spending leisure time. The private master bath is also quite well appointed, flaunting a stunning corner tub, a separate shower, his-and-hers walk-in closets and dual vanities.

- The kids get their space, too—a pair of good-sized bedrooms with ample closet space share a nearby hall bath.

Plan RD-1418

Bedrooms: 3	Baths: 2
Living Area:	
Main floor	1,418 sq. ft.
Total Living Area:	**1,418 sq. ft.**
Garage and storage	464 sq. ft.
Exterior Wall Framing:	2x4

Foundation Options:

Crawlspace
Slab
(All plans can be built with your choice of foundation and framing. A generic conversion diagram is available. See order form.)

BLUEPRINT PRICE CODE:	A

MAIN FLOOR

ORDER BLUEPRINTS ANYTIME!
CALL TOLL-FREE 1-800-820-1296

Plan RD-1418
Plan copyright held by home designer/architect

PRICES AND DETAILS
ON PAGES 12-15   103

Wide Angles Add Style

- The comfortably sized living areas of this gorgeous home are stylishly enhanced by wide, interesting angles.
- Past the covered front porch, the sidelighted front door brightens the living room just ahead.
- The spacious living room is warmed by a dramatic corner fireplace and opens to an angled, covered back porch.
- A stunning bayed dining room merges with the kitchen and its functional angled snack bar. Laundry facilities and access to the garage are nearby.
- The master suite is removed from the secondary bedrooms and features double doors to a deluxe private bath with an angled spa tub, a dual-sink vanity and a large walk-in closet.
- Another full bath serves the two additional bedrooms at the opposite end of the home.

Plan E-1426

Bedrooms: 3	Baths: 2

Living Area:

Main floor	1,420 sq. ft.
Total Living Area:	**1,420 sq. ft.**
Garage and mechanical	480 sq. ft.
Storage	60 sq. ft.
Exterior Wall Framing:	2x6

Foundation Options:

Crawlspace
Slab

(All plans can be built with your choice of foundation and framing. A generic conversion diagram is available. See order form.)

BLUEPRINT PRICE CODE: A

MAIN FLOOR

104   ***ORDER BLUEPRINTS ANYTIME!*** ***CALL TOLL-FREE 1-800-820-1296***   Plan E-1426   ***PRICES AND DETAILS*** ***ON PAGES 12-15***

Plan copyright held by home designer/architect

At One with the Sun

- An open floor plan and large windows on every side of this design allow you to take full advantage of the sun.
- The vaulted kitchen opens to a cheerful sun porch that's the perfect spot to start your day. A pass-through serving counter makes the kitchen available to the adjoining formal dining area.
- The dining and living rooms flow together nicely, and are enhanced by saoring ceilings and views of the large rear deck. A corner fireplace radiates warmth to the living area.
- The master bedroom has twin walk-in closets and a private bath. Another vaulted ceiling adds a spacious feel; sliding glass doors open to the deck.
- Another full bath services a nearby secondary bedroom that may be used as a cozy den or home office.
- The full basement offers more potential living space. A guest suite, a family room or a hobby and craft area would nicely round out the floor plan.

Plan B-91012

Bedrooms: 1+	Baths: 2
Living Area:	
Main floor	1,316 sq. ft.
Sun porch	105 sq. ft.
Total Living Area:	**1,421 sq. ft.**
Standard basement	1,421 sq. ft.
Garage	400 sq. ft.
Exterior Wall Framing:	2x4

Foundation Options:

Standard basement

(All plans can be built with your choice of foundation and framing. A generic conversion diagram is available. See order form.)

BLUEPRINT PRICE CODE:	A

REAR VIEW

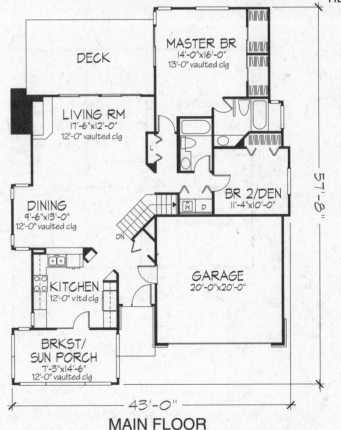

DECK

MASTER BR
14'-0"x16'-0"
13'-0" vaulted clg

LIVING RM
17'-6"x12'-0"
12'-0" vaulted clg

BR 2/DEN
11'-4"x10'-0"

DINING
9'-6"x13'-0"
12'-0" vaulted clg

GARAGE
20'-0"x20'-0"

KITCHEN
12'-0" vltd clg

BRKST/
SUN PORCH
7'-3"x14'-6"
12'-0" vaulted clg

57'-8"

43'-0"

DN

MAIN FLOOR

ORDER BLUEPRINTS ANYTIME!
CALL TOLL-FREE 1-800-820-1296

Plan B-91012

Plan copyright held by home designer/architect

PRICES AND DETAILS
ON PAGES 12-15

105

Appealing and Affordable

- This affordable home offers a choice of fetching exteriors—choose from brick, stucco or siding.
- Its simple yet appealing floor plan offers three bedrooms, two full baths and plenty of open living space.
- The spacious living room at the center of the home has a cathedral ceiling and a fireplace flanked by windows.

- A spacious bay with French doors to the backyard highlights the adjoining dining room. This appealing arrangement lets you enjoy the ambience of the fireplace while dining with family and friends.
- The large, sunny eat-in kitchen has generous counter space and a handy laundry closet near the garage entrance.
- The master bedroom features a dramatic corner window and a private, vaulted bath with a luxury tub; a large walk-in closet completes the picture.

Plan APS-1413

Bedrooms: 3	Baths: 2
Living Area:	
Main floor	1,428 sq. ft.
Total Living Area:	**1,428 sq. ft.**
Garage	419 sq. ft.
Exterior Wall Framing:	2x4

Foundation Options:

Slab

(All plans can be built with your choice of foundation and framing. A generic conversion diagram is available. See order form.)

BLUEPRINT PRICE CODE:	**A**

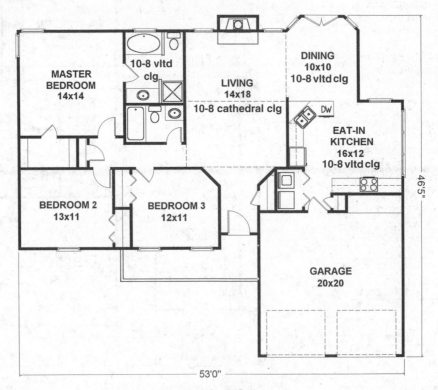

MAIN FLOOR

MASTER BEDROOM 14x14

10-8 vltd clg

LIVING 14x18 10-8 cathedral clg

DINING 10x10 10-8 vltd clg

EAT-IN KITCHEN 16x12 10-8 vltd clg

BEDROOM 2 13x11

BEDROOM 3 12x11

GARAGE 20x20

DW

46'5"

53'0"

Plan APS-1413

Plan copyright held by home designer/architect

PRICES AND DETAILS ON PAGES 12-15

Off to a Great Start!

- This beautiful one-story's charming looks, efficient floor plan and elegant amenities make it a great starter home.
- Half-round windows, decorative corner quoins and a covered front porch add character to the distinctive exterior.
- Past the double-door entry, the foyer flows into the vaulted living room, which boasts a handsome fireplace and a vaulted ceiling.
- The adjoining formal dining room is brightened by French doors to a covered patio. A convenient pass-through provides service from the kitchen, which enjoys a vaulted ceiling and a sunny breakfast nook with patio access.
- The luxurious master suite features a double walk-in closet. The roomy master bath includes a garden tub, a separate shower and a dual-sink vanity.
- Another full bath, a hallway linen closet and a laundry are convenient to the remaining rooms.

Plan B-93009

Bedrooms: 2+	Baths: 2
Living Area:	
Main floor	1,431 sq. ft.
Total Living Area:	**1,431 sq. ft.**
Standard basement	1,431 sq. ft.
Garage	380 sq. ft.
Exterior Wall Framing:	2x6

Foundation Options:

Standard basement

(All plans can be built with your choice of foundation and framing. A generic conversion diagram is available. See order form.)

BLUEPRINT PRICE CODE: **A**

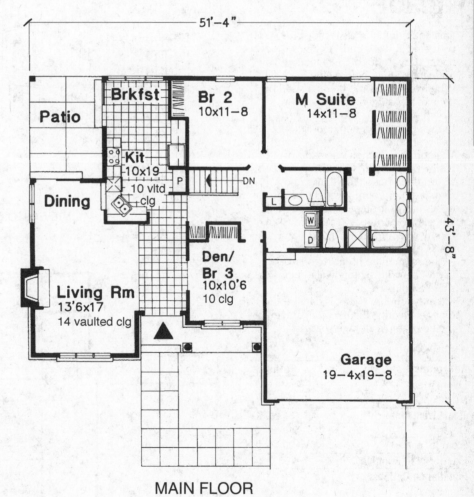

MAIN FLOOR

Br 2 10x11-8
M Suite 14x11-8
Patio
Brkfst
Kit 10x19 10 vltd clg
Dining
Living Rm 13'6x17 14 vaulted clg
Den/ Br 3 10x10'6 10 clg
Garage 19-4x19-8

51'-4"
43'-8"

ORDER BLUEPRINTS ANYTIME!
CALL TOLL-FREE 1-800-820-1296

Plan B-93009
Plan copyright held by home designer/architect

PRICES AND DETAILS
ON PAGES 12-15 107

Welcoming Facade

- This charming home's facade bids you welcome at day's end. Arched windows and a cozy front porch encourage you to linger a while before entering.
- When you do, you'll be impressed by the expansive, central living room, which enjoys a handsome corner fireplace and a French door leading out to a rear porch.
- The gourmet kitchen offers lots of cabinet space and a snack bar that serves the dinette. You'll also find a formal dining room—perfect for special occasions or for large families.
- The extravagant master suite boasts a roomy sleeping area, a good-sized walk-in closet and a private bath.
- At the right of the home, two large bedrooms with sizable walk-in closets share a full bath.
- A handy laundry closet is right off the dinette. Nearby, the two-car garage includes ample storage space.

Plan E-1416

Bedrooms: 3	Baths: 2
Living Area:	
Main floor	1,434 sq. ft.
Total Living Area:	**1,434 sq. ft.**
Garage	441 sq. ft.
Storage	98 sq. ft.
Exterior Wall Framing:	2x4

Foundation Options:

Crawlspace
Slab

(All plans can be built with your choice of foundation and framing. A generic conversion diagram is available. See order form.)

BLUEPRINT PRICE CODE:	A

VIEW INTO LIVING ROOM

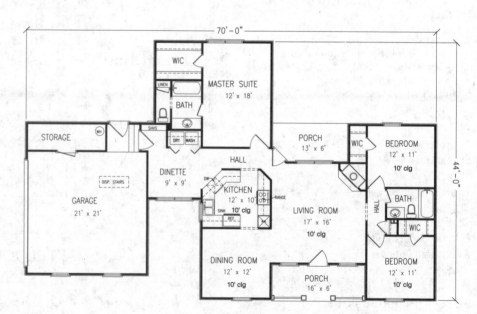

MAIN FLOOR

ORDER BLUEPRINTS ANYTIME!
CALL TOLL-FREE 1-800-820-1296

Plan E-1416
Plan copyright held by home designer/architect

PRICES AND DETAILS
ON PAGES 12-15

Flexible Boathouse

- Originally designed as part of a collection of boathouse plans, this fabulous outbuilding could be built to generate rental income—or could simply be used as a stand-alone home.
- Craftsman accents complement the home's attractive facade. Separate doors and a balcony overhang downplay the front-facing garage.

- On the lower floor, you'll find a bedroom and a full bath, as well as a utility room with laundry facilities.
- The kitchen is made for entertaining. It opens to a spacious dining area and a Great Room with a central fireplace, over which a breathtaking cathedral ceiling soars.
- This home is just the ticket for single adults, young couples or empty nesters looking for a cost-effective alternative to a larger home. This design will function equally well as a supplemental building to an existing home.

Plan COA-3-O

Bedrooms: 2	**Baths:** 2

Living Area:

Main floor	960 sq. ft.
Lower floor	480 sq. ft.
Total Living Area:	**1,440 sq. ft.**
Tuck-under garage	480 sq. ft.
Exterior Wall Framing:	2x4

Foundation Options:

Slab
(All plans can be built with your choice of foundation and framing. A generic conversion diagram is available. See order form.)

BLUEPRINT PRICE CODE: A

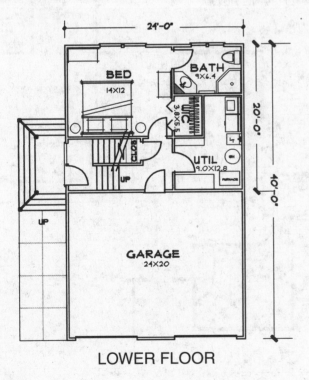

LOWER FLOOR

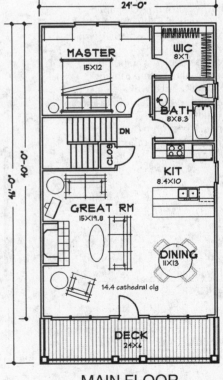

MAIN FLOOR

ORDER BLUEPRINTS ANYTIME!
CALL TOLL-FREE 1-800-820-1296

Plan COA-3-O
Plan copyright held by home designer/architect

**PRICES AND DETAILS
ON PAGES 12-15**   109

Quality Details Inside and Out

- A sparkling stucco finish, an eye-catching roofline and elegant window treatments hint at the quality features found inside this exquisite home.
- The airy entry opens to a large, central living room, which is embellished with a high ceiling and a dramatic fireplace.
- The living room flows into a nice-sized dining area. A covered side porch expands the entertaining area.
- A functional eating bar and pantry are featured in the adjoining U-shaped kitchen. The nearby hallway to the garage neatly stores a washer, a dryer and a laundry sink.
- Secluded to the back of the home is a private master suite with a romantic sitting area and a large walk-in closet. The master bath offers dual sinks and an exciting oval tub.
- Two secondary bedrooms and another bath are located on the other side of the living room and entry.

VIEW INTO LIVING ROOM

Plan E-1435

Bedrooms: 3	Baths: 2
Living Area:	
Main floor	1,442 sq. ft.
Total Living Area:	**1,442 sq. ft.**
Garage and storage	516 sq. ft.
Exterior Wall Framing:	2x4

Foundation Options:

Crawlspace

Slab

(All plans can be built with your choice of foundation and framing. A generic conversion diagram is available. See order form.)

BLUEPRINT PRICE CODE: **A**

MAIN FLOOR

   ORDER BLUEPRINTS ANYTIME! CALL TOLL-FREE 1-800-820-1296

Plan E-1435
Plan copyright held by home designer/architect

PRICES AND DETAILS ON PAGES 12-15

Lasting Appeal

- Strong lines and a partial stone veneer give this home a solid, lasting feel.
- Stroll from the covered front porch into the spacious living room, which counts a vaulted ceiling, a striking corner fireplace and tall transomed windows among its features.
- A formal dining area and bayed breakfast nook adjoin the kitchen, whose open design will be appreciated by the family chef. A pass-through is aimed toward the dining room and the living room for ease in entertaining.
- Accessed via sliding glass doors in the dining room, a rear deck provides the perfect space for grilling the day's catch, hosting a Sunday brunch or simply soaking up rays.
- Beyond the kitchen lies the master suite, which includes a walk-in closet, a cozy window seat and a private bath.
- Upstairs you'll find two more bedrooms and a full bath. A loft overlooking the living room might become a quiet reading corner.

Plan B-88050	
Bedrooms: 3	**Baths: 2½**
Living Area:	
Upper floor	476 sq. ft.
Main floor	972 sq. ft.
Total Living Area:	**1,448 sq. ft.**
Standard basement	972 sq. ft.
Garage	406 sq. ft.
Exterior Wall Framing:	2x4

Foundation Options:

Standard basement
(All plans can be built with your choice of foundation and framing. A generic conversion diagram is available. See order form.)

BLUEPRINT PRICE CODE: A

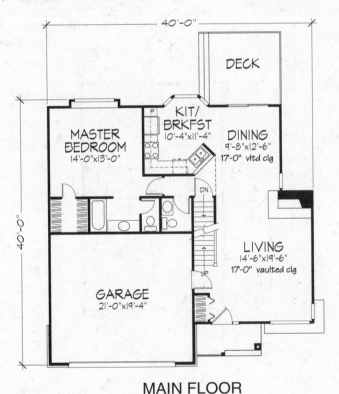

MAIN FLOOR

UPPER FLOOR

ORDER BLUEPRINTS ANYTIME!
CALL TOLL-FREE 1-800-820-1296

Plan B-88050
Plan copyright held by home designer/architect

PRICES AND DETAILS
ON PAGES 12-15 111

Perfect Chalet

- With expansive deck space and windows throughout, this chalet-style retreat is perfect for nature lovers.
- Three walls of windows create a panoramic view, drawing the living room, the dining room and the kitchen into one flowing space. A vaulted ceiling soars over all.
- Serve forth elaborate meals from the U-shaped kitchen or prepare hot drinks to enjoy around the rustic stove nearby.

An eating bar swiftly accommodates quick lunches and snacks.
- At the rear of the home, the master bedroom enjoys a private exit to the deck and shares a full bath with the second main-floor bedroom.
- Downstairs, the third bedroom opens to a family room, where sliding glass doors open to a small side deck.
- A laundry room and a full bath round out the lower floor, which adjoins the two-car garage, making winter visits even cozier.

Plan SUN-2695	
Bedrooms: 3	**Baths:** 2
Living Area:	
Main floor	1,000 sq. ft.
Lower floor	450 sq. ft.
Total Living Area:	**1,450 sq. ft.**
Garage	456 sq. ft.
Exterior Wall Framing:	2x6

Foundation Options:
Crawlspace
Slab
(All plans can be built with your choice of foundation and framing. A generic conversion diagram is available. See order form.)

BLUEPRINT PRICE CODE:	A

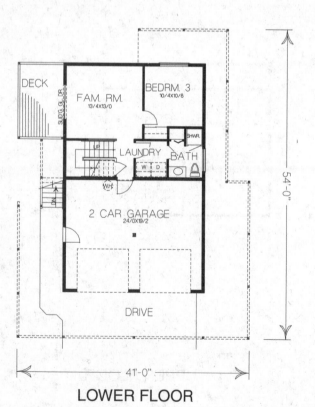

LOWER FLOOR

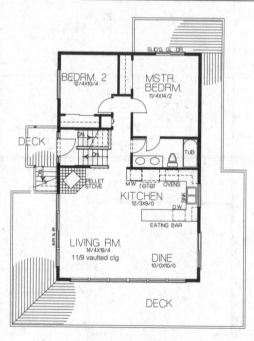

MAIN FLOOR

Plan SUN-2695

Plan copyright held by home designer/architect

**PRICES AND DETAILS
ON PAGES 12-15**

Stupendous Split-Foyer

- A glass door with bright sidelights and an arched transom makes this cozy split-foyer home a welcome sight.
- Inside, stairs lead up from the entry to the vaulted living areas.
- A warm fireplace highlights the enormous family room, which extends to a cheery sun room. The sun room shares the family room's vaulted ceiling and includes a bright wall of windows and access to a rear deck.
- The efficient galley-style kitchen unfolds to the adjacent breakfast nook.
- A lovely window arrangement brightens the elegant dining room.
- Across the home, the luxurious master bedroom boasts a unique tray ceiling, a cozy private deck and a huge walk-in closet. The deluxe master bath features a garden tub, a separate shower and a dual-sink vanity.
- The daylight basement offers plenty of space for future expansion.

Plan APS-1414

Bedrooms: 3+	Baths: 2–3
Living Area:	
Main floor	1,391 sq. ft.
Daylight basement (finished)	68 sq. ft.
Total Living Area:	**1,459 sq. ft.**
Daylight basement (unfinished)	520 sq. ft.
Tuck-under garage	595 sq. ft.
Exterior Wall Framing:	2x4

Foundation Options:

Daylight basement

(All plans can be built with your choice of foundation and framing. A generic conversion diagram is available. See order form.)

BLUEPRINT PRICE CODE: A

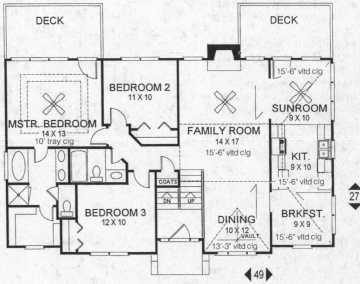

MAIN FLOOR

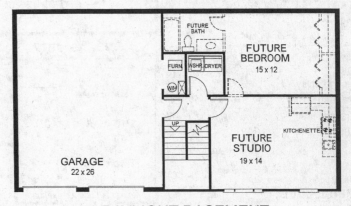

DAYLIGHT BASEMENT

ORDER BLUEPRINTS ANYTIME!
CALL TOLL-FREE 1-800-820-1296

Plan APS-1414
Plan copyright held by home designer/architect

PRICES AND DETAILS
ON PAGES 12-15
113

Victorian Form

- This beautiful home flaunts true-to-form Victorian styling in a modest one-story.
- A delightful, covered front porch and a stunning, sidelighted entry give way to the welcoming foyer.
- The foyer flows into the Great Room, which is warmed by a corner fireplace and topped by a stepped ceiling.
- Sliding French doors open to the backyard from both the Great Room and the adjoining formal dining room.
- On the other side of the open kitchen, a turreted breakfast room overlooks the front porch with cheery windows under an incredible high ceiling!
- The restful master suite is graced by a charming window seat and crowned by a stepped ceiling. A dressing area leads to the master bath, which offers a separate tub and shower.
- To the right of the foyer, two more bedrooms share a hall bath. One bedroom features an impressive vaulted ceiling.

Plan AX-94319

Bedrooms: 3	Baths: 2
Living Area:	
Main floor	1,466 sq. ft.
Total Living Area:	**1,466 sq. ft.**
Standard basement	1,498 sq. ft.
Garage, storage and utility	483 sq. ft.
Exterior Wall Framing:	2x4

Foundation Options:
Standard basement
Crawlspace
Slab
(All plans can be built with your choice of foundation and framing. A generic conversion diagram is available. See order form.)

BLUEPRINT PRICE CODE: **A**

VIEW INTO BREAKFAST ROOM

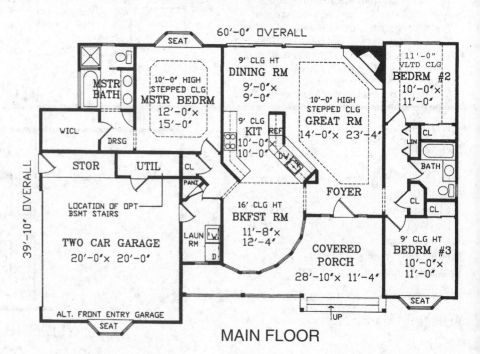

MAIN FLOOR

Plan AX-94319
Plan copyright held by home designer/architect

PRICES AND DETAILS
ON PAGES 12-15

Seasonal Chalet

- This handsome chalet-style vacation home is so comfortable you may find yourself using it all year long.
- An entry hallway leads back to the main-floor living spaces. To the right is a generous living room that flows into a dining area. A fireplace separates the two rooms, warming them both and providing a sense of definition.
- The walk-through kitchen opens directly into the dining area.
- Sliding doors in the living room access a large side deck. You'll love using this area as additional outdoor living space in warm weather.
- The main-floor bedroom, with dual closets and easy access to a full bath, would make a nice master bedroom.
- Upstairs, two secondary bedrooms share a full bath. Each bedroom boasts a private deck.

Plans H-881-1 & -1A

Bedrooms: 3	Baths: 2
Living Area:	
Upper floor	462 sq. ft.
Main floor	1,008 sq. ft.
Total Living Area:	**1,470 sq. ft.**
Daylight basement	560 sq. ft.
Tuck-under garage	448 sq. ft.
Exterior Wall Framing:	2x4
Foundation Options:	**Plan #**
Daylight basement	H-881-1
Crawlspace	H-881-1A

(All plans can be built with your choice of foundation and framing. A generic conversion diagram is available. See order form.)

BLUEPRINT PRICE CODE:	**A**

UPPER FLOOR

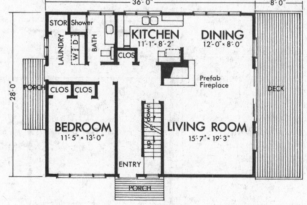

MAIN FLOOR

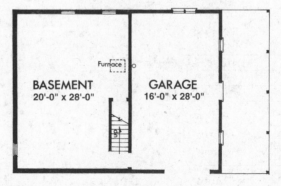

DAYLIGHT BASEMENT

Plans H-881-1 & -1A

Plan copyright held by home designer/architect

PRICES AND DETAILS
ON PAGES 12-15

A Novel Idea

- Create the tradition of reading a bedtime story aloud by the fire before the kids go upstairs to bed. Then select a grown-up book from the built-in living room bookshelves and enjoy the peace and quiet while buried deep in a bedtime story of your own. What a novel idea!

- Hectic mornings getting ready for work and school are a little less stressful when tackled in this free-flowing kitchen and dining area. Set the bag lunches on the serving bar, and then get breakfast to the table in a matter of a few steps.

- Less-harried mornings are a sunny delight. Take it slow and enjoy an unrushed meal in the window-lined dining room.

- The master bedroom offers homeowners a comfortable space all their own. The attached split bath means secluded bathing and getting-ready time.

- There's room for a growing family with two upstairs bedrooms and a full bath. Both bedrooms have walk-in closets, and there's a shared indoor balcony.

Plan L-1473-SA

Bedrooms: 3	Baths: 2
Living Area:	
Upper floor	528 sq. ft.
Main floor	945 sq. ft.
Total Living Area:	**1,473 sq. ft.**
Garage	494 sq. ft.
Exterior Wall Framing:	2x4

Foundation Options:

Slab

(All plans can be built with your choice of foundation and framing. A generic conversion diagram is available. See order form.)

BLUEPRINT PRICE CODE:	**A**

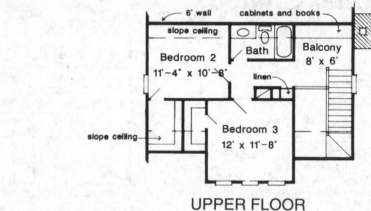

UPPER FLOOR

MAIN FLOOR

Plan L-1473-SA

Plan copyright held by home designer/architect

PRICES AND DETAILS
ON PAGES 12-15

FRONT VIEW

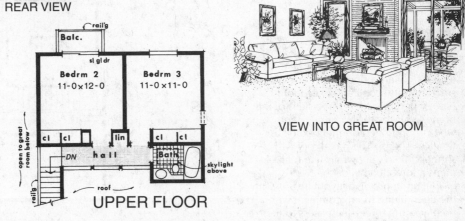

REAR VIEW

More for Less

- Big in function but small in square footage, this passive-solar plan can be built as a single-family home or as part of a multiple-unit complex.
- The floor plan flows visually from its open foyer to its high-ceilinged Great Room, where a high-efficiency fireplace is flanked by glass. Sliding glass doors open to a brilliant south-facing sun room that overlooks a backyard terrace.
- The eat-in kitchen has a pass-through to a bright dining area that opens to a nice side terrace.
- The master bedroom boasts a pair of tall windows, a deluxe private bath and three roomy closets.
- A handy laundry closet and a half-bath are located at the center of the floor plan, near the garage.
- Upstairs, a skylighted bath serves two more bedrooms, one with a private, rear-facing balcony.

VIEW INTO GREAT ROOM

Plan K-507-S

Bedrooms: 3	Baths: 2½
Living Area:	
Upper floor	397 sq. ft.
Main floor	915 sq. ft.
Sun room	162 sq. ft.
Total Living Area:	**1,474 sq. ft.**
Standard basement	915 sq. ft.
Garage	400 sq. ft.
Exterior Wall Framing:	2x4 or 2x6

Foundation Options:

Standard basement

Slab

(All plans can be built with your choice of foundation and framing. A generic conversion diagram is available. See order form.)

BLUEPRINT PRICE CODE: **A**

UPPER FLOOR

MAIN FLOOR

ORDER BLUEPRINTS ANYTIME!
CALL TOLL-FREE 1-800-820-1296

Plan K-507-S

Plan copyright held by home designer/architect

PRICES AND DETAILS
ON PAGES 12-15

117

Smart and Smarter

- This country home's smart, appealing exterior covers a floor plan that is even smarter in its scope and execution.
- A deep porch borders three sides of the home, while a sturdy chimney and well-proportioned dormers exude a timeless charm. The metal roof will shrug off heavy snowfalls and make ice dams a forgotten headache.
- Inside, an impressive layout begins with the open living room, complete with a fireplace and three-step access to the kitchen. Here, you'll find an island cooktop, bright windows and an adjoining dining room.
- The master suite occupies the rear half of the main floor. Its impressive private bath boasts a tub and a separate shower, plus a dual-sink vanity. Even the laundry facilities are included! As a final touch, private porch access is provided from the suite.
- On the upper floor, two bedrooms and a second bath flank a beautiful overlook to the living room, below.

Plan RLA-309

Bedrooms: 3	Baths: 2
Living Area:	
Upper floor	568 sq. ft.
Main floor	911 sq. ft.
Total Living Area:	**1,479 sq. ft.**
Standard basement	900 sq. ft.
Exterior Wall Framing:	2x4
Foundation Options:	

Standard basement

(All plans can be built with your choice of foundation and framing. A generic conversion diagram is available. See order form.)

BLUEPRINT PRICE CODE:	**A**

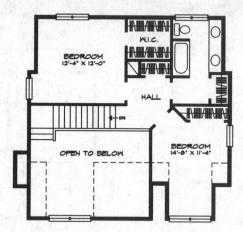

UPPER FLOOR

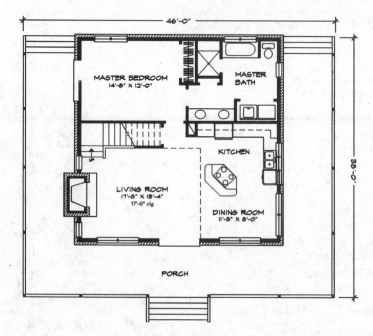

MAIN FLOOR

ORDER BLUEPRINTS ANYTIME! CALL TOLL-FREE 1-800-820-1296

Plan RLA-309

Plan copyright held by home designer/architect

PRICES AND DETAILS ON PAGES 12-15

Pastoral Perfection

- An expansive front porch, quaint shutters and warm wood siding lend this home its look of pastoral perfection.
- With a striking stepped ceiling, a cozy fireplace and a built-in entertainment area, the Great Room is a natural gathering spot. Three sets of sliding French doors offer a view to the gentle beauty of the outdoors.
- The nearby dining room shares a snack counter with the kitchen. Here, a windowed sink brightens daily chores.
- Cleverly separated from the other bedrooms for privacy, the master suite is topped by a dramatic stepped ceiling. The bath offers a large walk-in closet and ample preparation space.
- Across the home, two secondary bedrooms look out to the backyard and share another full bath.
- The laundry room is quietly and conveniently tucked between these bedrooms and the foyer.

Plan AX-5380

Bedrooms: 3	Baths: 2
Living Area:	
Main floor	1,480 sq. ft.
Total Living Area:	**1,480 sq. ft.**
Standard basement	1,493 sq. ft.
Garage and storage	610 sq. ft.
Exterior Wall Framing:	2x4

Foundation Options:

Standard basement
Crawlspace
Slab
(All plans can be built with your choice of foundation and framing. A generic conversion diagram is available. See order form.)

BLUEPRINT PRICE CODE: A

VIEW INTO GREAT ROOM

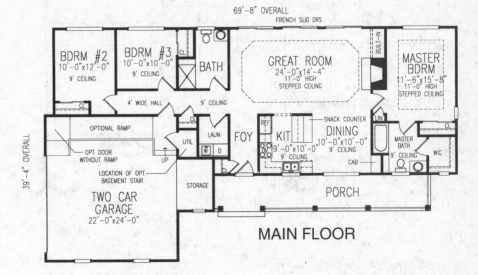

MAIN FLOOR

ORDER BLUEPRINTS ANYTIME!
CALL TOLL-FREE 1-800-820-1296

Plan AX-5380
Plan copyright held by home designer/architect

PRICES AND DETAILS
ON PAGES 12-15

119

Eye-Catching Chalet

- Steep rooflines, dramatic windows and wide cornices give this chalet a distinctive alpine appearance.
- The large living and dining area offers a striking vaulted ceiling and a breathtaking view of the outdoors through a soaring wall of windows. Sliding glass doors access an inviting wood deck.

- The efficient U-shaped kitchen shares an eating bar with the dining area.
- Two main-floor bedrooms share a hall bath, and laundry facilities are nearby.
- The upper floor hosts a master bedroom with a vaulted ceiling, plenty of storage space and easy access to a full bath with a shower.
- The pièce de résistance is a balcony with a vaulted ceiling, offering sweeping outdoor views as well as an overlook into the living/dining area below. Additional storage areas flank the balcony.

Plans H-886-3 & -3A

Bedrooms: 3	**Baths:** 2

Living Area:

Upper floor	486 sq. ft.
Main floor	994 sq. ft.
Total Living Area:	**1,480 sq. ft.**
Daylight basement	715 sq. ft.
Tuck-under garage	279 sq. ft.
Exterior Wall Framing:	2x6
Foundation Options:	**Plan #**
Daylight basement	H-886-3
Crawlspace	H-886-3A

(All plans can be built with your choice of foundation and framing. A generic conversion diagram is available. See order form.)

BLUEPRINT PRICE CODE:	**A**

DAYLIGHT BASEMENT

GENERAL USE
22'-4" x 18'-8"

STOR

GARAGE
12'-6" x 22'-4"

FURNACE RM
9'-10" x 21'-3"

furnace

MAIN FLOOR

23' - 8"

4' - 0"

BEDROOM
8'-10" x 11'-0"

BEDROOM
10'-0" x 13'-10"

CLOSET
5'-0"

W D

LIN

CLOSET
4'-0"

CLOSET
4'-0"

down

up

BATH

44' - 0"

DW Ref

KITCHEN
7'-1" x 8'-3"

R/O

DINING   LIVING
22'-7" x 22'-10"
20'-0" vaulted clg

10' - 0"

UPPER FLOOR

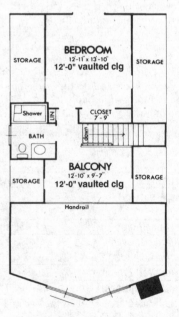

STORAGE

BEDROOM
12'-11" x 13'-10"
12'-0" vaulted clg

STORAGE

Shower

LIN

CLOSET
7'-9"

BATH

down

STORAGE

BALCONY
12'-10" x 9'-7"
12'-0" vaulted clg

STORAGE

Handrail

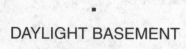

Plans H-886-3 & -3A

Plan copyright held by home designer/architect

PRICES AND DETAILS ON PAGES 12-15

Stellar Living

- This lovely one-story home's friendly front porch, bright windows and flowing floor plan will dazzle you with stellar comfort.
- You'll treasure quiet moments in the formal dining room, which offers a wonderful space for fine meals.
- Double doors not only close off the kitchen's noises, they also shield your culinary secrets from prying eyes!
- Your morning danish will taste better when accompanied by the warm sun and pleasant views afforded by the bayed breakfast nook.
- The Great Room serves as a fabulous gathering space when entertaining large crowds. The cheery fireplace, with its handsome hearth, brings warmth during the cold-weather months. In the summer, guests can pick up an icy drink from the kitchen's breakfast bar and relax on the backyard patio.
- More luxuries await you in the posh master bedroom's private bath, where an inviting corner tub is nestled between two windows.
- Children and guests have plenty of personal space in the two bedrooms on the opposite end of the home.

Plan KD-1494

Bedrooms: 3	Baths: 2
Living Area:	
Main floor	1,494 sq. ft.
Total Living Area:	**1,494 sq. ft.**
Garage and storage	475 sq. ft.
Exterior Wall Framing:	2x4

Foundation Options:

Slab

(All plans can be built with your choice of foundation and framing. A generic conversion diagram is available. See order form.)

BLUEPRINT PRICE CODE: A

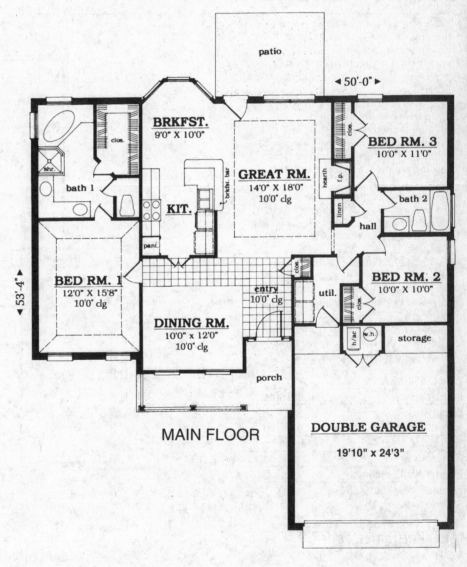

MAIN FLOOR

ORDER BLUEPRINTS ANYTIME!
CALL TOLL-FREE 1-800-820-1296

Plan KD-1494

Plan copyright held by home designer/architect

PRICES AND DETAILS
ON PAGES 12-15

121

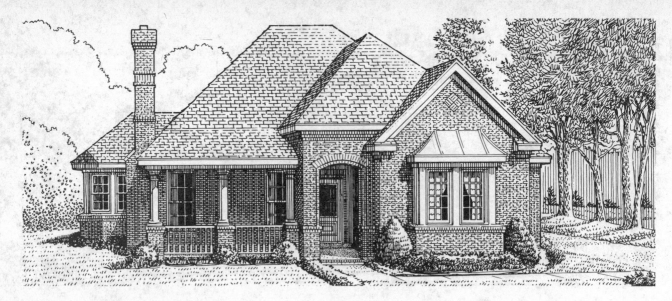

Cottage Charm

- Bigger on the inside than it appears on the outside, this lovely cottage will charm you and your friends at first glance with its steeply-pitched roofline, gently arched entry and columned front porch.
- The foyer gives way to a generously sized living room anchored by an inviting fireplace.
- Wrapped in windows, the dining area adjoins a U-shaped kitchen with two serving counters to accommodate a gathering of any size.
- Retire to the luxurious master suite and draw a soothing bath in the spa tub. A French door invites you to step out to a peaceful, private courtyard for a peek at the stars.
- Two additional bright bedrooms, one with a built-in desk, easily accommodate children or guests. The foremost bedroom is topped by a high ceiling.
- A utility room that leads from the kitchen to the two-car garage makes bringing in the groceries a snap.

Plan L-498-CSA

Bedrooms: 3	Baths: 2
Living Area:	
Main floor	1,496 sq. ft.
Total Living Area:	**1,496 sq. ft.**
Garage	504 sq. ft.
Exterior Wall Framing:	2x4

Foundation Options:

Slab

(All plans can be built with your choice of foundation and framing. A generic conversion diagram is available. See order form.)

BLUEPRINT PRICE CODE: **A**

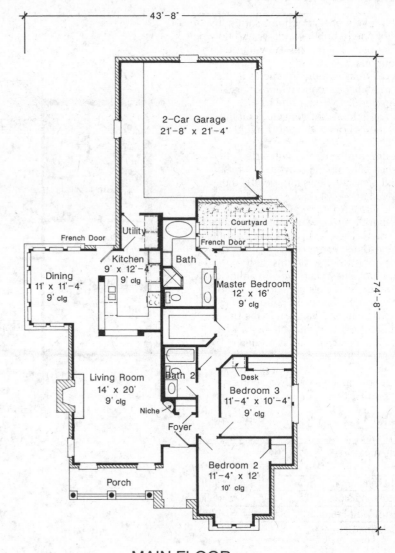

MAIN FLOOR

Plan L-498-CSA

Plan copyright held by home designer/architect

PRICES AND DETAILS
ON PAGES 12-15

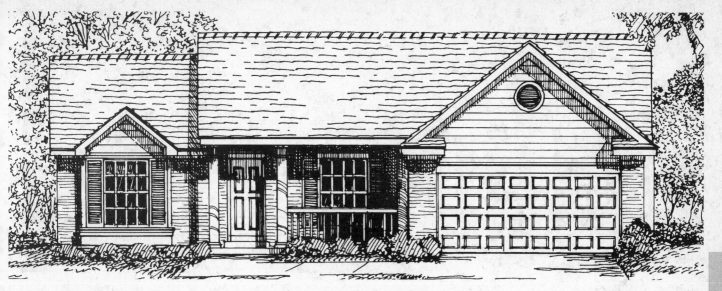

Wish You Were Here?

- This home's inviting front porch and welcoming interior is enough to make anyone wish for the sweet life within.
- With an air of mystery, the foyer allows guests a glimpse of the elegant dining room over a half-wall to the right.
- Ahead, the open living room leaves no room for guessing; its prominent fireplace practically begs you to pull up a chair and relax in the warmth.
- A serving bar brings a casual tone to your gatherings, and joins the living room to the kitchen. Here, you'll find vast counter space and an adjoining breakfast nook that should slow you down on those busy weekday mornings!
- Corner windows spruce up the master bedroom, which provides a pleasant oasis when the cares of your world press in. Past two roomy closets, a private bath awaits to spoil you, complete with a whirlpool tub, a separate shower and a dual-sink vanity.

Plan BRF-1502

Bedrooms: 3	Baths: 2
Living Area:	
Main floor	1,502 sq. ft.
Total Living Area:	**1,502 sq. ft.**
Daylight basement	1,502 sq. ft.
Garage	413 sq. ft.
Exterior Wall Framing:	2x4

Foundation Options:

Daylight basement

(All plans can be built with your choice of foundation and framing. A generic conversion diagram is available. See order form.)

BLUEPRINT PRICE CODE:	**B**

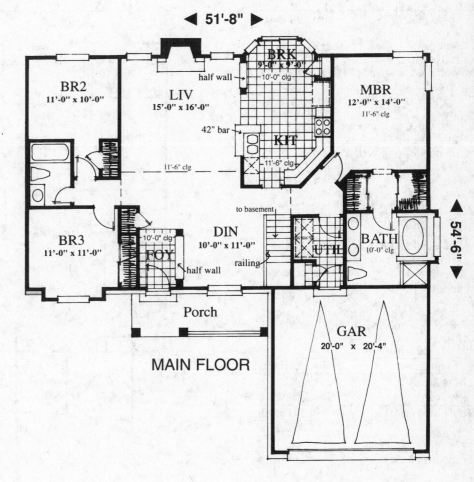

◄ 51'-8" ►

BR2 11'-0" x 10'-0"

LIV 15'-0" x 16'-0"

BRK 9'-0" x 9'-0"
10'-0" clg

half wall

MBR 12'-0" x 14'-0"
11'-6" clg

42" bar

KIT
11'-6" clg

11'-6" clg

BR3 11'-0" x 11'-0"

10'-0" clg

FOY

half wall

to basement

DIN 10'-0" x 11'-0"

UTIL

railing

BATH 10'-0" clg

54'-6"

Porch

GAR 20'-0" x 20'-4"

MAIN FLOOR

ORDER BLUEPRINTS ANYTIME!
CALL TOLL-FREE 1-800-820-1296

Plan BRF-1502
Plan copyright held by home designer/architect

PRICES AND DETAILS
ON PAGES 12-15

123

Grand Views on a Narrow Lot

- The popular Palladian window of this economical narrow-lot home smartly echoes the curved brick arch of the entryway.
- Inside, a grand view of the spacious central living room and the outdoors beyond greets you at the tiled foyer. To the left, an angled wall ends at an innovative media center and an attractive fireplace.
- The angled half-wall to the right serves as a convenient pass-through from the kitchen, which also includes a pantry and a sunny breakfast room.
- Two bedrooms and a full bath make up a small sleeping cluster at the front of the home.
- Secluded to the rear, the master suite effortlessly beckons for your retreat. The soothing garden tub, the cool breeze through the open French doors, and the gentle vault above your favorite king-sized bed are all the persuasion you'll need to spend your leisure time here!

Plan L-1507-TA

Bedrooms: 3	Baths: 2
Living Area:	
Main floor	1,507 sq. ft.
Total Living Area:	**1,507 sq. ft.**
Garage	452 sq. ft.
Exterior Wall Framing:	2x4

Foundation Options:

Slab

(All plans can be built with your choice of foundation and framing. A generic conversion diagram is available. See order form.)

BLUEPRINT PRICE CODE:	B

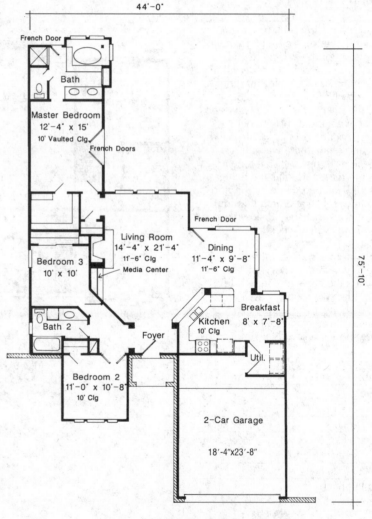

MAIN FLOOR

Plan L-1507-TA

Plan copyright held by home designer/architect

PRICES AND DETAILS ON PAGES 12-15

Cream of the Crop

- This country-style home's Great Room is the cream of the crop. Its prominent location at the center of the plan, plus its array of amenities—like a soaring ceiling and a fireplace flanked by French doors—result in ripe satisfaction.
- The picturesque front porch provides a sidelighted entry to the foyer, as well as a service entry to the mudroom.
- Just as the foyer spills into the Great Room, the Great Room flows out to a backyard terrace that will be a relaxing place for sunny, lazy brunches.
- Everything is within reach of the family chef in the well-planned, tidy kitchen, which includes a snack bar that serves the eye-catching dining room.
- The master suite—crowned by a tray ceiling—harbors an enormous walk-in closet. Its private bath has a soothing whirlpool tub and a separate shower.
- Across the home, two nice-sized bedrooms share a full hall bath.

VIEW INTO GREAT ROOM

REAR VIEW

Plan AHP-2010

Bedrooms: 3	Baths: 2
Living Area:	
Main floor	1,528 sq. ft.
Total Living Area:	**1,528 sq. ft.**
Standard basement	1,584 sq. ft.
Garage	466 sq. ft.
Exterior Wall Framing:	2x4 or 2x6

Foundation Options:

Standard basement

Crawlspace

Slab

(All plans can be built with your choice of foundation and framing. A generic conversion diagram is available. See order form.)

BLUEPRINT PRICE CODE: B

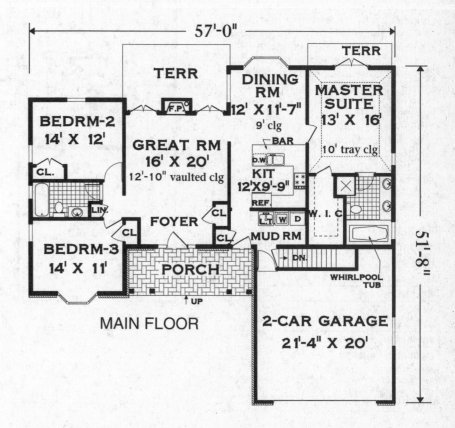

MAIN FLOOR

ORDER BLUEPRINTS ANYTIME!
CALL TOLL-FREE 1-800-820-1296

Plan AHP-2010
Plan copyright held by home designer/architect

PRICES AND DETAILS
ON PAGES 12-15

125

Family Magnet

- Pleasant, spacious living areas and plenty of bedrooms make this economical one-story home a magnet for growing families. The attractive exterior presents a beautiful image to guests and passersby.
- Hang a basketball hoop above the garage door and spend weekends honing your daughter's jump shot and crossover dribble.
- Step through the columned entry into the foyer. From there, an immediate left lands you in the formal dining room, highlighted by two gorgeous plant shelves. Straight ahead is the oversized living room, complete with a grand fireplace and views to the back deck.
- Perfectly poised to serve both eating areas, the kitchen is designed for easy efficiency. The adjacent breakfast nook walks out to the deck.
- The dynamic master suite offers ample closet space and a private bath with a soothing garden tub.
- On the opposite side of the home are the two secondary bedrooms, each with a big, cheery window and near a full-size bath.

Plan B-95007

Bedrooms: 3	Baths: 2
Living Area:	
Main floor	1,527 sq. ft.
Total Living Area:	**1,527 sq. ft.**
Standard basement	1,527 sq. ft.
Garage	448 sq. ft.
Exterior Wall Framing:	2x6

Foundation Options:

Standard basement
(All plans can be built with your choice of foundation and framing. A generic conversion diagram is available. See order form.)

BLUEPRINT PRICE CODE: B

MAIN FLOOR

VIEW INTO LIVING ROOM

Plan B-95007

Plan copyright held by home designer/architect

PRICES AND DETAILS ON PAGES 12-15

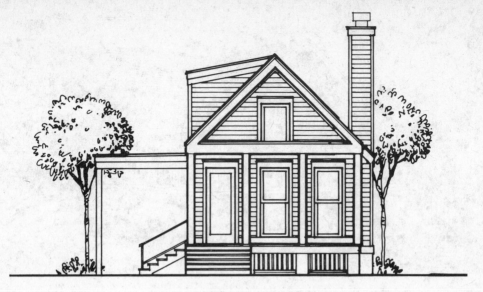

Fantastic Design

- With the help of a fantastic design, this home makes amazing use of space in an economical footprint.
- The front porch opens into the living room, which boasts a vaulted ceiling and a handsome fireplace. Two tall windows provide a view of the porch.
- The cozy, vaulted kitchen serves the living room via a pass-through, and the bright dining room over a snack bar.
- Past a spiral staircase, a bedroom with a walk-in closet is situated next to laundry facilities. A door leading out to the carport follows, as does a full bath.
- At the back of the home, the secluded master suite boasts access to a porch, while repeating the living area's vaulted ceiling. A dual-sink vanity and a walk-in closet form a neat dressing area outside the bath.
- Up the space-saving spiral staircase that's sure to delight any child and many adults, the bright loft can be used as another bedroom or a quiet study.

Plan LRK-91158

Bedrooms: 2+	Baths: 2
Living Area:	
Upper floor	256 sq. ft.
Main floor	1,278 sq. ft.
Total Living Area:	**1,534 sq. ft.**
Carport	261 sq. ft.
Exterior Wall Framing:	2x4

Foundation Options:

Crawlspace

(All plans can be built with your choice of foundation and framing. A generic conversion diagram is available. See order form.)

BLUEPRINT PRICE CODE:	**B**

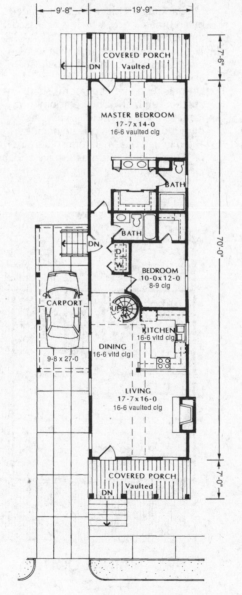

MAIN FLOOR

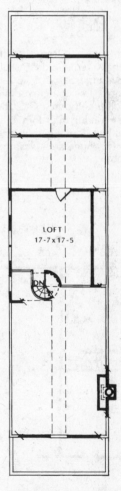

UPPER FLOOR

Plan LRK-91158

Plan copyright held by home designer/architect

PRICES AND DETAILS ON PAGES 12-15

Romantic Retreat

- The romance and appeal of the Alpine chalet have remained constant over time. With more than 1,500 sq. ft. of living area, this chalet would make a great full-time home or vacation retreat.
- The L-shaped living room, dining room and kitchen flow together for casual living. This huge area is warmed by a freestanding fireplace and surrounded by an ornate deck, which is accessed through sliding glass doors.
- The main-level bedroom, with its twin closets and adjacent bath, could serve as a nice master suite.
- Upstairs, two large bedrooms share another full bath. One bedroom features a walk-in closet, while the other boasts its own private deck.
- The daylight basement offers laundry facilities, plenty of storage space and an extra-long garage.

Plan H-858-2	
Bedrooms: 3	**Baths:** 2
Living Area:	
Upper floor	576 sq. ft.
Main floor	960 sq. ft.
Total Living Area:	**1,536 sq. ft.**
Daylight basement	530 sq. ft.
Tuck-under garage	430 sq. ft.
Exterior Wall Framing:	2x6
Foundation Options:	
Daylight basement	

(All plans can be built with your choice of foundation and framing. A generic conversion diagram is available. See order form.)

BLUEPRINT PRICE CODE:	B

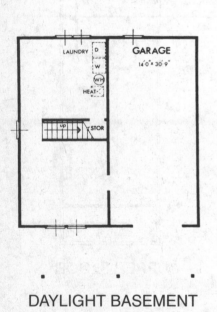

DAYLIGHT BASEMENT

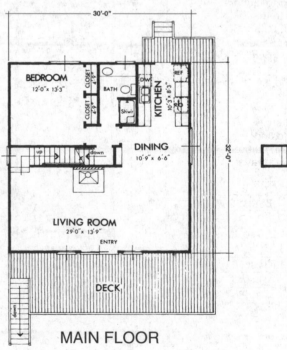

MAIN FLOOR

UPPER FLOOR

Plan H-858-2

Plan copyright held by home designer/architect

PRICES AND DETAILS
ON PAGES 12-15

Traditional Heritage

- A distinctive roofline and a covered wraparound porch reflect this charming home's traditional heritage.
- The roomy entry flows directly into the spacious, open living room. Enhanced by a cathedral ceiling, the living room is warmed by a fireplace and offers a French door to a backyard patio. A good-sized laundry room is nearby.

- The adjoining dining area shares porch access with the stylish gourmet kitchen, which includes an eating bar and a garden window over the sink.
- The master bedroom suite features a lavish private bath with a garden spa tub, a separate shower, a dual-sink vanity and a big walk-in closet.
- A second full bath, located at the end of the bedroom hall, is convenient to the two remaining bedrooms.
- The double carport includes a separate lockable storage area for your lawn, garden and sporting equipment.

Plan J-86142	
Bedrooms: 3	**Baths:** 2
Living Area:	
Main floor	1,536 sq. ft.
Total Living Area:	**1,536 sq. ft.**
Standard basement	1,536 sq. ft.
Carport and storage	520 sq. ft.
Exterior Wall Framing:	2x4

Foundation Options:

Standard basement
Crawlspace
Slab

(All plans can be built with your choice of foundation and framing. A generic conversion diagram is available. See order form.)

BLUEPRINT PRICE CODE: B

76-0

Storage
18-5 x 5-1

Patio

Carport
20-0 x 20-0

Util.

M.Bath

Master Bedroom
16-0 x 13-0

Living
17-0 x 16-0

Bath

Dining

40-0

Kitchen

Foyer

Bedroom
11-0 x 10-0

Bedroom
11-6 x 10-0

Porch

MAIN FLOOR

ORDER BLUEPRINTS ANYTIME!
CALL TOLL-FREE 1-800-820-1296

Plan J-86142
Plan copyright held by home designer/architect

PRICES AND DETAILS
ON PAGES 12-15

129

Classic Visual Appeal

- A classic brick facade and front-facing gables enhance this home's visual appeal. Inside, a built-in media center brings everyone together for movie night in the living room.
- A high ceiling crowns the spacious living room, where a fireplace adds a cozy touch. The adjacent, open dining room offers access to a rear porch.
- The efficient, L-shaped kitchen features a pantry closet and a handy snack bar that serves the dining area. Laundry facilities are just a few steps away in the adjoining utility room.
- The secluded master suite flaunts a gambrel ceiling, a generous walk-in closet and private access to the rear porch. A dual-sink vanity, a garden tub and a separate shower complete the nicely appointed master bath.
- Two secondary bedrooms round out the sleeping wing. Both offer plenty of closet space and are serviced by a full hall bath.

Plan L-563-FA

Bedrooms: 3	Baths: 2
Living Area:	
Main floor	1,541 sq. ft.
Total Living Area:	**1,541 sq. ft.**
Garage	567 sq. ft.
Exterior Wall Framing:	2x4

Foundation Options:

Slab
(All plans can be built with your choice of foundation and framing. A generic conversion diagram is available. See order form.)

BLUEPRINT PRICE CODE:	B

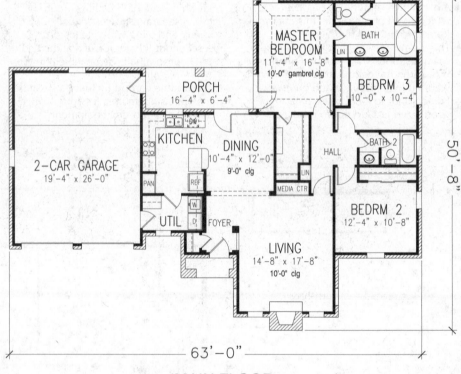

MAIN FLOOR

130   *ORDER BLUEPRINTS ANYTIME!*
CALL TOLL-FREE 1-800-820-1296

Plan L-563-FA
Plan copyright held by home designer/architect

PRICES AND DETAILS
ON PAGES 12-15

On Top of the World

- Sitting atop a sturdy pier foundation, this attractive home serves equally well as a relaxing retreat or for everyday living. With plenty of sleeping space and a large family room, all your friends and relatives will feel welcome here.
- Abundant windows ensure the central family room receives plenty of natural light, and its generous dimensions encourage large gatherings. Around the corner is the handy utility room.
- The U-shaped kitchen is a model of modern efficiency. It features a sleek design with counter space sufficient for even the most zealous chef.
- The breakfast nook adjoining the kitchen is ideal for catching a quick snack. Double doors lead to a rear deck—a great place to launch an adventurous backyard excursion!
- The spacious master suite features a large walk-in closet, three nice-sized windows and access to a shared bath.
- Upstairs, two good-sized bedrooms share an additional full bath.

Plan HDS-99-334

Bedrooms: 4	Baths: 2

Living Area:	
Upper floor	470 sq. ft.
Main floor	1,073 sq. ft.
Total Living Area:	**1,543 sq. ft.**
Exterior Wall Framing:	2x6

Foundation Options:

Pier
(All plans can be built with your choice of foundation and framing. A generic conversion diagram is available. See order form.)

BLUEPRINT PRICE CODE: **B**

MAIN FLOOR

UPPER FLOOR

ORDER BLUEPRINTS ANYTIME!
CALL TOLL-FREE 1-800-820-1296

Plan HDS-99-334
Plan copyright held by home designer/architect

PRICES AND DETAILS
ON PAGES 12-15   131

Universal Appeal

- As they observe its elegant window treatments and timeless brick exterior, passersby and guests will marvel at this appealing home.
- The central Great Room will be a surefire hit with young and old alike. For adult gatherings, there is plenty of room to mingle and converse. And what child wouldn't love to sneak an hors d'oeuvre from the breakfast bar and set up camp in front of the crackling fireplace?
- School lunches may be prepared more efficiently on the kitchen's island. Keep your snacks and sandwich bags in the handy pantry!
- If the outdoors calls to you on spring mornings, skip the bayed dining area and enjoy your tea and toast on the shaded backyard patio.
- Privacy and pampering are foremost in the master bedroom, with patio access a quick step away. In the master bath, an eye-pleasing plant shelf overlooks two walk-in closets and a dual-sink vanity with knee space.

Plan KD-1549

Bedrooms: 3	Baths: 2
Living Area:	
Main floor	1,549 sq. ft.
Total Living Area:	**1,549 sq. ft.**
Garage and storage	472 sq. ft.
Exterior Wall Framing:	2x4

Foundation Options:

Slab

(All plans can be built with your choice of foundation and framing. A generic conversion diagram is available. See order form.)

BLUEPRINT PRICE CODE:	B

MAIN FLOOR

Plan KD-1549

Plan copyright held by home designer/architect

**PRICES AND DETAILS
ON PAGES 12-15**

ELEVATION A

Exciting Exteriors

- Two exciting elevations are available with this striking stucco design. (Both are included with blueprint purchase.)
- With its modest width, this home is perfect for a narrow lot.
- The stately, covered front entry and elegant window treatments conceal a huge formal living and dining area that is topped by a stunning vaulted ceiling.
- A corner fireplace or media center highlights the adjoining family room, which also offers plenty of built-in shelving. Sliding glass doors open to a lovely covered patio with an optional summer kitchen.
- Wide, open spaces enhance the eat-in country kitchen, which overlooks the family room and features a long serving counter and a handy pantry. A tidy laundry closet and access to the two-car garage are nearby.
- Separated from two roomy secondary bedrooms, the master bedroom is a quiet retreat. It offers patio access and an oversized private bath with a huge walk-in closet, a luxurious corner tub and a dual-sink vanity with knee space.

ELEVATION B

SENSIBLE HOMES

Plan HDS-99-140

Bedrooms: 3	Baths: 2
Living Area:	
Main floor	1,550 sq. ft.
Total Living Area:	**1,550 sq. ft.**
Garage and storage	475 sq. ft.
Exterior Wall Framing:	2x4 or
	8-in. concrete block

Foundation Options:

Slab

(All plans can be built with your choice of foundation and framing. A generic conversion diagram is available. See order form.)

BLUEPRINT PRICE CODE: B

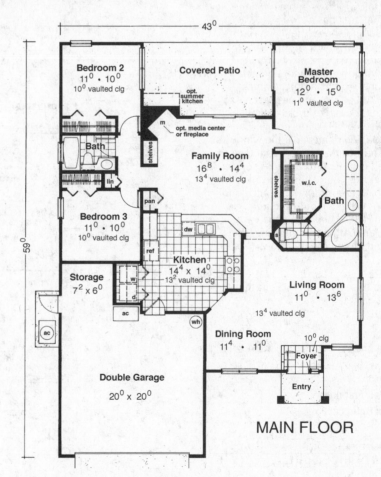

MAIN FLOOR

ORDER BLUEPRINTS ANYTIME!
CALL TOLL-FREE 1-800-820-1296

Plan HDS-99-140
Plan copyright held by home designer/architect

PRICES AND DETAILS
ON PAGES 12-15

133

A Country Classic

- The exterior of this cozy country-style home boasts a charming combination of woodwork and stone.
- A graceful, arched entryway leads into the spacious living room with a vaulted ceiling, tall windows and a fireplace.
- The dining area has a lovely view of a side patio and shares the living room's fireplace and vaulted ceiling.
- The impressive kitchen is brightened by a large window bank with skylights above, and it offers ample counter space, a full pantry and easy access to the dining room. For more casual meals, the kitchen offers ample space for a table and chairs near the windows.
- The main-floor master bedroom features a vaulted ceiling, plus a walk-in closet, a linen closet, a private, dual-sink master bath and sliding-door access to the patio. What a fabulous retreat!
- Two upper-floor bedrooms share another full bath and a view into the living and dining rooms below.

Plan B-87157

Bedrooms: 3	Baths: 2½
Living Area:	
Upper floor	452 sq. ft.
Main floor	1,099 sq. ft.
Total Living Area:	**1,551 sq. ft.**
Standard basement	1,099 sq. ft.
Garage	412 sq. ft.
Exterior Wall Framing:	2x4

Foundation Options:

Standard basement

(All plans can be built with your choice of foundation and framing. A generic conversion diagram is available. See order form.)

BLUEPRINT PRICE CODE: B

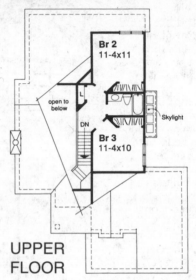

UPPER FLOOR

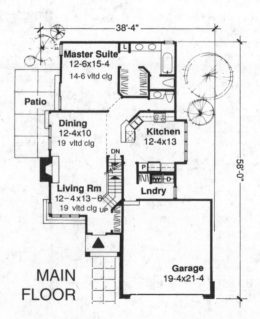

MAIN FLOOR

Plan B-87157

Plan copyright held by home designer/architect

PRICES AND DETAILS ON PAGES 12-15

Intimate Atmosphere

- Decorative wood detailing and an inviting covered front porch give this charming home its Victorian visage. In the front-facing living room, a bay window and a two-way fireplace create an intimate atmosphere.
- Sunlight floods the vast family room, which features an exciting media center wall and a French door that opens to a rear terrace.

- The kitchen provides lots of counter space and an eating bar for four that opens into the family room. Above the sink, a pair of windows drenches the scene with cheery natural light. The nearby laundry facilities let you perform multiple tasks at once.
- Upstairs, the master bedroom flaunts a cozy gas fireplace and two walk-in closets. A bayed area invites you to relax with a good book. The private bath includes a separate whirlpool tub and shower, plus a dual-sink vanity.
- Plans for a detached two-car garage are included with the blueprints.

Plan AHP-9560

Bedrooms: 3	Baths: 2½
Living Area:	
Upper floor	778 sq. ft.
Main floor	780 sq. ft.
Total Living Area:	**1,558 sq. ft.**
Standard basement	780 sq. ft.
Garage (detached)	484 sq. ft.
Exterior Wall Framing:	2x4 or 2x6

Foundation Options:
Standard basement
Crawlspace
Slab
(All plans can be built with your choice of foundation and framing. A generic conversion diagram is available. See order form.)

BLUEPRINT PRICE CODE:	B

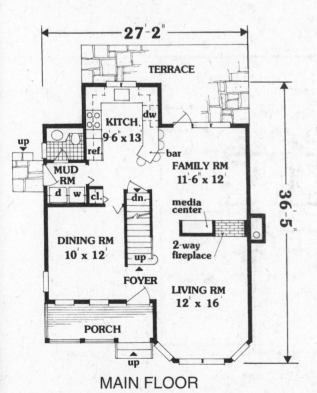

MAIN FLOOR

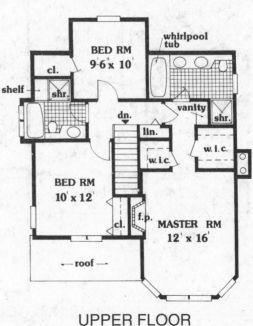

UPPER FLOOR

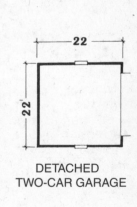

DETACHED
TWO-CAR GARAGE

ORDER BLUEPRINTS ANYTIME!
CALL TOLL-FREE 1-800-820-1296

Plan AHP-9560
Plan copyright held by home designer/architect

PRICES AND DETAILS
ON PAGES 12-15   135

Simple Appeal

- This home's appeal comes from its simple exterior and practical floor plan.
- A charming copper-top bay window adorns the facade, which boasts classic gables and a darling front porch.
- The sidelighted entry leads to the bright foyer that acts as a gallery, connecting all parts of the home. Straight ahead, past decorative columns, is the spacious living room. It features a well-appointed fireplace, a soaring cathedral ceiling and French doors to a rear porch that's perfect for grilling or stargazing.

- The bay window brightens the dining room and the kitchen, which allows for casual dining at the snack bar. A door leads to the rear porch or, if you choose, to a detached garage out back.
- On the opposite side of the home, clever storage fills every corner of the hallway. Two sizable bedrooms share a hall bath that boasts a dual-sink vanity.
- The master suite is crowned by a visually stunning cathedral ceiling. A walk-in closet and a lush private bath with a garden tub are added amenities.
- Laundry facilities are tucked into a closet off the master suite.

Plan HWG-1559-N

Bedrooms: 3	**Baths:** 2

Living Area:

Main floor	1,559 sq. ft.
Total Living Area:	**1,559 sq. ft.**
Exterior Wall Framing:	2x4

Foundation Options:

Crawlspace
(All plans can be built with your choice of foundation and framing. A generic conversion diagram is available. See order form.)

BLUEPRINT PRICE CODE:	B

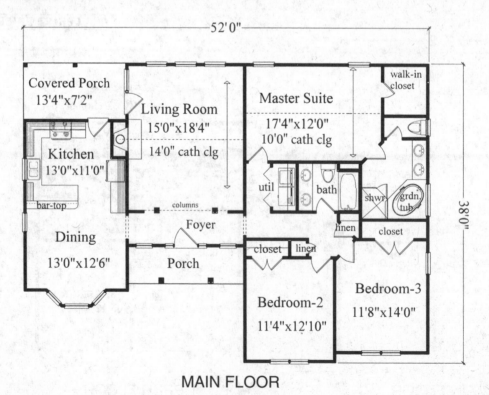

MAIN FLOOR

Plan HWG-1559-N
Plan copyright held by home designer/architect

PRICES AND DETAILS ON PAGES 12-15

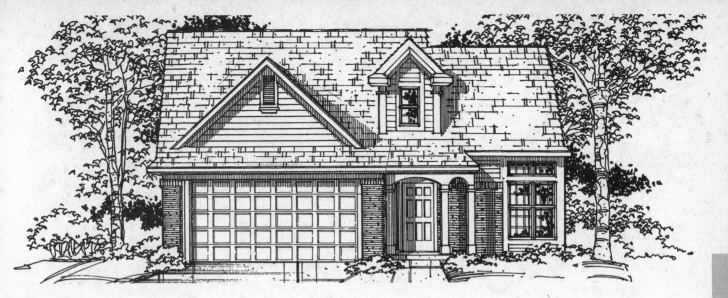

Open Spaces

- Spacious, bright living areas lend openness to this home's economical footprint.
- You'll fall in love with the adorable facade, which features a front porch with arched columns and a transom-topped window arrangement. A handsome dormer tops it all off.
- The living room's corner windows provide lots of natural light, which is maximized by a high ceiling. The adjoining formal dining room features easy access to the kitchen.
- The lovely kitchen enjoys a window above the corner sink, as well as a snack bar. Eat breakfast in the sunny morning room, where sliding glass doors lead to the backyard.
- The laundry room and a handy powder room are tucked into a hallway conveniently near the kitchen.
- The enchanting master suite boasts a huge walk-in closet, a dual-sink vanity, and a private bath with an inviting tub.
- Upstairs, the central hall leads to three good-sized bedrooms, two of which provide walk-in closets. A full bath and a linen closet service these bedrooms.

Plan LS-98810-GW

Bedrooms: 4	Baths: 2½
Living Area:	
Upper floor	593 sq. ft.
Main floor	996 sq. ft.
Total Living Area:	**1,589 sq. ft.**
Garage and storage	400 sq. ft.
Exterior Wall Framing:	2x4

Foundation Options:

Slab
(All plans can be built with your choice of foundation and framing. A generic conversion diagram is available. See order form.)

BLUEPRINT PRICE CODE:	**B**

SENSIBLE HOMES

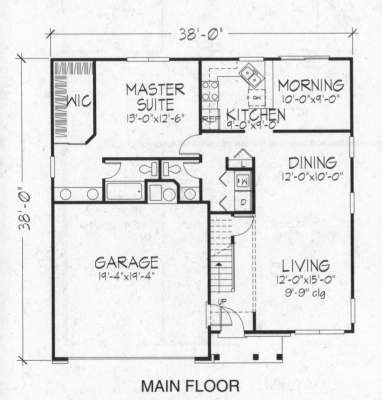

MAIN FLOOR

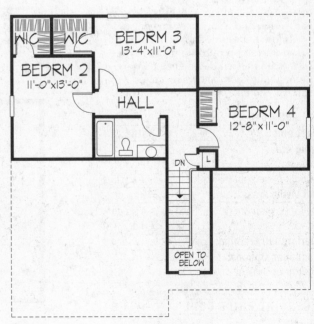

UPPER FLOOR

ORDER BLUEPRINTS ANYTIME!
CALL TOLL-FREE 1-800-820-1296

Plan LS-98810-GW
Plan copyright held by home designer/architect

PRICES AND DETAILS
ON PAGES 12-15

137

Smart Styling

- Smart curbside styling envelops this home's open interior plan with plenty of room to grow.
- The split-entry foyer leads up to the spacious living and dining area, which features a vaulted ceiling and a two-way fireplace.
- Around the corner, "acres" of counter and cupboard space fill the U-shaped kitchen, which boasts a pantry closet. A cozy breakfast nook is the perfect spot to mull over the morning paper.
- The master suite enjoys unmatched splendor. Secluded from the rest of the home, it features a vaulted ceiling, a huge walk-in closet and a sumptuous skylighted bath featuring his-and-hers vanities, a luxurious corner garden tub and a separate shower.
- Two more bedrooms and a full bath are found at the opposite end of the home.
- A large unfinished basement area next to the utility room allows space for storage, recreation or future expansion.

Plan APS-1510

Bedrooms: 3+	Baths: 2
Living Area:	
Main floor	1,507 sq. ft.
Daylight basement (finished)	72 sq. ft.
Total Living Area:	**1,579 sq. ft.**
Daylight basement (unfinished)	574 sq. ft.
Garage	754 sq. ft.
Exterior Wall Framing:	2x4

Foundation Options:

Daylight basement

(All plans can be built with your choice of foundation and framing. A generic conversion diagram is available. See order form.)

BLUEPRINT PRICE CODE:	**B**

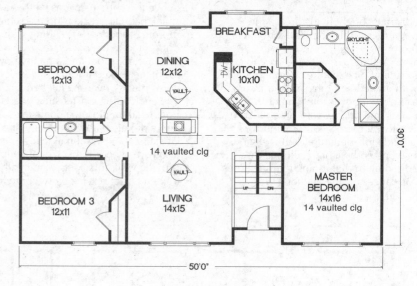

MAIN FLOOR

BEDROOM 2 12x13
DINING 12x12
BREAKFAST
KITCHEN 10x10
SKYLIGHT
14 vaulted clg
BEDROOM 3 12x11
LIVING 14x15
UP DN
MASTER BEDROOM 14x16 14 vaulted clg
VAULT
30'0"
50'0"

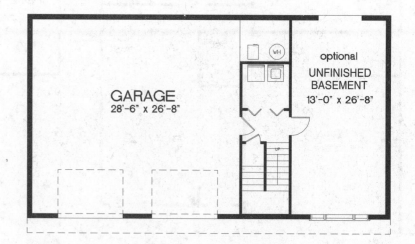

DAYLIGHT BASEMENT

GARAGE 28'-6" x 26'-8"
WH
optional UNFINISHED BASEMENT 13'-0" x 26'-8"
UP

Plan APS-1510

Plan copyright held by home designer/architect

PRICES AND DETAILS
ON PAGES 12-15

Functional Family Living

- This home is perfect for family living with its secluded sleeping wing, cozy family room and large activity area.
- Skylights can be used to brighten the covered entry and reception area as it leads to the living spaces.
- The living room and bayed dining room are warmed by a brick fireplace. Sliding glass doors open to a backyard terrace.
- The open kitchen features a handy snack bar that easily serves the cozy family room and the adjoining dinette .
- Just steps away, the smart mudroom boasts a wash room, convenient laundry facilities, plus garage access and a handy service entrance.
- The removed sleeping wing has four bedrooms. The generous master bedroom offers a private bath with a whirlpool tub and sliding glass doors to a secluded terrace.
- The three remaining bedrooms share a full bath with a dual-sink vanity.

Plan K-659-U

Bedrooms: 4	Baths: 2½
Living Area:	
Main floor	1,580 sq. ft.
Total Living Area:	**1,580 sq. ft.**
Standard basement	1,512 sq. ft.
Garage and storage	439 sq. ft.
Exterior Wall Framing:	2x4 or 2x6

Foundation Options:

Standard basement

Slab

(All plans can be built with your choice of foundation and framing. A generic conversion diagram is available. See order form.)

BLUEPRINT PRICE CODE:	**B**

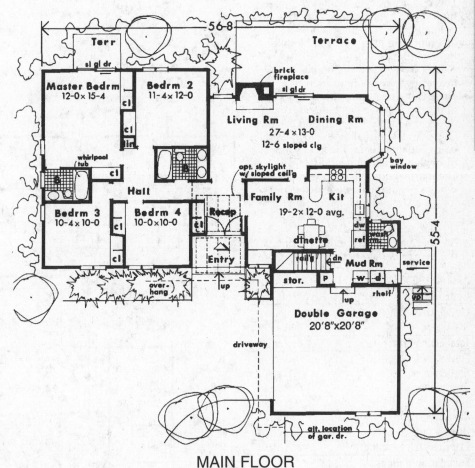

MAIN FLOOR

ORDER BLUEPRINTS ANYTIME!
CALL TOLL-FREE 1-800-820-1296

Plan K-659-U
Plan copyright held by home designer/architect

PRICES AND DETAILS
ON PAGES 12-15

139

Here and Now

- This country home's mammoth upper-floor future area can flex to meet your coming needs, but the main-floor amenities are fit to suit your lifestyle right here, right now.
- A cozy porch fronts the home, promising hours of relaxation.
- The bright Great Room boasts a media unit, a fireplace, a wet bar and French doors to a lovely screened porch.
- Guests in the formal dining room will enjoy looking out on the front yard through a wide bay window.
- The master bedroom features a bay window in the sleeping chamber, plus a long walk-in closet and a private bath with an oversized tub, a separate shower and a dual-sink vanity.
- Another bay window enhances one of the two secondary bedrooms.

Plan AX-00306

Bedrooms: 3+	Baths: 2
Living Area:	
Main floor	1,595 sq. ft.
Total Living Area:	**1,595 sq. ft.**
Future upper floor	813 sq. ft.
Screened porch	178 sq. ft.
Basement	1,595 sq. ft.
Garage	466 sq. ft.
Storage	24 sq. ft.
Utility room	22 sq. ft.
Exterior Wall Framing:	2x4

Foundation Options:

Daylight basement
Standard basement
Crawlspace
Slab

(All plans can be built with your choice of foundation and framing. A generic conversion diagram is available. See order form.)

BLUEPRINT PRICE CODE: B

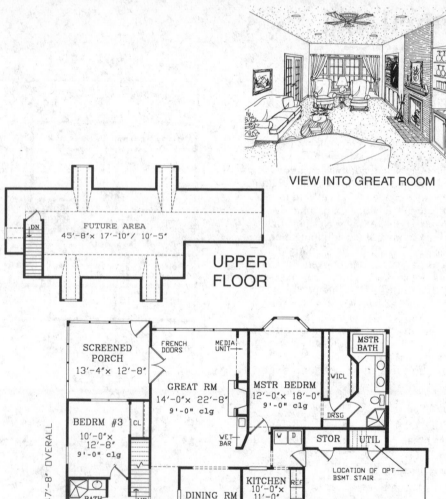

VIEW INTO GREAT ROOM

UPPER FLOOR

FUTURE AREA
45'-8" x 17'-10"/ 10'-5"

MAIN FLOOR

SCREENED PORCH
13'-4" x 12'-8"

GREAT RM
14'-0" x 22'-8"
9'-0" clg

MSTR BEDRM
12'-0" x 18'-0"
9'-0" clg

MSTR BATH

WICL

DRSG

FRENCH DOORS

MEDIA UNIT

BEDRM #3
10'-0" x 12'-8"
9'-0" clg

WET BAR

W   D

STOR   UTIL

LOCATION OF OPT BSMT STAIR

BATH

FOY

DINING RM
10'-0" x 13'-0"
9'-0" clg

KITCHEN
10'-0" x 11'-0"
9'-0" clg

REF

TWO CAR GARAGE
20'-0" x 21'-4"

BEDRM #2
11'-0" x 14'-0"
9'-0" clg

COV. PORCH

47'-8" OVERALL

59'-10" OVERALL

ORDER BLUEPRINTS ANYTIME!
CALL TOLL-FREE 1-800-820-1296

Plan AX-00306
Plan copyright held by home designer/architect

PRICES AND DETAILS
ON PAGES 12-15

Cape Cod Variation

- A handsome wraparound porch and stylish dormers with transom glass dress up this Cape Cod variation.
- Inside, a dramatic balcony creates immediate interest as it overlooks the living room and entry from high above. Complementing the lofty vaulted ceiling is a lovely boxed-out window.
- The kitchen and the dining area unite at the back of the home and include a neat pantry, a versatile island and access to the backyard. With everything at your fingertips, why dine out?
- When the dishes are done, slip into the private master suite on the main floor. Your daily worries will be long gone as you relax in the bubbly whirlpool tub.
- A skylighted bath shares the upper floor with two secondary bedrooms and a large attic storage area.
- A laundry room and a half-bath connect the home to the two-car garage.

VIEW INTO LIVING ROOM

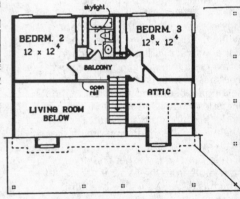

UPPER FLOOR

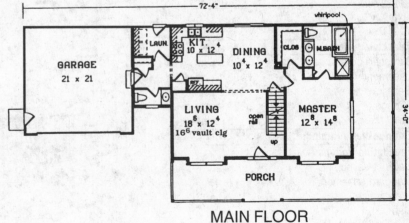

MAIN FLOOR

Plan GL-1581

Bedrooms: 3	Baths: 2½
Living Area:	
Upper floor	506 sq. ft.
Main floor	1,075 sq. ft.
Total Living Area:	**1,581 sq. ft.**
Attic storage space	137 sq. ft.
Standard basement	1,059 sq. ft.
Garage	441 sq. ft.
Exterior Wall Framing:	2x6

Foundation Options:

Standard basement

(All plans can be built with your choice of foundation and framing. A generic conversion diagram is available. See order form.)

BLUEPRINT PRICE CODE: B

ORDER BLUEPRINTS ANYTIME!
CALL TOLL-FREE 1-800-820-1296

Plan GL-1581
Plan copyright held by home designer/architect

PRICES AND DETAILS
ON PAGES 12-15   141

Single-Story with Sparkle

- A lovely facade with bay windows and dormers give this home extra sparkle.
- The Great Room anchors the floor plan, adjoining both the dining room and a screened porch. It also has a fireplace, a tray ceiling and a built-in wet bar.
- The eat-in kitchen utilizes a half-wall to stay connected with the Great Room, while the dining room offers a bay window that overlooks the porch. A convenient two-car garage is nearby.
- The master suite is set apart from two secondary bedrooms for privacy, and it includes a bay window, a tray ceiling, and a luxurious private bath.
- The two smaller bedrooms are off the main foyer and separated by a full bath.
- A mudroom with washer and dryer is accessible from the two-car garage, which is disguised with a beautiful bay window.

Plan AX-91312

Bedrooms: 3	Baths: 2
Living Area:	
Main floor	1,595 sq. ft.
Total Living Area:	**1,595 sq. ft.**
Screened porch	178 sq. ft.
Basement	1,595 sq. ft.
Garage	469 sq. ft.
Storage	21 sq. ft.
Utility room	18 sq. ft.
Exterior Wall Framing:	2x4

Foundation Options:

Daylight basement
Standard basement
Crawlspace
Slab

(All plans can be built with your choice of foundation and framing. A generic conversion diagram is available. See order form.)

BLUEPRINT PRICE CODE:	B

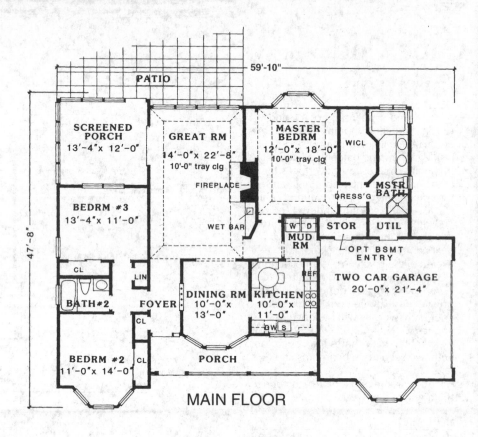

MAIN FLOOR

59'-10"

47'-8"

PATIO

SCREENED PORCH
13'-4" x 12'-0"

GREAT RM
14'-0" x 22'-8"
10'-0" tray clg

MASTER BEDRM
12'-0" x 18'-0"
10'-0" tray clg

WICL

MSTR BATH

DRESS'G

FIREPLACE

BEDRM #3
13'-4" x 11'-0"

WET BAR

W D

MUD RM

STOR

UTIL

OPT BSMT ENTRY

CL

LIN

BATH #2

FOYER

DINING RM
10'-0" x 13'-0"

KITCHEN
10'-0" x 11'-0"

REF

TWO CAR GARAGE
20'-0" x 21'-4"

CL

BEDRM #2
11'-0" x 14'-0"

PORCH

DW

VIEW INTO GREAT ROOM

Plan AX-91312

Plan copyright held by home designer/architect

PRICES AND DETAILS ON PAGES 12-15

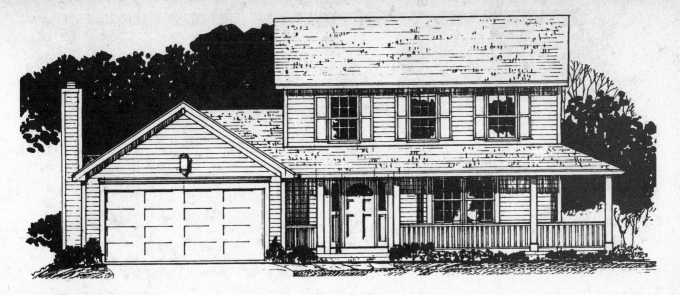

Great Family Choice

- Roominess and affordability make this traditional design a great family choice.
- The wraparound, covered front porch beckons guests to the sidelighted entry. Inside, the foyer features a coat closet and a nearby powder room.
- The living and dining rooms flow together for a large entertaining space.
- The expansive family room, the sunny dinette and the open kitchen form a more casual alternative along the rear of the home.
- The family room offers a fireplace option and a trio of windows. The dinette has sliding glass doors that access the backyard.
- The upper-floor master bedroom boasts a walk-in closet and private access to the main bath, which is shared with the two secondary bedrooms.

Plan GL-1597

Bedrooms: 3	Baths: 1½
Living Area:	
Upper floor	672 sq. ft.
Main floor	925 sq. ft.
Total Living Area:	**1,597 sq. ft.**
Standard basement	925 sq. ft.
Garage	413 sq. ft.
Exterior Wall Framing:	2x6

Foundation Options:

Standard basement

(All plans can be built with your choice of foundation and framing. A generic conversion diagram is available. See order form.)

BLUEPRINT PRICE CODE:	B

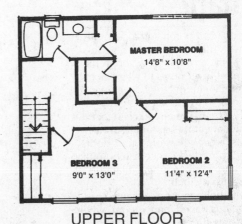

UPPER FLOOR

MASTER BEDROOM 14'8" x 10'8"

BEDROOM 3 9'0" x 13'0"

BEDROOM 2 11'4" x 12'4"

MAIN FLOOR

FAMILY ROOM 19'8" x 11'8"

DINETTE KITCHEN 16'10" x 11'4"

DINING ROOM 10'4" x 11'8"

LIVING ROOM 15'0" x 11'4"

GARAGE 20'0" x 20'8"

33'-8"

53'-0"

48'-0"

Plan GL-1597

Plan copyright held by home designer/architect

PRICES AND DETAILS ON PAGES 12-15

A Hint of Romance

- An ornate front porch and a decorative gable with fishscale shingles give this lovely home a romantic Victorian look.
- The central foyer flows to all areas of the home, including the convenient powder room to the left.
- Directly ahead, the airy kitchen features a functional eating bar and a sunny breakfast area with sliding glass doors to a backyard deck. Access to both the garage and a fully appointed laundry room is also a cinch.
- The formal dining room expands into the spacious bayed family room, where a handsome fireplace adds warmth and character to the room.
- Upstairs, the master bedroom boasts a bay window and an optional vaulted ceiling. Two closets and a private bath with a spa tub, a separate shower and twin vanities are also included.
- A second full bath and two more bedrooms complete the upper floor.

Plan APS-1514

Bedrooms: 3	Baths: 2½
Living Area:	
Upper floor	786 sq. ft.
Main floor	812 sq. ft.
Total Living Area:	**1,598 sq. ft.**
Garage	420 sq. ft.
Storage	140 sq. ft.
Exterior Wall Framing:	2x4

Foundation Options:

Crawlspace

Slab

(All plans can be built with your choice of foundation and framing. A generic conversion diagram is available. See order form.)

BLUEPRINT PRICE CODE:	**B**

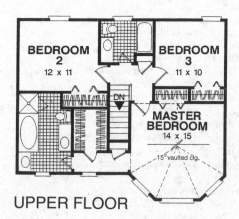

UPPER FLOOR

BEDROOM 2
12 x 11

BEDROOM 3
11 x 10

MASTER BEDROOM
14 x 15

15° vaulted clg.

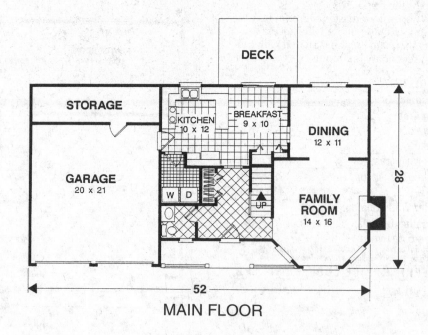

DECK

STORAGE

KITCHEN
10 x 12

BREAKFAST
9 x 10

DINING
12 x 11

GARAGE
20 x 21

W D

UP

FAMILY ROOM
14 x 16

28

52

MAIN FLOOR

ORDER BLUEPRINTS ANYTIME!
CALL TOLL-FREE 1-800-820-1296

Plan APS-1514

Plan copyright held by home designer/architect

PRICES AND DETAILS
ON PAGES 12-15

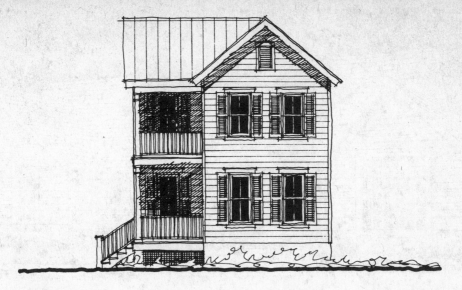

Charleston Form

- This charmer is a classic example of a "Charleston side yard" home. The side yard, in this case, would be located to the left of the home, overlooked by the stacked porches. If your lot so dictates, the plan could be "flipped" to place the overlook on the opposite side.

- The home's porches are deep and livable, with plenty of room for chairs or even a dinette set.

- Inside this well-proportioned home, you'll find a thoroughly modern floor plan that suits your lifestyle effortlessly. The living room unfolds from the entry porch and flows into the dining area and the kitchen. Access is easy from here to a backyard deck that's deep enough for a hungry family to dig into a barbecue.

- The foremost bedroom could easily serve as a home office.

- The master suite, a second bedroom and the laundry facilities occupy the upper floor.

- You don't need to settle for imitations that fall short of expectations. This is a flawless interpretation of a tried-and-true architectural form, and it could be yours today.

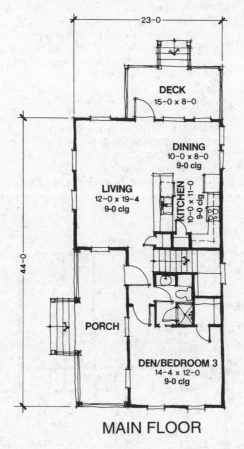

MAIN FLOOR

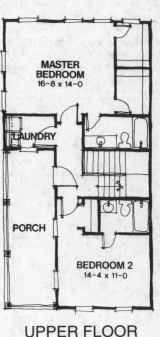

UPPER FLOOR

Plan WAA-9723-A

Bedrooms: 2+	Baths: 3
Living Area:	
Upper floor	786 sq. ft.
Main floor	820 sq. ft.
Total Living Area:	**1,606 sq. ft.**
Exterior Wall Framing:	2x4

Foundation Options:

Crawlspace
(All plans can be built with your choice of foundation and framing. A generic conversion diagram is available. See order form.)

BLUEPRINT PRICE CODE:	B

ORDER BLUEPRINTS ANYTIME!
CALL TOLL-FREE 1-800-820-1296

Plan WAA-9723-A
Plan copyright held by home designer/architect

PRICES AND DETAILS
ON PAGES 12-15   145

Timeless Accents

- The rustic exterior of this timeless country design is accented by broad, sturdy beams in the front gables that suggest a home that has been loved by your family for generations.
- A wide front porch welcomes you inside, where the gorgeous, open Great Room hosts family gatherings. It boasts a handy wet bar and a cozy fireplace, as well as a bright wall of windows overlooking the backyard. Stylish double doors open to the sunny screened porch.
- The master suite makes an elegant, restful retreat. The bayed sitting area, generous walk-in closet, separate dressing area and roomy master bath, defined by a corner whirlpool tub, will delight you.
- Enjoy the eating nook in the bright, front-facing kitchen. For special occasions, a doorway provides quick serving access to the dining room.
- Plentiful windows and large closets grace the two secondary bedrooms.
- Blueprints for this home include plans for an alternate, front-facing garage.

Plan AX-95368	
Bedrooms: 3	**Baths:** 2
Living Area:	
Main floor	1,595 sq. ft.
Total Living Area:	**1,595 sq. ft.**
Standard basement	1,595 sq. ft.
Screened porch	178 sq. ft.
Garage	455 sq. ft.
Storage	28 sq. ft.
Utility	25 sq. ft.
Exterior Wall Framing:	2x4

Foundation Options:
Standard basement
Crawlspace
Slab
(All plans can be built with your choice of foundation and framing. A generic conversion diagram is available. See order form.)

BLUEPRINT PRICE CODE:	B

MAIN FLOOR

SCREENED PORCH 13'-4" x 12'-8"

BEDRM #3 13'-4" x 11'-0"

47'-8" OVERALL

BATH

CL

GREAT RM 14'-0" x 22'-8" 10'-0" tray clg

WET BAR

MSTR BEDRM 12'-0" x 18'-0" 10'-0" tray clg

MSTR BATH

WICL

DRSG

STOR

W D

UTIL

FOY

DINING RM 10'-0" x 13'-0"

KITCHEN 10'-0" x 11'-0"

REF

LOCATION OF OPT BSMT STAIR

TWO CAR GARAGE 20'-0" x 21'-4"

BEDRM #2 11'-0" x 11'-0" 10'-0" clg

CL

DW

COV. PORCH

59'-10" OVERALL

Plan AX-95368
Plan copyright held by home designer/architect

PRICES AND DETAILS ON PAGES 12-15

At the Heart of the Home

- The family room, with its raised ceiling and row of windows, serves as the heart of this charming one-story, traditional-style home.
- A half-wall subtly separates the family room from the eating area, which is also accented by a wall of windows. It shares access to the backyard with the island kitchen, which offers the convenience of a big pantry.

- Across the home is the breathtaking master suite. Highlights include French doors opening to the backyard, a luxurious private bath with an oval tub and a separate shower, and a large walk-in closet.
- Two other bedrooms reside at the front of the home and share a full bath. Each contains a generous closet and boasts a pleasant window seat.
- There's no shortage of practical amenities in this design. The two-car garage includes an optional workbench with storage. The adjoining mudroom neatly houses the washer and dryer.

Plan KP-1004-A

Bedrooms: 3	**Baths:** 2

Living Area:	
Main floor	1,603 sq. ft.
Total Living Area:	**1,603 sq. ft.**
Basement	1,512 sq. ft.
Garage	601 sq. ft.
Exterior Wall Framing:	2x4

Foundation Options:

Daylight basement

Standard basement

(All plans can be built with your choice of foundation and framing. A generic conversion diagram is available. See order form.)

BLUEPRINT PRICE CODE:	B

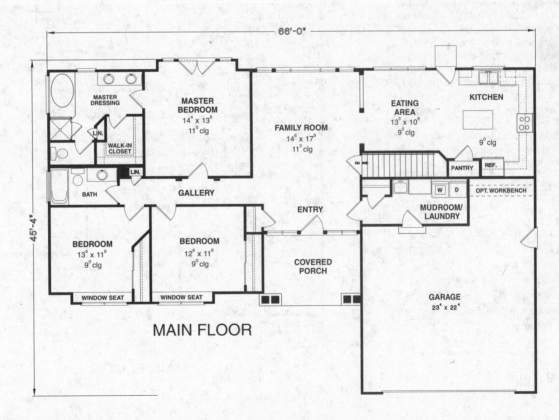

MAIN FLOOR

ORDER BLUEPRINTS ANYTIME!
CALL TOLL-FREE 1-800-820-1296

Plan KP-1004-A
Plan copyright held by home designer/architect

PRICES AND DETAILS
ON PAGES 12-15   147

European Adornment

- A stately European exterior adorns this quaint one-story.
- From the entry foyer, twin columns and half-walls introduce the living room, with its fireplace and tall windows.
- In the dining room, sliding glass doors open to a charming screen porch. A sunny patio is accessible through a screen door.
- The dining room is a few smooth steps from the kitchen, which boasts a spiffy breakfast bar and a breakfast corner for speedy morning meals.
- On the sleeping side of the home, the master bedroom sports a restful window seat and private access to the patio. The master bath flaunts a separate tub and shower, and a walk-through closet.
- A good-sized front bedroom is serviced by a hall bath.
- A cozy den or extra bedroom is brightened by a sheltered window with an arched transom.

Plan B-94012

Bedrooms: 2+	**Baths:** 2

Living Area:	
Main floor	1,606 sq. ft.
Total Living Area:	**1,606 sq. ft.**
Screen porch	87 sq. ft.
Standard basement	1,606 sq. ft.
Garage and storage	417 sq. ft.
Exterior Wall Framing:	8-in. concrete block

Foundation Options:

Standard basement

(All plans can be built with your choice of foundation and framing. A generic conversion diagram is available. See order form.)

BLUEPRINT PRICE CODE:	**B**

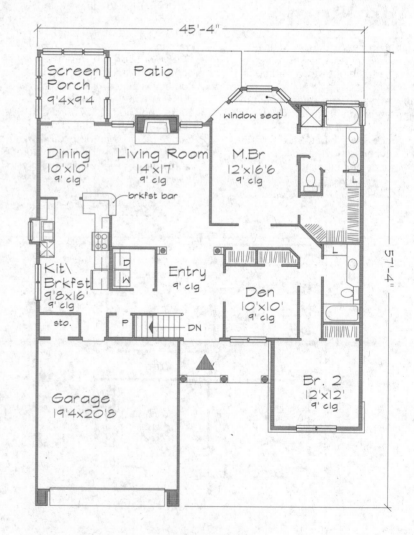

MAIN FLOOR

Plan B-94012

Plan copyright held by home designer/architect

PRICES AND DETAILS
ON PAGES 12-15

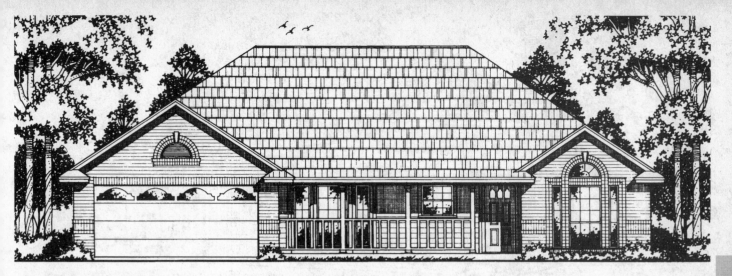

All the Best

- This stylish country home offers the best in amenities and comfortable touches.
- An inviting railed front porch flatters the entry, which opens immediately to the living areas.
- The massive living room will glow warmly with light from its central fireplace. A cozy backyard patio is easily accessed.
- A nifty breakfast bar separates the living room from the walk-through kitchen,

which flows into the bay-windowed dining room.
- Secluded from the rest of the home, the master bedroom is brightly lit by a tall, arched window arrangement. The sumptuous master bath boasts his-and-hers walk-in closets, a fabulous garden tub and a sit-down shower. The dual-sink vanity is enhanced by an overhead plant shelf and a makeup area.
- Two more bedrooms, one with an attractive window arrangement, share a convenient hall bath.

Plan KD-1606

Bedrooms: 3	**Baths:** 2

Living Area:	
Main floor	1,606 sq. ft.
Total Living Area:	**1,606 sq. ft.**
Garage and storage	453 sq. ft.
Exterior Wall Framing:	2x4

Foundation Options:

Slab
(All plans can be built with your choice of foundation and framing. A generic conversion diagram is available. See order form.)

BLUEPRINT PRICE CODE:	**B**

MAIN FLOOR

ORDER BLUEPRINTS ANYTIME!
CALL TOLL-FREE 1-800-820-1296

Plan KD-1606
Plan copyright held by home designer/architect

PRICES AND DETAILS
ON PAGES 12-15   149

Sweet Talker

- Sweet exterior details, including fishscale shingles, a covered front porch and pretty bay windows, entice family and guests to take a closer look at this cozy one-story home.
- Inside, the expansive family room boasts a warm fireplace for chilly evenings. The octagonal conversation area imbues everyday chats with unique charm.
- To the back of the home, the dining room flaunts a wall of windows and access to a side covered porch.

- The U-shaped kitchen supplies every amenity and plenty of work room. A center island adds convenience, while a windowed sink brightens the space.
- The master suite treats the owners of the home to a bay-windowed sitting area and a high ceiling in the bedroom, plus dual sinks and mirrored closet doors in the accommodating private bath.
- Two secondary bedrooms each house a walk-in closet, and share a hall bath nearby. The rear-facing bedroom is blessed with a corner window seat for reading or daydreaming.

Plan L-1614	
Bedrooms: 3	**Baths:** 2
Living Area:	
Main floor	1,614 sq. ft.
Total Living Area:	**1,614 sq. ft.**
Detached garage	544 sq. ft.
Exterior Wall Framing:	2x4
Foundation Options:	
Slab	

(All plans can be built with your choice of foundation and framing. A generic conversion diagram is available. See order form.)

BLUEPRINT PRICE CODE: B

DETACHED GARAGE

2-Car Garage
23'-4" x 23'-4"

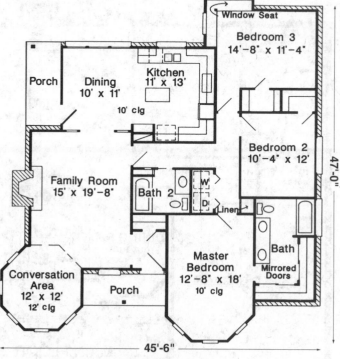

MAIN FLOOR

Plan L-1614
Plan copyright held by home designer/architect

PRICES AND DETAILS
ON PAGES 12-15

Tradition Updated

- The nostalgic exterior of this home gives way to dramatic vaulted ceilings and illuminating skylights inside.
- The front porch welcomes guests into the stone-tiled foyer. Beyond, the living and dining rooms merge together, forming an open entertaining area under a vaulted ceiling.
- The family room shares a vaulted ceiling and a cozy three-sided fireplace with the living room. A sunny skylight and sliding glass doors to a patio brighten the room.
- The skylighted island kitchen offers yet another vaulted ceiling and adjoins a cheery breakfast nook, which serves as the perfect spot for everyday meals.
- The master suite boasts a walk-in closet and a skylighted bath with a vaulted ceiling, a dual-sink vanity, a soaking tub and a separate shower.

Plan AX-90303-A

Bedrooms: 3	Baths: 2
Living Area:	
Main floor	1,615 sq. ft.
Total Living Area:	**1,615 sq. ft.**
Basement	1,615 sq. ft.
Garage	412 sq. ft.
Exterior Wall Framing:	2x4

Foundation Options:

Daylight basement
Standard basement
Crawlspace
Slab

(All plans can be built with your choice of foundation and framing. A generic conversion diagram is available. See order form.)

BLUEPRINT PRICE CODE: B

VIEW INTO FAMILY ROOM

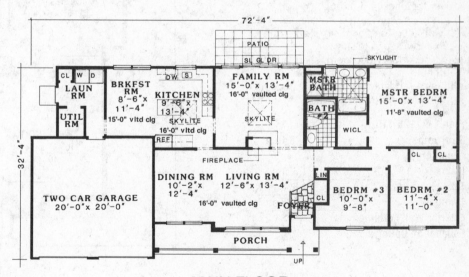

MAIN FLOOR

ORDER BLUEPRINTS ANYTIME!
CALL TOLL-FREE 1-800-820-1296

Plan AX-90303-A

Plan copyright held by home designer/architect

PRICES AND DETAILS
ON PAGES 12-15   151

City Mouse, Country Mouse

- This cozy cottage is at home in both the city and the country. Nestle comfortably within its walls, and burrow deep beneath its eaves.
- The spacious living room lies just off the foyer and features a fireplace, corner windows and a snuggly library alcove with a window, topped by a sloped ceiling. Hide out back here with a good book and your favorite munchies.
- From the living room enter the large dining room, which offers a media center, a boxed-out window, access to the back porch and a snack bar from the kitchen for quick meals.
- The secluded master suite looks out over the backyard through corner windows and boasts a private bath with a walk-in closet, dual sinks, a garden tub and a separate shower.
- Two secondary bedrooms share another full bath.
- Plans for a detached two-car garage are included with the blueprints.

Plan L-97125-TUDA

Bedrooms: 3	Baths: 2
Living Area:	
Main floor	1,621 sq. ft.
Total Living Area:	**1,621 sq. ft.**
Garage	528 sq. ft.
Exterior Wall Framing:	2x4

Foundation Options:
Crawlspace
Slab
(All plans can be built with your choice of foundation and framing. A generic conversion diagram is available. See order form.)

BLUEPRINT PRICE CODE:	B

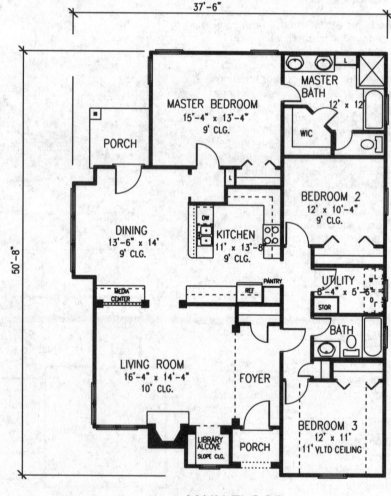

MAIN FLOOR

ORDER BLUEPRINTS ANYTIME!
CALL TOLL-FREE 1-800-820-1296

Plan L-97125-TUDA
Plan copyright held by home designer/architect

PRICES AND DETAILS
ON PAGES 12-15

Wraparound Deck Featured

- An expansive covered deck wraps around this home from the main entrance on the left side to the kitchen door on the right side.
- An oversized fireplace is the focal point of the vaulted living and dining room area. The living room's 10-ft.-high sloped ceiling is brightened by corner windows, while the dining area has sliding glass doors to access the adjoining deck.
- The kitchen is tucked into one corner, but the open counter space allows visual contact with the adjoining living areas beyond.
- Two good-sized main-floor bedrooms, each with sufficient closet space, are convenient to the hall bath.
- The basement level adds a roomy third bedroom, plus a huge general-use area and a tuck-under garage.

Plan H-806-2

Bedrooms: 3	Baths: 1

Living Area:

Main floor	952 sq. ft.
Daylight basement	673 sq. ft.
Total Living Area:	**1,625 sq. ft.**
Tuck-under garage	279 sq. ft.

Exterior Wall Framing:	2x6

Foundation Options:

Daylight basement
(All plans can be built with your choice of foundation and framing. A generic conversion diagram is available. See order form.)

BLUEPRINT PRICE CODE:	B

SENSIBLE HOMES

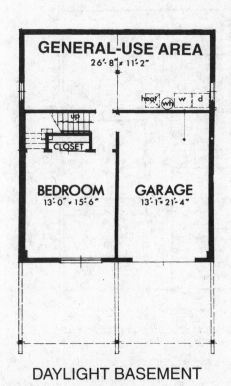

DAYLIGHT BASEMENT

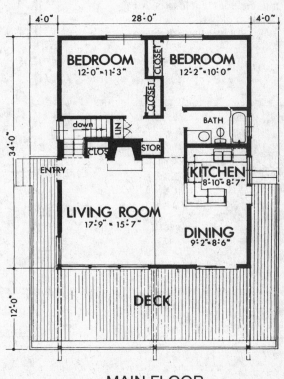

MAIN FLOOR

ORDER BLUEPRINTS ANYTIME!
CALL TOLL-FREE 1-800-820-1296

Plan H-806-2

Plan copyright held by home designer/architect

PRICES AND DETAILS
ON PAGES 12-15

153

Narrow Lot, Broad Appeal

- This compact, cozy and dignified plan makes great use of a small lot, while also offering an exciting interior design.
- In from the covered front porch, the living room features a warm fireplace and a cathedral ceiling.
- The bay-windowed dining room joins the living room to provide a spacious area for entertaining.
- The galley-style kitchen has easy access to a large pantry closet, the utility room and the carport.
- The master suite includes a deluxe bath and a roomy walk-in closet.
- Two secondary bedrooms share another bath off the hallway.
- A lockable storage area is located off the rear patio.

Plan J-86161

Bedrooms: 3	Baths: 2
Living Area:	
Main floor	1,626 sq. ft.
Total Living Area:	**1,626 sq. ft.**
Standard basement	1,626 sq. ft.
Carport	410 sq. ft.
Storage	104 sq. ft.
Exterior Wall Framing:	2x4

Foundation Options:

Standard basement
Crawlspace
Slab

(All plans can be built with your choice of foundation and framing. A generic conversion diagram is available. See order form.)

BLUEPRINT PRICE CODE:	B

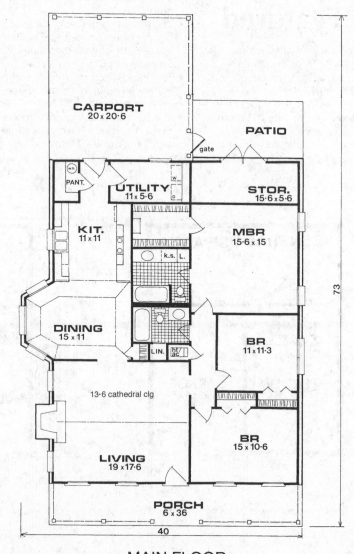

MAIN FLOOR

PRICES AND DETAILS ON PAGES 12-15

ORDER BLUEPRINTS ANYTIME! CALL TOLL-FREE 1-800-820-1296

Plan J-86161
Plan copyright held by home designer/architect

Indoor/Outdoor Pleasure

- For a scenic lake or mountain lot, this spectacular design takes full advantage of the views.
- A three-sided wraparound deck makes indoor/outdoor living a pleasure.
- The sunken living room—with a cathedral ceiling, a skylight, a beautiful fireplace and glass galore—is the heart of the floor plan.
- Both the formal dining room and the kitchen overlook the living room and the surrounding deck beyond.
- The main-floor master bedroom has a cathedral ceiling and private access to the deck and hall bath.
- Upstairs, two more bedrooms share a skylighted bath and flank a dramatic balcony sitting area that views to the living room below.

Plan AX-98607

Bedrooms: 3	Baths: 2
Living Area:	
Upper floor	531 sq. ft.
Main floor	1,098 sq. ft.
Total Living Area:	**1,629 sq. ft.**
Standard basement	894 sq. ft.
Garage	327 sq. ft.
Exterior Wall Framing:	2x4

Foundation Options:

Standard basement

Slab

(All plans can be built with your choice of foundation and framing. A generic conversion diagram is available. See order form.)

BLUEPRINT PRICE CODE: B

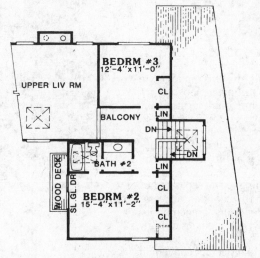

UPPER FLOOR

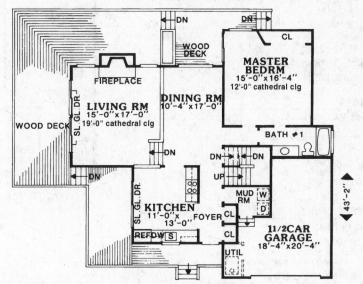

MAIN FLOOR

ORDER BLUEPRINTS ANYTIME!
CALL TOLL-FREE 1-800-820-1296

Plan AX-98607

Plan copyright held by home designer/architect

PRICES AND DETAILS
ON PAGES 12-15

155

Distinctive One-Story

- Bright, bold windows and eye-catching masonry details give this modern one-story home its distinctive look.
- The vaulted living room, located just past the inviting, light-filled entry, boasts a vaulted ceiling. The attractive fireplace, flanked by floor-to-ceiling windows, serves as the focal point of the room.
- The formal dining room, separated from the living room by columns, accesses a large rear deck through French doors.
- The modern kitchen includes a sunny breakfast area with access to a covered portion of the rear deck. A convenient laundry room is nearby.
- The luxurious master suite features a high ceiling and a bright sitting area with deck access. The master bath has a spa tub, a dual-sink vanity and a walk-in closet.
- Two additional bedrooms share a second full bath and are serviced by a hallway linen closet.

REAR VIEW

Plan B-91014

Bedrooms: 2+	Baths: 2
Living Area:.	
Main floor	1,633 sq. ft.
Total Living Area:	**1,633 sq. ft.**
Standard basement	1,633 sq. ft.
Garage	448 sq. ft.
Exterior Wall Framing:	2x6

Foundation Options:

Standard basement

(All plans can be built with your choice of foundation and framing. A generic conversion diagram is available. See order form.)

BLUEPRINT PRICE CODE:	B

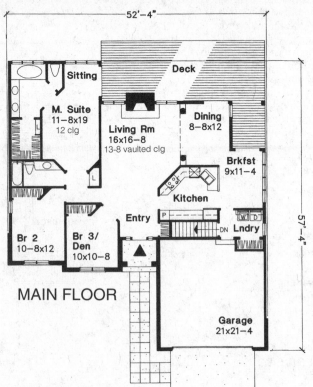

MAIN FLOOR

52'-4"

57'-4"

Sitting

Deck

M. Suite
11—8x19
12 clg

Living Rm
16x16-8
13-8 vaulted clg

Dining
8—8x12

Brkfst
9x11—4

Kitchen

Entry

Br 2
10—8x12

Br 3/
Den
10x10—8

Lndry

Garage
21x21—4

Friendly Country Charm

- An inviting front porch welcomes you to this friendly one-story home.
- The porch opens to a spacious central living room with a warm fireplace and functional built-in storage shelves.
- The bay window of the adjoining dining room allows a view of the backyard.

The dining area also enjoys an eating bar provided by the adjacent walk-through kitchen.
- The nice-sized kitchen also has a windowed sink and easy access to the laundry room and carport.
- Three bedrooms and two baths occupy the sleeping wing. The oversized master bedroom features a lovely boxed-out window, two walk-in closets and a private bath. The secondary bedrooms share the second full bath.

Plan J-8692	
Bedrooms: 3	**Baths:** 2
Living Area:	
Main floor	1,633 sq. ft.
Total Living Area:	**1,633 sq. ft.**
Standard basement	1,633 sq. ft.
Carport	380 sq. ft.
Exterior Wall Framing:	2x4
Foundation Options:	
Standard basement	
Crawlspace	
Slab	

(All plans can be built with your choice of foundation and framing. A generic conversion diagram is available. See order form.)

BLUEPRINT PRICE CODE:	B

SENSIBLE HOMES

VIEW INTO LIVING ROOM, DINING ROOM AND KITCHEN

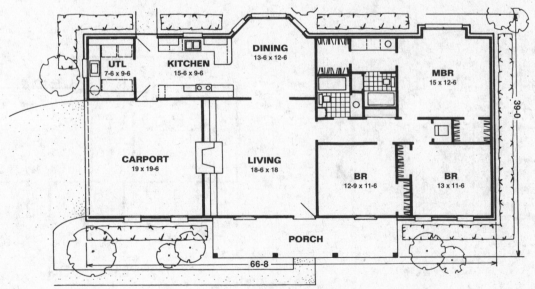

MAIN FLOOR

Plan J-8692

Plan copyright held by home designer/architect

PRICES AND DETAILS
ON PAGES 12-15

Simple Beauty

- This unassuming country home projects a peaceful air to the world.
- The classic front porch is a perfect place to reminisce with old friends. Inside, the high vaulted entry unfolds to the family room, where a fireplace serves as a striking focal point.
- Possessing its own quiet elegance, the adjoining dining area is equally suited for both casual meals and important social gatherings. Double windows look out over the inviting backyard deck; a French door lets you step out for a breath of fresh air.
- Clever and efficient touches abound in the kitchen, and include a smart serving counter angled to face the family and

dining rooms. A cheery skylight nicely punctuates the kitchen's vaulted ceiling, and a bright window gives the sink area visual appeal.
- A pocket door helps to segregate the laundry area and the master bedroom from the common living areas. In the master bath, a luxurious garden tub will help you to relax after a strenuous day.
- Your children will love their private upper-floor bedrooms, which offer dormers that are ideal for window seats. A split bath eases the bedtime routine and a balcony views the entry.
- A drive-under garage occupies half of the basement level.
- Upon request, a detached garage plan will be provided; a studio and bath above the garage measure 336 sq. ft.

Plan APS-1612	
Bedrooms: 3	**Baths:** 2½
Living Area:	
Upper floor	579 sq. ft.
Main floor	1,064 sq. ft.
Total Living Area:	**1,643 sq. ft.**
Daylight basement	490 sq. ft.
Tuck-under garage	520 sq. ft.
Exterior Wall Framing:	2x4
Foundation Options:	
Daylight basement	
Crawlspace	

(All plans can be built with your choice of foundation and framing. A generic conversion diagram is available. See order form.)

BLUEPRINT PRICE CODE:	B

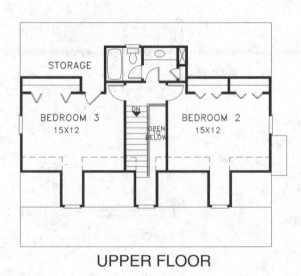

MAIN FLOOR

DECK

SKYLIGHT

DINING 12x12

KITCHEN 10x12

14' vltd clg

MASTER BEDRM 15x13

17' vltd clg

FAMILY ROOM 18x15

38

34

UPPER FLOOR

STORAGE

BEDROOM 3 15X12

BEDROOM 2 15X12

OPEN BELOW

ORDER BLUEPRINTS ANYTIME! CALL TOLL-FREE 1-800-820-1296

Plan APS-1612

Plan copyright held by home designer/architect

PRICES AND DETAILS ON PAGES 12-15

Welcome Home

- An inviting covered porch welcomes you home to this country-kissed ranch.
- Inside, a cathedral ceiling soars over the expansive living room, which boasts a fireplace flanked by windows.
- Bathed in sunlight from more windows, the dining room flaunts an elegant French door that opens to a delightful backyard porch.
- The gourmet kitchen features a planning desk, a pantry and a unique, angled bar—a great place to settle for an afternoon snack. Garage access is conveniently nearby.

- Smartly secluded in one corner of the home is the lovely and spacious master bedroom, crowned by a tray ceiling. Other amenities include huge his-and-hers walk-in closets and a private bath with a garden tub and a dual-sink vanity.
- Just outside the door to the master bedroom, a neat laundry closet is handy for last-minute loads.
- Two secondary bedrooms round out this wonderful design. The front-facing bedroom is complemented by a vaulted ceiling, while the rear bedroom offers a sunny window seat. A full bath accented by a stylish round window is shared by both rooms.

Plan J-91085

Bedrooms: 3	**Baths:** 2

Living Area:	
Main floor	1,643 sq. ft.
Total Living Area:	**1,643 sq. ft.**
Standard basement	1,643 sq. ft.
Garage	443 sq. ft.
Storage	37 sq. ft.

Exterior Wall Framing:	2x4

Foundation Options:

Standard basement
Crawlspace
Slab
(All plans can be built with your choice of foundation and framing. A generic conversion diagram is available. See order form.)

BLUEPRINT PRICE CODE:	**B**

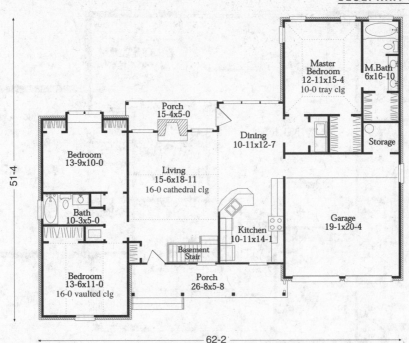

MAIN FLOOR

51-4

62-2

Bedroom
13-9x10-0

Bath
10-3x5-0

Bedroom
13-6x11-0
16-0 vaulted clg

Porch
15-4x5-0

Living
15-6x18-11
16-0 cathedral clg

Basement
Stair

Kitchen
10-11x14-1

Porch
26-8x5-8

Dining
10-11x12-7

Master
Bedroom
12-11x15-4
10-0 tray clg

M.Bath
6x16-10

Storage

Garage
19-1x20-4

ORDER BLUEPRINTS ANYTIME!
CALL TOLL-FREE 1-800-820-1296

Plan J-91085
Plan copyright held by home designer/architect

PRICES AND DETAILS
ON PAGES 12-15

159

Just Perfect

- This well-planned design is the perfect solution for a family in search of an affordable yet comfortable home.
- A quiet porch out front gives you a peaceful spot to retreat to with a book or just your thoughts. A charming rail lends warmth to the home.
- Inside, the formal dining room sits to the right of the entry. This is the ideal spot to entertain friends or celebrate a promotion with a good meal.
- At the core of the home, the living room awaits years of visiting, good

conversation, homework, TV watching and other regular activities. A handy bar between the living room and the kitchen holds chips, sodas and other refreshments during get-togethers.
- You will enjoy everyday dinners and leisurely breakfasts with coffee and the Sunday paper in the casual breakfast nook. A nearby door offers escape to a nice-sized covered patio.
- The cozy master suite makes getting out of bed even harder. In the skylighted bath, a dual-sink vanity and an oversized tub give the heads of the household extra-special treatment.

Plan KD-1648	
Bedrooms: 3	**Baths:** 2
Living Area:	
Main floor	1,648 sq. ft.
Total Living Area:	**1,648 sq. ft.**
Garage	446 sq. ft.
Storage	61 sq. ft.
Exterior Wall Framing:	2x4
Foundation Options:	

Slab
(All plans can be built with your choice of foundation and framing. A generic conversion diagram is available. See order form.)

BLUEPRINT PRICE CODE: B

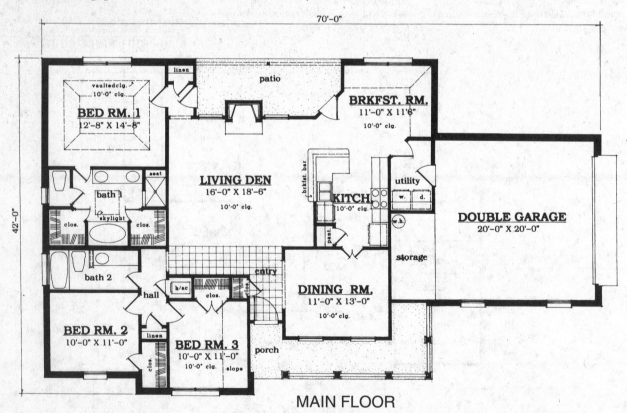

MAIN FLOOR

ORDER BLUEPRINTS ANYTIME!
CALL TOLL-FREE 1-800-820-1296

Plan KD-1648
Plan copyright held by home designer/architect

PRICES AND DETAILS
ON PAGES 12-15

Cottage Charm

- A charming front window with shutters and a gabled roof provide focal points for this European-style home's charming exterior.
- The interior of the home is no less inviting. Just inside the foyer, curl up with a good book in the study, which boasts a view of the front garden. Or join the party in the living room, warmed by the cozy fireplace.
- A half-wall separates the living and dining rooms. The dining room, just off the kitchen, provides access to the back porch. The island kitchen's serving bar bar eases the stovetop-to-table transition, besides adding workspace and a handy place for a quick meal or a cup of tea.
- For privacy, the two bedrooms lie at opposite ends of the home. The master suite is distinguished by a large walk-in closet, a relaxing oval tub and a separate shower, plus a dual-sink vanity.
- The home's facade is enhanced by the clever placement of the garage, which is accessed from the rear of the home or from the back porch. Extra storage area is found here.

Plan L-97144-TUDA

Bedrooms: 2+	Baths: 2
Living Area:	
Main floor	1,649 sq. ft.
Total Living Area:	**1,649 sq. ft.**
Garage	567 sq. ft.
Exterior Wall Framing:	2x4

Foundation Options:
Crawlspace
Slab
(All plans can be built with your choice of foundation and framing. A generic conversion diagram is available. See order form.)

BLUEPRINT PRICE CODE:	B

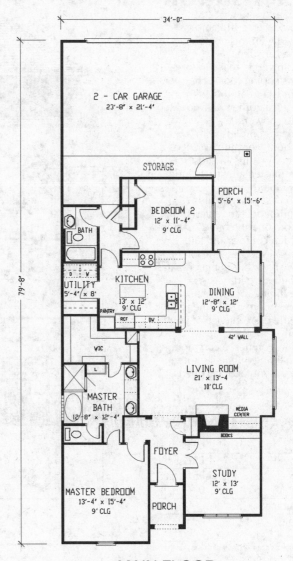

MAIN FLOOR

ORDER BLUEPRINTS ANYTIME!
CALL TOLL-FREE 1-800-820-1296

Plan L-97144-TUDA
Plan copyright held by home designer/architect

PRICES AND DETAILS
ON PAGES 12-15

161

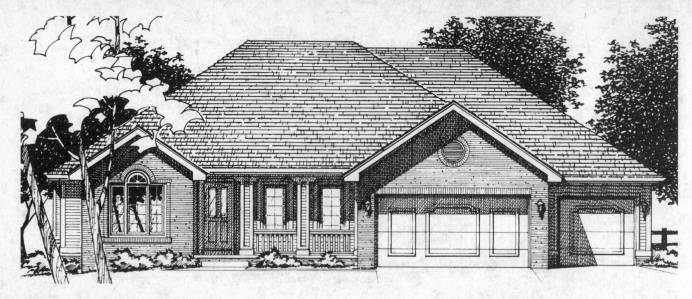

Suite Sensation

- Go ahead, you deserve it! Pamper yourself every day in this home's sensational master suite.
- A stepped ceiling adds space to the master suite's sleeping room. The oversized bath is a treat, too, with a dual-sink vanity, a corner whirlpool tub and a separate shower.
- An adjacent den, complete with a built-in wet bar, is quite versatile: Use it as a home office, convert it to a guest room or expand the master suite to include this area as an anteroom.
- The rest of the design is equally luxurious—and perfect for entertaining. The Great Room and the breakfast nook both feature high ceilings and tall, transom-topped windows. The kitchen offers a handy snack bar to the breakfast nook, and a butler's pantry eases serving to the dining room.
- A secondary bedroom resides near a full hall bath, for the convenience of your guests or family.
- The home's two porches accommodate outdoor entertaining, while the three-car garage meets your storage needs.

Plan DBI-2818

Bedrooms: 2+	Baths: 2
Living Area:	
Main floor	1,651 sq. ft.
Total Living Area:	**1,651 sq. ft.**
Standard basement	1,651 sq. ft.
Garage	677 sq. ft.
Exterior Wall Framing:	2x4

Foundation Options:

Standard basement
(All plans can be built with your choice of foundation and framing. A generic conversion diagram is available. See order form.)

BLUEPRINT PRICE CODE:	**B**

REAR VIEW

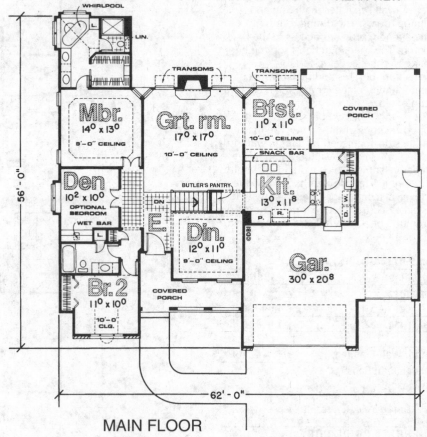

MAIN FLOOR

Plan DBI-2818

Plan copyright held by home designer/architect

PRICES AND DETAILS
ON PAGES 12-15

Something for Everyone

- The charming porches and Craftsman-inspired details of this home will capture your heart; the sensible layout will appeal to the utilitarian in you.
- The design's exterior is marked by tapered columns and projecting eaves, as well as a practical carport.
- Inside, the flowing floor plan offers porch access from almost every room in the house. A fireplace enhances the appeal of the large living room, while the kitchen and the dining room make a good team, sharing a handy peninsula.
- Each bedroom is blessed with a walk-in closet and lovely windows, but the master suite is set apart. It boasts an oversized walk-in closet and a luxurious bath, complete with a corner garden tub, a separate shower and a wide, dual-sink vanity.

Plan DW-1657

Bedrooms: 3	Baths: 2
Living Area:	
Main floor	1,657 sq. ft.
Total Living Area:	**1,657 sq. ft.**
Standard basement	1,657 sq. ft.
Detached garage	484 sq. ft.
Carport	282 sq. ft.
Exterior Wall Framing:	**2x4**

Foundation Options:

Standard basement
Crawlspace
Slab

(All plans can be built with your choice of foundation and framing. A generic conversion diagram is available. See order form.)

BLUEPRINT PRICE CODE:	**B**

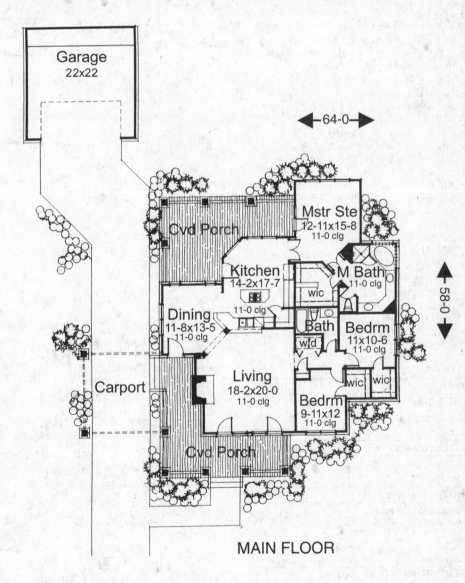

Garage 22x22

← 64-0 →

58-0

Cvd Porch

Mstr Ste 12-11x15-8 11-0 clg

Kitchen 14-2x17-7 11-0 clg

M Bath 11-0 clg

wic

Dining 11-8x13-5 11-0 clg

Bath

wic

Bedrm 11x10-6 11-0 clg

Carport

Living 18-2x20-0 11-0 clg

wic   wic

Bedrm 9-11x12 11-0 clg

Cvd Porch

MAIN FLOOR

ORDER BLUEPRINTS ANYTIME!
CALL TOLL-FREE 1-800-820-1296

Plan DW-1657
Plan copyright held by home designer/architect

PRICES AND DETAILS
ON PAGES 12-15

163

A New Angle

- This passive-solar design can be angled in various directions to take advantage of the sun's warming capabilities.
- A vestibule that traps outside air buffers an inviting reception area, which overlooks an exciting sun garden and a backyard terrace.
- To the right, a 12½-ft. sloped ceiling with a skylight adds serenity to the living and dining rooms. A high-efficiency fireplace warms the area, while sliding glass doors open to both the sun garden and the terrace.
- Another fireplace warms the casual living areas, where a handy snack bar for four separates the efficient U-shaped kitchen from the family room. A neat built-in shelf is a great place to display family photos or knickknacks.
- Across the home, the master suite includes a peaceful sitting area, a private terrace and access to the sun garden. The private bath features a luxurious whirlpool tub.
- Two additional bedrooms located across the hall share a full bath.

Plan K-526-C

Bedrooms: 3	Baths: 2
Living Area:	
Main floor	1,522 sq. ft.
Sun garden	140 sq. ft.
Total Living Area:	**1,662 sq. ft.**
Standard basement	1,522 sq. ft.
Garage	422 sq. ft.
Exterior Wall Framing:	2x4 or 2x6

Foundation Options:

Standard basement
Slab
(All plans can be built with your choice of foundation and framing. A generic conversion diagram is available. See order form.)

BLUEPRINT PRICE CODE:	B

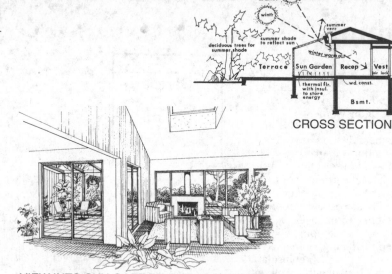

CROSS SECTION

VIEW INTO SUN GARDEN AND LIVING ROOM

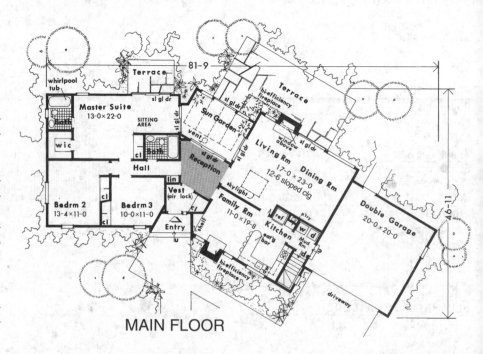

MAIN FLOOR

Plan K-526-C

Plan copyright held by home designer/architect

PRICES AND DETAILS
ON PAGES 12-15

Comfortable, Open Plan

- This comfortable home defines function and style, with a sharp window wall to brighten the central living areas.
- In from the broad front deck, the living/family room boasts a fireplace, a cathedral ceiling and soaring views. The fireplace visually sets off the dining room, which extends to the backyard patio through sliding doors.
- The galley-style kitchen offers a bright sink and an abundance of counter space, with a laundry closet and carport access nearby.
- The secluded and spacious master bedroom features private deck access, a walk-in closet and a private bath.
- On the other side of the home, two good-sized secondary bedrooms share another full bath.

Plan C-8160

Bedrooms: 3	Baths: 2

Living Area:

Main floor	1,669 sq. ft.
Total Living Area:	**1,669 sq. ft.**
Daylight basement	1,660 sq. ft.
Carport	413 sq. ft.
Storage	85 sq. ft.
Exterior Wall Framing:	2x4

Foundation Options:

Daylight basement
Crawlspace
Slab
(All plans can be built with your choice of foundation and framing. A generic conversion diagram is available. See order form.)

BLUEPRINT PRICE CODE:	B

SENSIBLE HOMES

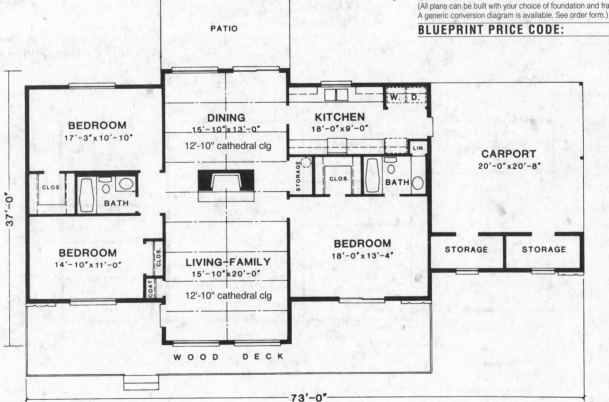

MAIN FLOOR

ORDER BLUEPRINTS ANYTIME!
CALL TOLL-FREE 1-800-820-1296

Plan C-8160
Plan copyright held by home designer/architect

PRICES AND DETAILS
ON PAGES 12-15

165

Rustic Welcome

- This rustic design boasts an appealing exterior with a covered front porch that offers guests a friendly welcome.
- Inside, the centrally located Great Room features a cathedral ceiling with exposed wood beams. A massive fireplace separates the living area from the large dining room, which offers access to a nice backyard patio.
- The galley-style kitchen flows between the formal dining room and the bayed

breakfast room, which offers a handy pantry and access to laundry facilities.
- The master suite features a walk-in closet and a compartmentalized bath.
- Across the Great Room, two additional bedrooms have extra closet space and share a second full bath.
- The side-entry garage gives the front of the home an extra-appealing and uncluttered look.
- The optional daylight basement offers expanded living space. The stairway (not shown) would be located along the wall between the dining room and the back bedroom.

Plan C-8460

Bedrooms: 3		**Baths: 2**
Living Area:		
Main floor		1,670 sq. ft.
Total Living Area:		**1,670 sq. ft.**
Daylight basement		1,600 sq. ft.
Garage		427 sq. ft.
Storage		63 sq. ft.
Exterior Wall Framing:		2x4

Foundation Options:
Daylight basement
Crawlspace
Slab
(All plans can be built with your choice of foundation and framing. A generic conversion diagram is available. See order form.)

BLUEPRINT PRICE CODE:	**B**

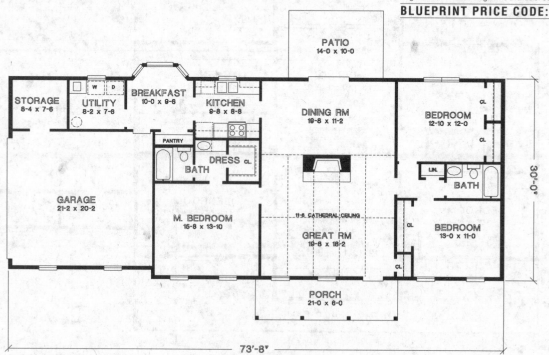

MAIN FLOOR

Plan C-8460

Plan copyright held by home designer/architect

PRICES AND DETAILS
ON PAGES 12-15

Beach Bum

- There's no way you'll feel like a fish out of water in this quaint coastal cottage. With plenty of porch space and an outdoor shower for washing away sea salt, this vacation home is a perfect fit for any beach bum.
- Head up the stairs to the front entrance and step into the bright dining room. The nearby island kitchen easily serves up fresh lobster dripping with butter or a creamy chowder on chilly nights.
- The two-story living room hosts family game nights or quiet evenings by the

fireplace. You'll want to step out to the rear porch for stargazing or to catch an ocean breeze.

- Two main-floor bedrooms share a hall bath and lie conveniently close to the laundry room.
- With front-facing windows, a huge walk-in closet and a private bath with an oversized shower and a dual-sink vanity, the master suite monopolizes the upper floor.
- The lower floor nicely houses plenty of garage space as well as convenient storage for bikes, fishing tackle and beach gear.

Plan SDC-002-B

Bedrooms: 3	Baths: 2

Living Area:	
Upper floor	402 sq. ft.
Main floor	1,260 sq. ft.

Total Living Area:	**1,662 sq. ft.**
Garage and storage	1,128 sq. ft.
Mechanical and shower	100 sq. ft.

Exterior Wall Framing:	2x4

Foundation Options:

Pole
(All plans can be built with your choice of foundation and framing. A generic conversion diagram is available. See order form.)

BLUEPRINT PRICE CODE: **B**

SENSIBLE HOMES

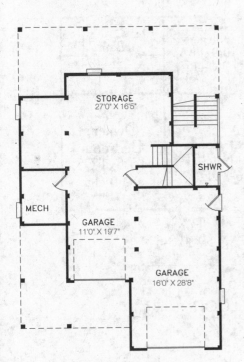

LOWER FLOOR

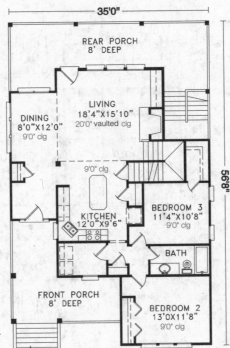

MAIN FLOOR

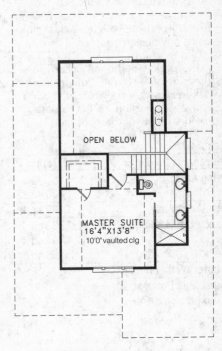

UPPER FLOOR

ORDER BLUEPRINTS ANYTIME!
CALL TOLL-FREE 1-800-820-1296

Plan SDC-002-B
Plan copyright held by home designer/architect

PRICES AND DETAILS
ON PAGES 12-15

167

Take It Outside

- Take a breather on this country-style home's expansive front porch, or relax with loved ones out on the wide-open backyard patio.
- Opening directly from the front porch, the spacious Great Room showcases a soaring ceiling and built-in bookcases that flank an inviting fireplace.
- The kitchen's angled snack bar conveniently serves both the Great Room and the dining room, which offers access to the carport and the back patio. The nearby walk-in pantry and laundry facilities ease household duties.
- The secluded owner's suite boasts a spacious sleeping area and two walk-in closets. Its private bath has a dual-sink vanity, a wide garden tub and a separate shower.
- Two secondary bedrooms occupy the other side of the home. Both feature walk-in closets and share a full bath.
- Storage space adjoining the carport provides plenty of room for tools.

Plan J-9720

Bedrooms: 3	Baths: 2
Living Area:	
Main floor	1,680 sq. ft.
Total Living Area:	**1,680 sq. ft.**
Standard basement	1,680 sq. ft.
Carport	484 sq. ft.
Storage	156 sq. ft.
Exterior Wall Framing:	2x4

Foundation Options:

Standard basement
Crawlspace
Slab

(All plans can be built with your choice of foundation and framing. A generic conversion diagram is available. See order form.)

BLUEPRINT PRICE CODE:	B

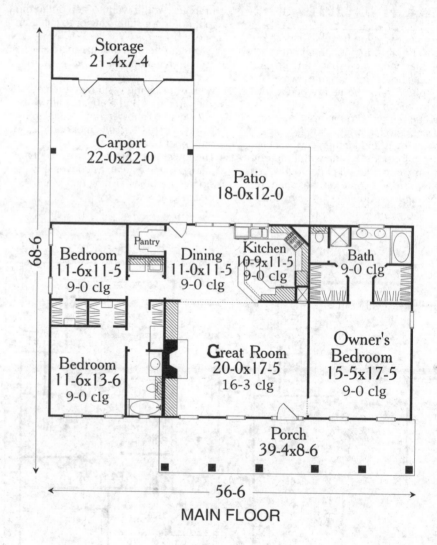

MAIN FLOOR

ORDER BLUEPRINTS ANYTIME!
CALL TOLL-FREE 1-800-820-1296

Plan J-9720
Plan copyright held by home designer/architect

PRICES AND DETAILS
ON PAGES 12-15

Porch Offers Three Entries

- Showy window treatments, stately columns and three sets of French doors give this Plantation-style home an inviting exterior.
- High ceilings in the living room, dining room and kitchen add volume to the economically-sized home.
- A corner fireplace and a view to the back porch are found in the living room. The porch is accessed from a door in the dining room.
- The adjoining kitchen features an angled snack bar that easily serves the dining room and the casual eating area.
- The secluded master suite offers a cathedral ceiling, a walk-in closet and a luxurious private bath with a spa tub and a separate shower.
- Across the home, two additional bedrooms share a second full bath.

Plan E-1602

Bedrooms: 3	Baths: 2
Living Area:	
Main floor	1,672 sq. ft.
Total Living Area:	**1,672 sq. ft.**
Standard basement	1,672 sq. ft.
Garage	484 sq. ft.
Storage	96 sq. ft.
Exterior Wall Framing:	2x6

Foundation Options:

Standard basement

Crawlspace

Slab

(All plans can be built with your choice of foundation and framing. A generic conversion diagram is available. See order form.)

BLUEPRINT PRICE CODE: B

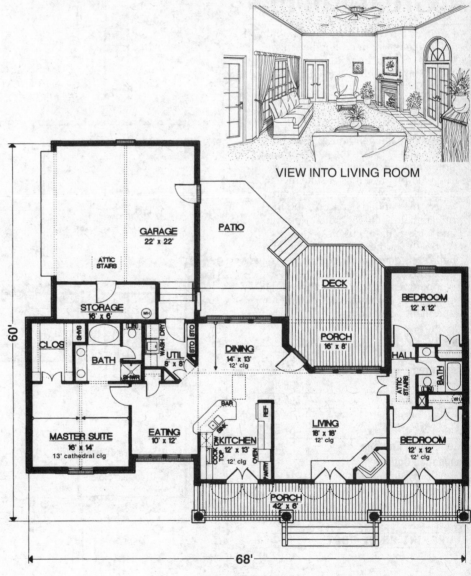

VIEW INTO LIVING ROOM

MAIN FLOOR

ORDER BLUEPRINTS ANYTIME!
CALL TOLL-FREE 1-800-820-1296

Plan E-1602
Plan copyright held by home designer/architect

PRICES AND DETAILS
ON PAGES 12-15

169

A Great Room

- Fanlights top two tall windows and the sidelighted front door, flooding this home's central Great Room with natural light. Built-in shelves flank a fireplace on one side of the room.
- Columns and a graceful arch introduce the dining room, where French doors open out to a patio. The adjoining galley-style kitchen houses a sizable pantry and accesses the garage, making unloading groceries a snap.
- The well-planned master suite reveals amenities galore. A bayed sitting area graces the vaulted bedroom, and the private bath includes a dual-sink vanity and wide walk-in closet.
- Across the home, two additional bedrooms offer handy built-in desks and generous closet space. They share a compartmentalized hall bath, and the entire wing enjoys privacy behind an optional pocket door.

Plan UD-142-C

Bedrooms: 3	Baths: 2½
Living Area:	
Main floor	1,698 sq. ft.
Total Living Area:	**1,698 sq. ft.**
Standard basement	1,698 sq. ft.
Garage	462 sq. ft.
Exterior Wall Framing:	2x4

Foundation Options:

Standard basement
Crawlspace
Slab

(All plans can be built with your choice of foundation and framing. A generic conversion diagram is available. See order form.)

BLUEPRINT PRICE CODE: **B**

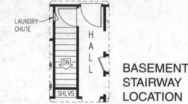

BASEMENT STAIRWAY LOCATION

MAIN FLOOR

Plan UD-142-C
Plan copyright held by home designer/architect

PRICES AND DETAILS
ON PAGES 12-15

Circular Dining Room Featured

- An attractive stone facade, innovative architectural features and a functional, light-filled floor plan are the hallmarks of this attractive design.
- Guests are welcomed in the skylighted gallery, which boasts a sloped ceiling. The living room features a stone fireplace and opens to the circular dining room.
- The dining room is highlighted by a curved wall of windows and a domed ceiling, making an expansive space for entertaining.
- The open kitchen is set up for efficient operation and adjoins the sunny dinette and the cozy family room.
- The bedrooms are zoned to the left, with the master suite including a private bath, a large walk-in closet and access to an outdoor terrace. The additional bedrooms share another full bath.

Plan K-663-N

Bedrooms: 3	Baths: 2
Living Area:	
Main floor	1,682 sq. ft.
Total Living Area:	**1,682 sq. ft.**
Standard basement	1,645 sq. ft.
Garage	453 sq. ft.
Exterior Wall Framing:	2x4 or 2x6

Foundation Options:

Standard basement

Slab

(All plans can be built with your choice of foundation and framing. A generic conversion diagram is available. See order form.)

BLUEPRINT PRICE CODE: B

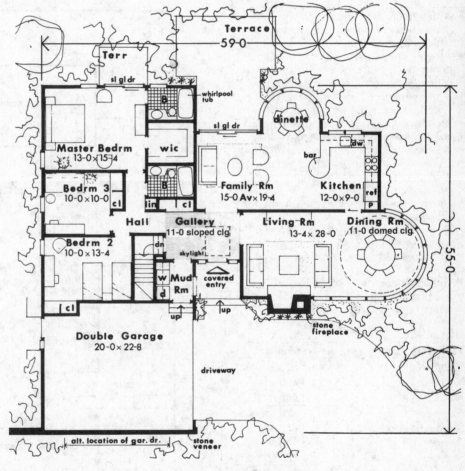

MAIN FLOOR

ORDER BLUEPRINTS ANYTIME!
CALL TOLL-FREE 1-800-820-1296

Plan K-663-N

Plan copyright held by home designer/architect

PRICES AND DETAILS
ON PAGES 12-15

171

Room to Grow

- With a future area upstairs, this home offers plenty of room for your family to grow in leaps and bounds.
- A lovely front porch leads into the Great Room, which features a cathedral ceiling, an entertainment center and a blazing fireplace. This will surely be a favorite room in the wintertime, when you can pop some popcorn, feed the fire and snuggle in to watch movies.
- The well-designed kitchen offers a corner sink, a roomy pantry closet and a dining area that flows into a gorgeous sun room.
- The owner's bedroom boasts a sunny sitting area, while the private bath enjoys two closets, a garden tub and a separate shower.
- Two more bedrooms, each with ample closet space, share a full hall bath.
- The upper-floor future area can be finished as desired. The possibilities are limited only by your imagination.

Plan J-9606

Bedrooms: 3+	Baths: 2
Living Area:	
Main floor	1,688 sq. ft.
Total Living Area:	**1,688 sq. ft.**
Future upper floor	816 sq. ft.
Standard basement	1,688 sq. ft.
Garage	443 sq. ft.
Storage	55 sq. ft.
Exterior Wall Framing:	2x4

Foundation Options:

Standard basement

Crawlspace

Slab

(All plans can be built with your choice of foundation and framing. A generic conversion diagram is available. See order form.)

BLUEPRINT PRICE CODE: **B**

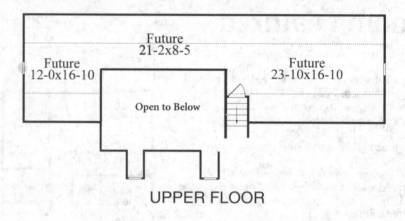

UPPER FLOOR

Future
21-2x8-5

Future
12-0x16-10

Future
23-10x16-10

Open to Below

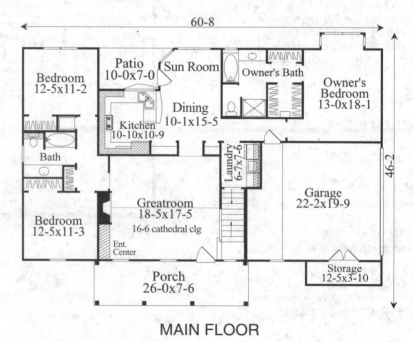

MAIN FLOOR

60-8

46-2

Bedroom
12-5x11-2

Patio
10-0x7-0

Sun Room

Owner's Bath

Owner's Bedroom
13-0x18-1

Dining
10-1x15-5

Kitchen
10-10x10-9

Bath

Laundry
6-7x7-6

Garage
22-2x19-9

Bedroom
12-5x11-3

Greatroom
18-5x17-5

16-6 cathedral clg

Ent. Center

Storage
12-5x3-10

Porch
26-0x7-6

ORDER BLUEPRINTS ANYTIME!
CALL TOLL-FREE 1-800-820-1296

Plan J-9606

Plan copyright held by home designer/architect

PRICES AND DETAILS
ON PAGES 12-15

Love at First Sight

- Who could resist this home's towering chimney, endearing boxed-out sitting area and intriguing side entry nestled into the left elevation? It's bound to be love at first sight.
- The foyer draws you into one large, cheerful expanse of living space. Extending from the sitting area and the corner fireplace at the front to the French door opening off the dining room at the back of the home, this generous space is perfect for formal and family gatherings alike.
- A convenient serving counter and an efficient design highlight the kitchen. Additional features include a pantry and a corner sink.
- An angled staircase, accented by a plant ledge, leads to the upper-floor sleeping quarters.
- The jewel of the master suite, the private bath includes a garden tub, a separate shower and a dual-sink vanity.
- Ample closet space and a shared hall bath serve the secondary bedrooms.

Plan L-692-PJA

Bedrooms: 3	Baths: 2½
Living Area:	
Upper floor	845 sq. ft.
Main floor	845 sq. ft.
Total Living Area:	**1,690 sq. ft.**
Garage	253 sq. ft.
Exterior Wall Framing:	2x4

Foundation Options:

Slab
(All plans can be built with your choice of foundation and framing. A generic conversion diagram is available. See order form.)

BLUEPRINT PRICE CODE:	**B**

SENSIBLE HOMES

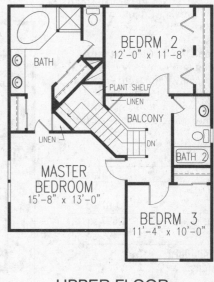

MAIN FLOOR

UPPER FLOOR

ORDER BLUEPRINTS ANYTIME!
CALL TOLL-FREE 1-800-820-1296

Plan L-692-PJA
Plan copyright held by home designer/architect

PRICES AND DETAILS
ON PAGES 12-15

173

Nostalgic Appeal

- Cedar shakes, rugged stone and a columned front porch give this home's facade a nostalgic appeal.
- Opening from the foyer, the spacious Great Room spotlights a vaulted ceiling, an expansive wall of windows and a built-in entertainment center. A cozy fireplace becomes the focal point of family activity.
- The adjacent island kitchen keeps the family cook close to the action. An angled snack bar serves the Great Room and the sunny breakfast nook, which offers access to a covered patio through French doors.
- Two suites flank the home's common areas, allowing family members and guests their privacy. One suite enjoys a private compartmentalized bath.
- A full hall bath with a dual-sink vanity serves the other suite, as well as a third bedroom.

Plan S-52099

Bedrooms: 3	Baths: 2
Living Area:	
Main floor	1,697 sq. ft.
Total Living Area:	**1,697 sq. ft.**
Garage	495 sq. ft.
Exterior Wall Framing:	2x6

Foundation Options:

Crawlspace

(All plans can be built with your choice of foundation and framing. A generic conversion diagram is available. See order form.)

BLUEPRINT PRICE CODE: **B**

VIEW INTO GREAT ROOM

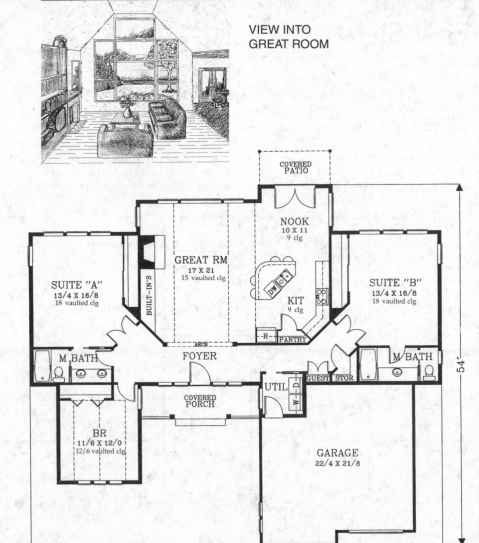

MAIN FLOOR

Plan S-52099

Plan copyright held by home designer/architect

PRICES AND DETAILS
ON PAGES 12-15

Captivating Showpiece

- This design is sure to be the showpiece of the neighborhood, with its captivating blend of traditional and contemporary features.
- The angled front porch creates an eye-catching look. Inside, the foyer, the dining room and the Great Room are expanded by tray ceilings and separated by columns.
- The dining room features a spectacular arched window, while the spacious Great Room hosts a fireplace framed by windows overlooking the rear terrace.
- The glass-filled breakfast room is given added impact by a tray ceiling. The adjoining kitchen offers an expansive island counter with an eating bar and a cooktop.
- A wonderful TV room or home office views out to the front porch.
- The master suite is highlighted by a tray ceiling and a sunny sitting area with a large picture window topped by an arched transom.

Plan AX-92322

Bedrooms: 3+	Baths: 2
Living Area:	
Main floor	1,699 sq. ft.
Total Living Area:	**1,699 sq. ft.**
Standard basement	1,740 sq. ft.
Garage/storage/utility room	480 sq. ft.
Exterior Wall Framing:	2x4

Foundation Options:

Standard basement

Crawlspace

Slab

(All plans can be built with your choice of foundation and framing. A generic conversion diagram is available. See order form.)

BLUEPRINT PRICE CODE: B

MAIN FLOOR

49'-10" OVERALL

60'-6" OVERALL

- TERRACE
- FIREPLACE
- MSTR BATH
- MSTR BEDRM 15'-0" x 15'-6" 9'-10" tray clg
- BRKFST RM 13'-6" x 10'-6" 9'-4" tray clg
- GREAT RM 13'-0" x 20'-0" 9'-4" tray clg
- WICL
- CL
- BEDRM # 2 11'-0" x 10'-0"
- KITCH'N 12'-0" x 11'-0"
- BATH #2
- CL
- S
- DW
- REF
- P
- FOYER 9'-4" clg
- DINING RM 12'-0" x 10'-0" 9'-4" tray clg
- W D
- MUD RM
- CL
- BEDRM #3 11'-0" x 10'-0"
- T.V. RM/ OFFICE 10'-0" x 12'-0"
- UTIL.
- STOR.
- UP
- OPT. BSMT. ENTRY
- PORCH UP
- TWO CAR GARAGE 19'-4" x 20'-0"

ORDER BLUEPRINTS ANYTIME!
CALL TOLL-FREE 1-800-820-1296

Plan AX-92322

Plan copyright held by home designer/architect

PRICES AND DETAILS ON PAGES 12-15

175

Surrounded by Ease and Light

- For your great escapes, why not escape conventionality altogether, and discover an entirely new kind of living? This octagonal design highlights an easy-living floor plan with clerestory windows in its layered roof.
- Kitchen, dining, and living areas address one another for flow and simplicity.

- Each bedroom enjoys access to a bath and a different view to the outdoors.
- The kitchen lies near a laundry room, plus pantry space, for utility efficiency.
- The living room's circular configuration is instantly cozy. A wide deck overlook gives it focus in the daytime; a huge fireplace gives it ambience at night.
- Order this plan with a basement, and double the size of your living area; customize the space as a relaxing recreation room, using a second fireplace as your anchor.

Plans H-821-1 & -1A	
Bedrooms: 3	**Baths:** 2½
Living Area:	
Main floor	1,699 sq. ft.
Total Living Area:	**1,699 sq. ft.**
Daylight basement	1,699 sq. ft.
Exterior Wall Framing:	2x4
Foundation Options:	**Plan #**
Daylight basement	H-821-1
Crawlspace	H-821-1A

(All plans can be built with your choice of foundation and framing. A generic conversion diagram is available. See order form.)

BLUEPRINT PRICE CODE: B

MAIN FLOOR

STAIRWAY AREA IN CRAWLSPACE VERSION

ORDER BLUEPRINTS ANYTIME!
CALL TOLL-FREE 1-800-820-1296

Plans H-821-1 & -1A
Plan copyright held by home designer/architect

PRICES AND DETAILS
ON PAGES 12-15

Suzanne Carmichael

Instant Impact

- Bold rooflines, interesting angles and unusual window treatments give this stylish home lots of impact.
- Inside, high ceilings and an open floor plan maximize the home's square footage. At only 28 feet wide, the home also is ideal for a narrow lot.
- A covered deck leads to the main entry, which features a sidelighted door, angled glass walls and a view of the striking open staircase.
- The Great Room is stunning, with its vaulted ceiling, energy-efficient woodstove and access to a large deck.
- A flat ceiling distinguishes the dining area, which shares an angled snack bar/cooktop with the step-saving kitchen. A laundry/mudroom is nearby.
- Upstairs, the master suite offers a sloped ceiling and a clerestory window. A walk-through closet leads to the private bath, which is enhanced by a skylighted, sloped ceiling.
- Another full bath and plenty of storage serve the other bedrooms, one of which has a sloped ceiling and a dual closet.

Plans H-1427-3A & -3B

Bedrooms: 3	Baths: 2½
Living Area:	
Upper floor	880 sq. ft.
Main floor	810 sq. ft.
Total Living Area:	**1,690 sq. ft.**
Daylight basement	810 sq. ft.
Garage	409 sq. ft.
Exterior Wall Framing:	2×4
Foundation Options:	**Plan #**
Daylight basement	H-1427-3B
Crawlspace	H-1427-3A

(All plans can be built with your choice of foundation and framing. A generic conversion diagram is available. See order form.)

BLUEPRINT PRICE CODE:	B

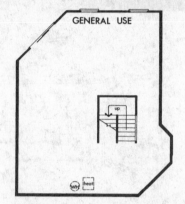

DAYLIGHT BASEMENT

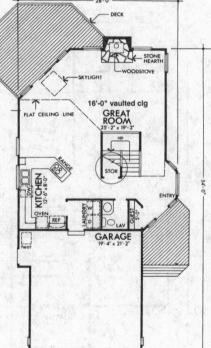

MAIN FLOOR

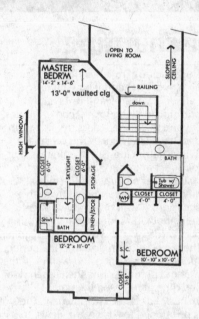

UPPER FLOOR

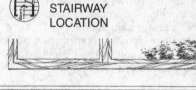

BASEMENT STAIRWAY LOCATION

VIEW INTO GREAT ROOM

ORDER BLUEPRINTS ANYTIME!
CALL TOLL-FREE 1-800-820-1296

Plans H-1427-3A & -3B
Plan copyright held by home designer/architect

PRICES AND DETAILS
ON PAGES 12-15

177

Enchanting!

- This gracious French-style home is the picture of enchantment, with its striking Palladian window and its beautiful brick facade with lovely corner quoins.
- Beyond the leaded-glass front door, the open entry introduces the versatile living room. Guests will enjoy visiting for hours in front of the crackling fire!
- Visible over a half-wall, the formal dining room is worthy of any festive occasion. A wall of windows offers delightful views to a porch and your backyard's award-winning landscaping.
- The bayed morning room is the perfect spot for orange juice and waffles. If the weather permits, open the French door and dine alfresco on the porch!
- A snack bar frames the kitchen. The sink is positioned for backyard views, to brighten those daily chores.
- The two-car garage is ideally located for easy unloading of groceries.
- Across the home, the master suite is a restful haven. Soak away your cares in the fabulous garden tub!
- Two secondary bedrooms, a nice hall bath and a central laundry room round out this enchanting plan.

Plan L-709-FA

Bedrooms: 3	Baths: 2
Living Area:	
Main floor	1,707 sq. ft.
Total Living Area:	**1,707 sq. ft.**
Garage	572 sq. ft.
Exterior Wall Framing:	2x4

Foundation Options:

Slab

(All plans can be built with your choice of foundation and framing. A generic conversion diagram is available. See order form.)

BLUEPRINT PRICE CODE: **B**

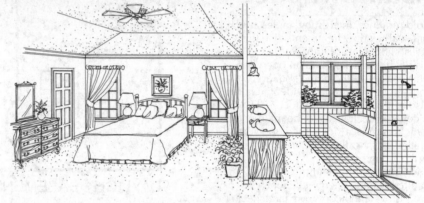

VIEW INTO MASTER SUITE

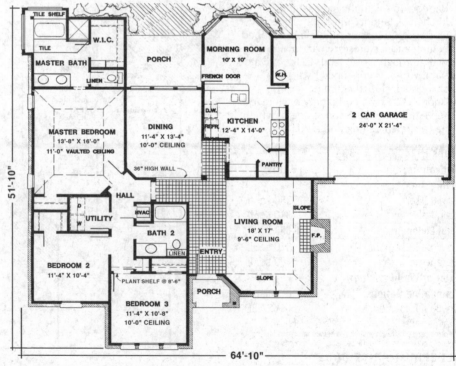

MAIN FLOOR

ORDER BLUEPRINTS ANYTIME!
CALL TOLL-FREE 1-800-820-1296

Plan L-709-FA

Plan copyright held by home designer/architect

PRICES AND DETAILS
ON PAGES 12-15

Perfect Repose

- This perfectly planned home is well suited to serve as the haven your family retreats to for repose and relaxation.
- The front porch includes just the right amount of space for your favorite two rocking chairs and a side table.
- Inside, the foyer flows into the generous Great Room, which will serve as home base for family gatherings. A fireplace flanked by a media center turns this room into a home theater.
- Nearby, sunlight pours into the versatile dining room. Along one wall, a beautiful built-in cabinet holds linens, china and other fine collectibles.
- For easy serving, the kitchen's snack bar extends to a peninsula counter. Serve casual meals on the back porch.
- A tray ceiling and a bay window in the master suite help to create a stylish oasis. A dressing area with a vanity table for morning preening leads to the master bath, where a skylight and a lofty vaulted ceiling brighten the room.

Plan AX-95347

Bedrooms: 3	Baths: 2½
Living Area:	
Main floor	1,709 sq. ft.
Total Living Area:	**1,709 sq. ft.**
Standard basement	1,709 sq. ft.
Garage and storage	448 sq. ft.
Enclosed storage	12 sq. ft.
Utility room	13 sq. ft.
Exterior Wall Framing:	2x4
Foundation Options:	
Standard basement	
Crawlspace	
Slab	

(All plans can be built with your choice of foundation and framing. A generic conversion diagram is available. See order form.)

BLUEPRINT PRICE CODE:	B

REAR VIEW

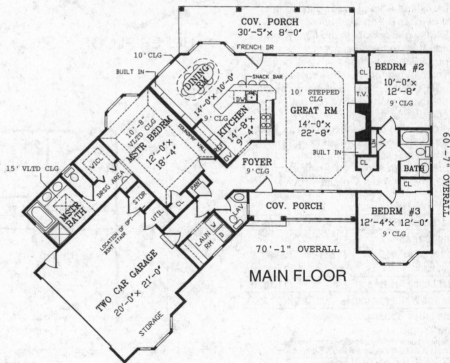

MAIN FLOOR

ORDER BLUEPRINTS ANYTIME!
CALL TOLL-FREE 1-800-820-1296

Plan AX-95347
Plan copyright held by home designer/architect

PRICES AND DETAILS
ON PAGES 12-15

179

Panoramic Prow View

- This glass-filled prow gable design is almost as spectacular as the panoramic view from inside.
- French doors open from the front deck into the dining room. A stunning window wall illuminates the adjoining living room, which flaunts a soaring cathedral ceiling.
- The open, corner kitchen is perfectly angled to service the dining room and the family room, while offering views of the front and rear decks. Its snack bar/island is ideal for displaying hors d'oeuvres or serving buffet-style meals.
- Sliding glass doors in the family room add light to this fun space, while providing an escape to a deck out back.
- The handy utility/laundry room also opens to the deck. Two bedrooms off the living room share a full bath, completing the main floor.
- A dramatic, open-railed stairway leads up to the secluded master bedroom, which boasts a dressing room and a private bath with a dual-sink vanity, a roomy tub and a separate shower.

Plan NW-196

Bedrooms: 3	Baths: 2
Living Area:	
Upper floor	394 sq. ft.
Main floor	1,317 sq. ft.
Total Living Area:	**1,711 sq. ft.**
Exterior Wall Framing:	2x6

Foundation Options:

Crawlspace

(All plans can be built with your choice of foundation and framing. A generic conversion diagram is available. See order form.)

BLUEPRINT PRICE CODE: B

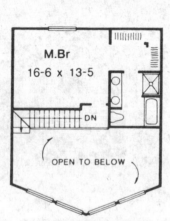

UPPER FLOOR

M.Br 16-6 x 13-5

OPEN TO BELOW

DN

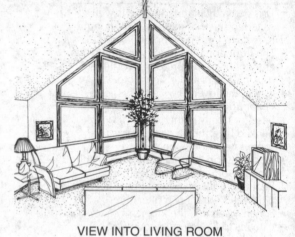

VIEW INTO LIVING ROOM

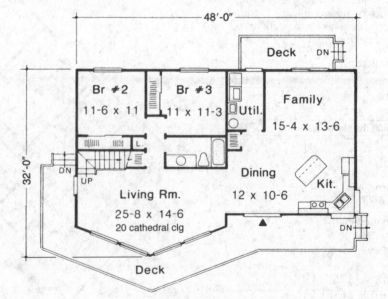

MAIN FLOOR

48'-0"

32'-0"

Deck DN

Br #2 11-6 x 11

Br #3 11 x 11-3

Util.

Family 15-4 x 13-6

DN UP

L.

Living Rm. 25-8 x 14-6 20 cathedral clg

Dining 12 x 10-6

Kit.

DN

Deck

Plan NW-196

Plan copyright held by home designer/architect

PRICES AND DETAILS ON PAGES 12-15

Tranquil Treasure

- Multiple decks, a stone fireplace and two lofts make this vacation home a real treasure. Spend tranquil evenings on the screened porch or soak up the rays on sunny afternoons on your choice of decks.
- As you enter the foyer, the Grand Room takes your breath away. With a soaring ceiling, sparkling windows and access to both the front screened porch and the rear decks, this room reigns supreme.

- Look up to the kitchen and dining areas, raised to accommodate panoramic views. The well-appointed kitchen is ready for a casual picnic on the deck or an indoor dinner party.
- The master suite includes a large walk-in closet, private bath and deck access. A charming loft, reached via a ship's ladder, would make a lovely library or computer room.
- Upstairs, a unique loft suite boasts a private deck, a full bath and a walk-in closet. It overlooks the Grand Room through two windows, which can be opened to take advantage of the fireplace's warmth.

Plan EOF-100

Bedrooms: 2	Baths: 2½
Living Area:	
Upper floor	460 sq. ft.
Main floor	1,283 sq. ft.
Total Living Area:	**1,743 sq. ft.**
Partial basement	352 sq. ft.
Detached one-car garage	350 sq. ft.
Detached two-car garage	525 sq. ft.
Exterior Wall Framing:	2x6

Foundation Options:

Partial basement

(All plans can be built with your choice of foundation and framing. A generic conversion diagram is available. See order form.)

BLUEPRINT PRICE CODE: B

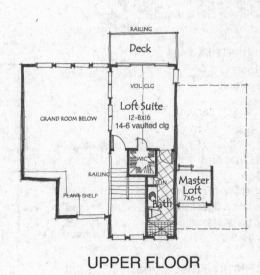

MAIN FLOOR

UPPER FLOOR

ORDER BLUEPRINTS ANYTIME!
CALL TOLL-FREE 1-800-820-1296

Plan EOF-100
Plan copyright held by home designer/architect

PRICES AND DETAILS
ON PAGES 12-15   181

REAR VIEW

FRONT VIEW

Bright Ideas!

- Four clerestory windows, a boxed-out window and wing walls sheltering the entry porch give this home definition.
- Inside, an open room arrangement coupled with vaulted ceilings, abundant windows and a sensational sun room make this home a definite bright spot.
- The living room features a vaulted ceiling, a warm woodstove and a glass-filled wall that offers views into the sun room. A patio door in the sun room opens to a large backyard deck.
- The adjoining dining room flows into the kitchen, which offers a versatile snack bar. A handy laundry room is just steps away, near the garage.
- Upstairs, the intimate bedroom suite includes a cathedral ceiling, a view to the living room, a walk-in closet and a private bath.
- The optional daylight basement boasts a spacious recreation room with a second woodstove, plus a fourth bedroom and a third bath. A shaded patio occupies the area under the deck.

Plans H-877-5A & -5B

Bedrooms: 3+	Baths: 2–3
Living Area:	
Upper floor	382 sq. ft.
Main floor	1,200 sq. ft.
Sun room	162 sq. ft.
Daylight basement	1,200 sq. ft.
Total Living Area:	**1,744/2,944 sq. ft.**
Garage	457 sq. ft.
Exterior Wall Framing:	2x6
Foundation Options:	**Plan #**
Daylight basement	H-877-5B
Crawlspace	H-877-5A

(All plans can be built with your choice of foundation and framing. A generic conversion diagram is available. See order form.)

BLUEPRINT PRICE CODE:	**B/D**

UPPER FLOOR

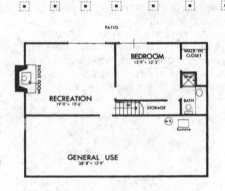

DAYLIGHT BASEMENT

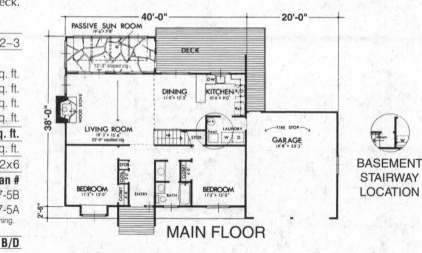

MAIN FLOOR

BASEMENT STAIRWAY LOCATION

ORDER BLUEPRINTS ANYTIME!
CALL TOLL-FREE 1-800-820-1296

Plans H-877-5A & -5B

Plan copyright held by home designer/architect

PRICES AND DETAILS ON PAGES 12-15

Mark Englund/Homestore™ Plans and Publications

Designed for Livability

- As you enter this excitingly spacious, traditional home, you see through the extensive windows to the backyard.
- This four-bedroom home was designed for the livability of the maturing family with the separation of the master suite.
- The formal dining room expands spatially to the living room while being set off by a decorative column and plant shelves.
- The bay that creates the morning room and the sitting area for the master suite also adds excitement to this plan, both inside and out.
- The master bath offers an exciting oval tub under glass and a separate shower, as well as a spacious walk-in closet and a dressing area.

Plan DD-1696

Bedrooms: 4	**Baths:** 2

Living Area:	
Main floor	1,748 sq. ft.
Total Living Area:	**1,748 sq. ft.**
Standard basement	1,748 sq. ft.
Garage	393 sq. ft.
Exterior Wall Framing:	2x4

Foundation Options:

Standard basement

Crawlspace

Slab

(All plans can be built with your choice of foundation and framing. A generic conversion diagram is available. See order form.)

BLUEPRINT PRICE CODE:	B

REAR VIEW

MAIN FLOOR

VIEW INTO LIVING ROOM, DINING ROOM AND KITCHEN

JUST-RIGHT HOMES

ORDER BLUEPRINTS ANYTIME!
CALL TOLL-FREE 1-800-820-1296

Plan DD-1696
Plan copyright held by home designer/architect

PRICES AND DETAILS
ON PAGES 12-15

183

Sun-Splashed One-Story

- This unique angled design offers spectacular backyard views, a delightful sun room and two enticing terraces.
- The reception hall opens to the huge combination living and dining area, which is enhanced by a high ceiling. A stone fireplace and walls of glass add to the expansive look and the inviting atmosphere.

- The adjoining family room, kitchen and nook are just as appealing. The family room features a built-in entertainment center and sliding glass doors that access the energy-saving sun room. The comfortable kitchen has a handy snack counter facing the sunny dinette. Utility areas are conveniently nearby.
- The master suite boasts a sloped ceiling, a private terrace, a large walk-in closet and a personal bath with a whirlpool tub. The two remaining bedrooms are near a hall bath.

Plan AHP-9330	
Bedrooms: 3	**Baths:** 2
Living Area:	
Main floor	1,626 sq. ft.
Sun room	146 sq. ft.
Total Living Area:	**1,772 sq. ft.**
Standard basement	1,542 sq. ft.
Garage	427 sq. ft.
Exterior Wall Framing:	2x4 or 2x6
Foundation Options:	
Standard basement	
Crawlspace	
Slab	

(All plans can be built with your choice of foundation and framing. A generic conversion diagram is available. See order form.)

BLUEPRINT PRICE CODE: B

VIEW INTO LIVING AND DINING ROOMS

MAIN FLOOR

184   *ORDER BLUEPRINTS ANYTIME!*
CALL TOLL-FREE 1-800-820-1296

Plan AHP-9330
Plan copyright held by home designer/architect

PRICES AND DETAILS
ON PAGES 12-15

JUST-RIGHT HOMES

Mark Englund/Homestore™ Plans and Publications

Free-Flowing Floor Plan

- A fluid floor plan with open indoor/outdoor living spaces characterizes this exciting luxury home.
- The stylish columned porch opens to a spacious living room and dining room expanse that overlooks the outdoor spaces. The breathtaking view also includes a dramatic corner fireplace.
- The dining area opens to a bright kitchen with an angled eating bar. The overall spaciousness of the living areas is increased with raised ceilings.
- A sunny, informal eating area adjoins the kitchen, and an angled set of doors opens to a convenient main-floor laundry room near the garage entrance.
- The vaulted master bedroom has a walk-in closet and a sumptuous bath with an oval tub.
- A separate wing houses two additional bedrooms and another full bath.
- Attic space is accessible from stairs in the garage and in the bedroom wing.

VIEW INTO LIVING ROOM

REAR VIEW

Plan E-1710

Bedrooms: 3	Baths: 2
Living Area:	
Main floor	1,792 sq. ft.
Total Living Area:	**1,792 sq. ft.**
Standard basement	1,792 sq. ft.
Garage	484 sq. ft.
Storage	96 sq. ft.
Exterior Wall Framing:	2x6

Foundation Options:

Standard basement

Crawlspace

Slab

(All plans can be built with your choice of foundation and framing. A generic conversion diagram is available. See order form.)

BLUEPRINT PRICE CODE:	B

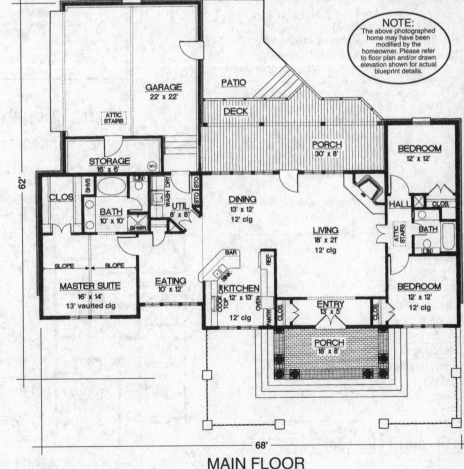

NOTE:
The above photographed home may have been modified by the homeowner. Please refer to floor plan and/or drawn elevation shown for actual blueprint details.

MAIN FLOOR

ORDER BLUEPRINTS ANYTIME!
CALL TOLL-FREE 1-800-820-1296

Plan E-1710

Plan copyright held by home designer/architect

PRICES AND DETAILS
ON PAGES 12-15

185

Fresh Air

- With its nostalgic look and country style, this lovely home brings a breath of fresh air into any neighborhood.
- Past the inviting wraparound porch, the foyer is brightened by an elliptical transom window above the front door.
- The adjoining formal dining room is defined by decorative columns and a stylish stepped ceiling.
- The bright and airy kitchen includes a pantry, a windowed sink and a sunny breakfast area with porch access.
- A stepped ceiling enhances the spacious Great Room, where a fireplace warms the area. Two sets of sliding glass doors open to a back porch.
- The lush master bedroom and a bayed sitting area boast high ceilings. The master bath showcases a circular spa tub embraced by a glass-block wall.
- Two more bedrooms share a second bath. The protruding bedroom includes a dramatic vaulted ceiling.
- Additional living space can be made available by finishing the upper floor.

Plan AX-93308

Bedrooms: 3+	Baths: 2
Living Area:	
Main floor	1,793 sq. ft.
Total Living Area:	**1,793 sq. ft.**
Future upper floor	779 sq. ft.
Standard basement	1,793 sq. ft.
Garage and utility	471 sq. ft.
Exterior Wall Framing:	2x4

Foundation Options:

Standard basement
Crawlspace
Slab

(All plans can be built with your choice of foundation and framing. A generic conversion diagram is available. See order form.)

BLUEPRINT PRICE CODE: B

VIEW INTO GREAT ROOM

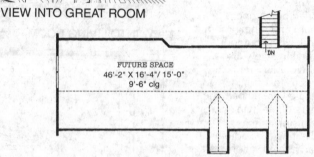

UPPER FLOOR

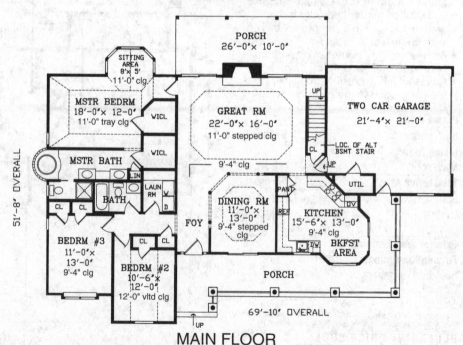

MAIN FLOOR

ORDER BLUEPRINTS ANYTIME!
CALL TOLL-FREE 1-800-820-1296

Plan AX-93308

Plan copyright held by home designer/architect

PRICES AND DETAILS
ON PAGES 12-15

Photos by Mark Englund/Homestore™ Plans and Publications

Masterful Master Suite

- This gorgeous home features front and rear covered porches and a master suite so luxurious it deserves its own wing.
- The expansive entry welcomes visitors into a spacious, skylighted living room, which boasts a handsome fireplace. The adjacent formal dining room overlooks the front porch.
- Designed for efficiency, the kitchen features an angled snack bar, a bayed eating area and views of the porch. An all-purpose utility room is conveniently located off the kitchen.
- The kitchen, eating area, living room and dining room are all heightened by high ceilings.
- The sumptuous and secluded master suite features a tub and a separate shower, a double-sink vanity, a walk-in closet with built-in shelves and a compartmentalized toilet.
- The two secondary bedrooms share a hall bath at the other end of the home. The rear bedroom offers porch access.
- The garage features built-in storage and access to unfinished attic space.

NOTE:
The photographed home may have been modified by the homeowner. Please refer to floor plan and/or drawn elevation shown for actual blueprint details.

VIEW INTO LIVING ROOM

Plan E-1811

Bedrooms: 3	Baths: 2
Living Area:	
Main floor	1,800 sq. ft.
Total Living Area:	**1,800 sq. ft.**
Garage and storage	634 sq. ft.
Exterior Wall Framing:	**2x6**

Foundation Options:

Crawlspace

Slab

(All plans can be built with your choice of foundation and framing. A generic conversion diagram is available. See order form.)

BLUEPRINT PRICE CODE:	**B**

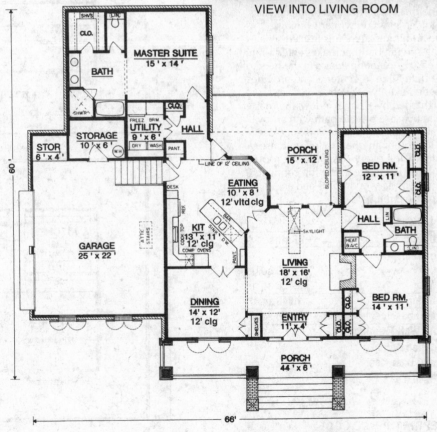

MAIN FLOOR

ORDER BLUEPRINTS ANYTIME!
CALL TOLL-FREE 1-800-820-1296

Plan E-1811

Plan copyright held by home designer/architect

PRICES AND DETAILS
ON PAGES 12-15

187

Rugged Look, Regal Feel

- This home's wraparound porch, stone exterior and metal roof give it the look of a rustic country lodge. Inside, you'll find amenities that treat you like royalty.
- Sunlight streams through a dormer window into the living room, where a vaulted ceiling adds to the space's generous proportions. A fireplace casts a golden glow on winter evenings.
- The adjoining kitchen is fronted by a long serving bar that makes entertaining as easy as pointing guests to the head of the buffet line. A center island provides needed extra work space.
- Brightened by a bay window, the master suite boasts a private bath with an oval soaking tub and a large walk-in closet.
- At the top of an open-railed staircase, a balcony loft overlooks the living room and the dining area. The loft connects two secondary bedrooms and an expansive full bath.

Plan DD-1850

Bedrooms: 3	Baths: 2½
Living Area:	
Upper floor	690 sq. ft.
Main floor	1,156 sq. ft.
Total Living Area:	**1,846 sq. ft.**
Standard basement	1,156 sq. ft.
Exterior Wall Framing:	2x4

Foundation Options:

Standard basement
Crawlspace
Slab

(All plans can be built with your choice of foundation and framing. A generic conversion diagram is available. See order form.)

BLUEPRINT PRICE CODE: **B**

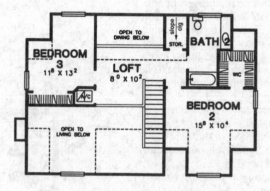

UPPER FLOOR

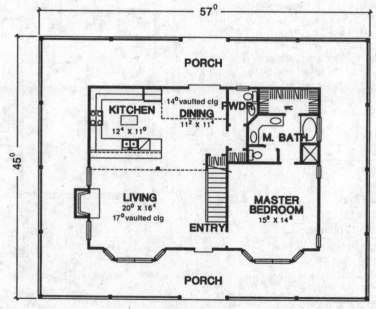

MAIN FLOOR

Plan DD-1850

Plan copyright held by home designer/architect

PRICES AND DETAILS
ON PAGES 12-15

Strength of Character

- The solid, permanent feel of brick and the intelligent, efficient floor plan of this stately one-story home give it an obvious strength of character.
- Guests are welcomed inside by an attractive raised foyer, from which virtually any room can be reached with just a few steps.
- With a high ceiling, a built-in bookcase, a gorgeous fireplace and French doors that lead to the backyard, the centrally located living room is well equipped to serve as a hub of activity.
- Smartly designed and positioned, the galley-style kitchen easily serves the cozy breakfast nook and the formal dining room.
- The beautiful master bedroom provides a nice blend of elegance and seclusion, and features a striking stepped ceiling, a large walk-in closet, a private bath and its own access to the backyard.
- Two additional bedrooms feature walk-in closets and share a full-sized bath.

Plan L-851-A

Bedrooms: 3	Baths: 2
Living Area:	
Main floor	1,849 sq. ft.
Total Living Area:	**1,849 sq. ft.**
Garage	437 sq. ft.
Exterior Wall Framing:	2x4

Foundation Options:

Slab

(All plans can be built with your choice of foundation and framing. A generic conversion diagram is available. See order form.)

BLUEPRINT PRICE CODE: B

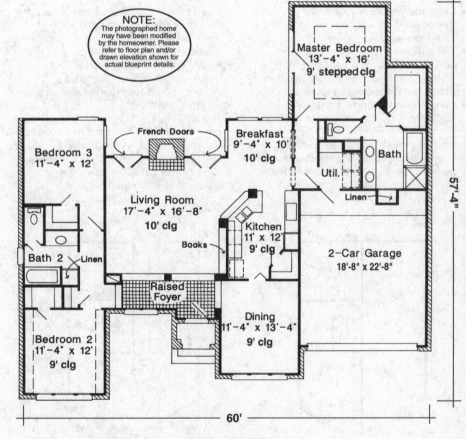

NOTE:
The photographed home may have been modified by the homeowner. Please refer to floor plan and/or drawn elevation shown for actual blueprint details.

Master Bedroom 13'-4" x 16' 9' stepped clg

Bath

Breakfast 9'-4" x 10' 10' clg

Util.

Linen

Bedroom 3 11'-4" x 12'

French Doors

Living Room 17'-4" x 16'-8" 10' clg

Kitchen 11' x 12' 9' clg

Books

2-Car Garage 18'-8" x 22'-8"

Bath 2

Linen

Raised Foyer

Dining 11'-4" x 13'-4" 9' clg

Bedroom 2 11'-4" x 12' 9' clg

57'-4"

60'

MAIN FLOOR

JUST-RIGHT HOMES

Bob Hallinen

Soaring Design

- Dramatic windows soar to the peak of this prowed chalet, offering unlimited views of outdoor scenery.
- The spacious living room flaunts a fabulous fireplace, a vaulted ceiling, a striking window wall and sliding glass doors to a wonderful wraparound deck.
- An oversized window brightens a dining area on the left side of the living room. The sunny, L-shaped kitchen is spacious and easily accessible.
- The secluded main-floor bedroom features two closets, plus convenient access to a full bath, a linen closet, a

good-sized laundry room and the rear entrance.
- A central, open-railed staircase leads to the upper floor, which contains two more bedrooms that have ample closet space and share a full bath.
- A skylighted balcony overlooks the living room below and offers a sweeping outdoor vista through the window wall.
- The optional daylight basement provides another fireplace in a versatile recreation room. The extra-long, tuck-under garage includes plenty of room for hobbies, while the service room offers additional storage space.

Plans H-930-1 & -1A

Bedrooms: 3	Baths: 2
Living Area:	
Upper floor	710 sq. ft.
Main floor	1,210 sq. ft.
Daylight basement	605 sq. ft.
Total Living Area:	**1,920/2,525 sq. ft.**
Tuck-under garage/shop	605 sq. ft.
Exterior Wall Framing:	2x6
Foundation Options:	**Plan #**
Daylight basement	H-930-1
Crawlspace	H-930-1A

(All plans can be built with your choice of foundation and framing. A generic conversion diagram is available. See order form.)

BLUEPRINT PRICE CODE:	**B/D**

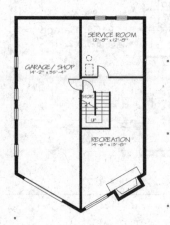

DAYLIGHT BASEMENT

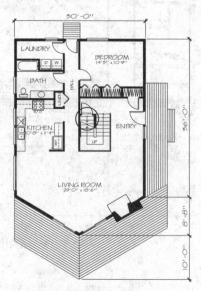

MAIN FLOOR

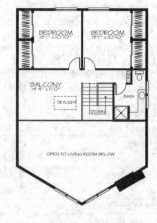

UPPER FLOOR

STAIRWAY AREA IN CRAWLSPACE VERSION

Plans H-930-1 & -1A

Plan copyright held by home designer/architect

PRICES AND DETAILS
ON PAGES 12-15

A Splash of Style

- Eye-catching keystones, arched window arrangements and a varied roofline give this home a refreshing splash of style.
- Inside, the raised entry leads to the dining room and the Great Room. A high, sloped ceiling expands the Great Room, which features a brick fireplace.
- A sunny bay brightens the cheery breakfast nook and the adjacent kitchen. A built-in desk, a pantry, an island workstation and a nearby powder room make the most of this busy area.
- A split staircase that overlooks the Great Room leads to the upper-floor bedrooms.
- A cathedral ceiling, a sunny bay and a plant ledge spice up the master suite. The private bath boasts a whirlpool tub under a sloped ceiling, two vanities and a separate shower.
- Three secondary bedrooms share a hall bath. The front bedroom has a built-in bookcase and a sloped ceiling, while an additional bedroom is topped by a cathedral ceiling.

Plan CC-1990-M

Bedrooms: 4	Baths: 2½
Living Area:	
Upper floor	967 sq. ft.
Main floor	1,023 sq. ft.
Total Living Area:	**1,990 sq. ft.**
Standard basement	1,023 sq. ft.
Garage	685 sq. ft.
Exterior Wall Framing:	2x4

Foundation Options:

Standard basement

(All plans can be built with your choice of foundation and framing. A generic conversion diagram is available. See order form.)

BLUEPRINT PRICE CODE: **B**

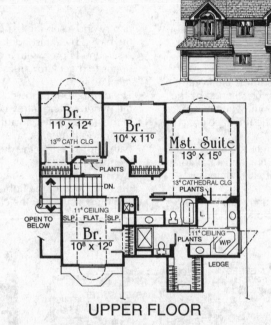

REAR VIEW

UPPER FLOOR

Br.
11⁰ x 12⁴
13¹⁰ CATH. CLG

Br.
10⁴ x 11⁰

Mst. Suite
13⁰ x 15⁰
13⁴ CATHEDRAL CLG
PLANTS

PLANTS

DN.

OPEN TO BELOW

11⁴ CEILING
SLP. FLAT SLP.

Br.
10⁸ x 12⁰

11⁴ CEILING
PLANTS

LEDGE

W/P

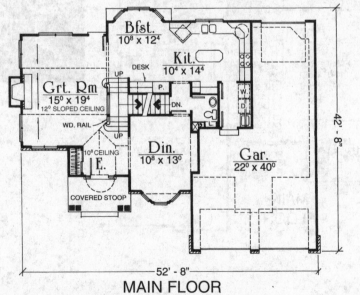

MAIN FLOOR

Bfst.
10⁸ x 12⁴

Kit.
10⁴ x 14⁴

UP   DESK

Grt. Rm
15⁰ x 19⁴
12⁰ SLOPED CEILING

WD. RAIL

UP

10⁸ CEILING

E.

Din.
10⁸ x 13⁰

Gar.
22⁰ x 40⁰

COVERED STOOP

52' - 8"

42' - 8"

ORDER BLUEPRINTS ANYTIME!
CALL TOLL-FREE 1-800-820-1296

Plan CC-1990-M
Plan copyright held by home designer/architect

PRICES AND DETAILS
ON PAGES 12-15

191

Classic Combo

- This snappy home combines classic touches with thoughtful design.
- Eye-catching arches frame the front porch. Inside, you'll be stunned by the expansive family room, where a vaulted ceiling and a majestic fireplace enhance the space.
- Double doors lead into the living room, where a vaulted ceiling and a Palladian window create an ideal spot for entertaining visitors.
- Through a graceful archway, the efficient kitchen includes a handy pantry and a serving bar overlooking the bayed breakfast nook.
- A screened porch with a vaulted ceiling opens to a deck for alfresco meals and relaxation.
- The dining room showcases a pair of tall windows and a tray ceiling.
- In the master suite, a vaulted ceiling, a separate sitting area, a lavish private bath and access to the deck create a wonderful retreat.
- Two more bedrooms share a bath on the other side of the home.
- The blueprints offer the choice of a two- or three-car garage.

Plan APS-1911	
Bedrooms: 3	Baths: 2½
Living Area:	
Main floor	1,992 sq. ft.
Total Living Area:	**1,992 sq. ft.**
Screened porch	192 sq. ft.
Standard basement	1,992 sq. ft.
Garage	649 sq. ft.
Exterior Wall Framing:	2x4

Foundation Options:

Standard basement
Crawlspace
Slab

(All plans can be built with your choice of foundation and framing. A generic conversion diagram is available. See order form.)

BLUEPRINT PRICE CODE: B

MAIN FLOOR

63'-0"

SCREENED PORCH 15'4" x 13'10"
13'-10" clg

DECK 11'0" x 7'6"

MASTER SUITE 21'4" x 15'0" 14'0" clg

SITTING 9' clg

BEDROOM 3 13'0" x 11'0" 9' clg

BRKFST 11'0" x 10'10" 9' clg

KITCHEN 13'8" x 9'6"

FAMILY ROOM 16'0" x 24'1" 13'-10" clg
10' clg

8' HIGH OPENING

PANTRY

LINEN

OPTIONAL STAIRS TO BASEMENT

DINING 11'0" x 12'0" 12' tray clg
9' clg

BEDROOM 2 13'0" x 11'0" 9' clg

LIVING 11'0" x 12'0" 13'-4" clg

PORCH 15'4" x 5'4"

3 CAR GARAGE 21'4" x 29'10"

2 CAR GARAGE OPTION

57'-2"

REAR VIEW

VIEW INTO FAMILY ROOM

Plan APS-1911

Plan copyright held by home designer/architect

PRICES AND DETAILS
ON PAGES 12-15

A Home Run

- The designer hit a home run with this plan. The compact square footage makes the home affordable, while the floor plan includes plenty of open spaces and amenities to please even the most demanding homeowners.
- A sunny transom above the front entry, gorgeous arched window arrangements and decorative keystones add flair to the otherwise modest exterior.
- Inside, the Great Room serves as the home's heart and soul. In this good-sized room, your family will celebrate birthdays, watch favorite movies and enjoy raucous games of Pictionary. Built-in cabinets by the fireplace hold your home entertainment system.
- The cheerful bayed dining room merges with the island kitchen. This convenient layout simplifies the chore of serving even the grandest meals, while a pantry closet nearby maximizes storage space.
- The master bedroom is secluded from the other bedrooms to ensure peace and quiet for the heads of the household. A raised tub under a beautiful window lends a touch of magnificence to the master bath.

Plan KD-1701

Bedrooms: 4	Baths: 2
Living Area:	
Main floor	1,701 sq. ft.
Total Living Area:	**1,701 sq. ft.**
Garage and storage	472 sq. ft.
Exterior Wall Framing:	2x4

Foundation Options:

Slab

(All plans can be built with your choice of foundation and framing. A generic conversion diagram is available. See order form.)

BLUEPRINT PRICE CODE: **B**

VIEW INTO
GREAT ROOM

MAIN FLOOR

ORDER BLUEPRINTS ANYTIME!
CALL TOLL-FREE 1-800-820-1296

Plan KD-1701
Plan copyright held by home designer/architect

PRICES AND DETAILS
ON PAGES 12-15   193

Large, Stylish Spaces

- This stylish brick home greets guests with a beautiful entry court that leads to the recessed front porch.
- Beyond the porch, the bright entry flows into the Great Room, which features a sloped ceiling. This airy space also offers a fireplace, a sunny dining area and sliding glass doors to a backyard patio.
- The kitchen has a walk-in pantry, an open serving counter above the sink and convenient access to the laundry facilities and the garage.
- Isolated from the secondary bedrooms, the master suite boasts a tray ceiling, an oversized walk-in closet and an exquisite bath with two distinct sink areas, a corner garden tub and a separate shower.
- The third bedroom, which features lovely double doors and a front-facing bay window, would also make a perfect home office.

Plan SDG-91188

Bedrooms: 2+	Baths: 2
Living Area:	
Main floor	1,704 sq. ft.
Total Living Area:	**1,704 sq. ft.**
Garage	484 sq. ft.
Exterior Wall Framing:	2x4

Foundation Options:

Slab

(All plans can be built with your choice of foundation and framing. A generic conversion diagram is available. See order form.)

BLUEPRINT PRICE CODE: B

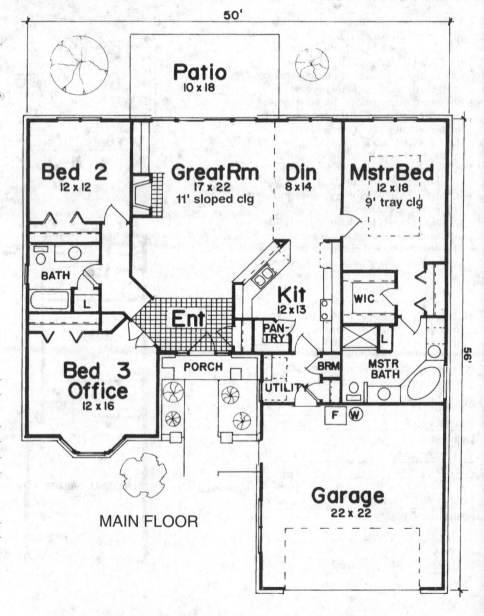

MAIN FLOOR

Plan SDG-91188

Plan copyright held by home designer/architect

PRICES AND DETAILS
ON PAGES 12-15

REAR VIEW

Year-Round Comfort

- Designed for the energy-conscious, this passive-solar home provides year-round comfort with much lower fuel costs.
- The open, airy interior is a delight. In the winter, sunshine penetrates deep into the living spaces. In the summer, wide overhangs shade the interior.
- The central living and dining rooms flow together, creating a bright, open space. Sliding glass doors open to a terrace and an enclosed sun spot.
- In the airy casual space, the kitchen has an eating bar and a sunny breakfast nook. The adjoining family room boasts a woodstove that warms the entire area.
- The master bedroom suite includes a private terrace, a personal bath and a walk-in closet. Two other bedrooms share another full bath.

FRONT VIEW

Plan K-392-T

Bedrooms: 3	Baths: 2½
Living Area:	
Main floor	1,592 sq. ft.
Sun spot	125 sq. ft.
Total Living Area:	**1,717 sq. ft.**
Partial basement	634 sq. ft.
Garage	407 sq. ft.
Exterior Wall Framing:	2x4 or 2x6

Foundation Options:

Partial basement

Slab

(All plans can be built with your choice of foundation and framing. A generic conversion diagram is available. See order form.)

BLUEPRINT PRICE CODE: **B**

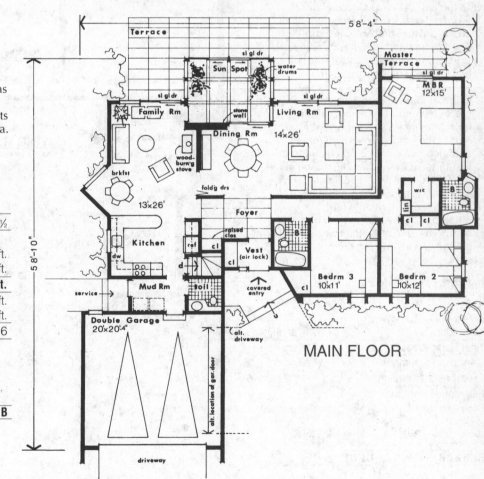

MAIN FLOOR

ORDER BLUEPRINTS ANYTIME!
CALL TOLL-FREE 1-800-820-1296

Plan K-392-T
Plan copyright held by home designer/architect

PRICES AND DETAILS
ON PAGES 12-15

195

French Charm

- The charming exterior of this French home exhibits an ornate assortment of keystones, quoins and arches.
- Inside the home, a high plant ledge adorns the tiled entry, which boasts a dramatic ceiling.
- To the left, the elegant formal dining room extends to the living room, which boasts a warm fireplace, neat built-in bookshelves and functional cabinets to store CDs or family photos. A striking high ceiling soars above both rooms.
- A convenient serving bar links the gourmet kitchen to the sunny bayed breakfast nook. The adjacent utility room includes a handy pantry closet.
- Across the home, a rear foyer offers entrance to a covered porch and to the luxurious master suite. The master suite features a high sloped ceiling, a window seat and a lush garden bath highlighted by a marble tub!
- A hall bath serves the two secondary bedrooms, one of which has a sloped ceiling, a walk-in closet and a built-in desk.

Plan RD-1714

Bedrooms: 3	Baths: 2
Living Area:	
Main floor	1,714 sq. ft.
Total Living Area:	**1,714 sq. ft.**
Garage and storage	470 sq. ft.
Exterior Wall Framing:	2x4

Foundation Options:

Crawlspace
Slab

(All plans can be built with your choice of foundation and framing. A generic conversion diagram is available. See order form.)

BLUEPRINT PRICE CODE:	B

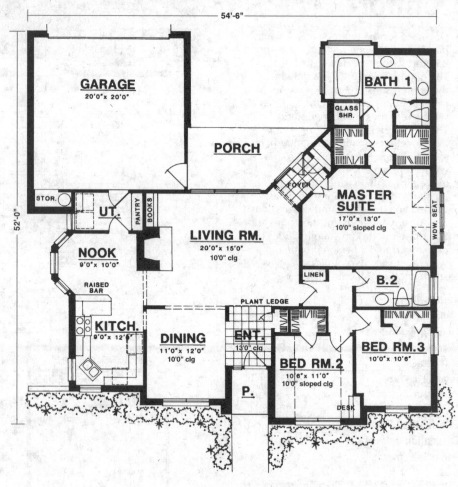

MAIN FLOOR

ORDER BLUEPRINTS ANYTIME!
CALL TOLL-FREE 1-800-820-1296

Plan RD-1714

Plan copyright held by home designer/architect

PRICES AND DETAILS
ON PAGES 12-15

Passive-Solar Features

- This design offers a flexible, angled layout that is suitable for a variety of lot shapes, plus the efficiency and convenience of passive-solar heating.
- The reception hall offers a pleasant view of the rear terrace, just beyond the dining room. To the left, the spacious living room is accented by a bow window and a stone fireplace.
- The sunny dining room boasts sliding glass doors to the rear terrace and to the glass-roofed solar room.
- The adjacent skylighted kitchen features a dinette with a sliding glass door to the solar room.
- The master suite features a private terrace, three walk-in closets and a master bath with a whirlpool tub.
- The skylighted upper floor holds two bedrooms, one with a balcony, the other with built-in shelves. Both have built-in desks.

Plan K-513-A

Bedrooms: 3	Baths: 2½
Living Area:	
Upper floor	416 sq. ft.
Main floor	1,172 sq. ft.
Solar room	140 sq. ft.
Total Living Area:	**1,728 sq. ft.**
Standard basement	1,176 sq. ft.
Garage and storage	520 sq. ft.
Exterior Wall Framing:	2x4 or 2x6

Foundation Options:

Standard basement

Slab

(All plans can be built with your choice of foundation and framing. A generic conversion diagram is available. See order form.)

BLUEPRINT PRICE CODE: B

VIEW INTO LIVING ROOM

UPPER FLOOR

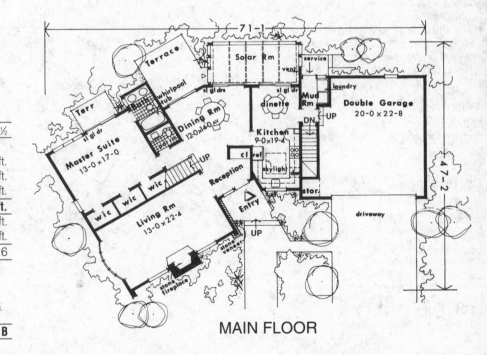

MAIN FLOOR

ORDER BLUEPRINTS ANYTIME!
CALL TOLL-FREE 1-800-820-1296

Plan K-513-A

Plan copyright held by home designer/architect

PRICES AND DETAILS
ON PAGES 12-15   197

Appealing, Angled Ranch

- This unique, angled ranch boasts a striking interior, which is highlighted by a dramatic domed ceiling at its center.
- The gabled entryway opens to a spacious pentagonal living area. A handsome fireplace, lots of glass and an adjoining backyard terrace are showcased, in addition to the fabulous domed ceiling.
- The dining room can be extended into the nearby den by opening the folding doors. The den features a sloped ceiling, an exciting solar bay and terrace access.
- A casual eating area and a nice-sized kitchen expand to the front of the home, ending at a windowed sink.
- The nearby mudroom area includes laundry facilities and an optional powder room.
- The sleeping wing offers four bedrooms, including an oversized master suite with a private terrace and a skylighted bath with dual sinks and a whirlpool tub. The secondary bedrooms share another full bath.

VIEW INTO DINING AND LIVING ROOMS

Plan K-669-N

Bedrooms: 4	Baths: 2–2½
Living Area:	
Main floor	1,728 sq. ft.
Total Living Area:	**1,728 sq. ft.**
Standard basement	1,545 sq. ft.
Garage and storage	468 sq. ft.
Exterior Wall Framing:	2x4 or 2x6

Foundation Options:

Standard basement

Slab

(All plans can be built with your choice of foundation and framing. A generic conversion diagram is available. See order form.)

BLUEPRINT PRICE CODE:	**B**

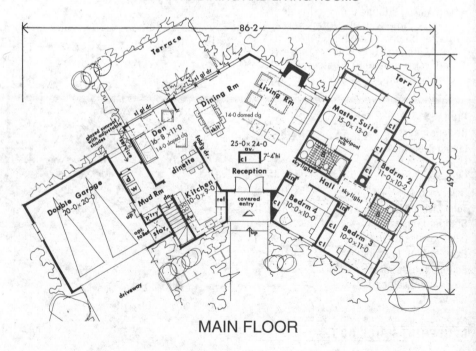

MAIN FLOOR

Plan K-669-N

Plan copyright held by home designer/architect

PRICES AND DETAILS
ON PAGES 12-15

Dynamic Design

- This dynamic five-sided design is perfect for scenic sites. The front (or street) side of the home is shielded by a two-car garage, while the back of the home hosts a glass-filled living area surrounded by a spectacular deck.
- The unique shape of the home allows for an unusually open and spacious interior design.
- The living/dining room is further expanded by a vaulted ceiling. The centrally located fireplace provides a focal point while distributing heat efficiently.
- The space-saving galley-style kitchen is connected to the living/dining area by a snack bar.
- A large main-floor bedroom has two closets and easy access to a full bath.
- The upper floor is highlighted by a breathtaking balcony overlook. Also, two bedrooms share a nice-sized bath.
- The optional daylight basement includes a huge recreation room.

Plans H-855-1 & -1A

Bedrooms: 3	Baths: 2
Living Area:	
Upper floor	625 sq. ft.
Main floor	1,108 sq. ft.
Daylight basement	1,108 sq. ft.
Total Living Area:	**1,733/2,841 sq. ft.**
Garage	346 sq. ft.
Exterior Wall Framing:	2x6
Foundation Options:	**Plan #**
Daylight basement	H-855-1
Crawlspace	H-855-1A

(All plans can be built with your choice of foundation and framing. A generic conversion diagram is available. See order form.)

BLUEPRINT PRICE CODE:	**B/D**

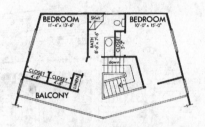

UPPER FLOOR

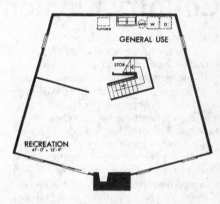

DAYLIGHT BASEMENT

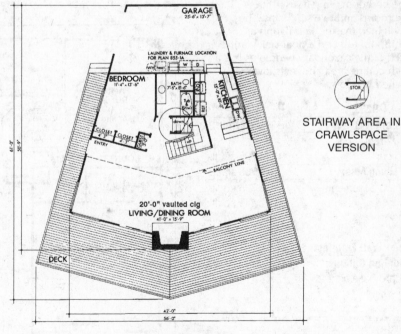

MAIN FLOOR

STAIRWAY AREA IN CRAWLSPACE VERSION

ORDER BLUEPRINTS ANYTIME!
CALL TOLL-FREE 1-800-820-1296

Plans H-855-1 & -1A
Plan copyright held by home designer/architect

PRICES AND DETAILS
ON PAGES 12-15   199

Skylighted Country Kitchen

- This country ranch-style home combines rustic wood posts and shutters with stylish curved glass.
- The foyer unfolds to the flowing formal areas. The living room and the dining room each offer a stepped ceiling and a view of one of the two porches.
- The skylighted country kitchen shares the family room's warm fireplace. The kitchen's central island cooktop and snack bar make serving a breeze!
- In addition to the fireplace, the family room also boasts gliding French doors to the adjacent porch.
- The bedroom wing houses three bedrooms and two full baths. The skylighted master bath flaunts a whirlpool tub and a dual-sink vanity.
- Each of the secondary bedrooms has a high ceiling area above its lovely arched window.

Plan AX-92321

Bedrooms: 3	Baths: 2
Living Area:	
Main floor	1,735 sq. ft.
Total Living Area:	**1,735 sq. ft.**
Standard basement	1,735 sq. ft.
Garage	449 sq. ft.
Storage	28 sq. ft.
Utility	28 sq. ft.
Exterior Wall Framing:	2x4

Foundation Options:

Standard basement
Crawlspace
Slab

(All plans can be built with your choice of foundation and framing. A generic conversion diagram is available. See order form.)

BLUEPRINT PRICE CODE: B

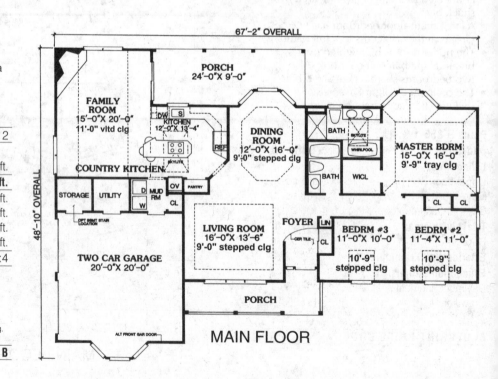

REAR VIEW

MAIN FLOOR

Plan AX-92321

Plan copyright held by home designer/architect

ORDER BLUEPRINTS ANYTIME!
CALL TOLL-FREE 1-800-820-1296

PRICES AND DETAILS
ON PAGES 12-15

Charming Guest Cottage

- A charming guest cottage makes this home a unique find.
- Incorporated with the detached garage, the cottage's cozy covered porch opens to a comfortable living area, which shares an efficient serving counter with the galley-style kitchen.
- A full bath and a bedroom with a large walk-in closet complete the cottage.
- The foyer of the main home unfolds to the spacious living room, which boasts a cathedral ceiling and a cozy fireplace.
- The sun-drenched dining room features French-door access to a covered porch.
- The efficient kitchen includes a neat serving counter and a handy laundry area behind pocket doors.
- Elegant double doors open to the master bedroom, which features another cathedral ceiling and attractive plant ledges above the two walk-in closets. The master bath flaunts a garden tub and a separate shower.
- French doors open to a cozy study, which could serve as a second bedroom.

Plan L-270-SA

Bedrooms: 2+	Baths: 3
Living Area:	
Main floor	1,268 sq. ft.
Guest cottage	468 sq. ft.
Total Living Area:	**1,736 sq. ft.**
Garage and storage	573 sq. ft.
Exterior Wall Framing:	2x4

Foundation Options:

Slab
(All plans can be built with your choice of foundation and framing. A generic conversion diagram is available. See order form.)

BLUEPRINT PRICE CODE:	B

REAR VIEW

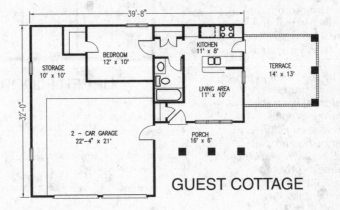

GUEST COTTAGE

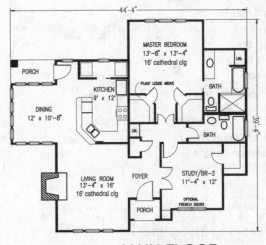

MAIN FLOOR

Plan L-270-SA

Plan copyright held by home designer/architect

PRICES AND DETAILS
ON PAGES 12-15

New-Fashioned Farmhouse

- Traditional styling combined with a highly contemporary floor plan update this farmhouse-inspired plan enough to take it into town.
- The home is embraced by a wraparound porch, which is accessible from the foyer and the family room.
- The floor plan is zoned for formal and casual living. The casual living spaces are oriented to the rear and integrated for family interaction. The family room's inviting fireplace can be seen from the adjoining kitchen, which features a snack bar and a bayed breakfast nook.
- The formal living and dining rooms allow you to entertain with confidence.
- The upper-floor master bedroom has a vaulted ceiling and his-and-hers walk-in closets. The suite includes a private, vaulted bath with an oval tub, a separate shower and dual sinks. Two more bedrooms share a full hall bath.

Plan S-62893

Bedrooms: 3	Baths: 2½
Living Area:	
Upper floor	774 sq. ft.
Main floor	963 sq. ft.
Total Living Area:	**1,737 sq. ft.**
Standard basement	930 sq. ft.
Garage	520 sq. ft.
Exterior Wall Framing:	2x6

Foundation Options:

Standard basement

Crawlspace

Slab

(All plans can be built with your choice of foundation and framing. A generic conversion diagram is available. See order form.)

BLUEPRINT PRICE CODE:	**B**

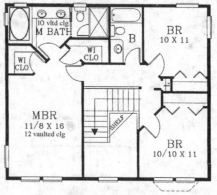

UPPER FLOOR

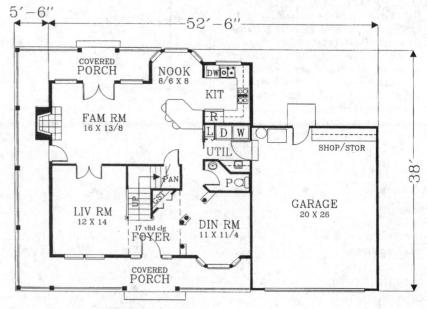

MAIN FLOOR

ORDER BLUEPRINTS ANYTIME!
CALL TOLL-FREE 1-800-820-1296

Plan S-62893

Plan copyright held by home designer/architect

PRICES AND DETAILS
ON PAGES 12-15

This Is It!

- This comfortable design is just the plan you're looking for. The affordable design includes all the features—both inside and out—today's family needs.
- The first days of spring will feel even better when you settle into a rocker on the porch and watch the kids play a game of Kick the Can in the front yard.
- Inside, the dining room awaits formal dinners. Built-in china cabinets replace the stairway to the basement in the crawlspace and slab versions.
- In the kitchen, a snack bar is the perfect place to feed the kids a snack. The sunshine that pours into the morning room will rouse the spirits of even the sleepiest family member.
- Friends and family will show up at your home to celebrate the Fourth of July on your fun-packed deck.
- In the busy living room, plenty of room is available to dance to your favorite music or gather the clan together to watch the newest release on video.
- When you need a break, retreat to the master suite, where you can savor the peace and quiet in the sitting area.

Plan DD-1716

Bedrooms: 3	Baths: 2
Living Area:	
Main floor	1,738 sq. ft.
Total Living Area:	**1,738 sq. ft.**
Standard basement	1,738 sq. ft.
Garage	425 sq. ft.
Exterior Wall Framing:	2x4

Foundation Options:

Standard basement

Crawlspace

Slab

(All plans can be built with your choice of foundation and framing. A generic conversion diagram is available. See order form.)

BLUEPRINT PRICE CODE: B

REAR VIEW

MAIN FLOOR

Plan DD-1716

Plan copyright held by home designer/architect

Eye-Catching Colonial

- Elegant bay windows embellish the rich brick exterior of this distinguished Colonial-style home.
- Inside, the entry is flanked by the formal living areas. The living room is warmed by a fireplace and separated from the family room by a decorative wood partition.
- The family room's two-story ceiling lends airiness to the room, while French doors open to a backyard terrace.
- The adjoining peninsula kitchen features a sloped ceiling, a tidy pantry closet and a circular dinette surrounded by windows.
- The secluded master bedroom has a cathedral ceiling, a large walk-in closet and French doors to a private terrace. The master bath features a whirlpool tub and a separate shower.
- Three more bedrooms are found upstairs and share a balcony overlook to the family room.

Plan AHP-9121

Bedrooms: 4	Baths: 2½
Living Area:	
Upper floor	557 sq. ft.
Main floor	1,183 sq. ft.
Total Living Area:	**1,740 sq. ft.**
Standard basement	1,183 sq. ft.
Garage and storage	440 sq. ft.
Exterior Wall Framing:	2x4 or 2x6

Foundation Options:
Standard basement
Crawlspace
Slab

(All plans can be built with your choice of foundation and framing. A generic conversion diagram is available. See order form.)

BLUEPRINT PRICE CODE: **B**

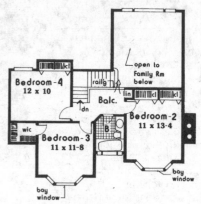

UPPER FLOOR

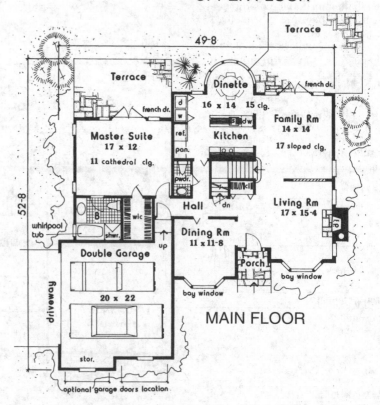

MAIN FLOOR

ORDER BLUEPRINTS ANYTIME!
CALL TOLL-FREE 1-800-820-1296

Plan AHP-9121
Plan copyright held by home designer/architect

PRICES AND DETAILS
ON PAGES 12-15

Breathtaking Open Space

- Soaring ceilings and an open floor plan add breathtaking volume to this charming country-style home.
- The inviting covered-porch entrance opens into the spacious living room, which boasts a spectacular cathedral ceiling. Two overhead dormers fill the area with natural light, while a fireplace adds warmth.
- Also under the cathedral ceiling, the kitchen and bayed breakfast room share an eating bar. Skylights brighten the convenient laundry room and the computer room, which provides access to a covered rear porch.
- The secluded master bedroom offers private access to another covered porch. The skylighted master bath has a walk-in closet and a sloped ceiling above a whirlpool tub.
- Optional upper-floor areas provide future expansion space for the needs of a growing family.

Plan J-9302

Bedrooms: 3+	Baths: 2

Living Area:

Main floor	1,745 sq. ft.
Total Living Area:	**1,745 sq. ft.**
Future upper floor	500 sq. ft.
Future area above garage	241 sq. ft.
Standard basement	1,745 sq. ft.
Garage and storage	559 sq. ft.
Exterior Wall Framing:	2x4

Foundation Options:

Standard basement
Crawlspace
Slab

(All plans can be built with your choice of foundation and framing. A generic conversion diagram is available. See order form.)

BLUEPRINT PRICE CODE:	B

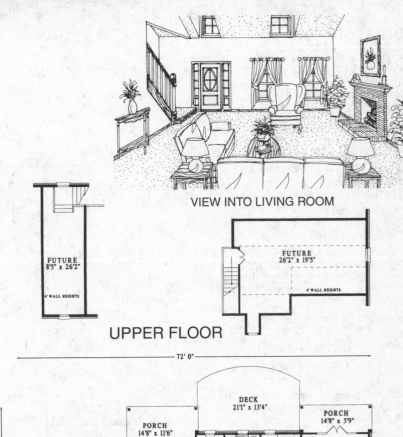

VIEW INTO LIVING ROOM

UPPER FLOOR

MAIN FLOOR

ORDER BLUEPRINTS ANYTIME!
CALL TOLL-FREE 1-800-820-1296

Plan J-9302
Plan copyright held by home designer/architect

PRICES AND DETAILS
ON PAGES 12-15

205

Simply Beautiful

- This four-bedroom design offers simplistic beauty, economical construction and ample space for both family life and formal entertaining—all on one floor.
- The charming cottage-style exterior gives way to a spacious interior. A vaulted, beamed ceiling soars above the huge living room, which features a massive fireplace, built-in bookshelves and access to a backyard patio.
- The deluxe master suite includes a dressing room, a large walk-in closet and a private bath.
- The three remaining bedrooms are larger than average and offer ample closet space.
- The efficient galley-style kitchen flows between a sunny bayed eating area and the formal dining room.
- A nice-sized storage area and a deluxe utility room are accessible from the two-car garage.

VIEW INTO LIVING ROOM

Plan E-1702

Bedrooms: 4	Baths: 2
Living Area:	
Main floor	1,751 sq. ft.
Total Living Area:	**1,751 sq. ft.**
Garage	484 sq. ft.
Storage	105 sq. ft.
Exterior Wall Framing:	2x4

Foundation Options:
Crawlspace
Slab
(All plans can be built with your choice of foundation and framing. A generic conversion diagram is available. See order form.)

BLUEPRINT PRICE CODE:	B

JUST-RIGHT HOMES

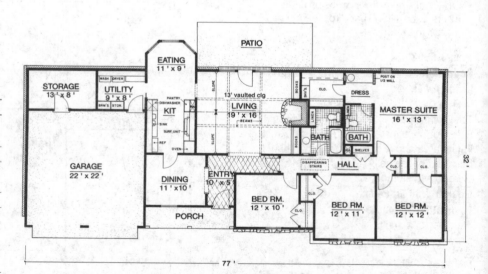

MAIN FLOOR

ORDER BLUEPRINTS ANYTIME! CALL TOLL-FREE 1-800-820-1296

Plan E-1702
Plan copyright held by home designer/architect

PRICES AND DETAILS ON PAGES 12-15

Open and Airy Design

- The open and airy design of this compact, affordable home makes the most of its space.
- Inside, the entry's 23½-ft. vaulted ceiling soars to the upper floor. Two decorative wood rails set off the entry from the living room. A corner fireplace topped by a wood mantel anchors the room, and French doors lead to the backyard.
- The good-sized dining room extends to the kitchen, where a handy island maximizes workspace, and a bright window adds light. Plenty of room is available for cooking and dining.
- Across the home, the secluded master bedroom is a great adult retreat. The private master bath boasts two separate vanities and a walk-in closet with convenient built-in shelves.
- At the top of the open staircase, a railed sitting area with a 16-ft. vaulted ceiling is ideal for a computer nook.
- Two spacious bedrooms are serviced by a centrally located hall bath.
- Plans for a detached two-car garage are also included in the blueprints.

Plan LS-94046-E

Bedrooms: 3	Baths: 2
Living Area:	
Upper floor	561 sq. ft.
Main floor	1,190 sq. ft.
Total Living Area:	**1,751 sq. ft.**
Standard basement	1,145 sq. ft.
Exterior Wall Framing:	2x6

Foundation Options:

Standard basement

(All plans can be built with your choice of foundation and framing. A generic conversion diagram is available. See order form.)

BLUEPRINT PRICE CODE: **B**

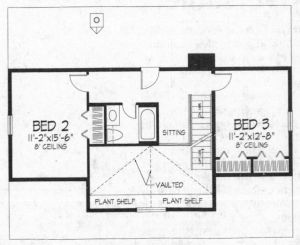

UPPER FLOOR

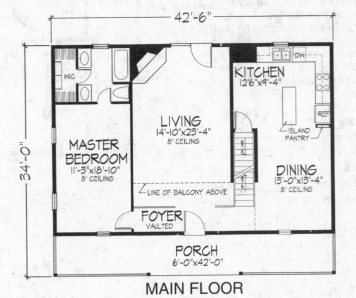

MAIN FLOOR

ORDER BLUEPRINTS ANYTIME!
CALL TOLL-FREE 1-800-820-1296

Plan LS-94046-E

Plan copyright held by home designer/architect

PRICES AND DETAILS
ON PAGES 12-15

207

Very Versatile!

- You won't find a more versatile design than this one! The attractive traditional facade gives way to a dramatic rear deck, making the home suitable for a lakeside lot. With its modest width and daylight basement, the home also adapts to a narrow or sloping site.
- A railed porch welcomes guests into the main entry and into the Great Room straight ahead. The Great Room flaunts a vaulted ceiling, a metal fireplace and sliding glass doors to the deck.
- The efficient U-shaped kitchen offers a pantry and presents a serving bar to the dining room.
- A convenient hall bath serves the quiet main-floor bedroom, which overlooks the scenic rear wood porch.
- Upstairs, a spacious loft allows dramatic views of the Great Room over a wood rail. A commodious storage closet is accessed from the loft.
- Double doors introduce the posh master suite, which boasts a walk-in closet, a whirlpool bath and attic access.
- The loft and the master bedroom are visually expanded by high ceilings.

Plan PI-92-373

Bedrooms: 2	Baths: 2
Living Area:	
Upper floor	546 sq. ft.
Main floor	1,212 sq. ft.
Total Living Area:	**1,758 sq. ft.**
Daylight basement	1,212 sq. ft.
Garage	475 sq. ft.
Exterior Wall Framing:	2x6

Foundation Options:

Daylight basement

(All plans can be built with your choice of foundation and framing. A generic conversion diagram is available. See order form.)

BLUEPRINT PRICE CODE: B

REAR VIEW

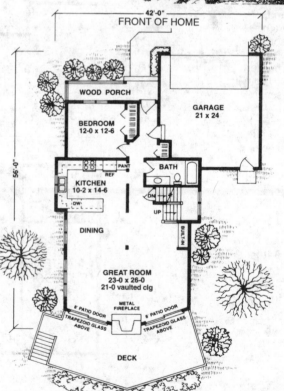

MAIN FLOOR

UPPER FLOOR

ORDER BLUEPRINTS ANYTIME!
CALL TOLL-FREE 1-800-820-1296

Plan PI-92-373

Plan copyright held by home designer/architect

PRICES AND DETAILS
ON PAGES 12-15

Dramatic Details

- The brick exterior of this elegant three-bedroom home is accented with copper roofing and multi-level wood trim.
- The interior drama begins at the vaulted foyer and continues to the adjoining activity areas.
- The splendid formal dining room is beautifully placed on a raised floor and surrounded by decorative columns.
- French doors brighten the spacious Great Room and attractively frame its handsome centered fireplace. The high ceiling vaults to the upper floor.
- Skylights illuminate the roomy kitchen, which overlooks a quaint breakfast area. A handy pass-through from the breakfast room allows the transfer of food and beverages to the Great Room.
- Isolated at the opposite end of the home, the master bedroom flaunts a stunning window, a cathedral ceiling, a huge walk-in closet and a private bath.
- Off the upper floor's balcony bridge are two more bedrooms and another bath.

Plan APS-1713

Bedrooms: 3	**Baths:** 2½
Living Area:	
Upper floor	425 sq. ft.
Main floor	1,334 sq. ft.
Total Living Area:	**1,759 sq. ft.**
Standard basement	1,272 sq. ft.
Garage	400 sq. ft.
Exterior Wall Framing:	2x4

Foundation Options:

Standard basement
(All plans can be built with your choice of foundation and framing. A generic conversion diagram is available. See order form.)

BLUEPRINT PRICE CODE:	**B**

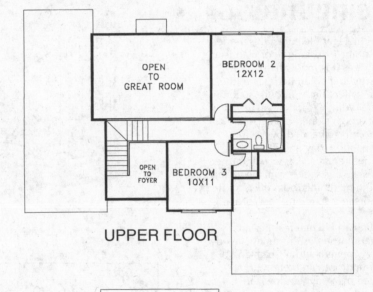

UPPER FLOOR

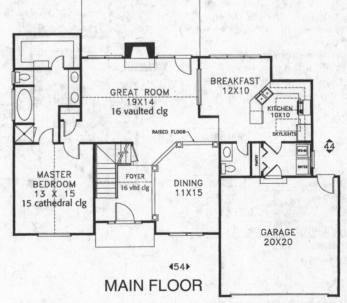

MAIN FLOOR

Plan APS-1713

Plan copyright held by home designer/architect

PRICES AND DETAILS
ON PAGES 12-15

Enticing Interior

- Filled with elegant features, this modern country home's exciting floor plan is as impressive as it is innovative.
- Past the inviting columned porch, the entrance gallery flows into the spacious living room/dining room area.
- Boasting a high sloped ceiling, the living room is enhanced by a semi-circular window bay and includes a handsome fireplace. A low wall further distinguishes this space from the gallery. The adjoining dining room offers sliding glass doors to a spacious backyard terrace.
- The skylighted kitchen features an eating bar that serves the sunny bayed dinette. A convenient half-bath and a laundry/mudroom are nearby.
- Brightened by a bay window, the luxurious master bedroom shows off his-and-hers walk-in closets. The master bath showcases a whirlpool garden tub under a glass sunroof.
- Two additional bedrooms—the smaller of which might make a nice home office or study—have plenty of closet space and share a skylighted hall bath.

Plan K-685-DA

Bedrooms: 3	Baths: 2½
Living Area:	
Main floor	1,760 sq. ft.
Total Living Area:	**1,760 sq. ft.**
Standard basement	1,700 sq. ft.
Garage	482 sq. ft.
Exterior Wall Framing:	2x4 or 2x6

Foundation Options:

Standard basement

Slab

(All plans can be built with your choice of foundation and framing. A generic conversion diagram is available. See order form.)

BLUEPRINT PRICE CODE: B

VIEW INTO LIVING AND DINING ROOMS

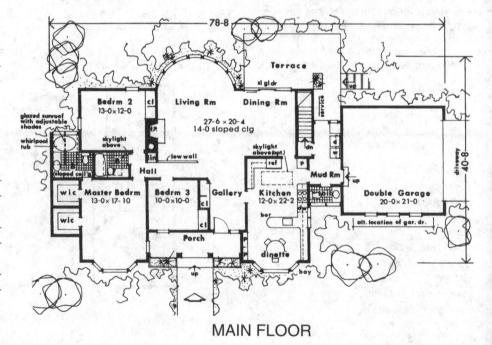

MAIN FLOOR

ORDER BLUEPRINTS ANYTIME! CALL TOLL-FREE 1-800-820-1296

Plan K-685-DA

Plan copyright held by home designer/architect

PRICES AND DETAILS ON PAGES 12-15

Rural Roots

- This nostalgic farmhouse reminds you of country life, bringing back memories or maybe just fond daydreams.
- Authentic Victorian details contribute to the comforting facade. Lovely fishscale shingles above the bay window and oval glass in the front door will command attention from visitors.
- Receive the long-awaited kinfolk on the delightful wraparound porch; you may want to sit a spell and catch up on family news!
- Then usher everyone into the family room, for memorable moments in front of the corner fireplace.

- When the feast is ready, eyes will sparkle as the turkey is presented in the bay-windowed dining room. A French door leads to the back porch for after-dinner chatting in the cool evening.
- The efficient kitchen handles meal preparation with ease. The "east" wall features a pantry and double ovens.
- The secluded master suite lets you unwind before a good night's rest. A fabulous bath and direct porch access make this suite really sweet!
- Two secondary bedrooms share a split bath. The bayed front bedroom boasts a raised ceiling and a walk-in closet.
- The blueprints include plans for a detached, two-car garage (not shown).

Plan L-1772	
Bedrooms: 3	**Baths:** 2
Living Area:	
Main floor	1,772 sq. ft.
Total Living Area:	**1,772 sq. ft.**
Detached garage	576 sq. ft.
Exterior Wall Framing:	2x4

Foundation Options:

Slab
(All plans can be built with your choice of foundation and framing. A generic conversion diagram is available. See order form.)

BLUEPRINT PRICE CODE:	B

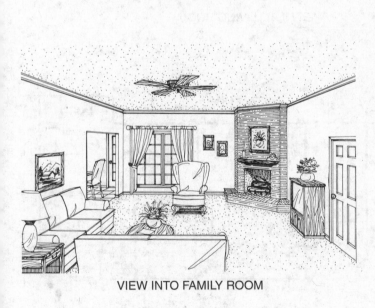

VIEW INTO FAMILY ROOM

MAIN FLOOR

ORDER BLUEPRINTS ANYTIME!
CALL TOLL-FREE 1-800-820-1296

Plan L-1772
Plan copyright held by home designer/architect

PRICES AND DETAILS
ON PAGES 12-15

211

Rustic, Relaxed Living

- The screened porch of this rustic home offers a cool place to dine on warm summer days. The covered front porch provides an inviting welcome and a place for pure relaxation.
- With its warm fireplace, the home's spacious living room is ideal for unwinding. The living room unfolds to a dining area that overlooks a backyard patio and opens to the screened porch.
- The U-shaped kitchen is centrally located and features a nice windowed sink. A handy pantry and a laundry room adjoin to the right.
- Three large bedrooms make up the home's sleeping wing. The master bedroom boasts a roomy private bath with a step-up spa tub, a separate shower and two walk-in closets.
- The secondary bedrooms share a compartmentalized hall bath.

VIEW INTO LIVING ROOM

Plan C-8650

Bedrooms: 3	Baths: 2
Living Area:	
Main floor	1,773 sq. ft.
Total Living Area:	**1,773 sq. ft.**
Screened porch	246 sq. ft.
Daylight basement	1,773 sq. ft.
Garage	441 sq. ft.
Exterior Wall Framing:	2x4

Foundation Options:

Daylight basement
Crawlspace
Slab

(All plans can be built with your choice of foundation and framing. A generic conversion diagram is available. See order form.)

BLUEPRINT PRICE CODE:	B

MAIN FLOOR

ORDER BLUEPRINTS ANYTIME! *CALL TOLL-FREE 1-800-820-1296*

Plan C-8650

Plan copyright held by home designer/architect

PRICES AND DETAILS *ON PAGES 12-15*

Casual Country Living

- With its covered wraparound porch, this gracious design is ideal for warm summer days or starry evenings.
- The spacious living room boasts a handsome brick-hearth fireplace and built-in shelving. French doors access the backyard.
- The open kitchen design provides plenty of space for food storage and preparation, with its pantry and oversized central island.
- Two mirror-image baths service the three bedrooms on the upper floor. Each secondary bedroom features a window seat and two closets. The master bedroom has a large walk-in closet and a private bath.
- A versatile hobby or sewing room is also included.
- An optional carport off the dining room is available upon request. Please specify when ordering.

Plan J-8895

Bedrooms: 3	Baths: 2½
Living Area:	
Upper floor	860 sq. ft.
Main floor	919 sq. ft.
Total Living Area:	**1,779 sq. ft.**
Standard basement	919 sq. ft.
Optional carport	462 sq. ft.
Exterior Wall Framing:	2x4

Foundation Options:

Standard basement

Crawlspace

Slab

(All plans can be built with your choice of foundation and framing. A generic conversion diagram is available. See order form.)

BLUEPRINT PRICE CODE:	B

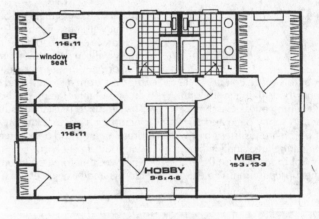

UPPER FLOOR

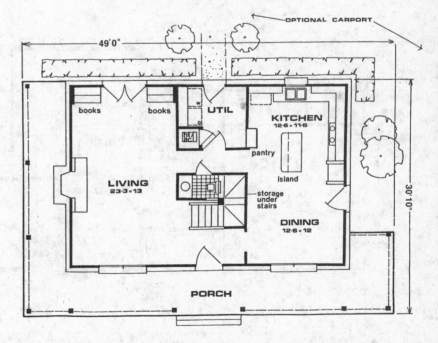

MAIN FLOOR

Plan J-8895

Plan copyright held by home designer/architect

PRICES AND DETAILS
ON PAGES 12-15

Classic Country-Style

- At the center of this rustic country-style home is an enormous living room with a flat beamed ceiling and a massive stone fireplace. A sunny patio and a covered rear porch are just steps away.
- The adjoining eating area and kitchen provide plenty of room for casual dining and meal preparation. The eating area is visually enhanced by a sloped ceiling with false beams. The kitchen includes a snack bar, a pantry closet and a built-in spice cabinet.
- The formal dining room gets plenty of pizzazz from a stone-faced wall and an arched planter facing the living room.
- The secluded master suite has it all, including a private bath, a separate dressing area and a large walk-in closet with built-in shelves.
- The two remaining bedrooms have big closets and easy access to a full bath.

Plan E-1808

Bedrooms: 3	**Baths:** 2

Living Area:

Main floor	1,800 sq. ft.
Total Living Area:	**1,800 sq. ft.**
Garage	506 sq. ft.
Storage	99 sq. ft.

Exterior Wall Framing: 2x4

Foundation Options:

Crawlspace
Slab
(All plans can be built with your choice of foundation and framing. A generic conversion diagram is available. See order form.)

BLUEPRINT PRICE CODE: B

MAIN FLOOR

ORDER BLUEPRINTS ANYTIME!
CALL TOLL-FREE 1-800-820-1296

Plan E-1808
Plan copyright held by home designer/architect

**PRICES AND DETAILS
ON PAGES 12-15**

Attention to Detail

- Quoins, keystones and columns on this home's welcoming brick exterior show that attention to detail truly makes a difference.
- Birthday parties begin by storing coats in one of two foyer closets and then unleashing the kids into the spacious Great Room, topped by a cathedral ceiling. A built-in entertainment center next to the fireplace keeps them busy, while the adults can visit and offer supervision nearby.
- Snacks are easily prepared in the roomy kitchen, where there's plenty of counter space. Set the cake in the sunny breakfast nook, or out on the back porch. If it's a gloomy day, blow out the candles in the formal dining room.
- Find peace and quiet in the master bedroom, tucked into the far right corner of th home. It has a walk-in closet and a private bath with a whirlpool tub.
- A second full bath is positioned between two more bedrooms.

Plan GL-1791

Bedrooms: 3	Baths: 2
Living Area:	
Main floor	1,791 sq. ft.
Total Living Area:	**1,791 sq. ft.**
Standard basement	1,791 sq. ft.
Garage	462 sq. ft.
Exterior Wall Framing:	2x4
Foundation Options:	

Standard basement

(All plans can be built with your choice of foundation and framing. A generic conversion diagram is available. See order form.)

BLUEPRINT PRICE CODE:	B

REAR VIEW

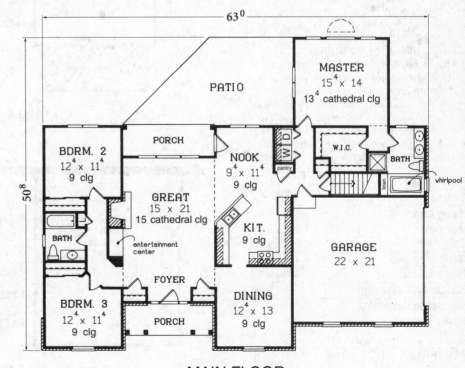

MAIN FLOOR

ORDER BLUEPRINTS ANYTIME!
CALL TOLL-FREE 1-800-820-1296

Plan GL-1791
Plan copyright held by home designer/architect

PRICES AND DETAILS
ON PAGES 12-15   215

Advantageous Vantage Points

- The raised living and deck areas of this charming home take full advantage of the beautiful surrounding views!
- Enter on the basement level, where you'll find a pair of spacious bedrooms, each with a walk-in closet and private access to a full-size bath.
- At the heart of the main floor is the huge Grand Room—the perfect space for casual or formal entertaining. Guests can gather around the cozy fireplace or, if the weather's cooperative, they can step out to the extra-large main deck to enjoy the evening air.
- Sunny and cheerful, the morning room also walks out to the main deck.
- The incredible master suite has a long list of special features: two closets, a dressing area, an expansive bath with a spa tub and a separate shower, plus a private deck to bring you nearer to the outdoors whenever the mood hits.
- A fourth bedroom may also serve as a secluded study if so desired.

Plan EOF-44

Bedrooms: 3+	Baths: 2
Living Area:	
Main floor	1,256 sq. ft.
Daylight basement	541 sq. ft.
Total Living Area:	**1,797 sq. ft.**
Tuck-under garage	460 sq. ft.
Exterior Wall Framing:	2x4
Foundation Options:	

Daylight basement
(All plans can be built with your choice of foundation and framing. A generic conversion diagram is available. See order form.)

BLUEPRINT PRICE CODE:	**B**

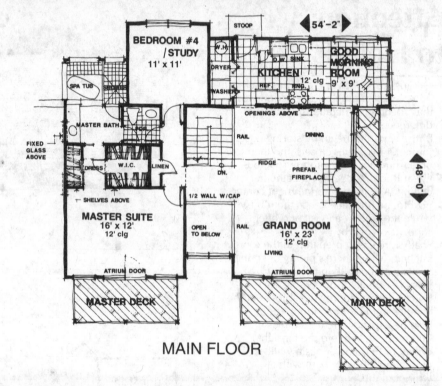

MAIN FLOOR

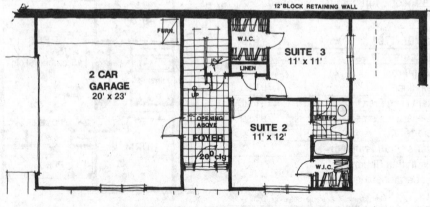

DAYLIGHT BASEMENT

ORDER BLUEPRINTS ANYTIME!
CALL TOLL-FREE 1-800-820-1296

Plan EOF-44

Plan copyright held by home designer/architect

PRICES AND DETAILS
ON PAGES 12-15

Fresh Country Air

- A skylighted screen porch, a fun backyard deck and an abundance of windows infuse this country-style home with air and light.
- An inviting front porch ushers neighbors into the spacious family room, where a fireplace warms chilly nights. On sunny days, enjoy the screened-in back porch, or head out onto the rear deck.
- The roomy kitchen boasts a built-in desk, a closet pantry and serving bars overlooking both the breakfast nook and the family room.
- A tray ceiling, his-and-hers walk-in closets and a light-filled sitting area highlight the master bedroom. The private master bath flaunts a dual-sink vanity and a garden tub.
- A versatile bonus room above the garage offers expansion opportunities.

Plan APS-1717

Bedrooms: 3+	Baths: 2
Living Area:	
Main floor	1,787 sq. ft.
Total Living Area:	**1,787 sq. ft.**
Future area	263 sq. ft.
Screen porch	153 sq. ft.
Standard basement	1,787 sq. ft.
Garage	466 sq. ft.
Exterior Wall Framing:	2x4

Foundation Options:

Standard basement

Crawlspace

Slab

(All plans can be built with your choice of foundation and framing. A generic conversion diagram is available. See order form.)

BLUEPRINT PRICE CODE: B

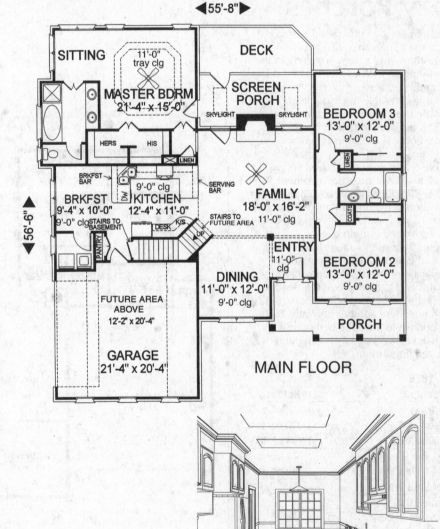

VIEW INTO
KITCHEN AND
BREAKFAST NOOK

Plan APS-1717

Plan copyright held by home designer/architect

PRICES AND DETAILS
ON PAGES 12-15

JUST-RIGHT HOMES

Cozy Porches

- Twin dormers give this raised one-story design the appearance of a two-story. Two porches and a deck supplement the main living areas with plenty of outdoor entertaining space.
- The large central living room features a dramatic fireplace, a high ceiling with a skylight and access to both porch areas. When dinner is ready, usher guests into the dining room.
- Double doors open to a bayed eating area, which overlooks the adjoining deck and includes a sloped ceiling. The open kitchen features an angled snack bar and a pantry closet, along with a menu desk and double ovens.
- The elegant master suite is tucked to one side of the home and overlooks the backyard and the deck. Handy laundry facilities and garage access are nearby.
- Across the home, two additional bedrooms share another full bath. You may choose to have the bedroom with porch access serve as a relaxing and secluded guest room.

Plan E-1826

Bedrooms: 3	Baths: 2
Living Area:	
Main floor	1,800 sq. ft.
Total Living Area:	**1,800 sq. ft.**
Garage and storage	574 sq. ft.
Enclosed storage	60 sq. ft.
Exterior Wall Framing:	2x6

Foundation Options:

Crawlspace

Slab

(All plans can be built with your choice of foundation and framing. A generic conversion diagram is available. See order form.)

BLUEPRINT PRICE CODE:	B

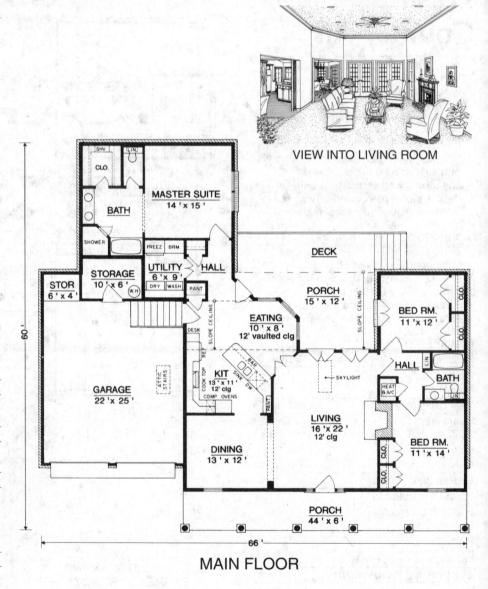

VIEW INTO LIVING ROOM

MAIN FLOOR

ORDER BLUEPRINTS ANYTIME!
CALL TOLL-FREE 1-800-820-1296

Plan E-1826

Plan copyright held by home designer/architect

PRICES AND DETAILS ON PAGES 12-15

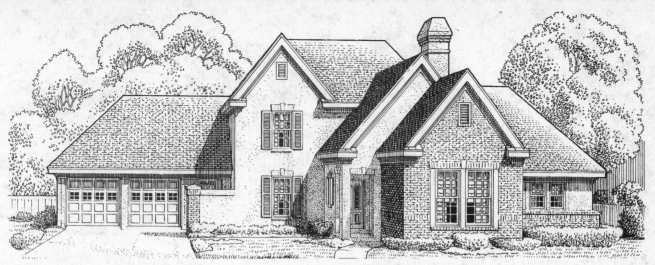

Fairy-Tale Feel

- Charming and whimsical, this comfy cottage jumps right out of the pages of your favorite fairy tale.
- Back in the real world, the home's inside spaces offer every modern convenience.
- Flowing from the foyer, the dining and living rooms are separated only by a lovely staircase. Imagine the parties you can host in this vast expanse! A nice fireplace adds ambience, while a French door opens onto a sunny patio.
- The open kitchen boasts an unusual layout; a central wet bar with a built-in wine rack facilitates the serving of refreshing beverages. Handy laundry facilities are nearby.
- The grocery shopper of the family will love the kitchen's proximity to the oversized two-car garage.
- The master suite is a relaxing haven. Its private bath and big walk-in closet make morning preparation easy.
- The children have their own space upstairs. A skylighted loft with bookshelves is a cozy spot to curl up with that favorite story. Walk-in closets and a shared, split bath give everyone a measure of comfort.

Plan L-867-HA

Bedrooms: 3	Baths: 2½
Living Area:	
Upper floor	603 sq. ft.
Main floor	1,262 sq. ft.
Total Living Area:	**1,865 sq. ft.**
Garage	478 sq. ft.
Exterior Wall Framing:	2x4

Foundation Options:

Slab

(All plans can be built with your choice of foundation and framing. A generic conversion diagram is available. See order form.)

BLUEPRINT PRICE CODE:	B

REAR VIEW

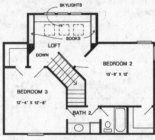

UPPER FLOOR

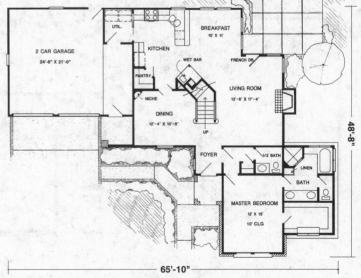

MAIN FLOOR

ORDER BLUEPRINTS ANYTIME!
CALL TOLL-FREE 1-800-820-1296

Plan L-867-HA

Plan copyright held by home designer/architect

PRICES AND DETAILS
ON PAGES 12-15

219

Outstanding One-Story

- This sharp one-story home has an outstanding floor plan, attractively enhanced by a stately brick facade.
- A vestibule introduces the foyer, which flows between the formal living spaces at the front of the home.
- The large living room features a sloped ceiling and dramatic, high windows. The spacious dining room has easy access to the kitchen.

- The expansive family room is the center of the home, with a beamed cathedral ceiling, a slate-hearth fireplace and sliding glass doors to a backyard terrace.
- The adjoining kitchen offers a snack bar and a sunny dinette framed by a curved window wall.
- Included in the sleeping wing is a luxurious master suite with a private bath. A skylighted dressing room and a big walk-in closet are also featured.
- The two secondary bedrooms share a hall bath that has a dual-sink vanity. A half-bath is near the mud/laundry room.

Plan K-278-M

Bedrooms: 3	Baths: 2½
Living Area:	
Main floor	1,803 sq. ft.
Total Living Area:	**1,803 sq. ft.**
Standard basement	1,778 sq. ft.
Garage	493 sq. ft.
Storage	58 sq. ft.
Exterior Wall Framing:	2x4 or 2x6

Foundation Options:

Standard basement
Slab
(All plans can be built with your choice of foundation and framing. A generic conversion diagram is available. See order form.)

BLUEPRINT PRICE CODE:	B

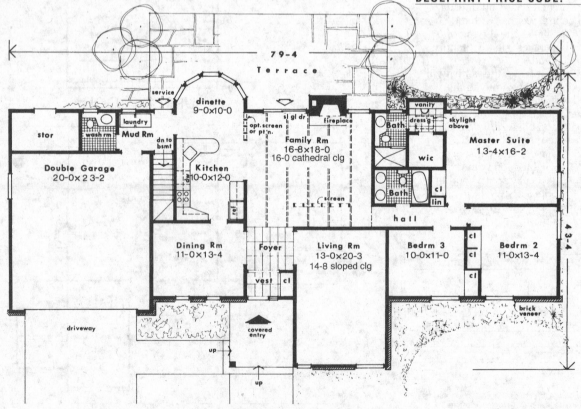

MAIN FLOOR

ORDER BLUEPRINTS ANYTIME!
CALL TOLL-FREE 1-800-820-1296

Plan K-278-M

Plan copyright held by home designer/architect

PRICES AND DETAILS
ON PAGES 12-15

Picture-Perfect

- Framed by decorative columns, the entry foyer in this traditional-style home invites your guests to head straight for the welcoming hearth in the spacious living room.
- The nearby dining room is easily served by the island kitchen and opens to a screen porch and a patio for meals in an al fresco setting.
- At the end of a busy day, curl up with a cup of hot chocolate and a good book on the bay window's seat in the master bedroom. A French door provides patio access. Later, pamper yourself with a soak in the private bath's garden tub.
- Beyond the full hall bath, another bedroom features a lovely elliptical transom window overlooking the front yard. A central den easily doubles as an extra bedroom.
- The attached garage leads directly to the kitchen, making unloading groceries a breeze on even the stormiest of days.
- A big and bright laundry/mudroom, a handy powder room and a railed front porch round out this home's fabulous floor plan.

Plan LS-20006-B

Bedrooms: 2+	Baths: 2½
Living Area:	
Main floor	1,806 sq. ft.
Total Living Area:	**1,806 sq. ft.**
Standard basement	1,806 sq. ft.
Garage	466 sq. ft.
Exterior Wall Framing:	2x6

Foundation Options:

Standard basement

(All plans can be built with your choice of foundation and framing. A generic conversion diagram is available. See order form.)

BLUEPRINT PRICE CODE: B

VIEW INTO LIVING AND DINING ROOMS

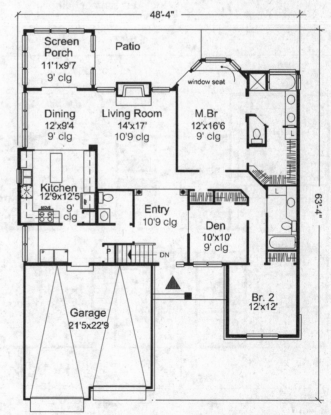

MAIN FLOOR

ORDER BLUEPRINTS ANYTIME!
CALL TOLL-FREE 1-800-820-1296

Plan LS-20006-B
Plan copyright held by home designer/architect

PRICES AND DETAILS
ON PAGES 12-15

221

Breezy Beauty

- A nostalgic covered front porch, a backyard deck and a sprawling screened porch combine to make this beautiful one-story home a breezy delight.
- The front entry opens into the Great Room, which is crowned by a soaring cathedral ceiling. A handsome fireplace is flanked by built-in bookshelves and cabinets.
- The large, bayed dining room offers a tray ceiling and deck access through French doors.

- The adjoining kitchen boasts plenty of counter space and a handy built-in recipe desk.
- From the kitchen, a side door leads to the screened porch. A wood floor and deck access highlight this cheery room.
- A quiet hall leads past a convenient utility room to the sleeping quarters.
- The secluded master bedroom is enhanced by a spacious walk-in closet. The private master bath includes a lovely garden tub, a separate shower and dual vanities.
- Two more bedrooms with walk-in closets share a hall bath.

Plan C-8905

Bedrooms: 3	**Baths:** 2
Living Area:	
Main floor	1,811 sq. ft.
Total Living Area:	**1,811 sq. ft.**
Screened porch	240 sq. ft.
Daylight basement	1,811 sq. ft.
Garage	484 sq. ft.
Exterior Wall Framing:	2x4

Foundation Options:
Daylight basement
Crawlspace
Slab
(All plans can be built with your choice of foundation and framing. A generic conversion diagram is available. See order form.)

BLUEPRINT PRICE CODE: B

JUST-RIGHT HOMES

MAIN FLOOR

DECK
28-0 x 12-0

BATH

GARDEN TUB

SHOWER

WALK-IN CLOSET

BEDROOM 2
11-0 x 13-6

WALK-IN CLOSET

DINING
12-0 x 13-6
9-0 TRAY CEILING

DRY WASH

UTILITY

DW

SINK

S UNIT

REF.

OVEN

KITCHEN
10-0 x 13-6

DESK

PANTRY

SCR. PORCH
12-0 x 20-0

GARAGE
22-0 x 22-0

CLOSET

50-0

38-4

MASTER BEDROOM
12-0 x 18-0

BATH

LINEN

HALL

DESK

COATS

BOOKS

12-0 CATHEDRAL CEILING W/ FALSE BEAMS

HEARTH

BEDROOM 3
12-0 x 11-4

WALK-IN CLOSET

GREAT ROOM
19-0 x 17-6

BOOKS

PORCH
25-0 x 6-0

89-6

ORDER BLUEPRINTS ANYTIME!
CALL TOLL-FREE 1-800-820-1296

Plan C-8905
Plan copyright held by home designer/architect

PRICES AND DETAILS
ON PAGES 12-15

Country Charm, Cottage Look

- An interesting combination of stone and stucco gives a charming cottage look to this attractive country home.
- Off the inviting sidelighted entry, the formal dining room is defined by striking columns.
- The dining room expands into the living room, which boasts a fireplace and built-in shelves. A French door provides access to a cute backyard patio.
- The galley-style kitchen unfolds to a sunny morning room.
- All of the living areas are expanded by high ceilings.
- The master bedroom features a nice bayed sitting area. The luxurious master bath boasts an exciting garden tub and a glass-block shower, as well as a big walk-in closet and a dressing area with two sinks.
- Across the home, two additional bedrooms with walk-in closets and private dressing areas share a tidy compartmentalized bath.

Plan DD-1790

Bedrooms: 3	Baths: 2½
Living Area:	
Main floor	1,812 sq. ft.
Total Living Area:	**1,812 sq. ft.**
Standard basement	1,812 sq. ft.
Garage	438 sq. ft.
Exterior Wall Framing:	2x4

Foundation Options:

Standard basement
Crawlspace
Slab

(All plans can be built with your choice of foundation and framing. A generic conversion diagram is available. See order form.)

BLUEPRINT PRICE CODE: **B**

REAR VIEW

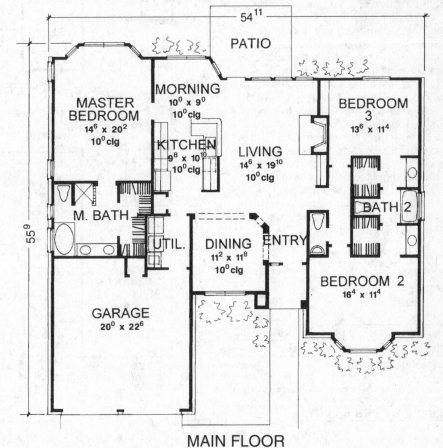

MAIN FLOOR

ORDER BLUEPRINTS ANYTIME!
CALL TOLL-FREE 1-800-820-1296

Plan DD-1790

Plan copyright held by home designer/architect

PRICES AND DETAILS
ON PAGES 12-15

223

Flexible Cottage

- This charming cottage is big enough to be a permanent home, yet small enough to fit on a narrow or lakeside lot.
- If you love to entertain, imagine the events you can host in the L-shaped living room! A two-sided fireplace serves as the focal point, while a corner window seat is great for conversation.
- Move the party into the glass-embraced dining room for a light meal or even a surprise birthday cake.
- A French door leads to a third party venue—your lovely backyard. Throw some horseshoes, fire up the barbecue or show off your prized fruit trees.
- Do you like to cook? Then you'll adore the open, U-shaped kitchen, complete with a pantry closet, double ovens and a brick cooktop.
- Was your nest recently emptied? You'll appreciate the main-floor master suite, with its vast sleeping area. The well-designed private bath opens to the backyard through a French door.
- Upstairs, children, boarders or guests are nicely accommodated by two bedrooms and a full bath.

Plan L-818-CSA

Bedrooms: 3	Baths: 2½
Living Area:	
Upper floor	486 sq. ft.
Main floor	1,330 sq. ft.
Total Living Area:	**1,816 sq. ft.**
Exterior Wall Framing:	2x4

Foundation Options:

Slab

(All plans can be built with your choice of foundation and framing. A generic conversion diagram is available. See order form.)

BLUEPRINT PRICE CODE: **B**

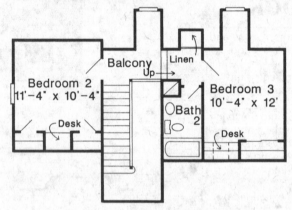

UPPER FLOOR

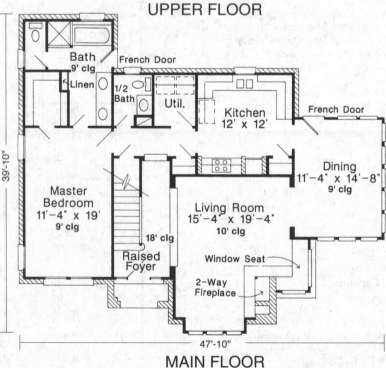

MAIN FLOOR

Plan L-818-CSA

Plan copyright held by home designer/architect

PRICES AND DETAILS
ON PAGES 12-15

Well Balanced

- A beautifully balanced facade plays against a well-planned interior in this country-style design.
- Twin gables with charming eave detailing complement a columned front porch, where double doors open into a fabulous Great Room. Spacious beyond expectations for a home of this square footage, the Great Room offers a fireplace, sliding-glass-door access to the backyard and a high ceiling.
- A serving bar defines the boundary between the Great Room and the kitchen. An adjacent breakfast nook opens out to a rear porch. The kitchen is well positioned to serve the porch, the nook and the formal dining room.
- The secluded master bedroom is topped by a stepped ceiling. The suite includes a walk-in closet and a private bath with a dual-sink vanity, a tub and separate shower, and a private toilet.
- The upper floor provides space for future expansion.

Plan AX-1303

Bedrooms: 3+	Baths: 2
Living Area:	
Main floor	1,823 sq. ft.
Total Living Area:	**1,823 sq. ft.**
Future upper floor	323 sq. ft.
Standard basement	1,823 sq. ft.
Garage and storage	473 sq. ft.
Exterior Wall Framing:	2x4

Foundation Options:

Standard basement
Crawlspace
Slab

(All plans can be built with your choice of foundation and framing. A generic conversion diagram is available. See order form.)

BLUEPRINT PRICE CODE: B

VIEW INTO GREAT ROOM AND KITCHEN

UPPER FLOOR

REAR VIEW

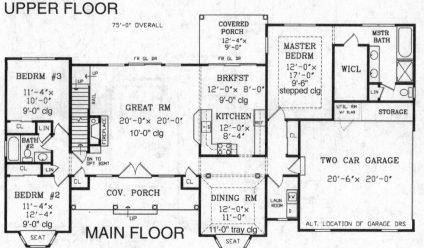

MAIN FLOOR

ORDER BLUEPRINTS ANYTIME!
CALL TOLL-FREE 1-800-820-1296

Plan AX-1303
Plan copyright held by home designer/architect

PRICES AND DETAILS
ON PAGES 12-15

225

Classic Styling

- Classic styling transcends the exterior and interior of this sprawling one-story.
- Outside, sweeping rooflines, arched windows and brick planters combine for an elegant curb appeal.
- The angled entry opens to a tiled foyer, which overlooks the spacious central living room. A handsome fireplace and a string of windows lend light and volume to this high-profile area.

- Unfolding to the right, the kitchen and dining room flow together, making the space seem even larger. A snack counter, a bar sink and a corner pantry are attractive kitchen efficiencies. Extra storage is offered in the nearby garage.
- The master suite is drenched in luxury with a romantic fireplace, a private porch and a grand Jacuzzi bath with lush surrounding plant shelves.
- Two good-sized secondary bedrooms share another full bath.

Plan L-824-EMB

Bedrooms: 3	Baths: 2

Living Area:	
Main floor	1,826 sq. ft.

Total Living Area:	**1,826 sq. ft.**
Garage and storage	534 sq. ft.

Exterior Wall Framing:	2x4

Foundation Options:

Slab
(All plans can be built with your choice of foundation and framing. A generic conversion diagram is available. See order form.)

BLUEPRINT PRICE CODE:	B

MAIN FLOOR

72'-4"

DINING
10'-8" x 13'
10' clg

STORAGE

2-CAR GARAGE
18' x 22'-4"

UTIL.

STORAGE

FRENCH DOORS

LIVING ROOM
23' x 15'-4"
9' clg

FIREPLACE

FIREPLACE

KITCHEN
11' x 15'
9' clg

MASTER BEDROOM
13'-8" x 18'
9' clg

FOYER

PLANTER

BATH 2

LINEN

BATH
10' clg

BEDROOM 2
10' x 13'-8"
9' clg

BEDROOM 3
10' x 11'-8"
11' clg

PLANTER

PLANTER

57'-0"

Plan L-824-EMB

Plan copyright held by home designer/architect

PRICES AND DETAILS
ON PAGES 12-15

JUST-RIGHT HOMES

Outdoor Surprises!

- A private entry courtyard topped by an intricate trellis draws attention to this beautiful brick home.
- The drama continues inside, where you'll find high ceilings, sprawling openness and breathtaking views of the many outdoor living spaces.
- The central hearth room is a great spot to welcome your guests and keep them entertained with its dazzling fireplace and media center combination.
- Appetizers and refreshments can be served at the long snack bar extending from the triangular kitchen.
- Plenty of space for formal mingling is offered in the spacious living and dining room expanse beyond. The screened porch, adjoining patio and panoramic views will inspire hours of conversation.
- Ideal for the empty nester, this home includes two private bedroom suites. The master suite boasts his-and-hers closets, vanities and toilets.
- The studio at the front of the home could also serve as an extra bedroom or home office.

Plan EOF-86-B

Bedrooms: 2+	Baths: 2½
Living Area:	
Main floor	1,830 sq. ft.
Total Living Area:	**1,830 sq. ft.**
Screened porch	134 sq. ft.
Garage	433 sq. ft.
Exterior Wall Framing:	2x4

Foundation Options:

Slab
(All plans can be built with your choice of foundation and framing. A generic conversion diagram is available. See order form.)

BLUEPRINT PRICE CODE: **B**

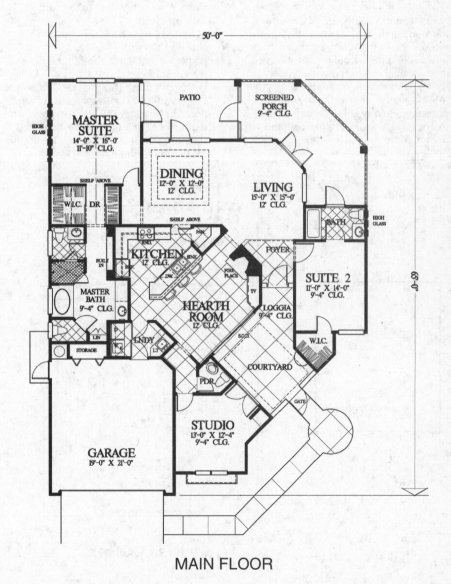

MAIN FLOOR

Plan EOF-86-B

Plan copyright held by home designer/architect

The Good Life

- The good life beckons from the rustic wraparound veranda of this charming farmhouse design.
- Inside, the living room features a cozy fireplace, a media center and a huge bay looking out to the veranda.
- Just past the living room, the dining room offers access to the veranda through a lovely set of French doors.
- A corner snack bar serving both the living and dining rooms highlights the galley kitchen.

- The main-floor master suite boasts a luxurious private bath with a corner garden tub and a separate shower, dual sinks, a private toilet and a spacious walk-in closet.
- Upstairs, two secondary bedrooms share a full hall bath. One flaunts a gorgeous bay while the other enjoys a walk-in closet.
- The upper floor also includes a storage closet, built-in bookshelves and French doors to a wonderful sun room reminiscent of a turn-of-the-century sleeping porch. Soak up the rays in this resplendent retreat.

Plan L-830-VACA	
Bedrooms: 3+	**Baths:** 2½
Living Area:	
Upper floor	578 sq. ft.
Main floor	1,141 sq. ft.
Sun room	78 sq. ft.
Storage	35 sq. ft.
Total Living Area:	**1,832 sq. ft.**
Garage	480 sq. ft.
Exterior Wall Framing:	2x4
Foundation Options:	
Slab	

(All plans can be built with your choice of foundation and framing. A generic conversion diagram is available. See order form.)

BLUEPRINT PRICE CODE:	**B**

2 - CAR GARAGE
20' x 24'

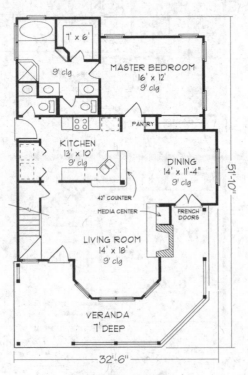

MAIN FLOOR

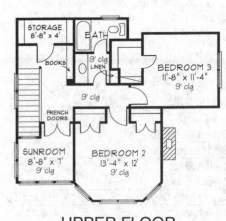

UPPER FLOOR

ORDER BLUEPRINTS ANYTIME!
CALL TOLL-FREE 1-800-820-1296

Plan L-830-VACA
Plan copyright held by home designer/architect

PRICES AND DETAILS
ON PAGES 12-15

Delightful Great Room

- An expansive Great Room with a vaulted ceiling, a warm corner fireplace and an angled wet bar highlights this tastefully appointed home.
- On the exterior, decorative plants thrive in the lush wraparound planter that leads to the sheltered entry. The foyer is brightened by a sidelight and a skylight.
- To the left, the kitchen offers an island cooktop with lots of room for food preparation and serving. The bayed breakfast nook is enhanced by bright windows and a vaulted ceiling.
- Formal dining is hosted in the space adjoining the Great Room. Graced by a lovely bay window, the room also offers French doors to a covered patio.
- In the sleeping wing of the home, the master bedroom features a sitting area and a walk-in closet. The private master bath boasts a relaxing Jacuzzi tub.
- Two secondary bedrooms share a full bath nearby. Laundry facilities are also convenient.

Plan S-52394

Bedrooms: 3	Baths: 2
Living Area:	
Main floor	1,841 sq. ft.
Total Living Area:	**1,841 sq. ft.**
Standard basement	1,789 sq. ft.
Garage	432 sq. ft.
Exterior Wall Framing:	2x6

Foundation Options:

Standard basement
Crawlspace
Slab

(All plans can be built with your choice of foundation and framing. A generic conversion diagram is available. See order form.)

BLUEPRINT PRICE CODE: **B**

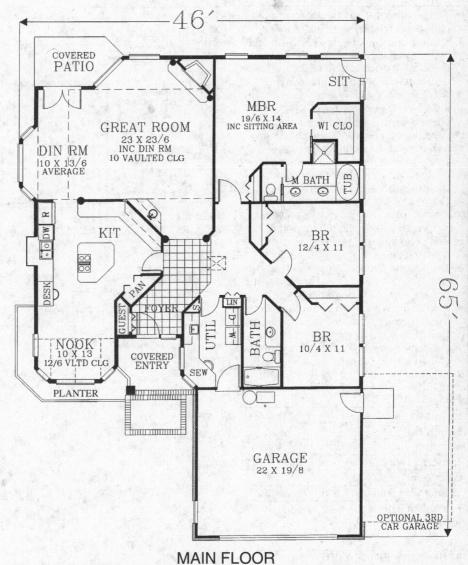

MAIN FLOOR

ORDER BLUEPRINTS ANYTIME!
CALL TOLL-FREE 1-800-820-1296

Plan S-52394

Plan copyright held by home designer/architect

PRICES AND DETAILS
ON PAGES 12-15

229

Golf, Anyone?

- Along with lovely arches that frame half-round windows, an interesting roofline and a livable layout, this home offers a parking space for your golf cart! If you have dreams of living by the golf course, this may be the plan for you.
- Transom-topped glass entry doors make a distinct first impression: This is a classy place! The tiled foyer and cavernous family room straight ahead indicate that it's comfortable, too.
- To the right of the foyer, a dramatic tray ceiling and a half-round window smartly promote the dining room.
- The nearby kitchen boasts an easy walk-through plan with a versatile angled serving bar. Access to a back porch, not to mention an optional bay window, deftly enhance the breakfast nook.
- Just past the kitchen, a hallway leads to two secluded bedrooms. Each has private access to a shared full bath.
- A vestibule with an art niche announces the entry to the master suite. An elegant tray ceiling and a porch door punctuate the bedroom, while a dual-sink vanity, a garden tub and a separate shower heighten the allure of the swank bath.

Plan HDS-99-355

Bedrooms: 3	Baths: 2½
Living Area:	
Main floor	1,834 sq. ft.
Total Living Area:	**1,834 sq. ft.**
Garage	743 sq. ft.
Exterior Wall Framing:	8-in. concrete block

Foundation Options:

Slab

(All plans can be built with your choice of foundation and framing. A generic conversion diagram is available. See order form.)

BLUEPRINT PRICE CODE:	**B**

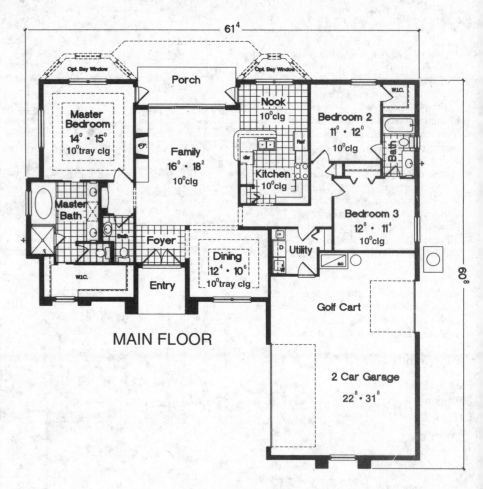

MAIN FLOOR

Plan HDS-99-355

Plan copyright held by home designer/architect

PRICES AND DETAILS
ON PAGES 12-15

Take a Look!

- Once you take a look at this delightful home, you're sure to be enchanted by its many amenities. Out front, a perfectly sized porch offers a warm welcome to visitors.
- Inside, the entry leads back to the Great Room, where a cathedral ceiling with exposed wood beams draws admiring glances from guests. The handsome fireplace maximizes the room's comforting nature.
- To the left, the bayed dining room and kitchen merge together, creating an

efficient space for family meals. A breakfast bar between the two rooms holds bulky serving dishes during dinner, while a pantry stores sundries.
- Across the home, a coffered ceiling, a private bath and two huge walk-in closets distinguish the master suite from the other bedrooms.
- A vaulted ceiling also tops the front-facing secondary bedroom.
- Above the garage, a bonus room provides space to grow. Depending on your needs, this spot would be great as a home office, a workshop or an extra bedroom. You decide!

Plan KD-1577

Bedrooms: 3+		Baths: 2
Living Area:		
Main floor		1,577 sq. ft.
Bonus room		274 sq. ft.
Total Living Area:		**1,851 sq. ft.**
Garage		438 sq. ft.
Exterior Wall Framing:		2x4

Foundation Options:

Crawlspace
Slab
(All plans can be built with your choice of foundation and framing. A generic conversion diagram is available. See order form.)

BLUEPRINT PRICE CODE:	**B**

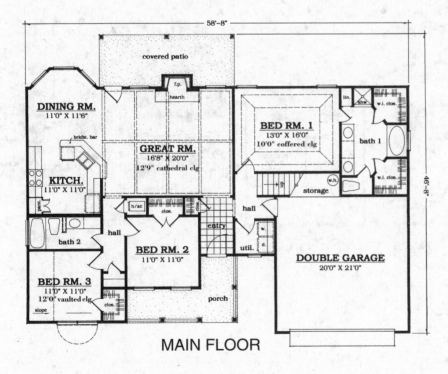

MAIN FLOOR

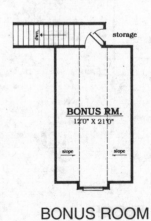

BONUS ROOM

ORDER BLUEPRINTS ANYTIME!
CALL TOLL-FREE 1-800-820-1296

Plan KD-1577
Plan copyright held by home designer/architect

PRICES AND DETAILS
ON PAGES 12-15

231

Unique Inside and Out

- This delightful design is as striking on the inside as it is on the outside.
- The focal point of the home is the huge Grand Room, which features a soaring, vaulted ceiling, high plant shelves and lots of glass, including a clerestory window. French doors flanking the fireplace lead to a spacious porch and two adjoining sun decks.
- The open, centrally located kitchen enjoys easy access from any room;

a full bath and a laundry area are located nearby.
- The two main-floor master suites are another unique design element of the home. Each suite showcases an airy, vaulted ceiling, a sunny window seat, a private bath, a walk-in closet and French doors that open to a sun deck.
- Upstairs, two guest suites under a vaulted peak overlook the gorgeous Grand Room below.
- The multiple suites make this design a perfect shared vacation home.
- The one-car garage at the rear of the home offers convenient access and additional storage space.

Plan EOF-13

Bedrooms: 4	Baths: 3
Living Area:	
Upper floor	443 sq. ft.
Main floor	1,411 sq. ft.
Total Living Area:	**1,854 sq. ft.**
Garage	264 sq. ft.
Storage	50 sq. ft.
Exterior Wall Framing:	2x6

Foundation Options:

Crawlspace
(All plans can be built with your choice of foundation and framing. A generic conversion diagram is available. See order form.)

BLUEPRINT PRICE CODE: **B**

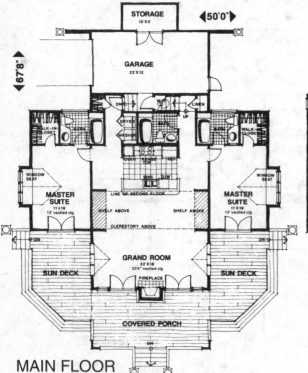

MAIN FLOOR

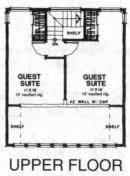

UPPER FLOOR

VIEW INTO GRAND ROOM

Plan EOF-13
Plan copyright held by home designer/architect

PRICES AND DETAILS
ON PAGES 12-15

Sun-Filled Living Areas

- Multiple windows flood the interior of this traditional two-story design with plenty of warm sunshine.
- Just off the two-story foyer, the formal dining room is crowned by an elegant, octagonal-shaped tray ceiling.
- A sun-filled living room and bayed breakfast area stretch across the back of the home. An open railing between the two areas allows the corner fireplace in the living room to be seen from both the nook and the island kitchen.
- In the kitchen, a pantry and a built-in desk aid the family chef. The half-bath and laundry room adjoining the garage allow you to clean up after a day spent working in the garden.
- Upstairs, the master suite features a lovely bay window, a big walk-in closet and a private bath with a dressing area, twin vanities and a lavish garden tub. Three secondary bedrooms and another full bath complete the design.

Plan OH-135	
Bedrooms: 4	**Baths:** 2½
Living Area:	
Upper floor	935 sq. ft.
Main floor	923 sq. ft.
Total Living Area:	**1,858 sq. ft.**
Standard basement	923 sq. ft.
Garage	400 sq. ft.
Exterior Wall Framing:	2x4

Foundation Options:

Standard basement
(All plans can be built with your choice of foundation and framing. A generic conversion diagram is available. See order form.)

BLUEPRINT PRICE CODE: B

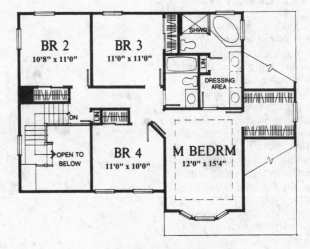

UPPER FLOOR

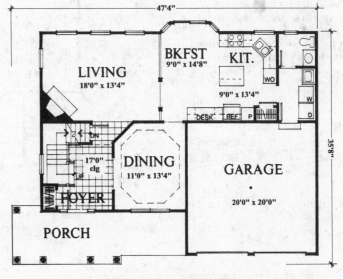

MAIN FLOOR

ORDER BLUEPRINTS ANYTIME!
CALL TOLL-FREE 1-800-820-1296

Plan OH-135
Plan copyright held by home designer/architect

PRICES AND DETAILS
ON PAGES 12-15

233

Classic Blend

- With decorative brick quoins, a columned porch and stylish dormers, the exterior of this classic one-story provides an interesting blend of Early American and European design.
- Just off the foyer, the bay-windowed formal dining room is enhanced by an stepped ceiling.
- The spacious Great Room, separated from the dining room by a columned arch, features a stepped ceiling, a built-in media center and a striking fireplace. Lovely French doors lead to a big backyard patio.
- The breakfast room, which shares an eating bar with the kitchen, boasts a sloped ceiling. French doors access a covered rear porch.
- The master bedroom has a tray ceiling, a sunny bay window and a roomy walk-in closet. The master bath features a whirlpool tub in a bayed nook and a separate shower.
- The front-facing bedroom is enhanced by a vaulted area over an arched transom window.

Plan AX-93304

Bedrooms: 3	Baths: 2
Living Area:	
Main floor	1,860 sq. ft.
Total Living Area:	**1,860 sq. ft.**
Standard basement	1,860 sq. ft.
Garage	434 sq. ft.
Exterior Wall Framing:	2x4

Foundation Options:

Standard basement
Crawlspace
Slab
(All plans can be built with your choice of foundation and framing. A generic conversion diagram is available. See order form.)

BLUEPRINT PRICE CODE:	B

VIEW INTO GREAT ROOM

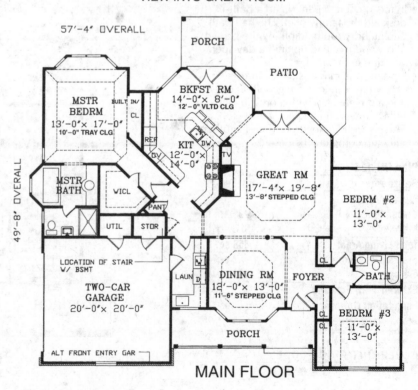

MAIN FLOOR

ORDER BLUEPRINTS ANYTIME! CALL TOLL-FREE 1-800-820-1296

Plan AX-93304

Plan copyright held by home designer/architect

PRICES AND DETAILS ON PAGES 12-15

Intriguing!

- A unique roofline and a rustic stone chimney grace the exterior of this intriguing two-story home.
- Past the covered entryway, the reception area offers a striking view of the formal spaces. A warm fireplace, a dramatic skylight and a sloped ceiling highlight the living room, while the dining room shows off a vaulted ceiling and a radiant curved glass wall!
- Folding doors open to the informal living areas, which include a cozy family room, a semi-circular dinette and a U-shaped kitchen equipped with a snack bar. Sliding glass doors in the family room open to an isolated terrace.
- An alternate layout that interchanges the kitchen and the family room is included with the blueprints.
- The secluded master bedroom suite offers a private terrace, a walk-in closet and a garden whirlpool bath. The main-floor laundry closet is close by.
- Off the upper-floor balcony are three additional bedrooms, a skylighted split bath and generous attic storage space.

Plan K-662-NA

Bedrooms: 4	Baths: 2½
Living Area:	
Upper floor	670 sq. ft.
Main floor	1,196 sq. ft.
Total Living Area:	**1,866 sq. ft.**
Standard basement	1,196 sq. ft.
Garage	418 sq. ft.
Exterior Wall Framing:	2x4 or 2x6
Foundation Options:	
Standard basement	
Slab	

(All plans can be built with your choice of foundation and framing. A generic conversion diagram is available. See order form.)

BLUEPRINT PRICE CODE:	B

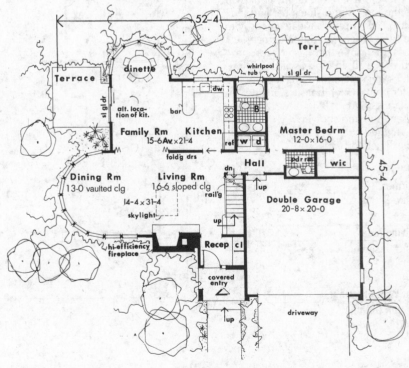

UPPER FLOOR

MAIN FLOOR

ORDER BLUEPRINTS ANYTIME!
CALL TOLL-FREE 1-800-820-1296

Plan K-662-NA
Plan copyright held by home designer/architect

PRICES AND DETAILS
ON PAGES 12-15   235

A Real Charmer

- A tranquil railed porch makes this country one-story a real charmer.
- The main entry opens directly into the Great Room, which serves as the home's focal point. A cathedral ceiling soars above, while a fireplace and a built-in cabinet for games make the space a fun gathering spot.
- Beautiful French doors expand the Great Room to a peaceful covered porch at the rear of the home. Open the doors and let in the fresh summer air!
- A bayed breakfast nook unfolds from the kitchen, where the family cook will love the long island snack bar and the pantry. The carport is located nearby to save steps when you unload groceries.
- Across the home, the master bedroom features a walk-in closet with built-in shelves. A cathedral ceiling tops the master bath, which boasts a private toilet, a second walk-in closet and a separate tub and shower.
- A skylighted hall bath services the two secondary bedrooms.

Plan J-9508

Bedrooms: 3	Baths: 2½
Living Area:	
Main floor	1,875 sq. ft.
Total Living Area:	**1,875 sq. ft.**
Standard basement	1,875 sq. ft.
Carport	418 sq. ft.
Storage	114 sq. ft.
Exterior Wall Framing:	2x4

Foundation Options:

Standard basement
Crawlspace
Slab
(All plans can be built with your choice of foundation and framing. A generic conversion diagram is available. See order form.)

BLUEPRINT PRICE CODE: B

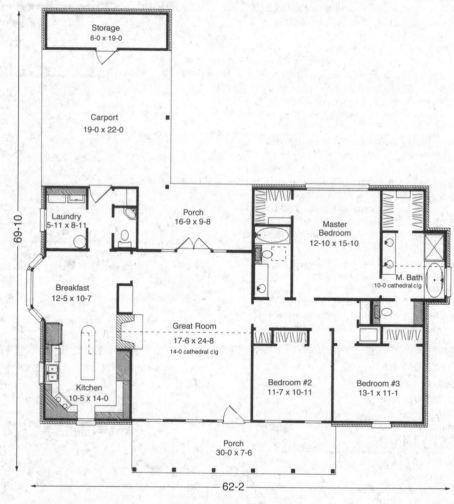

MAIN FLOOR

ORDER BLUEPRINTS ANYTIME! CALL TOLL-FREE 1-800-820-1296

Plan J-9508

Plan copyright held by home designer/architect

PRICES AND DETAILS ON PAGES 12-15

Familiarity
Breeds Content

- The familiar sight of this home's noble facade will bring ultimate contentment to you at the end of the day.
- From the foyer, double doors invite you into a quiet den or study. With its optional wet bar, this private space is a nice spot to unwind or surf the Internet before dinner.
- Presided over by a stunning fireplace, the huge central family room can host your larger gatherings. Sliding glass doors open to a covered patio that delivers a great view of the backyard. Why not line up some lawn chairs and cheer the participants of the family's croquet contest?
- A private entrance to the back patio enhances the master bedroom. Your morning will get off to the right start in the private bath, which boasts a large walk-in closet, a separate tub and shower, and a dual-sink vanity.
- When the kids stumble from their beds in the morning, they'll wake up quickly in the bright, bayed breakfast nook. The efficient layout of the kitchen lets you serve up their oatmeal in record time!

Plan HDS-99-287

Bedrooms: 3+	Baths: 2
Living Area:	
Main floor	1,869 sq. ft.
Total Living Area:	**1,869 sq. ft.**
Garage	470 sq. ft.
Exterior Wall Framing:	2×4

Foundation Options:

Slab
(All plans can be built with your choice of foundation and framing. A generic conversion diagram is available. See order form.)

BLUEPRINT PRICE CODE: B

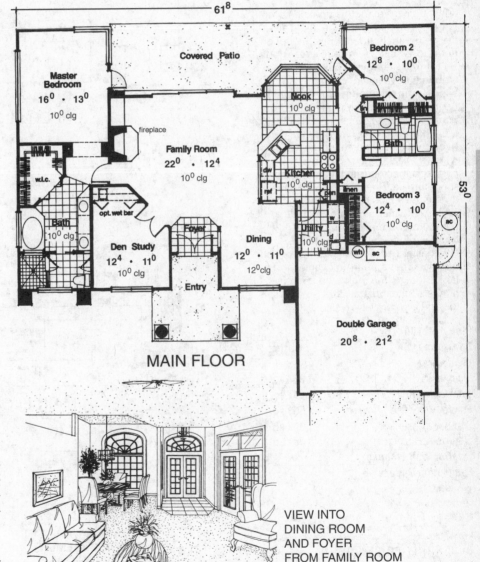

MAIN FLOOR

VIEW INTO
DINING ROOM
AND FOYER
FROM FAMILY ROOM

Plan HDS-99-287
Plan copyright held by home designer/architect

PRICES AND DETAILS
ON PAGES 12-15

JUST-RIGHT HOMES

Upscale Charm

- Country charm and the very latest in conveniences mark this upscale home. For extra appeal, all of the living areas are on the main floor, while the upper floor hosts space for future expansion.
- Set off from the foyer, the dining room is embraced by elegant columns. Arched windows in the dining room and in the bedroom across the hall echo the front porch detailing. Straight ahead, a wall of French doors in the family room overlooks a back porch and a large deck.
- A curved island snack bar smoothly connects the gourmet kitchen to the sunny breakfast area, which features a dramatic vaulted ceiling brightened by skylights. Other amenities include a computer room and a laundry/utility room with a recycling center.
- The master bedroom's luxurious private bath includes a dual-sink vanity and a large storage unit with a built-in chest of drawers. Other extras are a step-up spa tub and a separate shower.

Plan J-92100

Bedrooms: 3+	Baths: 2
Living Area:	
Main floor	1,877 sq. ft.
Total Living Area:	**1,877 sq. ft.**
Future upper floor	1,500 sq. ft.
Standard basement	1,877 sq. ft.
Garage and storage	551 sq. ft.
Exterior Wall Framing:	2x4

Foundation Options:

Standard basement
Crawlspace
Slab

(All plans can be built with your choice of foundation and framing. A generic conversion diagram is available. See order form.)

BLUEPRINT PRICE CODE:	B

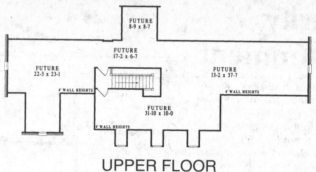

UPPER FLOOR

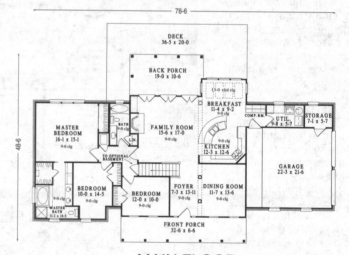

MAIN FLOOR

STAIRWAY AREA IN NON-BASEMENT VERSIONS

VIEW INTO FAMILY ROOM AND BREAKFAST NOOK

ORDER BLUEPRINTS ANYTIME! CALL TOLL-FREE 1-800-820-1296

Plan J-92100
Plan copyright held by home designer/architect

PRICES AND DETAILS ON PAGES 12-15

Distinguished Durability

- Sturdy tapered columns with brick pedestals give this unique home a feeling of durability and security.
- Off the foyer, the spacious living room is brightened by the incoming light of the double dormers above. The high ceiling and the glass-framed fireplace add further ambience. An atrium door opens to the wraparound porch.
- Decorative wood columns and a high ceiling enhance the dining room.
- The neat kitchen shares serving counters with the breakfast nook and the living room, for easy service to both locations. A central cooktop island and a built-in desk are other conveniences.
- The main bath has twin sinks and is easily accessible from the secondary bedrooms and the living areas.
- An oval garden tub, an isolated toilet and dual sinks are featured in the master bath. The master suite also boasts a cathedral ceiling, a huge walk-in closet and a private porch.

Plan DW-1883

Bedrooms: 3	Baths: 2
Living Area:	
Main floor	1,883 sq. ft.
Total Living Area:	**1,883 sq. ft.**
Standard basement	1,883 sq. ft.
Exterior Wall Framing:	2x4

Foundation Options:

Standard basement

Crawlspace

Slab

(All plans can be built with your choice of foundation and framing. A generic conversion diagram is available. See order form.)

BLUEPRINT PRICE CODE: **B**

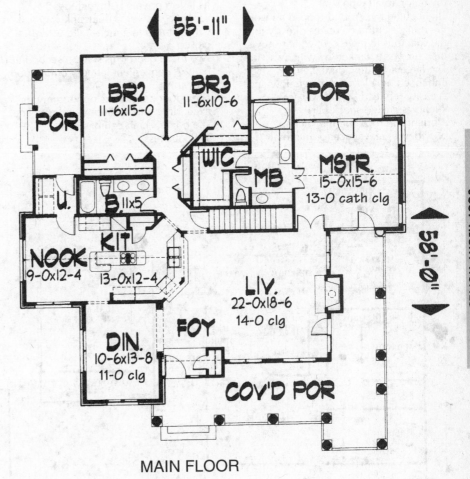

MAIN FLOOR

ORDER BLUEPRINTS ANYTIME!
CALL TOLL-FREE 1-800-820-1296

Plan DW-1883

Plan copyright held by home designer/architect

PRICES AND DETAILS
ON PAGES 12-15

239

Open Invitation

- The wide front porch of this friendly country-style home extends an open invitation to all who visit.
- Highlighted by a round-topped transom, the home's entrance opens directly into the spacious living room, which shows off a fireplace flanked by windows.
- The large adjoining dining area is enhanced by a lovely bay window and is easily serviced by the updated kitchen's angled snack bar.
- A bright sun room off the kitchen provides a great space for informal

meals or relaxation. Access to a back porch is nearby.
- The good-sized master bedroom is secluded from the other sleeping areas. Its lavish private bath includes a separate shower, a dual-sink vanity, a garden tub and a nice-sized walk-in closet.
- Two more bedrooms share a second full bath. A convenient laundry/utility room is nearby.
- The upper floor offers opportunity for expanding into additional living space.
- The home's high ceilings add spaciousness.

Plan J-91078	
Bedrooms: 3+	**Baths:** 2
Living Area:	
Main floor	1,879 sq. ft.
Total Living Area:	**1,879 sq. ft.**
Future upper floor	1,007 sq. ft.
Standard basement	1,846 sq. ft.
Garage	484 sq. ft.
Storage	132 sq. ft.
Exterior Wall Framing:	2x6

Foundation Options:
Standard basement
Crawlspace
Slab
(All plans can be built with your choice of foundation and framing. A generic conversion diagram is available. See order form.)

BLUEPRINT PRICE CODE: B

VIEW INTO DINING AND LIVING ROOMS

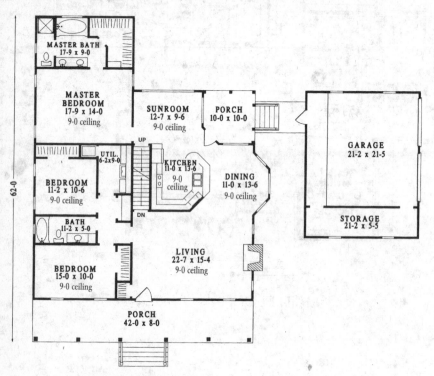

MAIN FLOOR

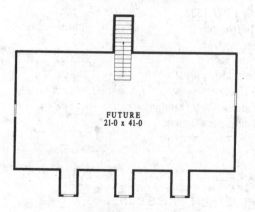

UPPER FLOOR

JUST-RIGHT HOMES

ORDER BLUEPRINTS ANYTIME!
CALL TOLL-FREE 1-800-820-1296

Plan J-91078

Plan copyright held by home designer/architect

PRICES AND DETAILS
ON PAGES 12-15

Great Expectations

- With its striking, columned front porch and plentiful windows, this home would make an ideal weekend haven or a cozy family dwelling.
- The heart of this abode is the sunken Great Room. With a warming fireplace, tall windows and a vaulted ceiling, it's sure to be a favorite gathering place. Sliding doors lead to the broad rear patio, perfect for morning coffee.

- The sun-drenched breakfast nook is ideal for intimate Sunday brunches with family or friends. The adjoining island kitchen features a garden view above the sink and additional storage in the nearby pantry.
- Across the entry, the master suite offers a vaulted ceiling, built-in bookshelves and a walk-in closet. The private bath boasts a sunny garden tub and a separate shower.
- Upstairs, the sun-drenched loft would make a great retreat for book-lovers and also leaves plenty of space for a home theater or office.

Plan GS-2002	
Bedrooms: 2+	**Baths:** 2
Living Area:	
Upper floor	279 sq. ft.
Main floor	1,615 sq. ft.
Total Living Area:	**1,894 sq. ft.**
Exterior Wall Framing:	2x6
Foundation Options:	

Crawlspace
(All plans can be built with your choice of foundation and framing. A generic conversion diagram is available. See order form.)

BLUEPRINT PRICE CODE:	**B**

MAIN FLOOR

PATIO
59-0

SOLARIUM

NOOK
10-10 x 12-8
12-8 vaulted clg

GREAT ROOM
21 x 18
25 vaulted clg

sunken floor

DN

CLST DN STOR

KITCHEN

UTIL

PNTR

ENTRY

UP

WH

COVERED PORCH

MASTER BEDROOM
14-2 x 14
12-4 vaulted clg

BOOK SHELVES

TUB

MSTR BATH

WALK-IN CLST

BATH

BEDROOM 2
10-4 x 10-6
11-8 sloped clg

FURN

D W

39-6

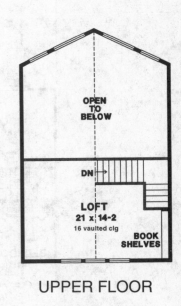

UPPER FLOOR

OPEN TO BELOW

DN

LOFT
21 x 14-2
16 vaulted clg

BOOK SHELVES

ORDER BLUEPRINTS ANYTIME!
CALL TOLL-FREE 1-800-820-1296

Plan GS-2002
Plan copyright held by home designer/architect

PRICES AND DETAILS
ON PAGES 12-15

241

Fantastic Family Living Space

- Luxury begins at the front door with this exciting one-story traditional home.
- The eye-catching front entry opens to an impressive vaulted foyer. Double doors lead to an unusual living room that can be used as a den, a home office or an extra bedroom.
- The formal dining room has easy access to the combination kitchen, breakfast room and family room. This fantastic family living space is punctuated by floor-to-ceiling windows, a tray ceiling, a fireplace and views of the rear deck.
- Double doors open to the vaulted master suite, which features French doors leading to the deck, just right for romantic moonlight strolls. There's also a luxurious bath with a corner spa tub, as well as a large walk-in closet.
- Two more bedrooms and another full bath are set apart across the home.
- A utility room near the two-car garage rounds out the floor plan.

Plan APS-1812

Bedrooms: 3+	Baths: 2
Living Area:	
Main floor	1,886 sq. ft.
Total Living Area:	**1,886 sq. ft.**
Standard basement	1,886 sq. ft.
Garage	400 sq. ft.
Exterior Wall Framing:	2x4

Foundation Options:

Standard basement
Crawlspace
Slab

(All plans can be built with your choice of foundation and framing. A generic conversion diagram is available. See order form.)

BLUEPRINT PRICE CODE: B

MAIN FLOOR

66

49

DECK

15 vltd clg

MASTER BEDROOM
19x13
15 vaulted clg

BEDROOM 2
14x10
9 clg

BREAKFAST
16x8
9 clg

W
D

FAMILY ROOM
18x14
12 tray clg

KITCHEN
13x9
9 clg

BEDROOM 3
14x11
9 clg

LIVING/
BR 4
12x11
9 clg

FOYER
12
vltd clg

DINING
12x13
9 clg

GARAGE
20x20

Plan APS-1812

Plan copyright held by home designer/architect

PRICES AND DETAILS
ON PAGES 12-15

Exemplary Colonial

- Inside this traditionally designed home is an exciting floor plan for today's lifestyles. The classic center-hall arrangement of this Colonial allows easy access to each of the living areas.
- Plenty of views are possible from the formal rooms at the front of the home, as well as from the informal areas at the rear.
- The spacious kitchen offers lots of counter space, a handy work island, a laundry closet and a sunny bayed breakfast nook.
- The adjoining family room shows off a fireplace and elegant double doors to the rear. An optional set of double doors opens to the living room.
- The beautiful master suite on the upper level boasts a vaulted ceiling, two closets, dual sinks, a garden tub and a separate shower.

Plan CH-100-A	
Bedrooms: 4	**Baths:** 2½
Living Area:	
Upper floor	923 sq. ft.
Main floor	965 sq. ft.
Total Living Area:	**1,888 sq. ft.**
Basement	952 sq. ft.
Garage	462 sq. ft.
Exterior Wall Framing:	2x4

Foundation Options:

Daylight basement

Standard basement

Crawlspace

(All plans can be built with your choice of foundation and framing. A generic conversion diagram is available. See order form.)

BLUEPRINT PRICE CODE: B

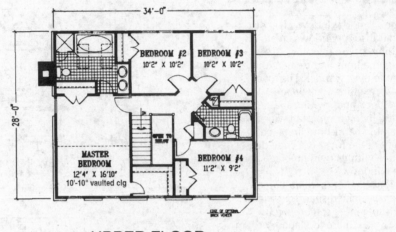

UPPER FLOOR

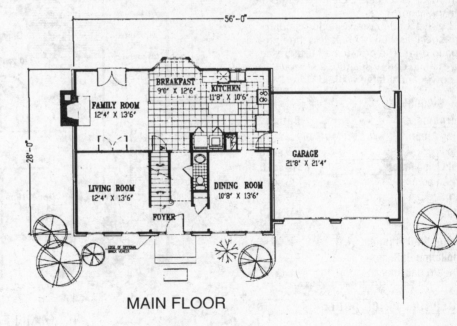

MAIN FLOOR

ORDER BLUEPRINTS ANYTIME!
CALL TOLL-FREE 1-800-820-1296

Plan CH-100-A

Plan copyright held by home designer/architect

PRICES AND DETAILS
ON PAGES 12-15

243

A Real Original

- This home's round window, elegant entry and transom windows create an eye-catching, original look.
- Inside, high ceilings and tremendous views let the eyes wander. The foyer provides an exciting look at an expansive deck and inviting spa through the living room's tall windows, which frame a handsome fireplace.
- To the right of the foyer is a cozy den or home office with its own fireplace and dramatic windows.
- The spacious kitchen/breakfast area features an oversized snack bar island and opens to a large screen porch. Within easy reach are the laundry room and the entrance to the garage.
- The bright formal dining room overlooks the deck and offers a clear view into the living room.
- The secluded master suite looks out to the deck as well, with access through a patio door. The private bath features a dynamite corner spa tub, a separate shower and a large walk-in closet.

Plan B-90065

Bedrooms: 2+	**Baths:** 2

Living Area:	
Main floor	1,889 sq. ft.
Total Living Area:	**1,889 sq. ft.**
Screen porch	136 sq. ft.
Standard basement	1,889 sq. ft.
Garage	406 sq. ft.
Storage	60 sq. ft.
Exterior Wall Framing:	2x6

Foundation Options:

Standard basement

(All plans can be built with your choice of foundation and framing. A generic conversion diagram is available. See order form.)

BLUEPRINT PRICE CODE: B

VIEW INTO LIVING ROOM

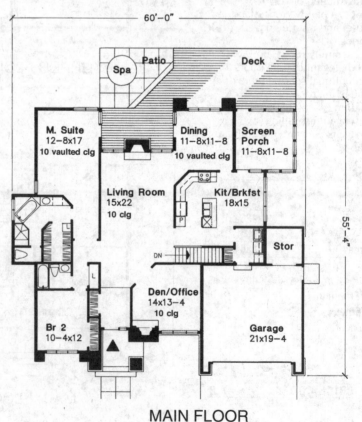

MAIN FLOOR

ORDER BLUEPRINTS ANYTIME! CALL TOLL-FREE 1-800-820-1296

Plan B-90065

Plan copyright held by home designer/architect

PRICES AND DETAILS ON PAGES 12-15

Garden Home with a View

- This clever design proves that privacy doesn't have to be compromised even in high-density urban neighborhoods. From within, views are oriented to a beautiful, lush entry courtyard and a covered rear porch.
- The exterior appearance is sheltered, but warm and welcoming.
- The innovative interior design centers on a unique kitchen, which directs traffic away from the working areas while still serving the entire home.
- The sunken family room features a vaulted ceiling and a warm fireplace.
- The master suite is highlighted by a sumptuous master bath with an oversized shower and a whirlpool tub, plus a large walk-in closet.
- The formal living room is designed and placed in such a way that it can become a third bedroom, a den, or an office or study room, depending on family needs and lifestyles.

Plan E-1824

Bedrooms: 2+	Baths: 2
Living Area:	
Main floor	1,891 sq. ft.
Total Living Area:	**1,891 sq. ft.**
Garage	506 sq. ft.
Storage	60 sq. ft.
Exterior Wall Framing:	2x4

Foundation Options:

Crawlspace

Slab

(All plans can be built with your choice of foundation and framing. A generic conversion diagram is available. See order form.)

BLUEPRINT PRICE CODE: B

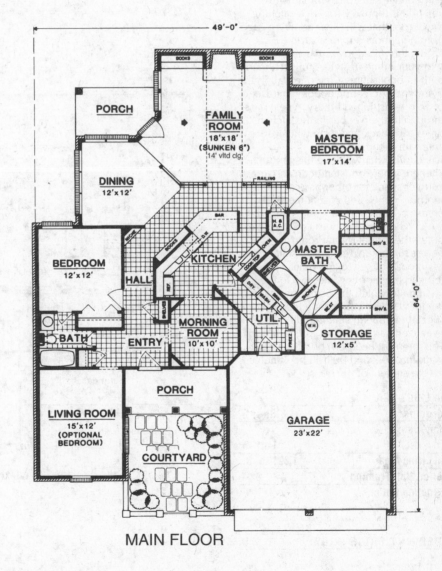

MAIN FLOOR

ORDER BLUEPRINTS ANYTIME!
CALL TOLL-FREE 1-800-820-1296

Plan E-1824
Plan copyright held by home designer/architect

PRICES AND DETAILS
ON PAGES 12-15

245

Quite a Cottage

- This cottage's inviting wraparound veranda is topped by an eye-catching metal roof that will draw admiring gazes from neighbors out for a stroll.
- Inside, the raised foyer ushers guests into your home in style. Straight ahead, built-in bookshelves line one wall in the living room, creating a look reminiscent of an old-fashioned library. A neat pass-through to the wet bar in the kitchen saves trips back and forth when you entertain friends.
- The family chef will love the gourmet kitchen, where an island cooktop frees counter space for other projects. For morning coffee and casual meals, the breakfast nook sets a cheery, relaxed tone. When appearances count, move out to the formal dining room.
- Across the home, the master suite serves as an oasis of peace and quiet. First thing in the morning, step out to the veranda to watch the rising sun soak up the mist. When you want a little extra special treatment, sink into the oversized garden tub for a long bath.
- The foremost bedroom boasts a large walk-in closet and built-in bookshelves for the student of the house.

Plan L-893-VSA

Bedrooms: 3	Baths: 2
Living Area:	
Main floor	1,891 sq. ft.
Total Living Area:	**1,891 sq. ft.**
Exterior Wall Framing:	2x4

Foundation Options:

Slab

(All plans can be built with your choice of foundation and framing. A generic conversion diagram is available. See order form.)

BLUEPRINT PRICE CODE:	**B**

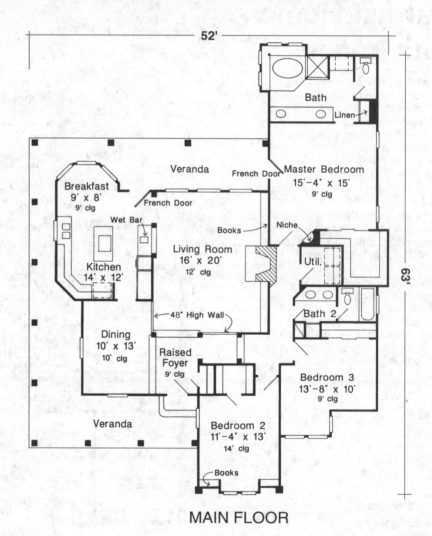

MAIN FLOOR

ORDER BLUEPRINTS ANYTIME! CALL TOLL-FREE 1-800-820-1296

Plan L-893-VSA

Plan copyright held by home designer/architect

PRICES AND DETAILS ON PAGES 12-15

Ultimate French Comfort

- Delightful interior touches coupled with a striking French facade make this home the ultimate in one-story comfort.
- In the sidelighted entry, an attractive overhead plant ledge captures the eye.
- The entry opens to the formal dining and living rooms—both of which boast high ceilings.
- In the living room, a handy wet bar and a media center flank a handsome fireplace. Large windows frame wide backyard views. Around the corner, French doors open to a back porch.
- Adjacent to the dining room, the kitchen offers a speedy serving bar. A bayed nook lights up with morning sun.
- Double doors open to the master bedroom, with its cute window seat and TV shelf. A high ceiling tops it off.
- Two walk-in closets with glamorous mirror doors flank the walkway to the master bath, which offers an exotic garden tub and a separate shower.
- One of the two roomy secondary bedrooms offers a walk-in closet, a built-in desk and a gorgeous window.

Plan RD-1895

Bedrooms: 3	Baths: 2
Living Area:	
Main floor	1,895 sq. ft.
Total Living Area:	**1,895 sq. ft.**
Garage and storage	485 sq. ft.
Exterior Wall Framing:	2x4

Foundation Options:

Crawlspace

Slab

(All plans can be built with your choice of foundation and framing. A generic conversion diagram is available. See order form.)

BLUEPRINT PRICE CODE: B

MAIN FLOOR

ORDER BLUEPRINTS ANYTIME!
CALL TOLL-FREE 1-800-820-1296

Plan RD-1895

Plan copyright held by home designer/architect

PRICES AND DETAILS
ON PAGES 12-15

247

Playful Floor Plan

- A high hip roof and a recessed entry give this home a smart-looking exterior. A dynamic floor plan—punctuated with angled walls, high ceilings and playful window treatments—gives the home an exciting interior.
- The sunken Great Room, the circular dining room and the angled island kitchen are the heartbeat of the home. The Great Room offers a vaulted ceiling, a fireplace, a built-in corner entertainment center and tall arched windows overlooking the backyard.

- An angled railing separates the Great Room from the open kitchen and dining room. An atrium door next to the glassed-in dining area leads to the backyard. The kitchen includes an island snack bar and a garden window.
- The master bedroom is nestled into one corner of the home for quiet and privacy. This deluxe suite features two walk-in closets and a luxurious whirlpool bath with a dual-sink vanity.
- An extra-large laundry area, complete with a clothes-folding counter and a coat closet, is accessible from the three-car garage.
- The home is expanded by high ceilings throughout.

Plan PI-90-435	
Bedrooms: 3	**Baths:** 2
Living Area:	
Main floor	1,896 sq. ft.
Total Living Area:	**1,896 sq. ft.**
Daylight basement	1,889 sq. ft.
Garage	667 sq. ft.
Exterior Wall Framing:	2x6
Foundation Options:	

Daylight basement
(All plans can be built with your choice of foundation and framing. A generic conversion diagram is available. See order form.)

BLUEPRINT PRICE CODE:	B

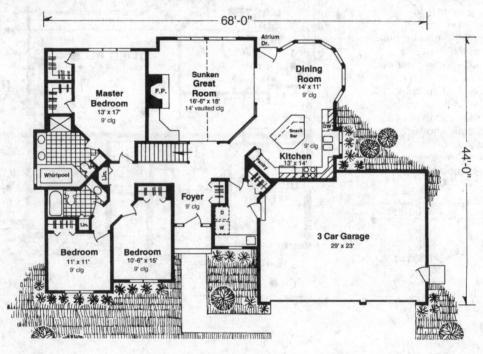

MAIN FLOOR

ORDER BLUEPRINTS ANYTIME!
CALL TOLL-FREE 1-800-820-1296

Plan PI-90-435
Plan copyright held by home designer/architect

PRICES AND DETAILS ON PAGES 12-15

Octagonal Dining Bay

- Classic traditional styling is recreated with a covered front porch and triple dormers with half-round windows.
- Off the entry porch, double doors reveal the reception area, with a walk-in closet and a half-bath.

- The living room features a striking fireplace and leads to the dining room, with its octagonal bay.
- The island kitchen overlooks the dinette and the family room, which features a second fireplace and sliding glass doors to a rear deck.
- Upstairs, the master suite boasts a walk-in closet and a whirlpool bath. A skylighted hallway connects three more bedrooms and another full bath.

Plan K-680-R	
Bedrooms: 4	**Baths:** 2½
Living Area:	
Upper floor	853 sq. ft.
Main floor	1,047 sq. ft.
Total Living Area:	**1,900 sq. ft.**
Standard basement	1,015 sq. ft.
Garage and storage	472 sq. ft.
Exterior Wall Framing:	2x4 or 2x6

Foundation Options:

Standard basement

Slab

(All plans can be built with your choice of foundation and framing. A generic conversion diagram is available. See order form.)

BLUEPRINT PRICE CODE: **B**

PRICES AND DETAILS ON PAGES 12-15

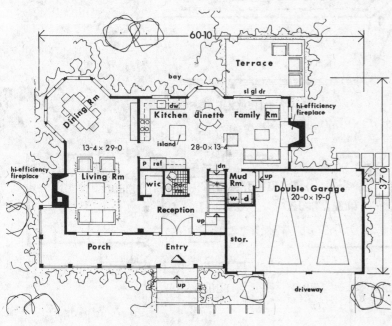

MAIN FLOOR

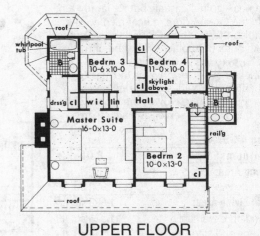

UPPER FLOOR

VIEW INTO LIVING AND DINING ROOMS

Plan K-680-R

Plan copyright held by home designer/architect

While Away an Afternoon

- The pretty porch that fronts this home provides plenty of room for whiling away an afternoon. Try a porch swing on one end and a cluster of comfortable wicker furniture on the other.
- Inside, columns introduce the living room and the dining room, on either side of the foyer. A tray ceiling lends elegance to the living room.
- At the rear of the home, the Great Room, the breakfast nook and the kitchen flow into one another, creating an easygoing, casual spot for family fun. In the Great Room, a neat media wall holds the TV, the VCR and the stereo. An angled fireplace adds a bit of rustic charm to the setting.
- Tucked away for privacy, the master bedroom provides a pleasant retreat. A stepped ceiling crowns the room, while a bay window serves as a sitting area.

Plan AX-5374

Bedrooms: 3	Baths: 2
Living Area:	
Main floor	1,902 sq. ft.
Total Living Area:	**1,902 sq. ft.**
Standard basement	1,925 sq. ft.
Garage and storage	534 sq. ft.
Utility room	18 sq. ft.
Exterior Wall Framing:	2x4

Foundation Options:

Standard basement

Crawlspace

Slab

(All plans can be built with your choice of foundation and framing. A generic conversion diagram is available. See order form.)

BLUEPRINT PRICE CODE: B

VIEW INTO GREAT ROOM

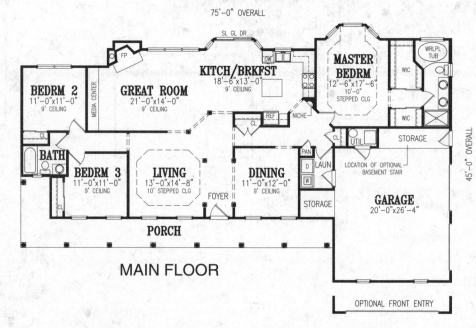

MAIN FLOOR

JUST-RIGHT HOMES

ORDER BLUEPRINTS ANYTIME!
CALL TOLL-FREE 1-800-820-1296

Plan AX-5374

Plan copyright held by home designer/architect

PRICES AND DETAILS
ON PAGES 12-15

Spacious and Open

- A brilliant wall of windows invites guests into the two-story-high foyer of this striking traditional home.
- At the center of this open floor plan, the sunken family room boasts a vaulted ceiling and a striking fireplace with flanking windows.
- The cozy dinette merges with the family room and the island kitchen, creating a spacious, open atmosphere. A pantry closet, a laundry room, a half-bath and garage access are all nearby.
- The formal living and dining rooms are found at the front of the home. The living room boasts a cathedral ceiling and a lovely window arrangement.
- The main-floor master bedroom has a tray ceiling, a walk-in closet and a lush bath designed for two.
- Upstairs, two bedrooms share another full bath and a balcony landing that overlooks the family room and foyer.

Plan A-2207-DS	
Bedrooms: 3	**Baths:** 2½
Living Area:	
Upper floor	518 sq. ft.
Main floor	1,389 sq. ft.
Total Living Area:	**1,907 sq. ft.**
Standard basement	1,389 sq. ft.
Garage	484 sq. ft.
Exterior Wall Framing:	2x6
Foundation Options:	
Standard basement	

(All plans can be built with your choice of foundation and framing. A generic conversion diagram is available. See order form.)

BLUEPRINT PRICE CODE:	B

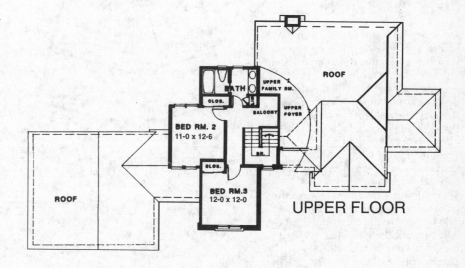

UPPER FLOOR

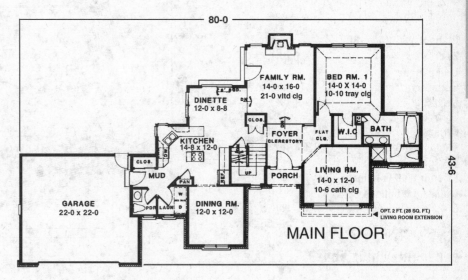

MAIN FLOOR

ORDER BLUEPRINTS ANYTIME!
CALL TOLL-FREE 1-800-820-1296

Plan A-2207-DS
Plan copyright held by home designer/architect

PRICES AND DETAILS
ON PAGES 12-15

251

Solar Design that Shines

- A passive-solar sun room, an energy-efficient woodstove and a panorama of windows make this design really shine.
- The open living/dining room features a vaulted ceiling, glass-filled walls and access to the dramatic decking. A balcony above gives the huge living/dining area definition while offering spectacular views.
- The streamlined kitchen has a convenient serving bar that connects it to the living/dining area.
- The main-floor bedroom features dual closets and easy access to a full bath. The laundry room, located just off the garage, doubles as a mudroom and includes a handy coat closet.
- The balcony hallway upstairs is bathed in natural light. The two nice-sized bedrooms are separated by a second full bath.

Plans H-855-3A & -3B

Bedrooms: 3	Baths: 2-3
Living Area:	
Upper floor	586 sq. ft.
Main floor	1,192 sq. ft.
Sun room	132 sq. ft.
Daylight basement	1,192 sq. ft.
Total Living Area:	**1,910/3,102 sq. ft.**
Garage	520 sq. ft.
Exterior Wall Framing:	2x6
Foundation Options:	**Plan #**
Daylight basement	H-855-3B
Crawlspace	H-855-3A

(All plans can be built with your choice of foundation and framing. A generic conversion diagram is available. See order form.)

BLUEPRINT PRICE CODE:	**B/E**

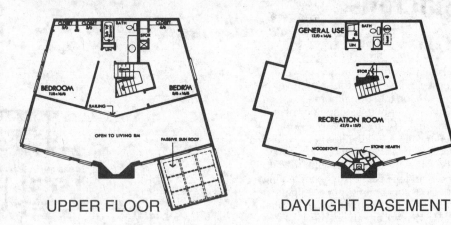

UPPER FLOOR   DAYLIGHT BASEMENT

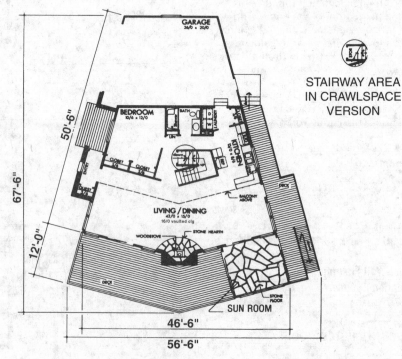

STAIRWAY AREA IN CRAWLSPACE VERSION

MAIN FLOOR

ORDER BLUEPRINTS ANYTIME! CALL TOLL-FREE 1-800-820-1296

Plans H-855-3A & -3B

Plan copyright held by home designer/architect

PRICES AND DETAILS ON PAGES 12-15

Good Move!

- With its front porch, shutters and graceful dormers, this home exudes comfort and livability. When you invite them in for the first time, family and friends will congratulate you on your good move.
- From the foyer flows the open expanse of the Great Room and the dining room. The Great Room boasts a corner fireplace and sliding glass doors to the rear porch.
- The island kitchen offers ample work space and a lovely bayed breakfast nook; enjoy your morning coffee amid the sun's cheery rays!
- A private office with an outside entrance contributes privacy and quiet to your home business. It can also serve as a fourth bedroom.
- The secluded master suite charms you with a stepped ceiling and a bright bay window. Its amenities include two walk-in closets and a vaulted bath with a dual-sink vanity, a private toilet and a whirlpool tub.
- Across the home, two secondary bedrooms share another full bath.

REAR VIEW

Plan AX-5378

Bedrooms: 3+	Baths: 2
Living Area:	
Main floor	1,914 sq. ft.
Total Living Area:	**1,914 sq. ft.**
Standard basement	1,925 sq. ft.
Garage and storage	482 sq. ft.
Exterior Wall Framing:	2x4

Foundation Options:

Standard basement
Crawlspace
Slab

(All plans can be built with your choice of foundation and framing. A generic conversion diagram is available. See order form.)

BLUEPRINT PRICE CODE:	**B**

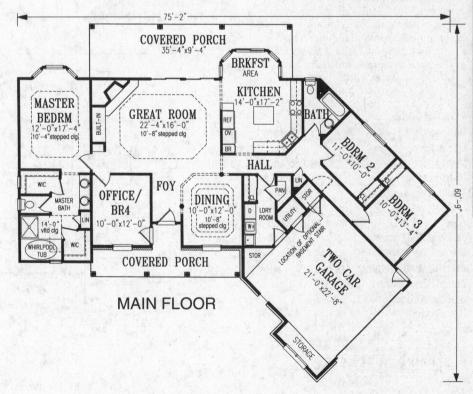

MAIN FLOOR

ORDER BLUEPRINTS ANYTIME!
CALL TOLL-FREE 1-800-820-1296

Plan AX-5378

Plan copyright held by home designer/architect

PRICES AND DETAILS
ON PAGES 12-15

253

Indoor/Outdoor Delights

- A curved porch in the front and a garden sun room in the back make this home an indoor/outdoor delight.
- Inside, a roomy kitchen is open to a five-sided, glassed-in dining room that looks out to the porch.
- The living room features a fireplace nestled into a radiant glass wall that adjoins the sunny garden room.
- Wrapped in windows, the garden room accesses the backyard as well as a storage area in the side-entry garage.
- The master suite is luxurious, featuring a sumptuous master bath with a garden tub, a corner shower and a big closet.
- The two secondary bedrooms have boxed-out windows and walk-in closets. They share a full bath.

Plan DD-1852

Bedrooms: 3+	Baths: 2
Living Area:	
Main floor	1,680 sq. ft.
Garden room	240 sq. ft.
Total Living Area:	**1,920 sq. ft.**
Future area	316 sq. ft.
Attic	309 sq. ft.
Standard basement	1,680 sq. ft.
Garage and storage	570 sq. ft.
Exterior Wall Framing:	2x4

Foundation Options:

Standard basement

Crawlspace

Slab

(All plans can be built with your choice of foundation and framing. A generic conversion diagram is available. See order form.)

BLUEPRINT PRICE CODE:	**B**

VIEW INTO
DINING ROOM
FROM KITCHEN

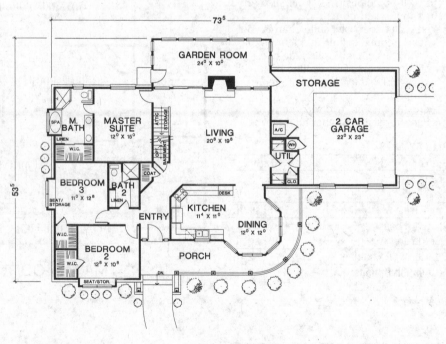

MAIN FLOOR

ORDER BLUEPRINTS ANYTIME!
CALL TOLL-FREE 1-800-820-1296

Plan DD-1852
Plan copyright held by home designer/architect

PRICES AND DETAILS
ON PAGES 12-15

Fond of French?

- Old country elegance and comfort are yours with this beautiful French traditional home.
- Central to all activities in the home, the large living room boasts the warmth of a fireplace and is complemented by built-in bookshelves.
- The convenient galley kitchen features a handy snack bar shared with the living room, and a breakfast nook for casual meals. A formal dining room lies between the kitchen and the foyer.
- "Luxurious" best describes the master suite, with an art niche to display your favorite sculpture, and a lavish bath that boasts dual sinks and a Jacuzzi tub. A roomy walk-in closet and built-in shelves are welcome additions, providing plenty of space for clothing and storage.
- Across the home, two secondary bedrooms share another full bath. A porch in the rear will tempt you to sit back and unwind on a sunny summer afternoon.

Plan L-925-FA

Bedrooms: 3	Baths: 2
Living Area:	
Main floor	1,923 sq. ft.
Total Living Area:	**1,923 sq. ft.**
Garage	490 sq. ft.
Exterior Wall Framing:	2x4

Foundation Options:

Slab

(All plans can be built with your choice of foundation and framing. A generic conversion diagram is available. See order form.)

BLUEPRINT PRICE CODE: B

MAIN FLOOR

ORDER BLUEPRINTS ANYTIME!
CALL TOLL-FREE 1-800-820-1296

Plan L-925-FA

Plan copyright held by home designer/architect

PRICES AND DETAILS
ON PAGES 12-15

255

Irresistible Master Suite

- This home's main-floor master suite is hard to resist, with its inviting window seat and delightful bath.
- A covered front entry topped by a dormer with a half-round window introduces the home.
- Inside, a tray ceiling and a picture window accent the formal dining room.
- Straight back, the Great Room features a high vaulted ceiling with a window wall facing the backyard. The fireplace can be enjoyed from the adjoining kitchen and breakfast area.
- The gourmet kitchen includes a corner sink, an island cooktop and a walk-in pantry. A vaulted ceiling expands the breakfast nook, which features a built-in desk and backyard deck access.
- The vaulted master suite offers a private bath with a walk-in closet, a garden tub, a separate shower and a dual-sink vanity with a sit-down makeup area.
- A stairway leads up to another full bath that serves two additional bedrooms.

Plan B-89061

Bedrooms: 3	Baths: 2½
Living Area:	
Upper floor	436 sq. ft.
Main floor	1,490 sq. ft.
Total Living Area:	**1,926 sq. ft.**
Standard basement	1,490 sq. ft.
Garage	400 sq. ft.
Exterior Wall Framing:	2x4

Foundation Options:

Standard basement

(All plans can be built with your choice of foundation and framing. A generic conversion diagram is available. See order form.)

BLUEPRINT PRICE CODE: **B**

REAR VIEW

MAIN FLOOR

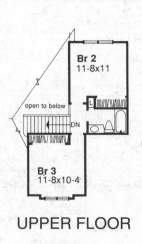

UPPER FLOOR

Plan B-89061

Plan copyright held by home designer/architect

PRICES AND DETAILS
ON PAGES 12-15

Decked-Out Chalet

- This gorgeous chalet is partially surrounded by a large and roomy deck that is great for indoor/outdoor living.
- The living and dining area shows off a fireplace with a raised hearth, plus large windows to take in the outdoor views. The area is further expanded by a vaulted ceiling in the dining room and sliding glass doors that lead to the deck.
- The kitchen offers a breakfast bar that separates it from the dining area. A convenient laundry room is nearby.
- The main-floor master bedroom is just steps away from a linen closet and a hall bath. Two upstairs bedrooms share a second full bath.
- The highlight of the upper floor is a balcony room with a vaulted ceiling, exposed beams and tall windows. A decorative railing provides an overlook into the dining area below.

Plans H-919-1 & -1A

Bedrooms: 3	Baths: 2
Living Area:	
Upper floor	869 sq. ft.
Main floor	1,064 sq. ft.
Daylight basement	475 sq. ft.
Total Living Area:	**1,933/2,408 sq. ft.**
Tuck-under garage	501 sq. ft.
Exterior Wall Framing:	2x6
Foundation Options:	**Plan #**
Daylight basement	H-919-1
Crawlspace	H-919-1A

(All plans can be built with your choice of foundation and framing. A generic conversion diagram is available. See order form.)

BLUEPRINT PRICE CODE:	B/C

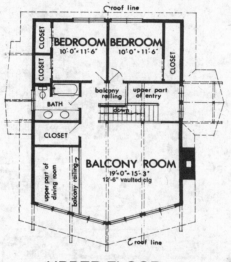

UPPER FLOOR

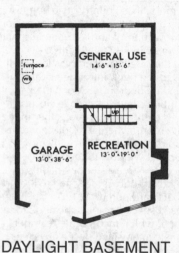

DAYLIGHT BASEMENT

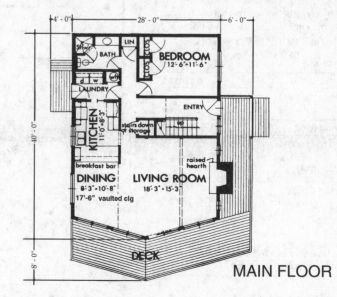

MAIN FLOOR

JUST-RIGHT HOMES

ORDER BLUEPRINTS ANYTIME!
CALL TOLL-FREE 1-800-820-1296

Plans H-919-1 & -1A
Plan copyright held by home designer/architect

PRICES AND DETAILS
ON PAGES 12-15

257

Morning Glory

- This melodious country-style home opens itself to the sights and sounds of nature with front and rear porches, and dazzling window treatments.
- From the sidelighted entry, a long hall leads to the right, introducing three secondary bedrooms. Along the way, you'll find plenty of storage closets.
- There's plenty of space to gather in the family room, where a fireplace warms the spirit. Bird-watchers will enjoy a boxed-out window to the rear.
- The cheery breakfast nook flaunts its own boxed-out window and a door to the backyard porch.
- A raised snack bar joins the nook to the kitchen, which incorporates cabinets into its center island. Just a few steps bring you to the formal dining room.
- The master suite is enhanced by a charming window seat. The private bath is packed with essentials, including twin walk-in closets, a whirlpool tub and a dual-sink vanity. The sit-down shower is sure to be a morning eye-opener!

Plan RD-1944

Bedrooms: 4	**Baths:** 2

Living Area:

Main floor	1,944 sq. ft.
Total Living Area:	**1,944 sq. ft.**
Standard basement	1,750 sq. ft.
Garage and storage	538 sq. ft.
Exterior Wall Framing:	2x4

Foundation Options:

Standard basement

Crawlspace

Slab

(All plans can be built with your choice of foundation and framing. A generic conversion diagram is available. See order form.)

BLUEPRINT PRICE CODE:	**B**

VIEW INTO FAMILY ROOM

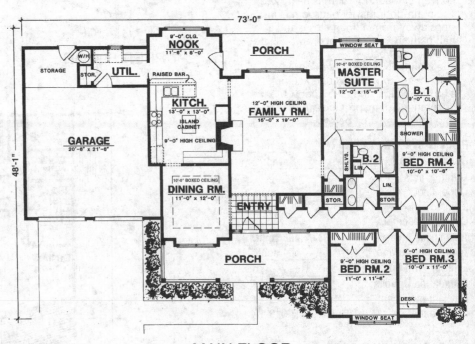

MAIN FLOOR

ORDER BLUEPRINTS ANYTIME!
CALL TOLL-FREE 1-800-820-1296

Plan RD-1944

Plan copyright held by home designer/architect

PRICES AND DETAILS
ON PAGES 12-15

Country Living

- A covered porch, half-round transom windows and three dormers give this home its warm, nostalgic appeal. Shuttered windows and a louvered vent beautify the side-entry, two-car garage.
- Designed for the ultimate in country living, the floor plan starts off with a dynamic Great Room that flows to a bayed dining area. A nice fireplace adds warmth, while a French door provides access to a backyard covered porch. A powder room is just steps away.
- A vaulted ceiling presides over the large country kitchen, which offers a bayed nook, an oversized breakfast bar and a convenient pass-through to the rear porch.
- The exquisite master suite boasts a tray ceiling, a bay window and an alcove for built-in shelves or extra closet space. Other amenities include a large walk-in closet and a compartmentalized bath.
- Upstairs, high ceilings enhance two more bedrooms and a second full bath. Each bedroom boasts a cozy dormer window and two closets.

Plan AX-93311

Bedrooms: 3	Baths: 2½
Living Area:	
Upper floor	570 sq. ft.
Main floor	1,375 sq. ft.
Total Living Area:	**1,945 sq. ft.**
Standard basement	1,280 sq. ft.
Garage	450 sq. ft.
Exterior Wall Framing:	2x4

Foundation Options:

Standard basement
Crawlspace
Slab

(All plans can be built with your choice of foundation and framing. A generic conversion diagram is available. See order form.)

BLUEPRINT PRICE CODE:	B

VIEW INTO GREAT ROOM

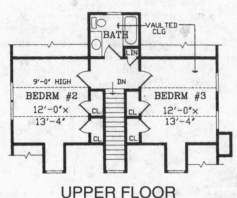

UPPER FLOOR

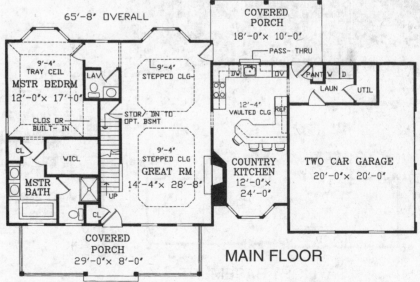

MAIN FLOOR

ORDER BLUEPRINTS ANYTIME!
CALL TOLL-FREE 1-800-820-1296

Plan AX-93311
Plan copyright held by home designer/architect

PRICES AND DETAILS
ON PAGES 12-15

259

Meant to Be

- One glimpse of the beautiful front view will tempt you, and a good look at the stunning rear view will convince you, that this home was meant to be yours!
- The vaulted, skylighted entry ushers you to the Great Room, which shows off a vaulted ceiling and features a cozy fireplace. Sliding glass doors provide speedy access to an incredible wraparound deck.
- Equipped for any sudden culinary inspirations, the well-planned kitchen features its own pantry. You'll also appreciate its close proximity to the garage when it's time to unload those heavy grocery bags.

- The master suite will take your breath away, with its walk-in closet and a secluded bath with dual sinks and a spa tub. Exquisite French doors create easy access to the deck.
- Imagine magical nights on the deck. With the kids at Grandma's house, put on some soft music and use the deck as your own private dance floor!
- A vast unfinished area in the daylight basement promises excitement. Turn it into a game room for the ultimate in entertainment. A fourth bedroom and a full bath complete the space.

Plan SUN-1310-C

Bedrooms: 3+	**Baths: 3½**
Living Area:	
Main floor	1,636 sq. ft.
Daylight basement (finished)	315 sq. ft.
Total Living Area:	**1,951 sq. ft.**
Daylight basement (unfinished)	730 sq. ft.
Garage	759 sq. ft.
Exterior Wall Framing:	2x6

Foundation Options:
Daylight basement
Crawlspace
Slab
(All plans can be built with your choice of foundation and framing. A generic conversion diagram is available. See order form.)

BLUEPRINT PRICE CODE:	**B**

REAR VIEW

DAYLIGHT BASEMENT

MAIN FLOOR

Plan SUN-1310-C

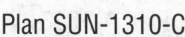

Plan copyright held by home designer/architect

PRICES AND DETAILS
ON PAGES 12-15

Long-Lasting Appeal

- The interesting roofline, attractive front deck and dramatic windows of this stylish sloping-lot home give it lasting contemporary appeal.
- The two-story entry opens up to the spacious living room, which boasts floor-to-ceiling windows and a vaulted ceiling with exposed beams.

- The adjoining dining area provides access to a wraparound railed deck.
- The updated kitchen offers a walk-in pantry, an eating bar and a breakfast nook with sliding glass doors to a second railed deck.
- A fireplace and access to a rear patio highlight the attached family room.
- Upstairs, a washer and dryer in the hall bath are convenient to all three bedrooms, making laundry a breeze.
- The master bedroom has a vaulted ceiling and a private bath.

Plan P-7737-4D

Bedrooms: 3	Baths: 2½
Living Area:	
Upper floor	802 sq. ft.
Main floor	1,158 sq. ft.
Total Living Area:	**1,960 sq. ft.**
Tuck-under garage	736 sq. ft.
Exterior Wall Framing:	2x6

Foundation Options:
Partial daylight basement
(All plans can be built with your choice of foundation and framing. A generic conversion diagram is available. See order form.)

BLUEPRINT PRICE CODE:	B

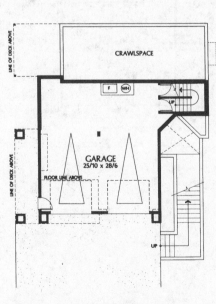

DAYLIGHT BASEMENT

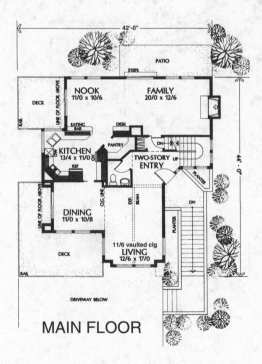

MAIN FLOOR

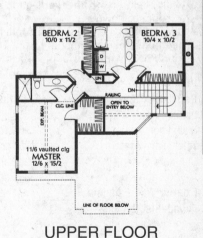

UPPER FLOOR

Morning Room with a View

- This modern-looking ranch is stylishly decorated with a pair of arched-window dormers, handsome brick trim and a covered front porch.
- Inside, the dining room is set off by columns, as it merges with the entry.
- The main living areas are oriented to the rear, where a huge central family room offers a patio view and a fireplace that may also be enjoyed from the bayed morning room and adjoining kitchen.
- The walk-through kitchen features a pantry, a snack bar to the family room and easy service to the formal dining room across the hall.
- The secluded master suite boasts a wide window seat and a private bath with a walk-in closet, a corner garden tub and a separate shower.
- Across the home, the three secondary bedrooms share another full bath. The fourth bedroom may double as a study.

Plan DD-1962-1

Bedrooms: 3+	Baths: 2
Living Area:	
Main floor	1,962 sq. ft.
Total Living Area:	**1,962 sq. ft.**
Standard basement	1,962 sq. ft.
Garage and storage	386 sq. ft.
Exterior Wall Framing:	2x4

Foundation Options:

Standard basement
Crawlspace
Slab

(All plans can be built with your choice of foundation and framing. A generic conversion diagram is available. See order form.)

BLUEPRINT PRICE CODE:	**B**

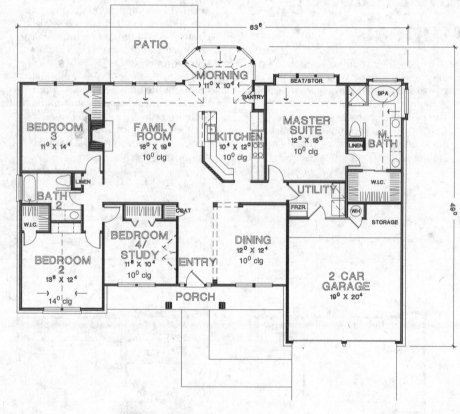

MAIN FLOOR

ORDER BLUEPRINTS ANYTIME!
CALL TOLL-FREE 1-800-820-1296

Plan DD-1962-1
Plan copyright held by home designer/architect

PRICES AND DETAILS
ON PAGES 12-15

Exploding Views

- This spectacular two-story has the style and that is perfect for your family.
- An exploding view from the two-story foyer is just a preview of the excitement that follows.
- Every major living space on the main floor has a view of the outdoors, whether it's looking over a pool area or the fifth tee.
- The expansive formal living and dining area is perfect for entertaining or candlelight dinners.

- The modern island kitchen overlooks the breakfast area and the family room, which boasts an exciting and functional media wall. Sliding glass doors open to the backyard.
- Luxurious double doors open to reveal the stunning master bedroom. Among its highlights are a private garden bath and a sparkling window wall. An optional second set of doors could access a nursery or a private study. Or, this room could be used as a conventional fourth bedroom.
- The home also offers your choice of elevation. Both elevations shown above are included in the working blueprints.

Plan HDS-99-145	
Bedrooms: 3+	**Baths:** 2½
Living Area:	
Upper floor	982 sq. ft.
Main floor	982 sq. ft.
Total Living Area:	**1,964 sq. ft.**
Garage	646 sq. ft.
Exterior Wall Framing:	2x4
Foundation Options:	
Slab	

(All plans can be built with your choice of foundation and framing. A generic conversion diagram is available. See order form.)

BLUEPRINT PRICE CODE:	**B**

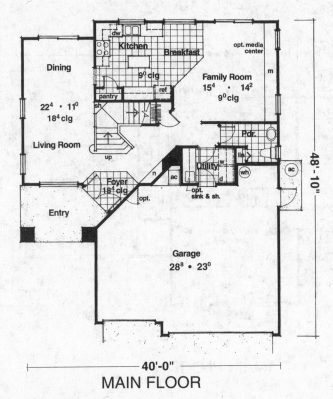

MAIN FLOOR

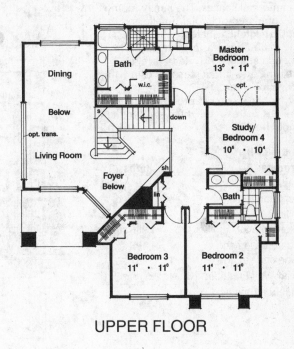

UPPER FLOOR

ORDER BLUEPRINTS ANYTIME!
CALL TOLL-FREE 1-800-820-1296

Plan HDS-99-145

Plan copyright held by home designer/architect

PRICES AND DETAILS
ON PAGES 12-15

263

Light-Filled Interior

- A stylish contemporary exterior and an open, light-filled interior define this two-level home.
- The covered entry leads to a central gallery. The huge living room and dining room combine to generate a spacious ambience that is enhanced by a cathedral ceiling and a warm fireplace with tall flanking windows.
- Oriented to the rear and overlooking a terrace and backyard landscaping are the informal spaces. The family room, the sunny semi-circular dinette and the modern kitchen share a snack bar.
- The main-floor master suite boasts a sloped ceiling, a private terrace, a dressing area and a personal bath with a whirlpool tub.
- Two to three extra bedrooms with high ceilings share a skylighted bath on the upper floor.

Plan K-683-D

Bedrooms: 3+	Baths: 2½
Living Area:	
Upper floor	491 sq. ft.
Main floor	1,475 sq. ft.
Total Living Area:	**1,966 sq. ft.**
Standard basement	1,425 sq. ft.
Garage and storage	487 sq. ft.
Exterior Wall Framing:	2x4 or 2x6

Foundation Options:

Standard basement
Slab

(All plans can be built with your choice of foundation and framing. A generic conversion diagram is available. See order form.)

BLUEPRINT PRICE CODE:	**B**

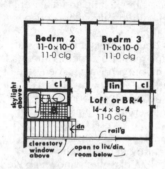

UPPER FLOOR

VIEW INTO DINING AND LIVING ROOMS

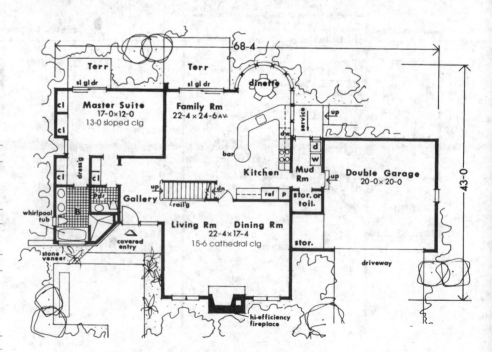

MAIN FLOOR

Plan K-683-D

Plan copyright held by home designer/architect

PRICES AND DETAILS
ON PAGES 12-15

Southern Comfort

- This sprawling three-bedroom design exemplifies the comfort and charm of Southern-style architecture.
- The columned front porch beckons you to relax on a Sunday afternoon.
- Inside, the formal dining room opens to the left of the foyer, which leads to the home's focal point—the large living room. Complete with a built-in entertainment center, a cozy fireplace and a snack bar, this space will attract

plenty of attention. Windows flanking the fireplace overlook the rear porch.
- Among the kitchen's many amenities are an island cooktop, a pantry closet and an adjoining breakfast area. The breakfast area accesses the rear porch through a French door.
- Secluded from the other bedrooms for privacy, the master suite is highlighted by two walk-in closets, a garden tub, a separate shower and a dual-sink vanity. The suite also enjoys private access to the rear porch.
- Across the home, two secondary bedrooms, one with a walk-in closet, share another full bath.

Plan L-1990-02A	
Bedrooms: 3	**Baths:** 2½
Living Area:	
Main floor	1,990 sq. ft.
Total Living Area:	**1,990 sq. ft.**
Garage	522 sq. ft.
Exterior Wall Framing:	2x4
Foundation Options:	

Slab

(All plans can be built with your choice of foundation and framing. A generic conversion diagram is available. See order form.)

BLUEPRINT PRICE CODE:	**B**

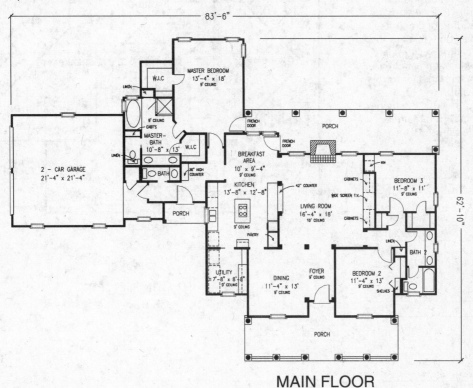

MAIN FLOOR

Plan L-1990-02A

Plan copyright held by home designer/architect

Outdoor Fête

- Who doesn't love an outdoor party? Front and rear porches and a spacious back deck make this design a natural for outside entertaining. The back porch features a spa and a summer kitchen.

- The interior is equally accommodating. Formal living and dining rooms flank the foyer, which leads into the stunning angled family room. A fireplace topped by a TV niche serves as the room's focal point. High above, a clerestory window illuminates the space.

- Columns define the entrance to the bright breakfast room and the kitchen, which boasts proximity to the two-car garage for easy unloading of groceries.

- When your guests are gone, relax in the master suite. A tray ceiling, a sitting area and a luxurious private bath make it a pampering retreat. A second bedroom is serviced by the hall bath.

- Plans are included for making the living room a third bedroom. A future area over the garage could be used as a studio or a playroom.

Plan APS-1914

Bedrooms: 2+	Baths: 3
Living Area:	
Main floor	1,992 sq. ft.
Total Living Area:	**1,992 sq. ft.**
Future area	247 sq. ft.
Standard basement	1,992 sq. ft.
Garage	590 sq. ft.
Mechanical	19 sq. ft.
Exterior Wall Framing:	2x4

Foundation Options:

Standard basement

Slab

(All plans can be built with your choice of foundation and framing. A generic conversion diagram is available. See order form.)

BLUEPRINT PRICE CODE: B

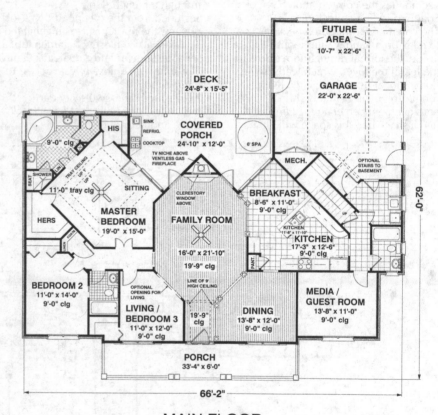

MAIN FLOOR

ORDER BLUEPRINTS ANYTIME!
CALL TOLL-FREE 1-800-820-1296

Plan APS-1914
Plan copyright held by home designer/architect

PRICES AND DETAILS
ON PAGES 12-15

Bright Outlook

- Brighten your perspective in this cozy, country-style home! Passersby will gaze admiringly at its glorious paned windows, accented by keystones and shutters; those within will enjoy viewing the great outdoors.
- A unique gallery introduces the magnificent Great Room, which showcases a fireplace flanked by two archtop windows. A sloped ceiling completes the picture of spaciousness.
- Flowing from the Great Room, the dining room offers access to a covered patio overlooking the backyard, and

also shares an angled snack counter with the island kitchen.
- An island cooktop, a gigantic walk-in pantry and a built-in desk distinguish the smart layout in the spacious kitchen. A window over the sink adds interest to those daily chores!
- Across the home, the master suite provides an ideal retreat. Its perks include a huge walk-in closet, a whirlpool tub, a separate shower, a private toilet and a dual-sink vanity. An arched window and private access to the patio create romance.
- Two additional bedrooms share a second full bath.

Plan DD-1982	
Bedrooms: 3	**Baths:** 2
Living Area:	
Main floor	1,993 sq. ft.
Total Living Area:	**1,993 sq. ft.**
Standard basement	1,993 sq. ft.
Garage and storage	538 sq. ft.
Exterior Wall Framing:	2x4
Foundation Options:	
Standard basement	
Crawlspace	
Slab	

(All plans can be built with your choice of foundation and framing. A generic conversion diagram is available. See order form.)

BLUEPRINT PRICE CODE:	B

MAIN FLOOR

MASTER SUITE
15⁴ x 15²
10⁰ CLG

COVERED PATIO

DINING
12¹⁰ x 11⁰
10⁰ SLOPED CLG

M. BATH
10⁰ CLG

WIC

GREAT ROOM
21⁸ X 21⁰
11⁷ CLG

ISLAND KITCHEN
13¹ X 13⁴

SPA

BATH 2

UTILITY
10⁰ CLG

DESK

OVEN/MICRO

PANTRY

GALLERY

13⁰ CLG

2-CAR GARAGE
27⁷ X 21⁰

BEDRM 3
12² x 11⁷
10⁰ SLOPED CLG

COVERED PORCH

BEDRM 2
11⁶ x 12²
10⁰ SLOPED CLG

COATS

STORAGE

75¹¹

53¹⁰

ORDER BLUEPRINTS ANYTIME!
CALL TOLL-FREE 1-800-820-1296

Plan DD-1982
Plan copyright held by home designer/architect

PRICES AND DETAILS
ON PAGES 12-15

267

Traditional Curb Appeal

- With an expansive front porch topped by a charming trio of dormers, this traditional country-style home offers the curb appeal you seek.
- Accessing both the formal dining room and a bayed morning room, the kitchen boasts a work island and an attractive, bow-shaped counter serving the living room. The mudroom and laundry facilities are just around the corner.
- Step through the spacious living room's French doors to the deck area. An optional barbecue and an outdoor spa make entertaining a breeze.
- The master suite enjoys a bayed sitting area, deck access, two walk-in closets and a private bath with separate vanities and a garden tub.
- Two more bedrooms share a full hall bath. Future space upstairs can be used as you desire.

Plan DD-1984

Bedrooms: 3+	Baths: 3
Living Area:	
Main floor	1,994 sq. ft.
Total Living Area:	**1,994 sq. ft.**
Future upper floor	1,316 sq. ft.
Standard basement	1,994 sq. ft.
Garage and storage	466 sq. ft.
Exterior Wall Framing:	2x4

Foundation Options:

Standard basement

Crawlspace

Slab

(All plans can be built with your choice of foundation and framing. A generic conversion diagram is available. See order form.)

BLUEPRINT PRICE CODE: B

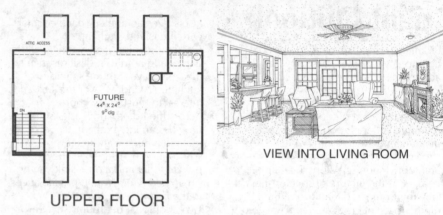

UPPER FLOOR

VIEW INTO LIVING ROOM

MAIN FLOOR

JUST-RIGHT HOMES

ORDER BLUEPRINTS ANYTIME!
CALL TOLL-FREE 1-800-820-1296

Plan DD-1984

Plan copyright held by home designer/architect

PRICES AND DETAILS
ON PAGES 12-15

On the Moor

- This lovely design, with its brick facade, keystones and corner quoins, would be right at home in the English countryside. It's a perfect choice for your special lot.
- A sheltered front porch gives way to the foyer, where a built-in corner display shelf waits to showcase your collection of Irish crystal.
- The formal dining room is visible over a half-wall. Here, sunlight streams through a triple window arrangement.
- Past decorative columns, the living room's inviting fireplace will have you

longing for winter's return. In the meantime, throw open the French doors that flank the fireplace, and enjoy the sounds and smells of a beautiful summer evening.

- The master suite is highlighted by a private bath that features a corner spa tub, a separate shower with a seat, a time-saving dual-sink vanity and a generous walk-in closet.
- Two secondary bedrooms also include walk-in closets. One of the rooms is brightened by a stunning Palladian window that gives the front of the home a look of pure elegance.

Plan L-1994-FA	
Bedrooms: 3	**Baths:** 2
Living Area:	
Main floor	1,994 sq. ft.
Total Living Area:	**1,994 sq. ft.**
Garage and storage	569 sq. ft.
Exterior Wall Framing:	2x4
Foundation Options:	
Slab	

(All plans can be built with your choice of foundation and framing. A generic conversion diagram is available. See order form.)

BLUEPRINT PRICE CODE: B

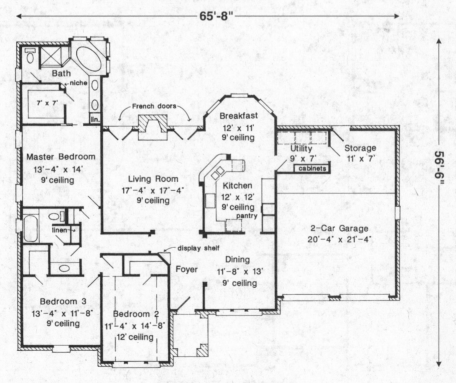

MAIN FLOOR

ORDER BLUEPRINTS ANYTIME!
CALL TOLL-FREE 1-800-820-1296

Plan L-1994-FA
Plan copyright held by home designer/architect

PRICES AND DETAILS
ON PAGES 12-15

269

Sprawling Brick Beauty

- Exquisite exterior details hint at the many exciting features you'll find inside this sprawling brick beauty.
- The raised foyer boasts a neat display niche above the coat closet to spark interest for your guests.
- Attractive formal spaces unfold from the foyer and share a lofty ceiling. The fireplace to the left is creatively nestled between built-in book cabinets. French doors whisk you to a lavish backyard covered porch.
- The kitchen and breakfast area flow together near the garage and laundry room for maximum mobility.
- Three bedrooms and two convenient dual-sink baths make up the sleeping wing. Entered through elegant double doors, the master suite offers the owners of the home a private library, garden bath and outdoor access.

Plan L-998-FA	
Bedrooms: 3	**Baths:** 2
Living Area:	
Main floor	1,996 sq. ft.
Total Living Area:	**1,996 sq. ft.**
Garage	449 sq. ft.
Exterior Wall Framing:	2x4
Foundation Options:	
Slab	

(All plans can be built with your choice of foundation and framing. A generic conversion diagram is available. See order form.)

BLUEPRINT PRICE CODE: B

JUST-RIGHT HOMES

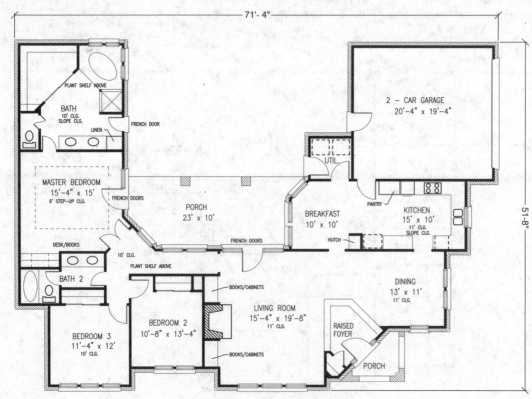

MAIN FLOOR

ORDER BLUEPRINTS ANYTIME!
CALL TOLL-FREE 1-800-820-1296

Plan L-998-FA
Plan copyright held by home designer/architect

PRICES AND DETAILS
ON PAGES 12-15

Relax on the Front Porch

- With its wraparound covered porch, this quaint two-story home makes summer evenings a breeze.
- Inside, a beautiful open stairway welcomes guests into the vaulted foyer, which connects the formal areas. The front-facing living and dining rooms have views of the covered front porch.
- French doors open from the living room to the family room, where a fireplace and corner windows warm and brighten this spacious activity area.
- The breakfast nook, set off by a half-wall, hosts a handy work desk and opens to the back porch.
- The country kitchen offers an oversized island, a pantry closet and illuminating windows flanking the corner sink.
- The upper-floor master suite boasts two walk-in closets and a private bath with a tub and a separate shower. Two more bedrooms, another full bath and a laundry room are also included.

Plan AGH-1997

Bedrooms: 3	**Baths:** 2½

Living Area:	
Upper floor	933 sq. ft.
Main floor	1,064 sq. ft.
Total Living Area:	**1,997 sq. ft.**
Standard basement	1,064 sq. ft.
Garage	662 sq. ft.
Exterior Wall Framing:	2x6

Foundation Options:

Standard basement

(All plans can be built with your choice of foundation and framing. A generic conversion diagram is available. See order form.)

BLUEPRINT PRICE CODE: **B**

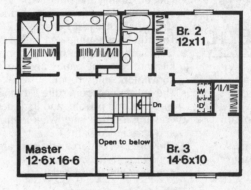

UPPER FLOOR

Br. 2 12x11

Master 12·6x16·6

Br. 3 14·6x10

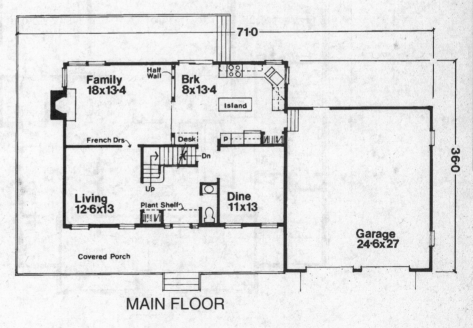

71·0

36·0

Family 18x13·4

Half Wall

Brk 8x13·4

Island

French Drs

Desk

P

Living 12·6x13

Plant Shelf

Dine 11x13

Garage 24·6x27

Covered Porch

MAIN FLOOR

Plan AGH-1997

Plan copyright held by home designer/architect

PRICES AND DETAILS ON PAGES 12-15

Interior Angles Add Excitement

- Interior angles add a touch of excitement to this one-story home.
- A pleasantly charming exterior combines wood and stone to give the plan a solid, comfortable look for any neighborhood.
- Formal living and dining rooms flank the entry, which leads into the large family room, featuring a fireplace, a vaulted ceiling and built-in bookshelves. A covered porch and a sunny patio are just steps away.
- The adjoining eating area with a built-in china cabinet angles off the roomy kitchen. Note the pantry and the convenient utility room.
- The master bedroom suite is both spacious and private, and includes a dressing room, a large walk-in closet and a secluded bath.
- The three secondary bedrooms are also zoned for privacy, and share a compartmentalized bath.

Plan E-1904

Bedrooms: 4	**Baths:** 2½

Living Area:

Main floor	1,997 sq. ft.
Total Living Area:	**1,997 sq. ft.**
Garage	484 sq. ft.
Storage	104 sq. ft.

Exterior Wall Framing: 2x4

Foundation Options:

Crawlspace
Slab

(All plans can be built with your choice of foundation and framing. A generic conversion diagram is available. See order form.)

BLUEPRINT PRICE CODE: B

MAIN FLOOR

ORDER BLUEPRINTS ANYTIME!
CALL TOLL-FREE 1-800-820-1296

Plan E-1904

Plan copyright held by home designer/architect

PRICES AND DETAILS
ON PAGES 12-15

Sense of Space

- A flowing design and optional upper-floor rooms make this home seem bigger than its footprint suggests.
- Just beyond the entry, the modest living room spills into a neat kitchen and dining area. A serving counter connects the kitchen and living room, making snack serving quick and easy.
- Two main-floor bedrooms offer ample closet space and nice views through sunny windows. A full bath with a tub is just steps from the bedrooms.
- On the upper floor, plans for optional bedrooms reveal a vast, versatile area.

Plan DD-768	
Bedrooms: 2+	Baths: 1
Living Area:	
Upper floor	309 sq. ft.
Main floor	768 sq. ft.
Total Living Area:	**1,077 sq. ft.**
Exterior Wall Framing:	2x4
Foundation Options:	
Crawlspace	
Slab	

(All plans can be built with your choice of foundation and framing. A generic conversion diagram is available. See order form.)

BLUEPRINT PRICE CODE:	A

MAIN FLOOR

UPPER FLOOR

Plan DD-768
Plan copyright held by home designer/architect

Entertain Easily

- This country-style home's open main floor makes entertaining delightful. A coat closet and a powder room near the entry add ease for guests.
- Glass doors in the dining room brighten meals and open to the backyard.
- The efficient kitchen, with lots of cupboard space and a convenient serving bar, is sure to delight the cook.
- On the upper floor are three bedrooms, a deluxe full bath and a laundry area that's hidden by folding doors.

Plan PIC-7666	
Bedrooms: 3	Baths: 1½
Living Area:	
Upper floor	626 sq. ft.
Main floor	540 sq. ft.
Total Living Area:	**1,166 sq. ft.**
Standard basement	540 sq. ft.
Garage	242 sq. ft.
Exterior Wall Framing:	2x6
Foundation Options:	
Standard basement	

(All plans can be built with your choice of foundation and framing. A generic conversion diagram is available. See order form.)

BLUEPRINT PRICE CODE:	A

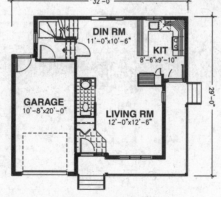

MAIN FLOOR

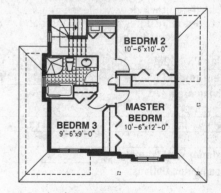

UPPER FLOOR

Plan PIC-7666
Plan copyright held by home designer/architect

PRICES AND DETAILS
ON PAGES 12-15

50 NEW DESIGNS!

A Great Room

- With this home's Great Room at your disposal, everything suddenly becomes easier! Neither slumber parties nor dinner parties are complicated—just move activities into the Great Room. The fireplace and cathedral ceiling add interest, while a back patio adds space.
- The snug kitchen has plenty of sunlight. It teams up with the dining room via an efficient eating bar.
- Sleeping quarters include two bedrooms at the front of the home and a private master suite at the back. A hallway hosts laundry facilities, linen storage and a full bath near the Great Room.

Plan CHD-122

Bedrooms: 3	Baths: 2
Living Area:	
Main floor	1,234 sq. ft.
Total Living Area:	**1,234 sq. ft.**
Storage	45 sq. ft.
Exterior Wall Framing:	2x4

Foundation Options:

Slab

(All plans can be built with your choice of foundation and framing. A generic conversion diagram is available. See order form.)

BLUEPRINT PRICE CODE:	**A**

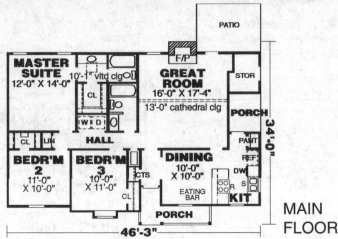

Plan CHD-122

Plan copyright held by home designer/architect

Timeless

- While away a summer afternoon on either the front or the rear porch of this timeless design, which fosters easy living for all ages and abilities.
- Entertain guests in the living room or the dining room—both share a cozy three-sided fireplace—and serve each area from the well-appointed kitchen.
- Located to the left of the entry are the two bedrooms, which share a large bath with a dual-sink vanity.
- The front-facing bedroom boasts a boxed-out window, while the main bedroom features a walk-in closet and direct access to the rear porch.

Plan PSC-1269

Bedrooms: 2	Baths: 1
Living Area:	
Main floor	1,269 sq. ft.
Total Living Area:	**1,269 sq. ft.**
Garage	672 sq. ft.
Exterior Wall Framing:	2x4

Foundation Options:

Crawlspace

Slab

(All plans can be built with your choice of foundation and framing. A generic conversion diagram is available. See order form.)

BLUEPRINT PRICE CODE:	**A**

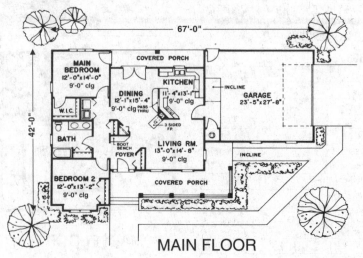

Plan PSC-1269

Plan copyright held by home designer/architect

ORDER BLUEPRINTS ANYTIME! CALL TOLL-FREE 1-800-820-1296

PRICES AND DETAILS ON PAGES 12-15

Fit to Welcome

- Especially nice for a narrow or corner lot, this plan incorporates clever angles into its design to help it fit in anywhere.
- For example, because the front door angles directly into the Great Room, it feels more like a familiar back-door entrance than a formal front passage. Visitors will immediately feel welcome!
- The Great Room expands out to a patio for alfresco meals or conversation. For dining indoors, the kitchen and dining room are eager—and able—to please. The kitchen's open layout eases that transition from the stovetop to the tabletop, while optional French doors in the dining room brighten the area.
- A laundry closet within the kitchen helps confine chores to one space.
- Two nearly identical bedrooms are tucked neatly into a nearby wing, where they share a full bath and linen storage.
- On the other side of the home, the master suite enjoys a little seclusion. A private bath and a sizable walk-in closet assist in creating this quiet environment.
- An attached two-car garage adjoins the dining room and kitchen, so you can shuttle groceries inside with ease!

Plan HDS-99-387

Bedrooms: 3	Baths: 2

Living Area:	
Main floor	1,284 sq. ft.
Total Living Area:	**1,284 sq. ft.**
Garage	375 sq. ft.
Exterior Wall Framing:	8-in. concrete block

Foundation Options:
Slab
(All plans can be built with your choice of foundation and framing. A generic conversion diagram is available. See order form.)

BLUEPRINT PRICE CODE:	**A**

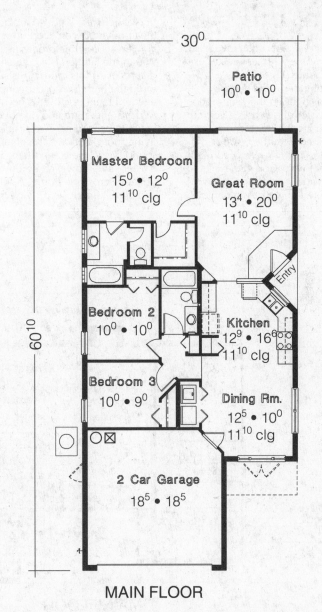

MAIN FLOOR

Plan HDS-99-387
Plan copyright held by home designer/architect

PRICES AND DETAILS
ON PAGES 12-15

50 NEW DESIGNS!

Fills the Bill

- Combining the elements you crave in a livable family home with a practical use of space, this home fills the bill.
- A pretty sidelight marks the home's entry and sheds light on the wide-open living room, which showcases a central fireplace and a French door leading to a back patio. Joined with the nearby dining room, the living room becomes a perfect spot for parties and gatherings.
- The kitchen's wide, angled snack bar makes such entertaining possible. Not only is this a place for snacks and

hors d'oeuvres, it is also a place where the family chef can keep up with the conversation while preparing food.
- Within the kitchen is a cute eating nook that receives lots of luscious sunlight through charming corner windows. An efficient laundry closet is housed here.
- At day's end, retreat to one of three enticing bedrooms. Two reside off the living room, with a full bath acting as a sound barrier between them. The master suite, however, enjoys ultimate privacy across the home. A split bath and a walk-in closet provide all the luxury you need.

Plan HDS-99-339	
Bedrooms: 3	**Baths: 2**
Living Area:	
Main floor	1,300 sq. ft.
Total Living Area:	**1,300 sq. ft.**
Garage	448 sq. ft.
Exterior Wall Framing:	2x4
Foundation Options:	

Slab
(All plans can be built with your choice of foundation and framing. A generic conversion diagram is available. See order form.)

| **BLUEPRINT PRICE CODE:** | **A** |

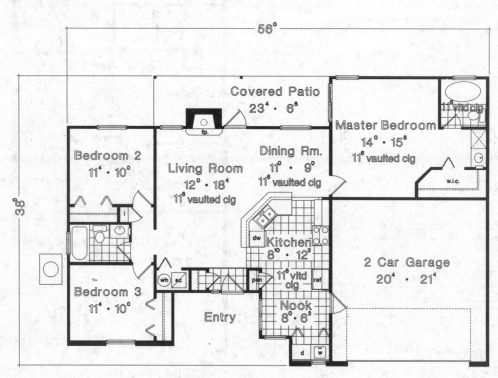

MAIN FLOOR

Plan HDS-99-339

Plan copyright held by home designer/architect

PRICES AND DETAILS
ON PAGES 12-15

In a League of Its Own

- Imaginative use of design space and plenty of natural light set this home apart from the rest.
- An unusual angled entry introduces the home. The Great Room, dining room and kitchen—with a shared high, airy ceiling—work together in an open floor plan to bring your family together during meals and leisure time. The windows and glass patio doors allow light to surround the living space.
- The efficiency of the spacious island kitchen is enhanced by a serving counter, making the stove-to-table transition easy.
- The home's master suite features a high ceiling, a walk-in closet and a bath with the option of either a conventional tub or a corner private spa tub. Glass block adds light and a measure of privacy to the bath.
- Two more bedrooms are situated toward the front of the home. A nearby hall bath contains two handy closets.

Plan HDS-99-388

Bedrooms: 3	Baths: 2
Living Area:	
Main floor	1,309 sq. ft.
Total Living Area:	**1,309 sq. ft.**
Garage	383 sq. ft.
Exterior Wall Framing:	8-in. concrete block

Foundation Options:

Slab

(All plans can be built with your choice of foundation and framing. A generic conversion diagram is available. See order form.)

BLUEPRINT PRICE CODE: A

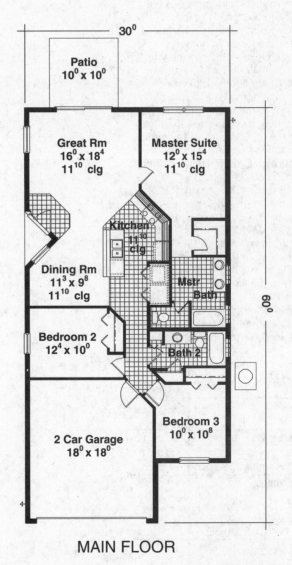

MAIN FLOOR

ORDER BLUEPRINTS ANYTIME!
CALL TOLL-FREE 1-800-820-1296

Plan HDS-99-388
Plan copyright held by home designer/architect

PRICES AND DETAILS
ON PAGES 12-15

277

A Clean Slate

- Keystones, shutters and an angled entry add interest to the facade of this modest, Mediterranean-style home.
- Upon entry, the Great Room greets you with a fresh, clean slate. Arrange your furniture however you wish, wherever you wish. The only details to work around are the entrance to a side patio and the door to the master suite.
- An open dining room borders the tiled entry and the easy, comfortable kitchen. Add the kitchen's serving bar and the roomy patio, and you have more dining options than you'd expect.
- A short hall leads to two bedrooms, a full bath with ample linen storage and the garage. If you don't need both bedrooms for sleeping, turn one into a den or your home office. It's up to you!
- At the other end of the home is a roomy master suite with a high ceiling. A dual-sink vanity and a garden tub embellish the private bath.
- The Great Room, dining room and kitchen all feature high ceilings, creating a lofty feeling throughout the rooms.

Plan HDS-99-389

Bedrooms: 3	Baths: 2
Living Area:	
Main floor	1,309 sq. ft.
Total Living Area:	**1,309 sq. ft.**
Garage	383 sq. ft.
Exterior Wall Framing:	8-in. concrete block

Foundation Options:
Slab
(All plans can be built with your choice of foundation and framing. A generic conversion diagram is available. See order form.)

BLUEPRINT PRICE CODE:	**A**

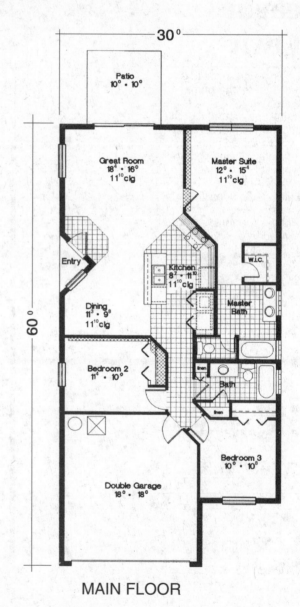

MAIN FLOOR

ORDER BLUEPRINTS ANYTIME!
CALL TOLL-FREE 1-800-820-1296

Plan HDS-99-389
Plan copyright held by home designer/architect

PRICES AND DETAILS
ON PAGES 12-15

Vertical Appeal

- Porch columns and roofline details on this Victorian-style home draw attention to its vertical appearance. The sense of height is also promoted by an unobtrusive, lower-level garage.
- Just in from the charming front porch, a spacious, tiled entry greets you. It boasts a practical coat closet and plenty of room for a hall table or a storage bench.
- Dual doors lead into the living room, which overlooks the porch via a sunny bay window. Sharing in this generous splay of natural light, the adjoining

formal dining room is further brightened by a trio of windows.
- Another pair of doors announces the cozy eating nook and up-to-date kitchen, which share an eating bar.
- A powder room near the nook does double duty: A laundry station with a washer and dryer stands at one end.
- Upstairs, the living room's bay window is repeated in the master bedroom, the largest of the three bedrooms; all are situated upstairs for quiet and privacy.
- A sizable bath with an oversized shower also shows off a free-standing oval tub.

Plan PIC-20989	
Bedrooms: 3	**Baths:** 1½
Living Area:	
Upper floor	666 sq. ft.
Main floor	666 sq. ft.
Total Living Area:	**1,332 sq. ft.**
Daylight basement	387 sq. ft.
Garage	279 sq. ft.
Exterior Wall Framing:	2x6
Foundation Options:	

Daylight basement
(All plans can be built with your choice of foundation and framing. A generic conversion diagram is available. See order form.)

BLUEPRINT PRICE CODE: A

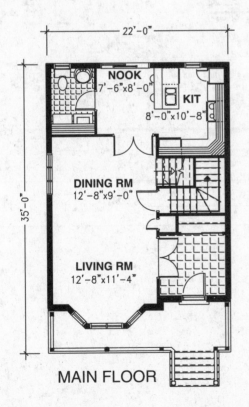

MAIN FLOOR

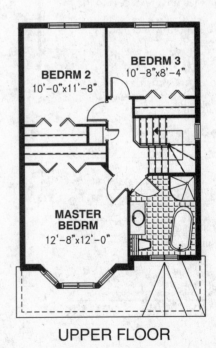

UPPER FLOOR

ORDER BLUEPRINTS ANYTIME!
CALL TOLL-FREE 1-800-820-1296

Plan PIC-20989
Plan copyright held by home designer/architect

PRICES AND DETAILS
ON PAGES 12-15

279

Attractive Amenities

- An open floor plan and large windows make the most of this compact home, which provides easy living for all ages and abilities.
- The good-sized living room features a romantic fireplace and flows easily into both the kitchen and the dining room. Kids and adults alike will enjoy meals on the go at the breakfast bar, while more formal dinners can be served in the dining room or on the back patio.
- The magnificent owner's suite offers separate vanities and his-and-hers closets, as well as private access to the split bath.
- The second bedroom works equally well as a guest room or a nursery and commands a private vanity in the shared bath.
- The attached garage provides direct entrance to the kitchen—a real comfort on cold or rainy days.

Plan PSC-1336

Bedrooms: 2	Baths: 1
Living Area:	
Main floor	1,336 sq. ft.
Total Living Area:	**1,336 sq. ft.**
Garage	392 sq. ft.
Exterior Wall Framing:	2x4

Foundation Options:

Crawlspace
Slab

(All plans can be built with your choice of foundation and framing. A generic conversion diagram is available. See order form.)

BLUEPRINT PRICE CODE: A

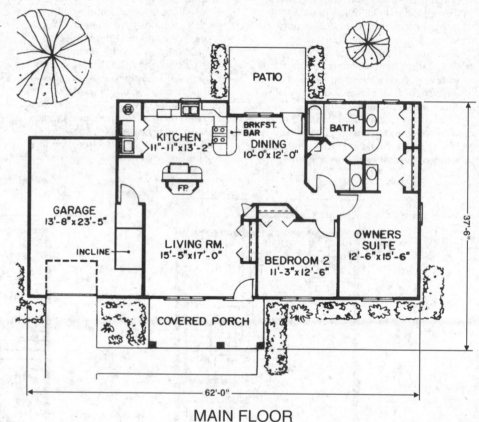

MAIN FLOOR

ORDER BLUEPRINTS ANYTIME!
CALL TOLL-FREE 1-800-820-1296

Plan PSC-1336
Plan copyright held by home designer/architect

PRICES AND DETAILS ON PAGES 12-15

Touch of Flair

- Keystones crown the front windows and other points of interest along this home's facade, while columns span the porch and add a touch of flair to this space-efficient home.
- A high ceiling and a tall, front-facing window grant the formal dining room its panache. Combine it with the central living room, which boasts a fireplace and access to a back porch, and you're able to host a variety of affairs.
- A great deal of counter space and easy access to the dining room highlight the well-planned kitchen. The sizable, sun-drenched eating nook is nearby.
- The master suite's entry lies within a small vestibule that also houses the washer and dryer, a coat closet and bookshelves. Along with a secluded location, amenities such as a sloped ceiling and a luxurious bath make the master suite an enticing spot.
- On the other side of the home, a short hall near the front entry reveals two additional bedrooms. A full bath with a garden tub and a neighboring linen niche in the hall round out this wing of the home.

Plan RD-1374

Bedrooms: 3	Baths: 2
Living Area:	
Main floor	1,374 sq. ft.
Total Living Area:	**1,374 sq. ft.**
Garage and storage	488 sq. ft.
Exterior Wall Framing:	2x4

Foundation Options:

Crawlspace

Slab

(All plans can be built with your choice of foundation and framing. A generic conversion diagram is available. See order form.)

BLUEPRINT PRICE CODE:	**A**

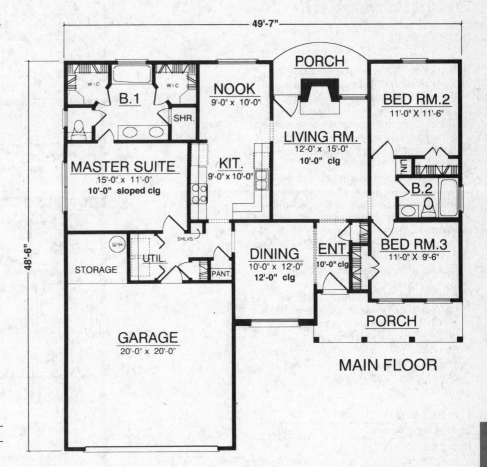

MAIN FLOOR

Plan RD-1374

Plan copyright held by home designer/architect

PRICES AND DETAILS
ON PAGES 12-15

50 NEW DESIGNS!

Single-Level Living

- You'll love the advantages of single-level living in this cozy home. Its narrow width makes it suitable for virtually any lot.
- The side entry introduces guests to the expansive Great Room. Sliding glass doors access a backyard patio—a perfect place to set up the grill!
- The spacious eat-in kitchen can easily accommodate family meals or entertain friends in an intimate setting. A utility closet simplifies laundry duties.
- In one corner of the home, the quiet master suite boasts a walk-in closet and a private bath with a dual-sink vanity and separate tub and shower areas.
- Two secondary bedrooms share a hall bath. One of the bedrooms features double doors and is located near the entry; it could easily serve as a home office, a guest room or a den.
- Overhead plant shelves add splashes of greenery for visual interest. A linen closet and a double garage round out the floor plan.

Plan HDS-99-377

Bedrooms: 2+	Baths: 2
Living Area:	
Main floor	1,396 sq. ft.
Total Living Area:	**1,396 sq. ft.**
Garage	374 sq. ft.
Exterior Wall Framing:	8-in. concrete block

Foundation Options:

Slab

(All plans can be built with your choice of foundation and framing. A generic conversion diagram is available. See order form.)

BLUEPRINT PRICE CODE: A

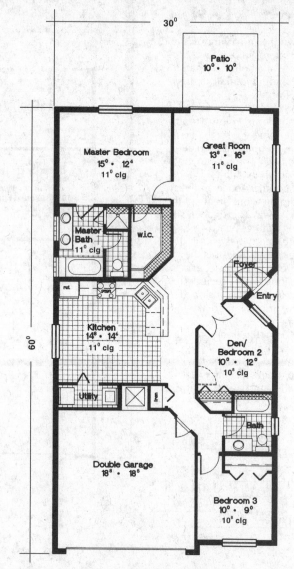

MAIN FLOOR

Plan HDS-99-377

Plan copyright held by home designer/architect

PRICES AND DETAILS
ON PAGES 12-15

It's a Snap!

- Baking, cooking and cleaning up a big feast can be simply a snap—in the right environment. This pretty home provides a grand kitchen with ample counter space and a hard-working layout.
- At last, you won't be cramped! The kitchen and the nook combined provide enough room to host a sizable table for casual family meals. Large windows make the most of natural light.
- Slim columns separate the nook from the large living and dining rooms, which sit prominently at the center of

the home. A back patio could be used for dining alfresco or extending the living space during a boisterous party.
- Windows along one wall in the master suite afford a wide view of the backyard. The deluxe, split master bath presents an oversized shower, a dual-sink vanity and access to the outdoors.
- At the front of the home, the third bedroom is a good candidate for a home office. Its double-door entry from the foyer separates the room from the sleeping wing, making it more suitable for greeting business associates. A garden tub enhances the nearby bath.

Plan HDS-99-340	
Bedrooms: 3	**Baths:** 2
Living Area:	
Main floor	1,428 sq. ft.
Total Living Area:	**1,428 sq. ft.**
Garage	424 sq. ft.
Exterior Wall Framing:	8-in. concrete block
Foundation Options:	
Slab	

(All plans can be built with your choice of foundation and framing. A generic conversion diagram is available. See order form.)

BLUEPRINT PRICE CODE: **A**

MAIN FLOOR

Patio

Master Suite
15⁰ · 12⁰

Master Bath

linen

w.i.c.

Bath 2

linen

Living Rm.
18⁰ · 15⁰
8⁴ vaulted clg

Nook
15¹⁰ · 13⁶

Kitchen

dw · sink

ref

Laun.

a/c

w.h.

Bedroom 2
11⁰ · 10⁰

Bedroom 3
11⁰ · 10⁰

Foyer

Dining Rm.
9⁸ · 9⁰
8⁴ vaulted clg

Entry

2 Car Garage
19⁶ · 20⁸

60⁰

38⁰

ORDER BLUEPRINTS ANYTIME!
CALL TOLL-FREE 1-800-820-1296

Plan HDS-99-340
Plan copyright held by home designer/architect

PRICES AND DETAILS
ON PAGES 12-15
283

Pretty, Petite

- Pretty and petite, this nostalgic charmer will surely win you over.
- A darling porch fronts the home, and revels in ample space for you to recline, read or rock lightly on a porch swing.
- Inside, the living and dining rooms are just as laid back: Nestled along an open hallway, they share free-flowing space that suits all your entertaining needs.
- In equipping you for parties, the kitchen also delivers. A sizable island with an angled snack bar provides a pivot point for all your meal preparation and cleanup, while creating a nice spot for light meals, chats or homework.
- Around the corner, a compact laundry room lies out of the way of your guests. A handy closet is the perfect place to hang your coat when you come in through the garage.
- Two secondary bedrooms share the back corner of the home, where a full bath is convenient to both.
- The master suite, on the other hand, enjoys a private bath with both an elaborate tub and a separate shower. A big walk-in closet with storage shelves is an added amenity.

Plan PIC-10791

Bedrooms: 3	Baths: 2
Living Area:	
Main floor	1,438 sq. ft.
Total Living Area:	**1,438 sq. ft.**
Standard basement	1,438 sq. ft.
Garage	513 sq. ft.
Exterior Wall Framing:	2x6

Foundation Options:

Standard basement
(All plans can be built with your choice of foundation and framing. A generic conversion diagram is available. See order form.)

BLUEPRINT PRICE CODE:	**A**

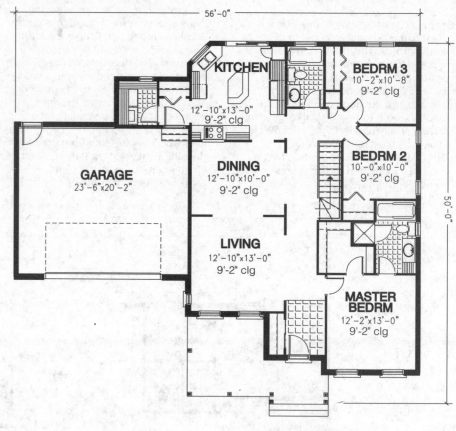

MAIN FLOOR

ORDER BLUEPRINTS ANYTIME!
CALL TOLL-FREE 1-800-820-1296

Plan PIC-10791

Plan copyright held by home designer/architect

PRICES AND DETAILS
ON PAGES 12-15

Just What You Need

- Modest and flexible, this vacation home is also ideal for a single dweller or a small family. Common living areas on the main floor, sleeping quarters on the upper floor and porches at the front and back constitute this simple plan.
- The foyer opens directly into the living room, which receives ample sunlight from windows on three walls.
- Past the stairs to the upper floor, a powder room and the compact kitchen

are situated at the center of the plan for your convenience.
- A family room and dining spot merge at the back of the home, allowing you to create whatever furniture arrangements you desire. Double doors open out to the back porch.
- The kitchen's sink and serving counter extend into the dining area, making kitchen duty less solitary. Nearby, an out-of-the-way door reveals space for a stacked washer and dryer.
- Two large bedrooms—each with a walk-in closet—and a full bath are nestled on the upper floor. A closet in the hallway adds storage space.

Plan HDS-99-341	
Bedrooms: 2	**Baths:** 1½
Living Area:	
Upper floor	705 sq. ft.
Main floor	737 sq. ft.
Total Living Area:	**1,442 sq. ft.**
Standard basement	705 sq. ft.
Exterior Wall Framing:	2x4
Foundation Options:	
Standard basement	
Crawlspace	
Slab	

(All plans can be built with your choice of foundation and framing. A generic conversion diagram is available. See order form.)

BLUEPRINT PRICE CODE:	A

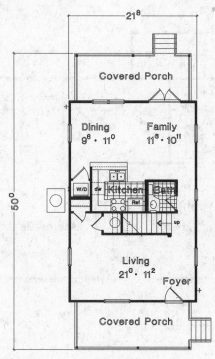

MAIN FLOOR

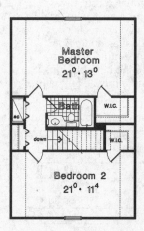

UPPER FLOOR

ORDER BLUEPRINTS ANYTIME!
CALL TOLL-FREE 1-800-820-1296

Plan HDS-99-341
Plan copyright held by home designer/architect

PRICES AND DETAILS
ON PAGES 12-15

285

50 NEW DESIGNS!

Family Comfort

- A low roofline and a simple, ranch-style layout make this a perfect family home, and a good fit for any neighborhood. Something about its unassuming looks, which include a welcoming front porch, will fill you with genuine peace and familial comfort.

- Though the porch is big enough for a swing, you won't want to obscure the view afforded by the picture window in the family room. A fireplace further enhances this happy gathering spot.

- A bay window brightens the nook and the kitchen, where a peninsula serving bar is a handy spot for snacks on the go or fancy hors d'oeuvres. The laundry room close by provides a door leading to the cost-effective carport and storage.

- Three bedrooms down the hall offer all the space you need. For regular residents or occasional guests, two secondary bedrooms—each with dual closets—will be much appreciated. A full hall bath is convenient to both.

- Dual doors mark the entrance to the master suite, which includes built-ins, a walk-in closet and a private full bath.

Plan HDS-99-411

Bedrooms: 3	Baths: 2
Living Area:	
Main floor	1,442 sq. ft.
Total Living Area:	**1,442 sq. ft.**
Carport	437 sq. ft.
Storage	64 sq. ft.
Exterior Wall Framing:	2x4

Foundation Options:
Crawlspace
(All plans can be built with your choice of foundation and framing. A generic conversion diagram is available. See order form.)

BLUEPRINT PRICE CODE: A

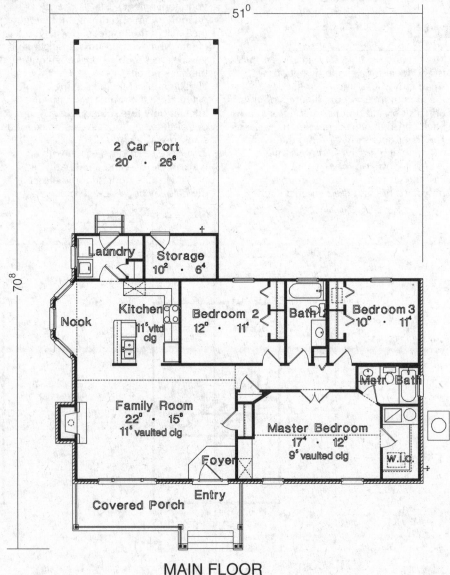

MAIN FLOOR

Plan HDS-99-411

Plan copyright held by home designer/architect

PRICES AND DETAILS
ON PAGES 12-15

As It Appears

- Brick on three sides of this handsome home puts forth an attractive front to your neighbors, whether they are next door or across the street. And just as it appears outside, so its layout is inside.
- A lovely formal dining room lies just off the entry—a show-stopper for anyone walking in the door. Fortunately, a half-wall in this room overlooks the Great Room and its central fireplace, so your guests will be quickly diverted to still more lovely areas of the home.
- The Great Room is just as its name implies: grand in proportion as well as style. A French door to the rear of the room leads out back, while a high plant shelf sits atop one of its bordering walls.
- A sunny breakfast nook lies around the corner, and is serviced by the kitchen. The efficiency of the kitchen is due to its compact, galley-style layout.
- Enjoying a bit of seclusion in a back hallway, two secondary bedrooms—one with a walk-in closet—share a full bath. The master suite revels in privacy of its own, complete with a skylighted bath that features a gorgeous spa tub. Day's end can't come fast enough!

Plan CHD-1425

Bedrooms: 3	Baths: 2
Living Area:	
Main floor	1,449 sq. ft.
Total Living Area:	**1,449 sq. ft.**
Garage and storage	499 sq. ft.
Exterior Wall Framing:	2x4

Foundation Options:

Crawlspace

Slab

(All plans can be built with your choice of foundation and framing. A generic conversion diagram is available. See order form.)

BLUEPRINT PRICE CODE: A

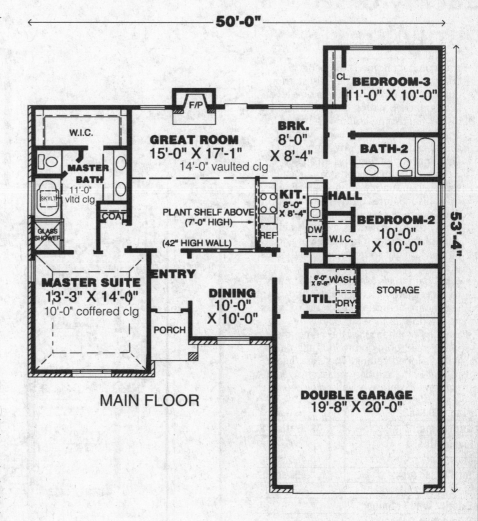

MAIN FLOOR

ORDER BLUEPRINTS ANYTIME!
CALL TOLL-FREE 1-800-820-1296

Plan CHD-1425
Plan copyright held by home designer/architect

PRICES AND DETAILS
ON PAGES 12-15

287

Plenty of Amenities

- This compact home is the perfect choice for a young family just starting out, or for anyone desiring a one-level layout packed with plenty of amenities.
- Inside, handsome columns separate the entry from the dining room, where a boxed-out window draws light inside.
- The adjacent kitchen has an angled work area, which extends as a raised serving bar. A cozy adjoining eating nook also features a boxed-out window.
- Back-porch access is available in the family room. However, a sloped ceiling, a fireplace, built-in bookshelves and ample sunlight sources indicate that it's just as well to stay indoors.
- A full bath that's adjacent to the family room is shared by the home's two secondary bedrooms. Each bedroom sits near a door to the split bath.
- Situated at the front of the home, the master bedroom commands attention with a sloped ceiling. The extravagant master bath includes a glass shower, a garden tub and two walk-in closets.

Plan RD-1450

Bedrooms: 3	Baths: 2
Living Area:	
Main floor	1,450 sq. ft.
Total Living Area:	**1,450 sq. ft.**
Garage and storage	465 sq. ft.
Exterior Wall Framing:	2x4
Foundation Options:	
Crawlspace	
Slab	

(All plans can be built with your choice of foundation and framing. A generic conversion diagram is available. See order form.)

BLUEPRINT PRICE CODE:	A

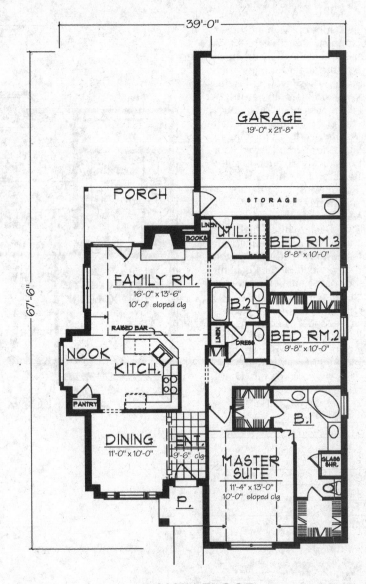

MAIN FLOOR

Plan RD-1450
Plan copyright held by home designer/architect

PRICES AND DETAILS
ON PAGES 12-15

50 NEW DESIGNS!

In a Tight Spot

- Tight lots require innovative plans, which is why this lovely Victorian-style, narrow-lot home rises above the rest.
- A neat porch patterned after a classic wraparound fronts this home, and leads past a sidelighted entry into the living and dining rooms. Together, these rooms create a prime spot for both small- and large-scale entertaining.
- When it's time for preparing and serving the evening meal, you'll appreciate the kitchen's efficiency. Its location allows you to serve meals in the dining room

with ease, while concealing any prep mess from guests in the living room.
- A half-bath with laundry facilities lies to one side of the kitchen. Garage access is a few steps down from here.
- For privacy and convenience, all three bedrooms are located on the upper floor. The master bedroom includes a sitting area that's tucked into a bayed turret. With panoramic views of the landscape, you can enjoy nature's splendor at any time of the day.
- A boxed-out window expands the space in another bedroom. All three share a luxurious full bath.

Plan PIC-2996	
Bedrooms: 3	**Baths:** 1½
Living Area:	
Upper floor	848 sq. ft.
Main floor	604 sq. ft.
Total Living Area:	**1,452 sq. ft.**
Standard basement	604 sq. ft.
Garage	258 sq. ft.
Exterior Wall Framing:	2x6
Foundation Options:	

Standard basement
(All plans can be built with your choice of foundation and framing. A generic conversion diagram is available. See order form.)

BLUEPRINT PRICE CODE:	A

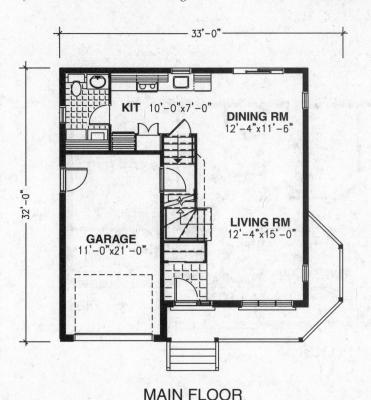

MAIN FLOOR

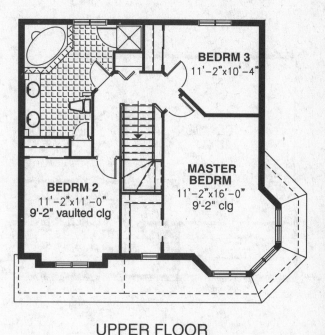

UPPER FLOOR

Plan PIC-2996
Plan copyright held by home designer/architect

PRICES AND DETAILS
ON PAGES 12-15

50 NEW DESIGNS!

Low Profile

- This narrow-lot home keeps a low, lean profile—the image shown above is actually a series of closely situated homes. It looks snug, but you won't feel cramped inside. There's plenty of room to roam.
- Because of a recessed side entry, guests bypass your sleeping quarters and head straight to the home's common areas.
- Situated adjacent to the entry, the dining room features a partial view of the kitchen and eating area fostered by a unique wall of vertical railings.

- Through a pair of doors, an eating nook and the kitchen luxuriate under a sloped ceiling and a skylight. Cute shutters above the sink open to the living room, letting in more light.
- A fantastic vaulted ceiling, a corner fireplace and lots of glass brighten the big living room.
- On the other side of the home, the posh master suite is topped by another vaulted ceiling. A huge oval tub in the private bath imparts more luxury.
- A second bedroom has access to another full bath, either through its broad walk-in closet or via the hallway.

Plan E-1415	
Bedrooms: 2	**Baths: 2**
Living Area:	
Main floor	1,459 sq. ft.
Total Living Area:	**1,459 sq. ft.**
Garage	484 sq. ft.
Storage	80 sq. ft.
Exterior Wall Framing:	2x6

Foundation Options:
Slab
(All plans can be built with your choice of foundation and framing. A generic conversion diagram is available. See order form.)

BLUEPRINT PRICE CODE:	**A**

77' – 0"

28' – 0"

GARAGE
22' X 22'

DISAP. STAIRS

FIREPLACE

LIVING ROOM
18' x 16'
14'-6" vaulted clg

BEDROOM
12' x 12'

WIC

KNEE SPACE

BATH

AC

MASTER SUITE
14' x 16'
14' vaulted clg

PANTRY

DW SINK REFRIG.

KITCHEN & EATING
17' x 12'

SKYLIGHT

BRM RANGE

DINING ROOM
13' x 12'

ENTRY

KNEE SPACE

BATH

WIC

STOR.

W
D

UTIL.

PORCH
11' x 6'

◄ FRONT

MAIN FLOOR

Plan E-1415
Plan copyright held by home designer/architect

PRICES AND DETAILS
ON PAGES 12-15

50 NEW DESIGNS!

Line 'em Up!

- An innovative floor plan allows this home to serve well on a narrow lot, and in fact equips it to reside alongside others of its kind—the absence of windows on one side protects your privacy, up and down the line!
- Off the entry, the living and dining rooms form one combined gathering space. Down the hall, the galley-style kitchen boasts an efficient layout that allows service to either the dining room or the cozy breakfast nook. French doors in the nook lead out back for alfresco meals.
- A lovely arched window at the front of the home graces the secondary bedroom. Amenities here include a closet that walks through to a full bath with linen storage and a skylight.
- Another full bath is incorporated into the master suite at the rear of the home. A walk-in closet provides ample storage, plus suitable space for dressing. French doors in the bedroom lead to the sideyard, perfect for a terrace that stretches to the living and dining rooms.
- The attached two-car garage with storage is accessed via a back service entry, which not only saves space but also face—that is, preserves the facade!

Plan E-1513

Bedrooms: 2	Baths: 2
Living Area:	
Main floor	1,500 sq. ft.
Total Living Area:	**1,500 sq. ft.**
Garage and storage	578 sq. ft.
Exterior Wall Framing:	2x6

Foundation Options:

Slab

(All plans can be built with your choice of foundation and framing. A generic conversion diagram is available. See order form.)

BLUEPRINT PRICE CODE: B

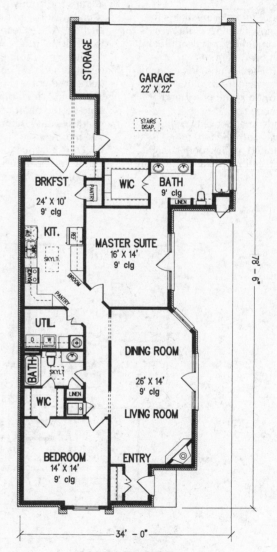

MAIN FLOOR

PRICES AND DETAILS ON PAGES 12-15

Plan E-1513

Plan copyright held by home designer/architect

50 NEW DESIGNS!

I'm Speechless

- Where can you find a home that is the right size for new families or retirees, packed with amenities and beautiful in an unassuming way? Hmm.
- That's right. This charming home begins with a pretty facade marked by a large, arched window, a petite porch and stately brick accents.
- The foyer leads to either of two spots—the sleeping wing to the left, or the expansive vaulted family room straight ahead. A focal-point fireplace highlights this space.

- A dining nook with a bay window adjoins the family room and is served via a snack bar in the well-appointed kitchen. A door leads from the kitchen to the utility room, which hosts laundry facilities, a sizable pantry and access to the attached side-entry garage.
- Across the home are two secondary bedrooms—including the vaulted, front-facing bedroom with the arched window—and the full bath they share. The master suite is also in this wing, which is a bonus for couples with small children. The luxurious private bath is a special place for you to be pampered.

Plan DHI-6	
Bedrooms: 3	**Baths: 2**
Living Area:	
Main floor	1,522 sq. ft.
Total Living Area:	**1,522 sq. ft.**
Garage	458 sq. ft.
Exterior Wall Framing:	2x4

Foundation Options:

Slab

(All plans can be built with your choice of foundation and framing. A generic conversion diagram is available. See order form.)

BLUEPRINT PRICE CODE:	**B**

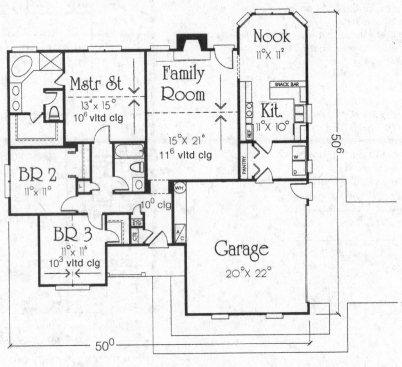

MAIN FLOOR

Plan DHI-6
Plan copyright held by home designer/architect

PRICES AND DETAILS
ON PAGES 12-15

Circle of Friends

- This smart design strikes the right balance between your need for privacy and your wish for neighborhood camaraderie.
- Just inside the entry, a spacious living room offers a pleasing first view of the home's interior. A fireplace is centrally situated for all to enjoy.
- Columns delineate the dining room, where sunlight streams through a row of windows along one wall. Opposite is the efficient kitchen, where a window over the sink will make your chores more pleasant.
- Beyond the common living areas, the bedroom wing is tucked away at the back of the home. The master suite boasts a sizable bedroom that accesses a side porch. The master bath includes a dual-sink vanity and lots of room for two of you to prepare for the day. A walk-in closet provides lots of storage.
- The second bedroom also features a walk-in closet, plus private access to a full hall bath.

Plan E-1509

Bedrooms: 2	Baths: 2
Living Area:	
Main floor	1,538 sq. ft.
Total Living Area:	**1,538 sq. ft.**
Garage	484 sq. ft.
Storage	48 sq. ft.
Exterior Wall Framing:	2x4

Foundation Options:

Slab
(All plans can be built with your choice of foundation and framing. A generic conversion diagram is available. See order form.)

BLUEPRINT PRICE CODE: B

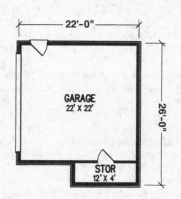

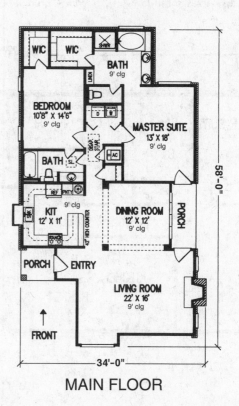

MAIN FLOOR

ORDER BLUEPRINTS ANYTIME!
CALL TOLL-FREE 1-800-820-1296

Plan E-1509
Plan copyright held by home designer/architect

PRICES AND DETAILS
ON PAGES 12-15

293

50 NEW DESIGNS!

Slim and Sleek

- Sleek, slender and well planned to meet atypical living needs, this plan really delivers.
- Beyond the spacious two-car garage and storage, a columned porch provides shelter for the entry. A handy utility room and bookshelves are close by.
- A skylighted vestibule off the porch leads to a secluded bedroom suite. A walk-through closet connects the bedroom to a full bath that is joined to the rest of the interior. Offering privacy and also convenient access to the rest of the home, this suite is ideal for in-laws.

- Two dining areas flank the entry—a large, accommodating dining room and a charming breakfast nook. The nearby kitchen's U-shaped layout is efficient for all aspects of meal preparation, service and clean-up.
- Down the hall, the living room is well-situated to enjoy lovely, wooded backyard views. A corner fireplace enhances the ambience of this delightful gathering space.
- You'll enjoy many luxuries in the master suite, where a split bath with a walk-in closet and a skylight affords the space and comfort you deserve. As a bonus, French doors lead outside.

Plan E-1516	
Bedrooms: 2	**Baths:** 2
Living Area:	
Main floor	1,542 sq. ft.
Total Living Area:	**1,542 sq. ft.**
Garage	484 sq. ft.
Storage	40 sq. ft.
Exterior Wall Framing:	2x4
Foundation Options:	

Slab
(All plans can be built with your choice of foundation and framing.
A generic conversion diagram is available. See order form.)

BLUEPRINT PRICE CODE:	B

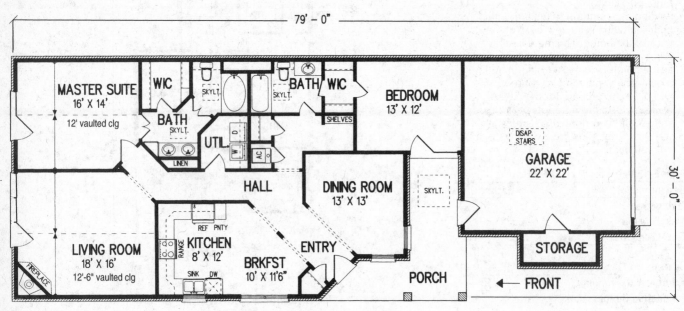

MAIN FLOOR

Plan E-1516
Plan copyright held by home designer/architect

PRICES AND DETAILS
ON PAGES 12-15

50 NEW DESIGNS!

One of a Kind

- Ideal for a narrow lot or as part of a series of row houses, this one-of-a-kind design packs a lot of space into a clever floor plan. Brick adds a stately, sturdy touch to the exterior.
- A diminutive porch introduces the entrance to the living and dining rooms, which constitute one grand space. A corner fireplace adds rustic allure, while a French door in an angled alcove provides quick passage to the outdoors.
- Across the hall, the U-shaped kitchen employs an efficient design—which

includes a pass-through—to better serve the adjoining breakfast room. Three French doors brighten the entire space and access a back porch.
- The master suite benefits from similar design features. French doors lead directly outside, while a set of double doors opens out to reveal a private bath. Inside, dual sinks offer spots for two to get ready for the day.
- A separate bedroom suite adjoins a walk-through closet that connects to a full hall bath. French doors in this bedroom lead out to the front porch, making it ideal for independent guests.

Plan E-1514

Bedrooms: 2	**Baths:** 2

Living Area:	
Main floor	1,548 sq. ft.
Total Living Area:	**1,548 sq. ft.**
Garage	492 sq. ft.
Storage	32 sq. ft.
Exterior Wall Framing:	2x4

Foundation Options:

Slab
(All plans can be built with your choice of foundation and framing. A generic conversion diagram is available. See order form.)

BLUEPRINT PRICE CODE:	B

Floor Plan

79' - 0"

30' - 0"

PORCH 5' X 14'

BRKFST 14' X 9'

RANGE

KIT. 10' X 10'

DW SINK

REF.

UTIL.

W. D

BATH

WIC

BEDROOM 17' X 13'

DISAP. STAIRS

GARAGE 22' X 22'

AC

BATH

SKYLT.

MASTER SUITE 16' X 15'

WIC

LIVING & DINING 26' X 16' 12' sloped clg

FIREPLACE

PORCH 9' X 13'

STORAGE

← FRONT

MAIN FLOOR

ORDER BLUEPRINTS ANYTIME!
CALL TOLL-FREE 1-800-820-1296

Plan E-1514
Plan copyright held by home designer/architect

PRICES AND DETAILS
ON PAGES 12-15

295

Traditional Treasure

- This traditional treasure is built to meet the needs of a growing family.
- The entryway to this home makes way for a handy coat closet and a compact powder room.
- The Great Room highlights this home, with its crackling fireplace and huge, open spaces.
- Both the bayed breakfast nook and the more formal dining room are easily served by the kitchen, which boasts plenty of counter space.
- An attached two-car garage provides direct access to the kitchen—a real blessing on cold or rainy days.
- Upstairs, the master suite showcases a coffered ceiling, while the private bath features dual sinks and a skylight above the oval tub.
- Two additional bedrooms share a full bath, while an extra room above the garage makes a great playroom.

Plan CHD-153

Bedrooms: 3+	Baths: 2½
Living Area:	
Upper floor	803 sq. ft.
Main floor	792 sq. ft.
Total Living Area:	**1,595 sq. ft.**
Future space	318 sq. ft.
Garage	432 sq. ft.
Storage	56 sq. ft.
Exterior Wall Framing:	2x4

Foundation Options:

Slab
(All plans can be built with your choice of foundation and framing. A generic conversion diagram is available. See order form.)

BLUEPRINT PRICE CODE:	B

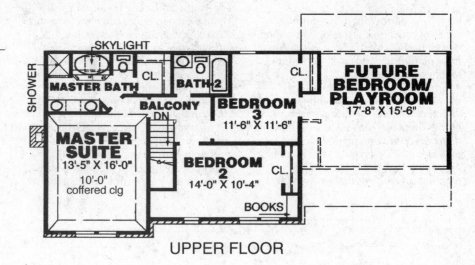

UPPER FLOOR

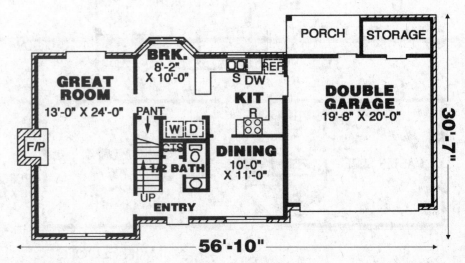

MAIN FLOOR

ORDER BLUEPRINTS ANYTIME!
CALL TOLL-FREE 1-800-820-1296

Plan CHD-153
Plan copyright held by home designer/architect

PRICES AND DETAILS
ON PAGES 12-15

Compact Charmer

- If you enjoy entertaining and desire a little luxury to spice up your life without emptying your wallet, you'll love this modern, compact charmer.
- A gorgeous entry framed by sidelights and a lovely transom provides a gracious welcome to your guests. Usher them straight down the hall into the Great Room, and get the party started.
- A central fireplace and ample media shelves make this the place to be. Bright

windows and French doors lining the back wall illuminate events, while an angled snack bar in the kitchen adds flavor to any gathering.
- For special occasions, or whenever you choose, enjoy a nice meal in the dining room. A china niche and tall windows enhance this snazzy supper setting.
- Across the hall, two bedrooms share a full bath. Use the rearmost bedroom—or perhaps the dining room?—as a study or much-needed home office.
- The master suite is cleverly hidden away from the action, and includes such pampering amenities as a split bath with dual sinks and a spa tub. *Yes!*

Plan ICON-103106-B	
Bedrooms: 2+	Baths: 2
Living Area:	
Main floor	1,595 sq. ft.
Total Living Area:	**1,595 sq. ft.**
Standard basement	1,595 sq. ft.
Garage	459 sq. ft.
Exterior Wall Framing:	2x4

Foundation Options:

Standard basement

(All plans can be built with your choice of foundation and framing. A generic conversion diagram is available. See order form.)

BLUEPRINT PRICE CODE:	B

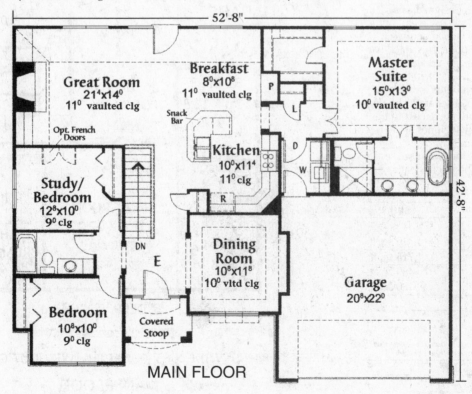

MAIN FLOOR

ORDER BLUEPRINTS ANYTIME!
CALL TOLL-FREE 1-800-820-1296

Plan ICON-103106-B
Plan copyright held by home designer/architect

PRICES AND DETAILS
ON PAGES 12-15

297

50 NEW DESIGNS!

Achieve Balance

- A pleasing symmetrical design and front-and-back porches set this home apart from the rest.
- The versatile Great Room, with its fireplace and adaptable, central location, is set to become the most-used room of this home. The kitchen lies adjacent to the Great Room in the open floor plan and, with its island and commodious storage, is well prepared to handle any culinary feat.
- The breakfast area is designed as a formal enough spot for any meal, but some may choose to place another table in the Great Room. The snack bar in the kitchen makes for added versatility.
- The master bedroom offers a walk-in closet, a garden tub, a separate shower and—best of all—private access to the back porch. Laundry facilities are housed just down the hall.
- Across the home reside two more bedrooms, which share a full bath.

Plan DP-1716

Bedrooms: 3	Baths: 2
Living Area:	
Main floor	1,716 sq. ft.
Total Living Area:	**1,716 sq. ft.**
Detached garage	480 sq. ft.
Storage	120 sq. ft.
Exterior Wall Framing:	2x4

Foundation Options:

Slab

(All plans can be built with your choice of foundation and framing. A generic conversion diagram is available. See order form.)

BLUEPRINT PRICE CODE: B

GARAGE

44'-0" WIDE X 65'-0" DEPTH - WITHOUT GARAGE

MAIN FLOOR

ORDER BLUEPRINTS ANYTIME!
CALL TOLL-FREE 1-800-820-1296

Plan DP-1716

Plan copyright held by home designer/architect

PRICES AND DETAILS
ON PAGES 12-15

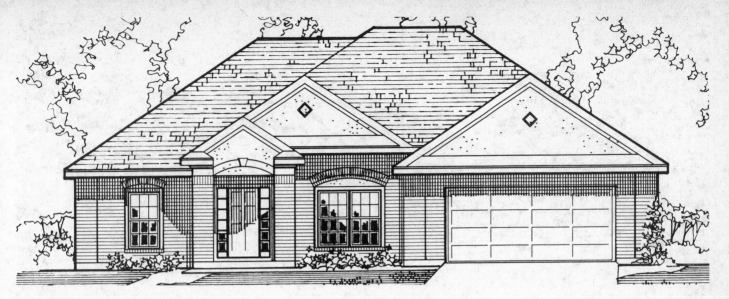

Soft Sunny Spot

- Despite this home's formidable facade, its interior boasts a casual elegance that is especially found in the sunny breakfast nook and screened porch.

- These light-filled spaces will be among your family's favorites. Not only is the nook ideal for casual meals, it can be a great spot for board games, puzzles, crafts and homework, as need arises.

- The screened porch has a private entrance from the master suite, where a full bath with dual sinks makes all the difference on hectic mornings.

- Don't forget to admire the rest of the home's living spaces! The Great Room, for example, is extra spacious, making it a perfect site for entertaining. The nearby dining room lies just past decorative columns, ready for special occasions or day-to-day dining.

- The kitchen has an efficient design that's just right for any meal. A snack bar helps you serve food with ease, while a laundry room and the two-car garage lie just across the hall.

- In a quiet wing of their own, two secondary bedrooms share a full bath.

Plan PJG-140908

Bedrooms: 3	Baths: 2
Living Area:	
Main floor	1,724 sq. ft.
Total Living Area:	**1,724 sq. ft.**
Screened porch	157 sq. ft.
Garage	508 sq. ft.
Mechanical	16 sq. ft.
Exterior Wall Framing:	2x4

Foundation Options:

Slab

(All plans can be built with your choice of foundation and framing. A generic conversion diagram is available. See order form.)

BLUEPRINT PRICE CODE: **B**

REAR VIEW

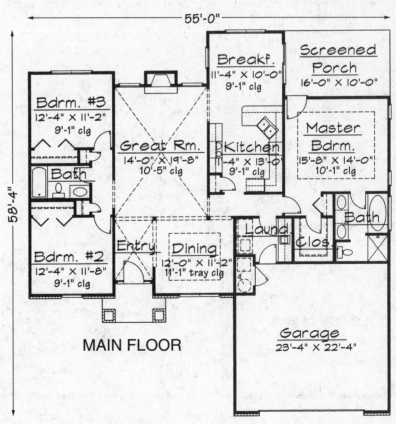

MAIN FLOOR

ORDER BLUEPRINTS ANYTIME!
CALL TOLL-FREE 1-800-820-1296

Plan PJG-140908

Plan copyright held by home designer/architect

PRICES AND DETAILS
ON PAGES 12-15

299

Quaint, Cozy

- Styled to fit nicely on a narrow lot, this quaint, cozy home will be a practical addition to any neighborhood.
- A slightly recessed entry leads down the hall into the living room, where a sunny panel of windows and a focal-point fireplace are sure to brighten any occasion. The placement of the living room at the back of the home puts it out of earshot of noisy street traffic, and close to the serenity of the backyard.
- The master suite also enjoys such a strategic location. Deep and spacious, it

includes a skylighted private bath with an oval tub, a separate shower and dual sinks. Perfect privacy just for you!
- When you're up for entertaining, consider planning a fancy meal, just so you can serve it in the captivating dining room. No pressure, but the meal better taste good if it's going to distract guests from this room's pretty windows!
- Casual meals are best in the eat-in kitchen, where a boxed-out window over the sink provides tons of space for your herb garden and other plants.
- A second bedroom off the entry may be enclosed as a quiet suite.

Plan E-1714	
Bedrooms: 2	Baths: 2
Living Area:	
Main floor	1,733 sq. ft.
Total Living Area:	1,733 sq. ft.
Detached garage	484 sq. ft.
Storage	72 sq. ft.
Exterior Wall Framing:	2x4

Foundation Options:

Slab
(All plans can be built with your choice of foundation and framing. A generic conversion diagram is available. See order form.)

BLUEPRINT PRICE CODE:	B

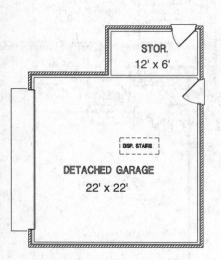

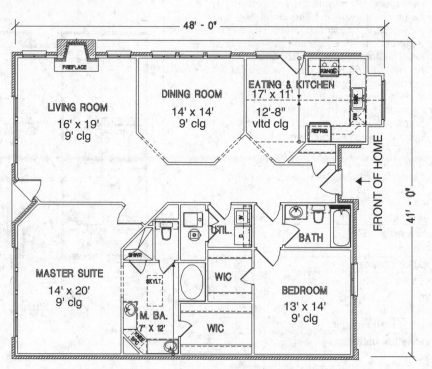

MAIN FLOOR

ORDER BLUEPRINTS ANYTIME!
CALL TOLL-FREE 1-800-820-1296

Plan E-1714
Plan copyright held by home designer/architect

PRICES AND DETAILS
ON PAGES 12-15

Grand-Packed

- Proving that livability and style are compatible, this home packs a lot of space—not to mention grandeur—into a modest-sized floor plan.

- A wide staircase leads to the sidelighted entry. Mimicking the look of the entry, a Palladian window arrangement in the living room dresses up the lovely brick exterior, as well as the open interior.

- Well lighted and warmed by a two-sided fireplace, the living and dining rooms create an ideal area for hosting parties or family events. A vaulted ceiling in the sunken living room further enhances the appeal of these spaces.

- With an island cooktop and more than enough counter space, the kitchen is perfect for concocting any delectable. The adjoining nook receives extra light from a bay with sliding glass doors— what a delightful spot for breakfast!

- Two sizable bedrooms constitute the sleeping wing. Dual doors introduce the master suite, where a large walk-in closet accommodates two wardrobes. A deluxe bath with every amenity is shared between the bedrooms. Laundry facilities are tucked into a nearby closet.

Plan PIC-6225

Bedrooms: 2	Baths: 1
Living Area:	
Main floor	1,749 sq. ft.
Total Living Area:	**1,749 sq. ft.**
Standard basement	1,749 sq. ft.
Garage	448 sq. ft.
Exterior Wall Framing:	2x6

Foundation Options:

Standard basement

(All plans can be built with your choice of foundation and framing. A generic conversion diagram is available. See order form.)

BLUEPRINT PRICE CODE:	B

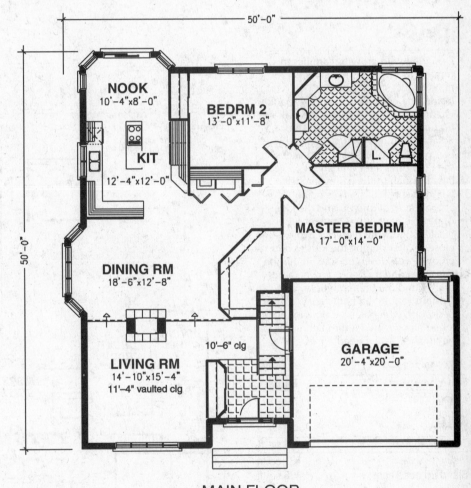

MAIN FLOOR

ORDER BLUEPRINTS ANYTIME!
CALL TOLL-FREE 1-800-820-1296

Plan PIC-6225

Plan copyright held by home designer/architect

**PRICES AND DETAILS
ON PAGES 12-15**

301

Growing Spaces

- Designed with growing families in mind, this lovely home is perfect for families just starting out.
- Inside, the entry flows into the spacious Great Room, complete with a striking fireplace and a high ceiling. The adjacent dining room, accented by a bay window, offers backyard access for the little ones after dinner.
- Pass through to the galley kitchen, where a snack bar serves up an afternoon treat for you and the kids.
- Another bay window brightens the master suite, which enjoys two walk-in closets. After putting the kids to bed, enjoy a well-deserved soak in the spa tub. A secondary bedroom and a full bath round out the main floor.
- Upstairs, a full hall bath serves a third bedroom, which can be built to include a bed alcove. Two future bedrooms can be finished as the need arises.

Plan LM-2172

Bedrooms: 3+	**Baths: 3**

Living Area:	
Upper floor	314 sq. ft.
Main floor	1,436 sq. ft.
Total Living Area:	**1,750 sq. ft.**
Future bedrooms	461 sq. ft.
Standard basement	1,436 sq. ft.
Garage	395 sq. ft.
Exterior Wall Framing:	2x4

Foundation Options:

Standard basement

(All plans can be built with your choice of foundation and framing. A generic conversion diagram is available. See order form.)

BLUEPRINT PRICE CODE:	**B**

REAR VIEW

OPTIONAL BUILT-IN BED

BED-3
12'X10'

LIN.   LIN.

BA.

HALL

DN.   UPPER ENTRY

FUTURE BED

FUTURE BED

UPPER FLOOR

DINING
12'X11'
9' clg

GREAT ROOM
15'X20'
10' clg

MASTER SUITE
16'X14'
9' clg

KIT.
12'X11'

PTY.

DN

UP

ENTRY

SALON BATH

GARAGE
20'X20'

BED-2
10'X10'
12' sloped clg

50'-0"

49'-0"

MAIN FLOOR

ORDER BLUEPRINTS ANYTIME! CALL TOLL-FREE 1-800-820-1296

Plan LM-2172

Plan copyright held by home designer/architect

PRICES AND DETAILS ON PAGES 12-15

Multi-Level Masterpiece

- This home's clever multi-level design creates an easy flow from room to room, giving your family the feeling of a masterful amount of space.
- The country-style facade is bolstered by a sidelighted front door and a lovely porch lined with windows and rails.
- Inside, the entry allows you to go down one level to the basement, or step directly into the spacious living area. Along the living area's bayed wall, a

cozy fireplace is framed by windows. An adjacent wall features three windows looking onto the porch.

- Up one level, the dining area greets you from its neat overlook position. The kitchen, which includes a broad wall of counter space, is open to the roomy, bayed breakfast area.
- Life is easy in the master suite, which is embellished by a walk-in closet, a bayed area with windows overlooking the backyard, and a space-saving salon bath with a tub and a separate shower.
- Two additional bedrooms, a full bath and a convenient laundry closet are on the uppermost level.

Plan LM-2352-1	
Bedrooms: 3	**Baths:** 2
Living Area:	
Main floor	1,316 sq. ft.
Lower floor	447 sq. ft.
Total Living Area:	**1,763 sq. ft.**
Partial basement	608 sq. ft.
Garage	462 sq. ft.
Exterior Wall Framing:	2x4

Foundation Options:

Partial basement
(All plans can be built with your choice of foundation and framing. A generic conversion diagram is available. See order form.)

BLUEPRINT PRICE CODE: B

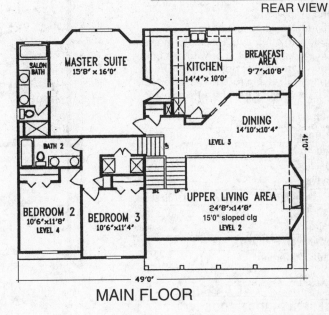

REAR VIEW

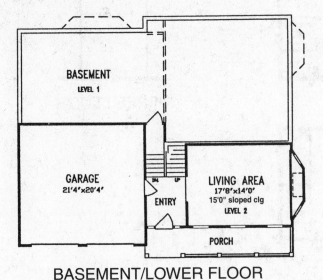

BASEMENT/LOWER FLOOR

MAIN FLOOR

ORDER BLUEPRINTS ANYTIME!
CALL TOLL-FREE 1-800-820-1296

Plan LM-2352-1
Plan copyright held by home designer/architect

PRICES AND DETAILS
ON PAGES 12-15

303

50 NEW DESIGNS!

All in a Row

- Long and lean, this home is designed for a narrow lot or a grouping of row houses, as shown above. It modestly sports a smart plan that's ideal for a family of two—or a few.
- Inside, you'll discover more space than you dared to imagine! In the dining and living room area, the slow slope of the vaulted ceiling and windows that line the wall lend depth and brightness.
- Two openings from the dining/living room enter the home's central hall. The first leads to a bedroom at the front of the home that may be used as a suite: A full bath is beyond the walk-in closet.
- Across from the second opening, the sunny kitchen is ideally located for serving formal meals. Skylights illuminate the well-equipped kitchen and the roomy breakfast nook. Off of the nook, a porch leads to the garage and ample storage.
- The master suite features a luxurious bath with a tub and a separate shower.
- On the upper floor, a private den opens you to an array of possibilities. Office, library or sewing room? Whatever you decide, it will surely be a haven.

Plan E-1715

Bedrooms: 2+	Baths: 2
Living Area:	
Upper floor	208 sq. ft.
Main floor	1,560 sq. ft.
Total Living Area:	**1,768 sq. ft.**
Garage	484 sq. ft.
Storage	132 sq. ft.
Exterior Wall Framing:	2x4

Foundation Options:

Slab
(All plans can be built with your choice of foundation and framing. A generic conversion diagram is available. See order form.)

BLUEPRINT PRICE CODE: **B**

ORDER BLUEPRINTS ANYTIME! CALL TOLL-FREE 1-800-820-1296

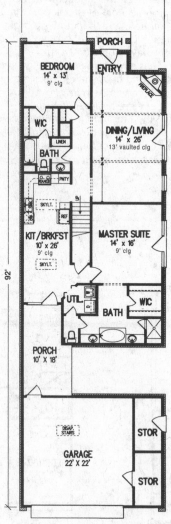

MAIN FLOOR

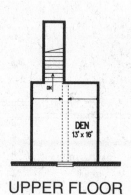

UPPER FLOOR

Plan E-1715

Plan copyright held by home designer/architect

PRICES AND DETAILS ON PAGES 12-15

Gallant Beauty

- Balanced, practical and yet stunningly beautiful, this gallant one-story home is just right for your family's needs.
- Past the dual-door entry, a tiled foyer opens into the living areas. Formal living and dining rooms flank the foyer, while the family room straight ahead is well equipped for day-to-day life. Here, media shelves flank a central fireplace, while sliding doors lead to a back patio.
- Merging with this fabulous casual spot is the bayed breakfast room. A snack bar serves this sunny area and fronts the

well-planned kitchen. Nearly every gourmet amenity is at your disposal here, including a step-in pantry and a handy planning desk, where you may pay bills, do homework or write letters.
- A utility room leading to the two-car garage and offering laundry facilities lies in smart proximity to the kitchen.
- Double doors are a lavish introduction to the master suite. The bright, spacious bedroom boasts direct access to the patio, and adjoins a deluxe private bath with a walk-in closet.
- Two additional bedrooms—and a possible third—share a separate wing.

Plan HDS-99-369	
Bedrooms: 3+	**Baths:** 2–3
Living Area:	
Main floor (3-bedroom)	1,783 sq. ft.
Main floor (4-bedroom)	1,999 sq. ft.
Total Living Area:	**1,783/1,999 sq. ft.**
Garage	409 sq. ft.
Exterior Wall Framing:	2x4

Foundation Options:
Slab
(All plans can be built with your choice of foundation and framing. A generic conversion diagram is available. See order form.)

BLUEPRINT PRICE CODE: B

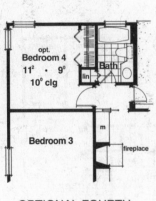

OPTIONAL FOURTH BEDROOM

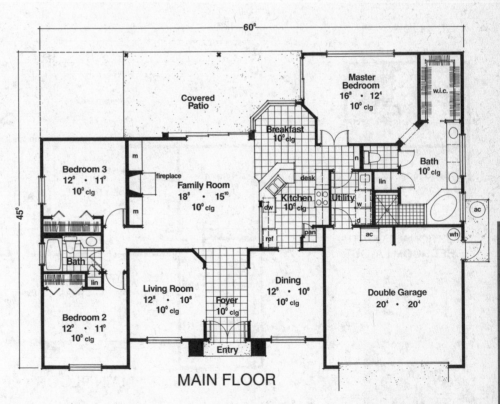

MAIN FLOOR

ORDER BLUEPRINTS ANYTIME!
CALL TOLL-FREE 1-800-820-1296

Plan HDS-99-369
Plan copyright held by home designer/architect

PRICES AND DETAILS
ON PAGES 12-15

305

50 NEW DESIGNS

Ten-Four!

- With ten-foot ceilings and a possible four bedrooms, this perfect plan will let you say, "over and out" to the lengthy home-search process.
- The grand, columned entry ushers guests through double doors and into the tiled foyer. The formal living and dining rooms provide a proper welcome on either side.
- Straight ahead, the fun family room is the hub of the home. Media shelves hold your TV and DVD player, while flanking a crackling fireplace. Sliding

glass doors open to a covered patio that is large enough for parties or bridge tournaments.
- The fabulous kitchen will get your creative juices flowing. Special features include a pantry, a menu desk and an angled serving bar. A bright breakfast nook overlooks a back patio.
- The master bedroom grants patio access and backyard views. The private bath hosts a corner tub, a separate shower and dual sinks.
- Two or three additional bedrooms and one or two more baths round out this gorgeous plan.

Plan HDS-99-370	
Bedrooms: 3+	**Baths:** 2–3
Living Area:	
Main floor (3 bedrooms)	1,783 sq. ft.
Main floor (4 bedrooms)	1,999 sq. ft.
Total Living Area:	**1,783/1,999 sq. ft.**
Garage	409 sq. ft.
Exterior Wall Framing:	2x4
Foundation Options:	

Slab
(All plans can be built with your choice of foundation and framing. A generic conversion diagram is available. See order form.)

BLUEPRINT PRICE CODE:	**B**

OPTIONAL FOURTH
BEDROOM LAYOUT

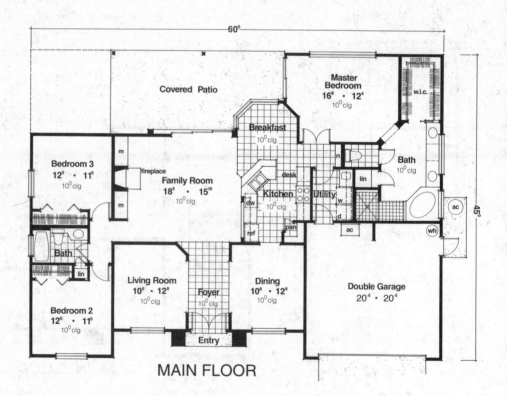

MAIN FLOOR

ORDER BLUEPRINTS ANYTIME!
CALL TOLL-FREE 1-800-820-1296

Plan HDS-99-370

Plan copyright held by home designer/architect

PRICES AND DETAILS
ON PAGES 12-15

Nifty Neotrad!

- Exuding neotraditional charm while boasting a thoroughly modern plan, this home is a winner inside and out.
- Gentle arches and sturdy columns impart the front porch with a dreamy look. Inside, the romance continues in the enviable master suite, where a prominent bay window provides not only ample light, but also a cozy sitting area. A private bath that is pampering yet modest complements the bedroom.
- Across the hall, pocket doors reveal the dining room. Suitable for fancy or laid-back meals, this room fits any mood. A

closet within the dining room expands its use to include a home office or a guest room, depending on your needs.
- The cavernous family room down the hall features a handsome fireplace flanked by shelves—just the place to be on chilly nights. On balmy evenings, step out back to a screened porch for bug-free relaxation or dining.
- A snack bar joins the kitchen to the family room, and is one of many delights. A full bath and a utility room nearby are added conveniences.
- Two secondary bedrooms and a smart split bath fill the upper floor. Expansion space awaits your family's future needs.

Plan LRK-96292

Bedrooms: 3+	**Baths:** 3

Living Area:	
Upper floor	556 sq. ft.
Main floor	1,228 sq. ft.
Total Living Area:	**1,784 sq. ft.**
Screened porch	192 sq. ft.
Porte cochere	546 sq. ft.
Storage	18 sq. ft.
Exterior Wall Framing:	2x4

Foundation Options:

Crawlspace
(All plans can be built with your choice of foundation and framing. A generic conversion diagram is available. See order form.)

BLUEPRINT PRICE CODE: B

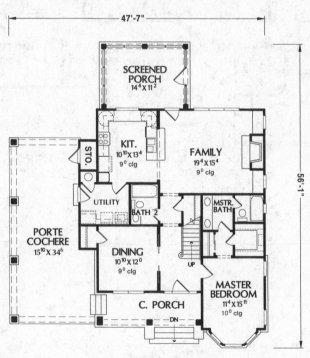

MAIN FLOOR

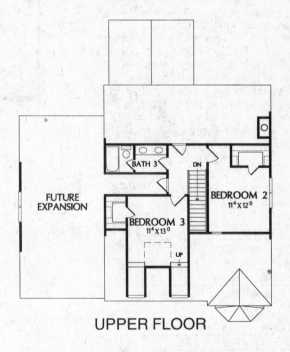

UPPER FLOOR

ORDER BLUEPRINTS ANYTIME!
CALL TOLL-FREE 1-800-820-1296

Plan LRK-96292
Plan copyright held by home designer/architect

PRICES AND DETAILS
ON PAGES 12-15

307

Winning Windows

- If natural light is a joy of your world, take a closer look at this bright and airy home. Its windows will win your heart!
- The sidelighted entry flows seamlessly into the dining room off to the right, where a niche provides the perfect space for a china hutch. Little separates this area from the Great Room, where transoms top every window.
- A snack bar extends into the Great Room from a large island in the kitchen. Extra counter space provides the elbow room you need to whip up gourmet delights, while a built-in desk affords you a quiet spot to form plans of attack.
- In the master suite, a bay window illuminates the bedroom, while a lavish garden tub beckons from one corner of the private bath. Gorgeous windows even grace the huge walk-in closet!
- Two sizable bedrooms on the other side of the home share a full hall bath. A neat little display niche in the hallway provides a special spot for your travel treasures or amateur art from the kids.

Plan ICON-103144-B

Bedrooms: 3	Baths: 2
Living Area:	
Main floor	1,790 sq. ft.
Total Living Area:	**1,790 sq. ft.**
Standard basement	1,790 sq. ft.
Garage	504 sq. ft.
Exterior Wall Framing:	2x4
Foundation Options:	

Standard basement
(All plans can be built with your choice of foundation and framing. A generic conversion diagram is available. See order form.)

BLUEPRINT PRICE CODE:	B

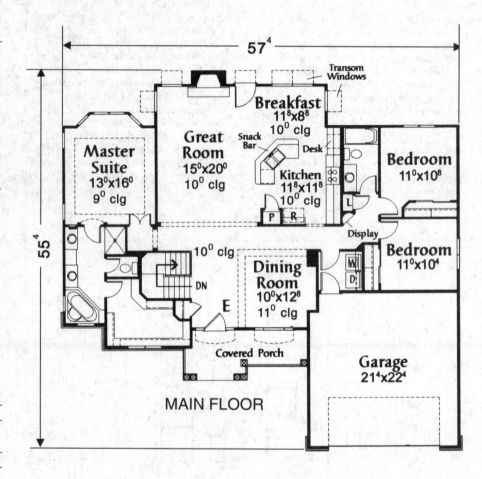

MAIN FLOOR

ORDER BLUEPRINTS ANYTIME!
CALL TOLL-FREE 1-800-820-1296

Plan ICON-103144-B

Plan copyright held by home designer/architect

PRICES AND DETAILS ON PAGES 12-15

Best of Show

- Sure to be the best home on the block, this clever design incorporates the space you need into a thoughtful, stylish package that's full of character.
- Classic detailing tops the entry porch and carport, nicely complementing the siding accents above. Pretty windows are proportionately placed along the perimeter of the plan.
- Just off the entry, a spacious study works nicely as a home office. Its proximity to a full bath doubles this room's use as a guest room when the need arises.
- Down the hall, the U-shaped kitchen is neatly arranged so that everything you need is within reach. A wide pass-through window allows you to set snacks out for guests in the sunken living/dining room, not to mention stay involved in the conversation.
- On special nights, you'll enjoy spending time on the screen porch, or possibly grilling out on the adjacent rear deck.
- The upper floor hosts two sizable bedrooms, including the vaulted master suite. Within this retreat is a practical bath with dual sinks, plus two walk-in closets. A huge balcony is a neat bonus.

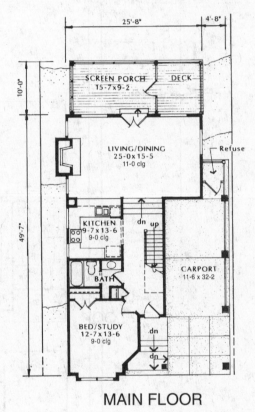

MAIN FLOOR

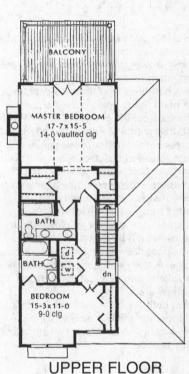

UPPER FLOOR

Plan LRK-90101

Bedrooms: 2+	Baths: 3
Living Area:	
Upper floor	855 sq. ft.
Main floor	980 sq. ft.
Total Living Area:	**1,835 sq. ft.**
Screen porch	242 sq. ft.
Carport	360 sq. ft.
Exterior Wall Framing:	2x4

Foundation Options:

Crawlspace

(All plans can be built with your choice of foundation and framing. A generic conversion diagram is available. See order form.)

BLUEPRINT PRICE CODE:	B

ORDER BLUEPRINTS ANYTIME!
CALL TOLL-FREE 1-800-820-1296

Plan LRK-90101
Plan copyright held by home designer/architect

PRICES AND DETAILS
ON PAGES 12-15

309

50 NEW DESIGNS

A Whole New Level

- This well-planned home will raise your expectations for split-level designs a notch or two, with its smart use of space and attention to detail.
- Up a half-level from the two-car garage, the main living areas cluster around a generous central gathering area. You'll find that with a fireplace and nearby access to the kitchen, your family will cluster around this area too.
- For those quiet afternoons, or on occasions when you'd like to entertain your friends, the intimate living and dining rooms stand ready.
- Meanwhile, the kids can play in their rooms, which lie down a side hallway.
- The upper-floor master suite crowns the home. A true retreat, the bedroom offers a vaulted sitting area along its front-facing Palladian window, while the salon bath awaits you after a long day.
- All these amenities come wrapped in an eye-pleasing exterior with an attractive entry portico.

Plan LM-2409

Bedrooms: 3	**Baths:** 2

Living Area:	
Upper floor	440 sq. ft.
Main floor	1,422 sq. ft.
Total Living Area:	**1,862 sq. ft.**
Standard basement	1,422 sq. ft.
Garage	497 sq. ft.
Exterior Wall Framing:	2x4

Foundation Options:

Standard basement

(All plans can be built with your choice of foundation and framing. A generic conversion diagram is available. See order form.)

BLUEPRINT PRICE CODE:	B

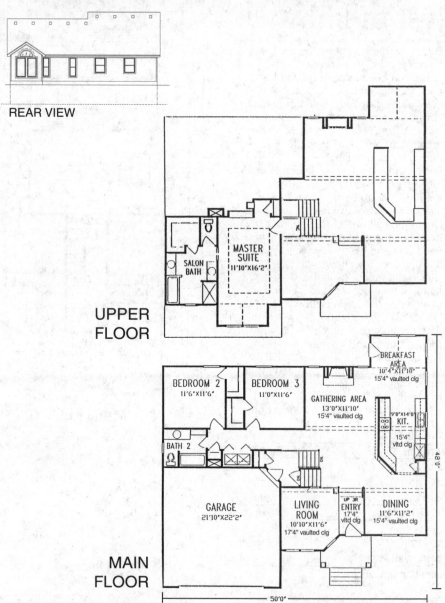

REAR VIEW

UPPER FLOOR

MASTER SUITE 11'10"x16'2"

SALON BATH

MAIN FLOOR

BEDROOM 2 11'6"x11'6"

BEDROOM 3 11'0"x11'6"

BATH 2

GARAGE 21'10"x22'2"

LIVING ROOM 10'10"x11'6" 17'4" vaulted clg

ENTRY 17'4" vltd clg

GATHERING AREA 13'0"x11'10" 15'4" vaulted clg

BREAKFAST AREA 10'4"x11'10" 15'4" vaulted clg

KIT. 9'0"x14'0" 15'4" vltd clg

DINING 11'6"x11'2" 15'4" vaulted clg

48'0"

50'0"

Plan LM-2409
Plan copyright held by home designer/architect

PRICES AND DETAILS ON PAGES 12-15

Narrow, Classic Southern Home

- You'll enjoy the Southern charm and classic architecture of this attractive sideyard home. And it will fit on even the most narrow of city lots!
- Stacked front porches bring back memories of simpler times and beckon visitors to sit a spell.
- Inside, columns separate the dining room from the living room, where a fireplace adds a warm ambience.
- The open kitchen adjoins the sunny breakfast nook, where you'll enjoy casual meals and snacks all day long.
- Perfect for guests, a study or extra bedroom is secluded at the rear of the home. A handy full bath is nearby.
- Upstairs, the master bedroom boasts a private porch and two walk-in closets. The private master bath includes a spa tub and a separate shower.
- A secondary bedroom with its own bath rounds out the upper floor.
- The two-car garage faces the alley, to keep the front of the home beautiful and uncluttered.

Plan LRK-95130

Bedrooms: 2+	Baths: 3
Living Area:	
Upper floor	801 sq. ft.
Main floor	1,092 sq. ft.
Total Living Area:	**1,893 sq. ft.**
Garage	539 sq. ft.
Exterior Wall Framing:	2x4

Foundation Options:

Slab
(All plans can be built with your choice of foundation and framing. A generic conversion diagram is available. See order form.)

BLUEPRINT PRICE CODE: B

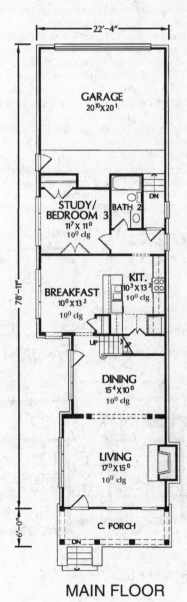

MAIN FLOOR

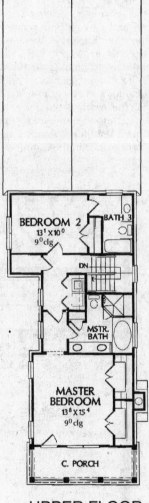

UPPER FLOOR

Plan LRK-95130

Plan copyright held by home designer/architect

PRICES AND DETAILS ON PAGES 12-15

Full of Pleasure

- Every country homestead should be graced with a plan like this one! Even in a rustic location, you'll still never want for pleasures in this home.
- Dormers and a sweet front porch imbue the exterior with a cozy charm, while brick accents dress up its simple look.
- Inside, the living room is the heart of the home. Clever bookshelves, a built-in media center and a warming fireplace establish this room as the place to be.
- A row of windows in the living room overlooks a rear porch that is accessed via a French door in the dining room. A

boxed-out window increases the floor space in this pretty dining spot.
- The kitchen includes a raised bar that is great for serving meals in the dining room or for snacking on light fare. A walk-in pantry affords ample storage for the canned fruits of your labor.
- Down the hall, two sizable bedrooms sit on either side of a handy utility room with laundry facilities. A full hall bath is convenient to both bedrooms.
- Not to be outdone by any other room in the home, the master suite offers so many amenities, it needs a wing of its own! A bayed sitting area and a marble tub are among the finest features.

Plan RD-1659-10	
Bedrooms: 3+	**Baths:** 2
Living Area:	
Main floor	1,659 sq. ft.
Bonus room	250 sq. ft.
Total Living Area:	**1,909 sq. ft.**
Garage	515 sq. ft.
Storage	17 sq. ft.
Exterior Wall Framing:	2x4

Foundation Options:

Crawlspace
Slab
(All plans can be built with your choice of foundation and framing. A generic conversion diagram is available. See order form.)

BLUEPRINT PRICE CODE:	B

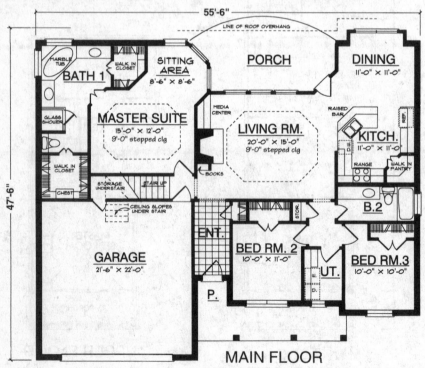

MAIN FLOOR

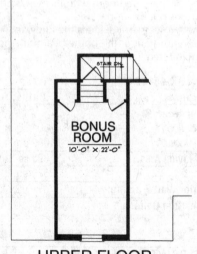

UPPER FLOOR

Plan RD-1659-10

Plan copyright held by home designer/architect

PRICES AND DETAILS
ON PAGES 12-15

50 NEW DESIGNS

This Is One Great Room!

- The wide-open Great Room at the center of this charming traditional home really lives up to its name!
- A crackling fireplace in the Great Room sets a comfortable tone, while the room's generous measurements allow space for large parties. Three windows provide views of a backyard patio and the greenery beyond.
- The island kitchen offers an angled serving counter and a nearby pantry.

- Bright and cheery, the versatile dining room offers patio access.
- A sloped ceiling enhances the master suite, where several windows bring in natural light. The master bath features a garden tub and a separate shower, plus a sizable walk-in closet.
- Two additional bedrooms face the front yard and share a full hall bath.
- Rounding out the floor plan, a handy utility room hosts the washer and dryer.
- The two-car garage is entered at the right side of the home, leaving the facade beautiful and uncluttered. And speaking of the front, twin dormers and stately columns add style and grace.

Plan DD-1932	
Bedrooms: 3	**Baths: 2**
Living Area:	
Main floor	1,933 sq. ft.
Total Living Area:	**1,933 sq. ft.**
Standard basement	1,933 sq. ft.
Garage	393 sq. ft.
Exterior Wall Framing:	2x4

Foundation Options:

Standard basement
Crawlspace
Slab
(All plans can be built with your choice of foundation and framing. A generic conversion diagram is available. See order form.)

BLUEPRINT PRICE CODE:	**B**

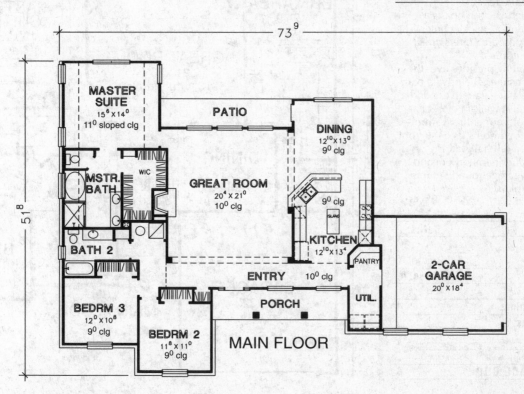

Plan DD-1932

Plan copyright held by home designer/architect

50 NEW DESIGNS

European Elements

- This attractive one-story incorporates European details into its facade for a comfortable, nostalgic look. Stucco, stacked stone and keystone accents will remind you of the gracious architecture of the Old World.
- Inside, the sidelighted entry shares a vaulted ceiling with the open dining room and the expansive Great Room. Three windows provide backyard views, while a corner fireplace adds warmth and character.
- The walk-through kitchen boasts a sizable pantry and a snack counter. The adjoining breakfast area offers direct access to the outdoors.
- A lovely tray ceiling presides over the peaceful master suite. The private bath showcases a relaxing garden tub and a separate shower. A walk-in closet has enough room for your entire wardrobe.
- Two additional bedrooms face the front yard and share a full hall bath.
- A convenient laundry/mudroom and a roomy two-car garage round out this space-efficient plan.

Plan LM-2425

Bedrooms: 3	Baths: 2

Living Area:

Main floor	1,935 sq. ft.
Total Living Area:	**1,935 sq. ft.**
Garage	458 sq. ft.
Exterior Wall Framing:	2x4

Foundation Options:

Slab

(All plans can be built with your choice of foundation and framing. A generic conversion diagram is available. See order form.)

BLUEPRINT PRICE CODE:	**B**

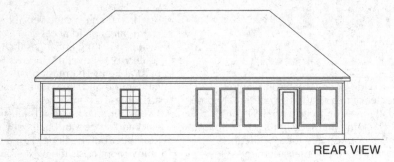

REAR VIEW

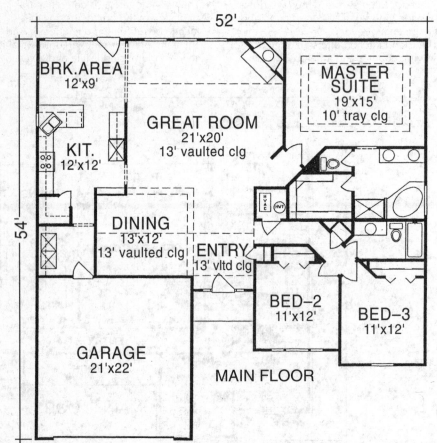

MAIN FLOOR

52'

54'

BRK. AREA 12'x9'

KIT. 12'x12'

GREAT ROOM 21'x20' 13' vaulted clg

MASTER SUITE 19'x15' 10' tray clg

DINING 13'x12' 13' vaulted clg

ENTRY 13' vltd clg

GARAGE 21'x22'

BED-2 11'x12'

BED-3 11'x12'

Plan LM-2425

Plan copyright held by home designer/architect

**PRICES AND DETAILS
ON PAGES 12-15**

Open to the Possibilities

- Openness characterizes this design's living and dining rooms, equipping these spaces with plenty of possibilities for entertaining friends or enjoying a peaceful, casual evening.
- Besides imparting light and gentle warmth, a three-way fireplace creates a subtle barrier between the living and dining rooms. Both rooms include useful built-in features.

- A pass-through connects the dining room and the kitchen, where an island workstation overlooks the cheery morning room.
- The master suite resides on the main floor, giving you all the privacy and convenience you desire.
- A fun loft at the top of the stairs looks down on the living room below. Imagine your home office or an enviable playroom for the kids here. Depending on your space needs, this area may be finished off to complement the other upper-floor bedrooms, which share a full bath.

Plan DD-1935	
Bedrooms: 3+	**Baths:** 2½
Living Area:	
Upper floor	682 sq. ft.
Main floor	1,256 sq. ft.
Total Living Area:	**1,938 sq. ft.**
Standard basement	1,256 sq. ft.
Garage	350 sq. ft.
Exterior Wall Framing:	2x4
Foundation Options:	
Standard basement	
Crawlspace	
Slab	

(All plans can be built with your choice of foundation and framing. A generic conversion diagram is available. See order form.)

BLUEPRINT PRICE CODE:	B

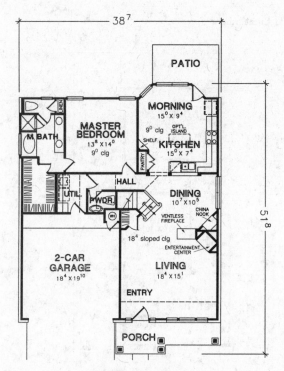

MAIN FLOOR

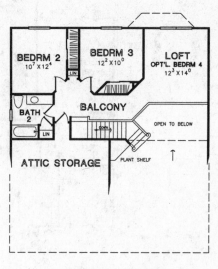

UPPER FLOOR

Plan DD-1935

Plan copyright held by home designer/architect

PRICES AND DETAILS ON PAGES 12-15

Different Is Good

- Interested in a home that's a departure from the "cookie-cutter" plans of your new development? This home's striking porch and turret are an exciting start.
- The interior is just as stimulating. High above the bayed dining room, clerestory windows draw in natural light from within the turret. The dining room opens through four elegant columns to

the family room, where a fireplace and French doors to a back patio make it a natural spot for casual entertaining.
- Convenient to both of these rooms, the kitchen extends an angled snack bar to a bright bayed morning room nearby.
- The master bedroom boasts a boxed-out window and leads to a private bath that includes a sizable walk-in closet.
- Three secondary bedrooms, each of which includes private access to one of two full baths, are situated along a quiet hallway on the opposite side of the home.

Plan DD-1949	
Bedrooms: 4	**Baths:** 3
Living Area:	
Main floor	1,950 sq. ft.
Total Living Area:	**1,950 sq. ft.**
Standard basement	1,950 sq. ft.
Exterior Wall Framing:	2x4

Foundation Options:

Standard basement
Crawlspace
Slab

(All plans can be built with your choice of foundation and framing. A generic conversion diagram is available. See order form.)

BLUEPRINT PRICE CODE:	B

MAIN FLOOR

Plan DD-1949

Plan copyright held by home designer/architect

PRICES AND DETAILS
ON PAGES 12-15

50 NEW DESIGNS

To the Max

- For maximum privacy, living space and style on a narrow lot or among other row houses, this design is the answer. Quoins add sophistication to the handsome brick exterior.
- The recessed entry leads down a hallway to the spacious vaulted living room, which features a fireplace and French doors that open out to a rear porch. Columns mark the adjacent formal dining room.
- Double doors in the kitchen hide meal messes from the dining room. When

guests are visiting in the living room, offer them drinks and snacks via a shuttered pass-through. The breakfast nook is a great spot for casual meals, as is a cozy side porch that's perfect for "tea for two."

- The master suite revels in secluded comfort at the rear of the home. The amenity-packed bath includes an oval garden tub that receives secondhand light from a window in a neat atrium.
- The enclosed atrium—an ideal retreat—is reached from one of the secondary bedrooms, which includes private access to a shared hall bath.

Plan E-1914

Bedrooms: 3	**Baths:** 2

Living Area:

Main floor	1,964 sq. ft.
Total Living Area:	**1,964 sq. ft.**
Garage	484 sq. ft.
Storage	70 sq. ft.
Exterior Wall Framing:	2x6

Foundation Options:

Slab

(All plans can be built with your choice of foundation and framing. A generic conversion diagram is available. See order form.)

BLUEPRINT PRICE CODE:	B

MAIN FLOOR

84' - 0"

44' - 0"

- WIC
- M. BATH 13'6" sloped clg
- ATRIUM
- BA.
- WIC
- BEDROOM 3 14' X 13' 13'6" vaulted clg
- ← FRONT
- BEDROOM 2 14' X 13' 9' clg
- MASTER SUITE 15'6" X 18' 9' clg
- ENTRY
- STORAGE
- UTIL.
- LIVING ROOM 17'8" X 20' 13' vaulted clg
- DINING ROOM 13' X 10'4" 9' clg
- PNTY
- GARAGE 22' X 22'
- PORCH
- KITCHEN 14' X 10'4"
- BRKFST 8' X 12' 9' clg
- OVEN
- REF
- PORCH

50 NEW DESIGNS

ORDER BLUEPRINTS ANYTIME!
CALL TOLL-FREE 1-800-820-1296

Plan E-1914
Plan copyright held by home designer/architect

PRICES AND DETAILS
ON PAGES 12-15

317

Get Focused

- When was the last time you were all really *together*? Maybe the solution to staying connected lies in a home plan that encourages gathering. This design features a free-flowing interior with focused living spaces that are bound to bring your family closer.
- The most notable room for this purpose is the living room. A bay window harvests light at one end of the room, and is complemented by two wide windows on another side. A corner fireplace adds ambience.

- The adjacent kitchen boasts ample work space and extends a serving counter to the nearby bayed breakfast room. A formal dining room awaits you opposite the living room, offering a spot for special-occasion meals.
- When your evening together is over, send the kids or your guests to their cozy bedrooms, which share a quiet vestibule off the main hall, along with a shared full bath and linen storage.
- Another secluded hallway leads to the master suite, where a sizable closet and a private bath with enviable amenities pampers you.

Plan DD-1975	
Bedrooms: 3	**Baths:** 2
Living Area:	
Main floor	1,975 sq. ft.
Total Living Area:	**1,975 sq. ft.**
Standard basement	1,975 sq. ft.
Garage and storage	472 sq. ft.
Exterior Wall Framing:	2x4
Foundation Options:	

Standard basement
Crawlspace
Slab
(All plans can be built with your choice of foundation and framing. A generic conversion diagram is available. See order form.)

BLUEPRINT PRICE CODE:	B

MAIN FLOOR

Plan DD-1975

PRICES AND DETAILS
ON PAGES 12-15

Safe and Sound

- Comfortable. Safe. Secure. That's how you'll feel in this charming two-story plan, which is the perfect fit on an infill or narrow lot. Stacked front porches not only provide unique comfort, they also encourage interaction with neighbors and "eyes on the street."
- The interior is surprisingly roomy, considering the design's slim footprint. A sizable living room with a fireplace and built-ins flows past a pair of columns into the formal dining room.
- Ample storage and bright windows characterize the kitchen and breakfast room, which share space beyond the dining room. These "everyday" rooms are satisfyingly well planned.
- A flexible study or secondary bedroom and a full bath complete the main floor.
- The upper floor contains two bedrooms, including the master suite, where highlights include a private bath, dual walk-in closets and an exciting balcony. A convenient private bath graces the secondary bedroom as well.
- Want a facade-saving secret? Take a hint from this plan, which tucks the garage away at the back of the home.

Plan LRK-94202-B

Bedrooms: 2+	Baths: 3
Living Area:	
Upper floor	848 sq. ft.
Main floor	1,145 sq. ft.
Total Living Area:	**1,993 sq. ft.**
Garage and storage	480 sq. ft.
Exterior Wall Framing:	2x4

Foundation Options:
Slab
(All plans can be built with your choice of foundation and framing. A generic conversion diagram is available. See order form.)

BLUEPRINT PRICE CODE:	B

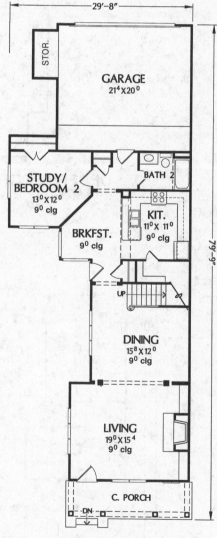

MAIN FLOOR

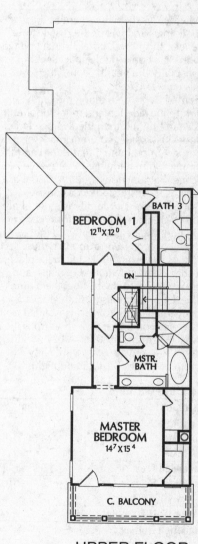

UPPER FLOOR

Plan LRK-94202-B

Plan copyright held by home designer/architect

PRICES AND DETAILS
ON PAGES 12-15

50 NEW DESIGNS

Cottage Feel

- Whether it's the varied gables, the sparkling windows or the rustic stone veneer, this home has a distinct cottage look. The comfortable spaces within, especially the hearth room, also foster this fairy-tale feel.
- Framed by an arch along the pretty porch, the sidelighted French-door entry is a tad brighter than the average Dutch door! Just inside, columns mark the borders of both the Great Room and the dining room, allowing for a free-flowing space that functions well for casual as well as sophisticated occasions.
- Nonetheless, your family is more likely to congregate in the area formed by the kitchen, the hearth room and the dinette. Open to one another, these spaces share amenities like a fireplace, a snack bar and vaulted ceilings, and are designed to invite "together" time.
- The main-floor master suite enjoys a convenient location that is isolated from the common areas, as well as from the kids' bedrooms upstairs. A bay window and a full, private bath with many extras promise luxurious days and nights.

Plan ICON-153149-B

Bedrooms: 3	Baths: 2½
Living Area:	
Upper floor	423 sq. ft.
Main floor	1,573 sq. ft.
Total Living Area:	**1,996 sq. ft.**
Standard basement	1,573 sq. ft.
Garage	469 sq. ft.
Exterior Wall Framing:	2x4

Foundation Options:

Standard basement
(All plans can be built with your choice of foundation and framing. A generic conversion diagram is available. See order form.)

BLUEPRINT PRICE CODE: B

UPPER FLOOR

MAIN FLOOR

ORDER BLUEPRINTS ANYTIME!
CALL TOLL-FREE 1-800-820-1296

Plan ICON-153149-B

Plan copyright held by home designer/architect

PRICES AND DETAILS
ON PAGES 12-15